# Clojure Cookbook

*Luke VanderHart and Ryan Neufeld*

Beijing • Cambridge • Farnham • Köln • Sebastopol • Tokyo

**Clojure Cookbook**

by Luke VanderHart and Ryan Neufeld



Printed in the United States of America.

Published by O'Reilly Media, Inc., 1005 Gravenstein Highway North, Sebastopol, CA 95472.

O'Reilly books may be purchased for educational, business, or sales promotional use. Online editions are also available for most titles (*http://my.safaribooksonline.com*). For more information, contact our corporate/institutional sales department: 800-998-9938 or *corporate@oreilly.com*.

**Editor:** Meghan Blanchette
**Production Editor:** Kristen Brown
**Copyeditor:** Amanda Kersey
**Proofreader:** Rachel Head
**Indexer:** Judith McConville
**Cover Designer:** Karen Montgomery
**Interior Designer:** David Futato
**Illustrator:** Rebecca Demarest

March 2014: First Edition

**Revision History for the First Edition:**

2014-03-04: First release

See *http://oreilly.com/catalog/errata.csp?isbn=9781449366179* for release details.



ISBN: 978-1-449-36617-9

[LSI]

# Table of Contents

# Preface

The primary goal of this book is to provide mid-length examples of Clojure code that go beyond the basics, with a focus on real-world, everyday applications (as opposed to more conceptual or academic issues).

Unlike many of the other books on Clojure written to date, the organizing theme of this book is not the language itself, or its features and capabilities. Instead, it focuses on specific *tasks* that developers face (regardless of what language they're using) and shows an example of how to use Clojure to solve each of those specific problems.

As such, this book is not and cannot be truly comprehensive; there are infinite possible example problems. However, we do hope we've documented some of the more common ones that most programmers encounter frequently, and that by induction readers will be able to learn some common patterns, approaches, and techniques that will serve them well as they design solutions for their own unique problems.

## How This Book Was Written

An important thing you should understand about this book is that it is, first and foremost, a group effort. It is not authored by one or two people. It isn't even the work of a single, well-defined group. Instead, it is the collaborative product of more than 60 of the best Clojurists from all over the world, from all backgrounds. These authors use Clojure every day on real applications, ranging from aerospace to social media, banking to robotics, AI research to e-commerce.

As such, you will see a lot of diversity in the recipes presented. Some are quick and to the point. Others are more deliberate, presenting digestible yet penetrating insights into the philosophy and implementation of certain aspects of Clojure.

We hope that there is something in this book for readers of diverse interests. We believe that it will be useful not only as a reference for looking up solutions to specific problems, but also as a worthwhile survey of the variety and expressivity that Clojure is capable of. As we edited submissions, we were astonished by the number of concepts and techniques that were new to us, and will hopefully be new to our readers as well.

Something else that we discovered while writing and editing was how difficult it was to draw a circumference around what we wanted to cover. Every single recipe is a beautiful, endless fractal, touching multiple topics, each of which deserves a recipe, a chapter, or a book of its own. But each recipe also needs to stand on its own. Each one should provide some useful nugget of information that readers can understand and take away with them.

We sincerely hope that we have balanced these goals appropriately, and that you find this book useful without being tedious, and insightful without being pedantic.

## Audience

Anyone who uses Clojure will, we hope, be able to get something out of this book. There are a lot of recipes on truly basic things that beginners will find useful, but there are also many recipes on more specialized topics that advanced users should find useful for getting a head start on implementation.

That said, if you're completely new to Clojure, this probably isn't the book to start with —at least, not by itself. It covers a great many useful topics, but not as methodically or as thoroughly as a good introductory text. See the following section for a list of general Clojure books you may find useful as prior or supplemental texts.

## Other Resources

One thing that this book is not, and could never be, is complete. There is too much to cover, and by presenting information in a task-oriented recipe format we have inherently precluded ourselves from methodical, narrative explanation of the features and capabilities of the whole language.

For a more linear, thorough explanation of Clojure and its features, we recommend one of the following books:

- *Clojure Programming* (O'Reilly, 2012), by Chas Emerick, Brian Carper, and Christophe Grand. A good, comprehensive, general-purpose Clojure book focusing on the language and common tasks, oriented toward beginner Clojure programmers.
- *Programming Clojure*, 2nd ed. (Pragmatic Bookshelf, 2012), by Stuart Halloway and Aaron Bedra. The first book on Clojure, this is a clear, comprehensive introductory tutorial on the Clojure language.
- *Practical Clojure* (Apress, 2010), by Luke VanderHart and Stuart Sierra. This is a terse, no-nonsense explanation of what Clojure is and what its features do.

- *The Joy of Clojure* (Manning, 2011), by Michael Fogus and Chris Houser. This is a slightly more advanced text that really digs into the themes and philosophies of Clojure.
- *ClojureScript: Up and Running* (O'Reilly, 2012), by Stuart Sierra and Luke VanderHart. While *Clojure Cookbook* and the other Clojure books listed here focus mainly or entirely on Clojure itself, ClojureScript (a dialect of Clojure that compiles to JavaScript) has gained considerable uptake. This book introduces ClojureScript and how to get started with it, and covers the similarities and differences between ClojureScript and Clojure.

Finally, you should look at the source code for this book itself, which is freely available on GitHub (*http://bit.ly/clj-ckbk*). The selection of recipes available online is larger than that in the print version, and we are still accepting pull requests for new recipes that might someday make it into a future edition of this book.

# Structure

The chapters in this book are for the most part groupings of recipes by theme, rather than strictly categorical. It is entirely possible for a recipe to be applicable to more than one chapter—in these cases, we have simply tried to place it where we think the majority of readers will likely look first.

A *recipe* consists of three primary parts and one secondary: problem, solution, discussion, and "see also." A recipe's problem statement lays out a task or obstacle to be overcome. Its solution tackles the problem head-on, illustrating a particular technique or library that effectively accomplishes the task. The discussion rounds everything out, exploring the solution and any caveats that may come with it. Finally, we tie off each recipe with a "see also" section, pointing you, the reader, to any additional resources or recipes that will assist you in enacting the described solution.

## Chapter Listing

The book is composed of the following chapters:

- Chapter 1, *Primitive Data*, and Chapter 2, *Composite Data*, cover Clojure's built-in primitive and composite data structures, and explain many common (and less common) ways one might want to use them.
- Chapter 3, *General Computing*, is a grab bag of useful topics that are generally applicable in many different application areas and project domains, from Clojure features such as Protocols to alternate programming paradigms such as logic programming with `core.logic` or asynchronous coordination with `core.async`.

- Chapter 4, *Local I/O*, deals with all the ways in which your program can interact with the local computer upon which it is running. This includes reading fromand writing to standard input and output streams, creating and manipulating files, serializing and deserializing files, etc.
- Chapter 5, *Network I/O and Web Services*, contains recipes with similar themes to Chapter 4, *Local I/O*, but instead deals with *remote* communication over a network. It includes recipes on a variety of network communication protocols and libraries.
- Chapter 6, *Databases*, demonstrates techniques and tools for connecting to and using a variety of databases. Special attention is given to Datomic, a datastore that shares and extends much of Clojure's underlying philosophy of value, state, and identity to persistent storage.
- Chapter 7, *Web Applications*, dives in-depth into one of the most common applications for Clojure: building and maintaining dynamic websites. It provides comprehensive treatment of Ring (the most popular HTTP server library for Clojure), as well as tools for HTML templating and rendering.
- Chapter 8, *Performance and Production*, explains what to do with a Clojure program once you have one, going over common patterns for packaging, distributing, profiling, logging, and associated ongoing tasks over the lifetime of an application.
- Chapter 9, *Distributed Computation*, focuses on cloud computing and using Clojure for heavyweight distributed data crunching. Special attention is given to Cascalog, a declarative Clojure interface to the Hadoop MapReduce framework.
- Last but not least, Chapter 10, *Testing*, covers a variety of techniques for ensuring the integrity and correctness of your code and data, ranging from traditional unit and integration tests to more comprehensive generative and simulation testing, and even optional compile-time validations using static typing with `core.typed`.

## Software Prerequisites

To follow along with the recipes in this book you will need valid installations of the Java Development Kit (JDK) and Clojure's de facto build tool, Leiningen. We recommend version 7 of the JDK, but a minimum of 6 will do. For Leiningen, you should have at least version 2.2.

If you don't have Java installed (or would like to upgrade), visit the Java Download Page (*http://bit.ly/java-download*) for instructions on downloading and installing the Java JDK.

To install Leiningen, follow the installation instructions on Leiningen's website (*http://leiningen.org/*). If you already have Leiningen installed, get the latest version by executing the command **lein upgrade**. If you aren't familiar with Leiningen, visit the tutorial (*http://bit.ly/lein-tutorial*) to learn more.

The one thing you *won't* need to manually install is Clojure itself; Leiningen will do this for you on an ad hoc basis. To verify your installation, run **lein repl** and check your Clojure version:

```
$ lein repl
# ...
user=> *clojure-version*
{:major 1, :minor 5, :incremental 1, :qualifier nil}
```

Some recipes have accompanying online materials available on GitHub. If you do not have Git installed on your system, follow the setup instructions (*https://help.github.com/articles/set-up-git*) to enable you to check out a GitHub repository locally.

Some recipes—such as the database recipes—require further software installations. Where this is the case, recipes will include additional information on installing those tools.

## Conventions Used in This Book

Being a book full of solutions, you'll find no shortage of Clojure source code in this book. Clojure source code appears in a monospace font, like this:

```
(defn add
  [x y]
  (+ x y))
```

When a Clojure expression is evaluated for a return value, that value is denoted with a comment followed by an arrow, much like it would appear on the command line:

```
(add 1 2)
;; -> 3
```

Where appropriate, code samples may omit or ellipsize return value comments. The two most common places you'll see this are when defining a function/var or shortening lengthy output:

```
;; This would return #'user/one, but do you really care?
(def one 1)

(into [] (range 1 20))
;; -> [1 2 ... 20]
```

When an expression produces output to `STDOUT` or `STDERR`, it is denoted by a comment (`*out*` or `*error*`, respectively), followed by a comment with each line of output:

```
(do (println "Hello!")
    (println "Goodbye!"))
;; -> nil
;; *out*
;; Hello!
;; Goodbye!
```

## REPL Sessions

Seeing that *REPL-driven development* is in vogue at present, it follows that this be a REPL-driven book. REPLs (read-eval-print loops) are interactive prompts that evaluate expressions and print their results. The Bash prompt, `irb`, and the `python` prompt are examples of REPLs. Nearly every recipe in this book is designed to be run at a Clojure REPL.

While Clojure REPLs are traditionally displayed as `user=> ...`, this book aims for readers to be able to copy and paste all of the examples in a recipe and see the indicated results. As such, samples omit `user=>` and comment out any output to make things easier. This is especially helpful if you're following along on a computer: you can blindly copy and paste code samples without worrying about trying to run noncode.

When an example is *only* relevant in the context of a REPL, we will retain the traditional REPL style (with `user=>`). What follows is an example of each, a REPL-only sample and its simplified version.

*REPL-only*:

```
user=> (+ 1 2)
3
user=> (println "Hello!")
Hello!
nil
```

*Simplified*:

```
(+ 1 2)
;; -> 3

(println "Hello!")
;; *out*
;; Hello!
```

## Console/Terminal Sessions

Console sessions (e.g., shell commands) are denoted by monospace font, with lines beginning with a dollar sign (`$`) indicating a shell prompt. Output is printed without a leading `$`:

```
$ lein version
Leiningen 2.0.0-preview10 on Java 1.6.0_29 Java HotSpot(TM) 64-Bit Server VM
```

A backslash (\) at the end of a command indicates to the console that the command continues on the next line.

### Our Golden Boy, lein-try

Clojure is not known for its extensive standard library. Unlike languages like Perl or Ruby, Clojure's standard library is comparatively small; Clojure chose *simplicity* and *power* instead. As such, Clojure is a language full of libraries, not built-ins (well, except for Java).

Since so many of the solutions in this book rely on third-party libraries, we developed `lein-try` (*https://github.com/rkneufeld/lein-try*). `lein-try` is a small plug-in for Leiningen (*http://leiningen.org/*), Clojure's de facto project tool, that lets you quickly and easily try out various Clojure libraries.

To use `lein-try`, ensure you have Leiningen installed, then edit your user profile (*~/.lein/profiles.clj*) as follows:

```
{:user {:plugins [[lein-try "0.4.1"]]}}
```

Now, inside of a project or out, you can use the **`lein try`** command to launch a REPL with access to whichever library you please:

```
$ lein try clj-time
#...
user=>
```

Long story short: where possible, you'll see instructions on which `lein-try` command to execute above recipes that use third-party libraries. You'll find an example of trying recipes with `lein-try` in Recipe 3.4, "Trying a Library Without Explicit Dependencies" on page 128.

If a recipe *cannot* be run via `lein-try`, we have made efforts to include adequate instructions on how to run that recipe on your local machine.

## Typesetting Conventions

The following typographic conventions are used in this book:

*Italic*
: Used for URLs, filenames, pathnames, and file extensions. New terms are also italicized when they first appear in the text, and italics are used for emphasis.

`Constant width`
: Used for function and method names and their arguments; for data types, classes, and namespaces; in examples to show both input and output; and in regular text to show literal code.

**`Constant width bold`**
: Used to indicate commands that you should enter literally at the command line.

*<replaceable-value>*
: Elements of pathnames, commands, function names, etc. that should be replaced with user-supplied values are shown in angle brackets.

The names of libraries follow one of two conventions: libraries with proper names are displayed in plain text (e.g., "Hiccup" or "Swing"), while libraries with names meant to mimic code symbols are displayed in constant-width text (e.g., `core.async` or `clj-commons-exec`).

This element signifies a tip or suggestion.

This element signifies a general note.

This element indicates a warning or caution.

## Using Code Examples

Supplemental material (code examples, exercises, etc.) is available for download at *http://bit.ly/clj-ckbk*.

This book is here to help you get your job done. In general, if example code is offered with this book, you may use it in your programs and documentation. You do not need to contact us for permission unless you're reproducing a significant portion of the code. For example, writing a program that uses several chunks of code from this book does not require permission. Selling or distributing a CD-ROM of examples from O'Reilly books does require permission. Answering a question by citing this book and quoting example code does not require permission. Incorporating a significant amount of example code from this book into your product's documentation does require permission.

We appreciate, but do not require, attribution. An attribution usually includes the title, author, publisher, and ISBN. For example: "*Clojure Cookbook* by Luke VanderHart and Ryan Neufeld (O'Reilly). Copyright 2014 Cognitect, Inc., 978-1-449-36617-9."

If you feel your use of code examples falls outside fair use or the permission given above, feel free to contact us at *permissions@oreilly.com*.

## Safari® Books Online

*Safari Books Online* is an on-demand digital library that delivers expert content in both book and video form from the world's leading authors in technology and business.

Technology professionals, software developers, web designers, and business and creative professionals use Safari Books Online as their primary resource for research, problem solving, learning, and certification training.

Safari Books Online offers a range of product mixes and pricing programs for organizations, government agencies, and individuals. Subscribers have access to thousands of books, training videos, and prepublication manuscripts in one fully searchable database from publishers like O'Reilly Media, Prentice Hall Professional, Addison-Wesley Professional, Microsoft Press, Sams, Que, Peachpit Press, Focal Press, Cisco Press, John Wiley & Sons, Syngress, Morgan Kaufmann, IBM Redbooks, Packt, Adobe Press, FT Press, Apress, Manning, New Riders, McGraw-Hill, Jones & Bartlett, Course Technology, and dozens more. For more information about Safari Books Online, please visit us online.

## How to Contact Us

Please address comments and questions concerning this book to the publisher:

O'Reilly Media, Inc.
1005 Gravenstein Highway North
Sebastopol, CA 95472
800-998-9938 (in the United States or Canada)
707-829-0515 (international or local)
707-829-0104 (fax)

We have a web page for this book, where we list errata, examples, and any additional information. You can access this page at *http://oreil.ly/clojure-ckbk*.

To comment or ask technical questions about this book, send email to *bookquestions@oreilly.com*.

For more information about our books, courses, conferences, and news, see our website at *http://www.oreilly.com*.

Find us on Facebook: *http://facebook.com/oreilly*

Follow us on Twitter: *http://twitter.com/oreillymedia* or *https://twitter.com/clojurecookbook*

Watch us on YouTube: *http://www.youtube.com/oreillymedia*

## Acknowledgments

This book would not have been possible without the selfless contributions of many within the Clojure community. Over 65 Clojurists rose to the occasion, submitting recipes, proofreading, and offering their input on the direction of the book. Ultimately, this is the community's book—we're just honored to have been able to help put it together. Those contributors are:

- Adam Bard, adambard (*https://github.com/adambard*) on GitHub
- Alan Busby, thebusby (*https://github.com/thebusby*) on GitHub
- Alex Miller, puredanger (*https://github.com/puredanger*) on GitHub
- Alex Petrov, ifesdjeen (*https://github.com/ifesdjeen*) on GitHub
- Alex Robbins, alexrobbins (*https://github.com/alexrobbins*) on GitHub
- Alex Vzorov, 0rca (*https://github.com/0rca*) on GitHub
- Ambrose Bonnaire-Sergeant, frenchy64 (*https://github.com/frenchy64*) on GitHub
- arosequist (*https://github.com/arosequist*)
- Chris Allen, bitemyapp (*https://github.com/bitemyapp*) on GitHub
- Chris Ford, ctford (*https://github.com/ctford*) on GitHub
- Chris Frisz, cjfrisz (*https://github.com/cjfrisz*) on GitHub
- Clinton Begin, cbegin (*https://github.com/cbegin*) on GitHub
- Clinton Dreisbach, cndreisbach (*https://github.com/cndreisbach*) on GitHub
- Colin Jones, trptcolin (*https://github.com/trptcolin*) on GitHub
- Craig McDaniel, cpmcdaniel (*https://github.com/cpmcdaniel*) on GitHub
- Daemian Mack, daemianmack (*https://github.com/daemianmack*) on GitHub
- Dan Allen, mojavelinux (*https://github.com/mojavelinux*) on GitHub
- Daniel Gregoire, semperos (*https://github.com/semperos*) on GitHub
- Dmitri Sotnikov, yogthos (*https://github.com/yogthos*) on GitHub
- Edmund Jackson, ejackson (*https://github.com/ejackson*) on GitHub

- Eric Normand, ericnormand (*https://github.com/ericnormand*) on GitHub
- Federico Ramirez, gosukiwi (*https://github.com/gosukiwi*) on GitHub
- Filippo Diotalevi, fdiotalevi (*https://github.com/fdiotalevi*) on GitHub
- fredericksgary (*https://github.com/fredericksgary*)
- Gabriel Horner, cldwalker (*https://github.com/cldwalker*) on GitHub
- Gerrit, gerritjvv (*https://github.com/gerritjvv*) on GitHub
- Guewen Baconnier, guewen (*https://github.com/guewen*) on GitHub
- Hoàng Minh Thắng, myguidingstar (*https://github.com/myguidingstar*) on GitHub
- Jason Webb, bigjason (*https://github.com/bigjason*) on GitHub
- Jason Wolfe, w01fe (*https://github.com/w01fe*) on GitHub
- Jean Niklas L'orange, hyPiRion (*https://github.com/hyPiRion*) on GitHub
- Joey Yang, joeyyang (*https://github.com/joeyyang*) on GitHub
- John Cromartie, jcromartie (*https://github.com/jcromartie*) on GitHub
- John Jacobsen, eigenhombre (*https://github.com/eigenhombre*) on GitHub
- John Touron, jwtouron (*https://github.com/jwtouron*) on GitHub
- Joseph Wilk, josephwilk (*https://github.com/josephwilk*) on GitHub
- jungziege (*https://github.com/jungziege*)
- jwhitlark (*https://github.com/jwhitlark*)
- Kevin Burnett, burnettk (*https://github.com/burnettk*) on GitHub
- Kevin Lynagh, lynaghk (*https://github.com/lynaghk*) on GitHub
- Lake Denman, ldenman (*https://github.com/ldenman*) on GitHub
- Leonardo Borges, leonardoborges (*https://github.com/leonardoborges*) on GitHub
- Mark Whelan, mrwhelan (*https://github.com/mrwhelan*) on GitHub
- Martin Janiczek, Janiczek (*https://github.com/Janiczek*) on GitHub
- Matthew Maravillas, maravillas (*https://github.com/maravillas*) on GitHub
- Michael Fogus, fogus (*https://github.com/fogus*) on GitHub
- Michael Klishin, michaelklishin (*https://github.com/michaelklishin*) on GitHub
- Michael Mullis, mmullis (*https://github.com/mmullis*) on GitHub
- Michael O'Church, michaelochurch (*https://github.com/michaelochurch*) on GitHub
- Mosciatti S., siscia (*https://github.com/siscia*) on GitHub
- nbessi (*https://github.com/nbessi*)

- Neil Laurance, toolkit (*https://github.com/toolkit*) on GitHub
- Nurullah Akkaya, nakkaya (*https://github.com/nakkaya*) on GitHub
- Osbert Feng, osbert (*https://github.com/osbert*) on GitHub
- Prathamesh Sonpatki, prathamesh-sonpatki (*https://github.com/prathamesh*) on GitHub
- R.T. Lechow, rtlechow (*https://github.com/rtlechow*) on GitHub
- Ravindra R. Jaju, jaju (*https://github.com/jaju*) on GitHub
- Robert Stuttaford, robert-stuttaford (*https://github.com/robert-stuttaford*) on GitHub
- Russ Olsen, russolsen (*https://github.com/russolsen*) on GitHub
- Ryan Senior, senior (*https://github.com/senior*) on GitHub
- Sam Umbach, sumbach (*https://github.com/sumbach*) on GitHub
- Sandeep Nangia, nangia (*https://github.com/nangia*) on GitHub
- Steve Miner, miner (*https://github.com/miner*) on GitHub
- Steven Proctor, stevenproctor (*https://github.com/stevenproctor*) on GitHub
- temacube (*https://github.com/temacube*)
- Tobias Bayer, codebrickie (*https://github.com/codebrickie*) on GitHub
- Tom White, dribnet (*https://github.com/dribnet*) on GitHub
- Travis Vachon, travis (*https://github.com/travis*) on GitHub
- Stefan Karlsson, zclj (*https://github.com/zclj*) on GitHub

Our biggest contributors also deserve special thanks: Adam Bard, Alan Busby, Alex Robbins, Ambrose Bonnaire-Sergeant, Dmitri Sotnikov, John Cromartie, John Jacobsen, Robert Stuttaford, Stefan Karlsson, and Tom Hicks. All together, these outstanding individuals contributed almost a third of the book's recipes.

Thanks also to our technical reviewers, Alex Robbins, Travis Vachon, and Thomas Hicks. These fine gentlemen scoured the book for technical errors in record time, in the 11th hour no less. Where a regular technical reviewer would merely submit textual descriptions of problems, these folks went above and beyond, often submitting pull requests *fixing* the very errors they were reporting. All in all, they were a pleasure to work with and the book is much better because of their involvement.

Finally, thanks to our employer, Cognitect, for giving us time to work on the book, and to all of our colleagues who offered advice, feedback, and best of all, more recipes!

## Ryan Neufeld

First, a huge thanks to Luke. It was Luke who originally pitched the idea for the book, and I'm very grateful that he extended an invitation for me to join him in authoring it. They say the best way to learn something is to write a book on it—this couldn't be any closer to the truth. Working on the book has really rounded out my Clojure skills and taken them to the next level.

And, most importantly, I have to thank my family for putting up with me through the process of writing the book. Getting this thing off the ground has been a Herculean task and I couldn't have done it without the love and support of my wife Jackie and daughter Elody. If it hadn't been for the hundreds upon hundreds of hours of evenings, weekends, and vacation time I usurped from them, I wouldn't have been able to write this book.

## Luke VanderHart

Most of all, I'd like to thank my coauthor Ryan, who worked incredibly hard to make the book happen.

Also, all of my coworkers at Cognitect provided lots of thoughts and ideas, and most importantly were a sounding board for the many questions that arose during the writing and editing process. Many thanks for that, as well as for providing the opportunity to write code in Clojure all day, every day.

CHAPTER 1

# Primitive Data

## 1.0. Introduction

Clojure is a fantastic language for tackling hard problems. Its *simple* tools let us software developers build up layer upon layer of abstractions until we've tackled some of the world's most difficult problems with ease. Like chemistry, every great Clojure program boils down to simple atoms—these are our primitives.

Standing on the shoulders of the Java giants from days of yore, Clojure leverages a fantastic array of battle-hardened types present in the Java Virtual Machine (JVM):[1] strings, numeric types, dates, Universally Unique Identifiers (UUIDs)—you name it, Clojure has it all. This chapter dives into the primitives of Clojure and how to accomplish common tasks.

### Strings

Almost every programming language knows how to work with and deal in strings. Clojure is no exception, and despite a few differences, Clojure provides the same general capabilities as most other languages. Here are a few key differences we think you should know about.

First, Clojure strings are backed by Java's UTF-16 strings. You don't need to add comments to files to indicate string encoding or worry about losing characters in translation. Your Clojure programs are ready to communicate in the world beyond A–Z.

Second, unlike languages like Perl or Ruby that have extensive string libraries, Clojure has a rather Spartan built-in string manipulation library. This may seem odd at first, but Clojure prefers simple and composable tools; all of the plethora of collection-

1. The JVM is where Java bytecode is executed. The Clojure compiler targets the JVM by emitting bytecode to be run there; thus, you have all of the native Java types at your disposal.

modifying functions in Clojure are perfectly capable of accepting strings—they're collections too! For this reason, Clojure's string library is unexpectedly small. You'll find that small set of very string-specific functions in the `clojure.string` namespace.

Clojure also embraces its host platform (the JVM) and does not duplicate functionality already adequately performed by Java's `java.lang.String` class. Using Java interop in Clojure is not a failure—the language is designed to make it straightforward, and using the built-in string methods is usually just as easy as invoking a Clojure function.

We suggest you "require as" the `clojure.string` namespace when you need it. Blindly `:use`-ing a namespace is always annoying,[2] and often results in collisions/confusion. Prefixing everything with `clojure.string` is kind of odd, so we prefer to alias it to `str` or `s`:

```
(require '[clojure.string :as str])

(str/blank? "")
;; -> true
```

## Numeric Types

The veneer between Clojure and Java is a little thicker over the numeric types. This isn't necessarily a bad thing, though. While Java's numeric types can be extremely fast or arbitrarily precise, numerics overall don't have the prettiest set of interfaces to work with. Clojure unifies the various numeric types of Java into one coherent package, with clear escape hatches at every turn.

The recipes on numeric types in this chapter will show you how to work with these hatches, showing you how to be as fast or precise or expressive as you desire.

## Dates

Dates and times have a long and varied history in the Java ecosystem. Do you want a `Date`, `Time`, `DateTime`, or `Calendar`? Who knows. And why are these APIs all so wonky? The recipes in this chapter should hopefully illuminate how and when to use the appropriate built-in types and when to look to an external library when built-ins aren't sufficient (or are just too darned difficult to use).

2. By using `use`, you introduce numerous new symbols into your project's namespaces without leaving any clues as to where they came from. This is often confusing and frustrating for maintainers of the code base. We highly suggest you avoid `use`.

# 1.1. Changing the Capitalization of a String

by Ryan Neufeld

## Problem

You need to change the capitalization of a string.

## Solution

Use `clojure.string/capitalize` to capitalize the first character in a string:

```
(clojure.string/capitalize "this is a proper sentence.")
;; -> "This is a proper sentence."
```

When you need to change the case of all characters in a string, use `clojure.string/lower-case` or `clojure.string/upper-case`:

```
(clojure.string/upper-case "loud noises!")
;; -> "LOUD NOISES!"

(clojure.string/lower-case "COLUMN_HEADER_ONE")
;; -> "column_header_one"
```

## Discussion

Capitalization functions only affect letters. While the functions `capitalize`, `lower-case`, and `upper-case` may modify letters, characters like punctuation marks or digits will remain untouched:

```
(clojure.string/lower-case "!&$#@#%^[]")
;; -> "!&$#@#%^[]"
```

Clojure uses UTF-16 for all strings, and as such its definition of what a letter is is liberal enough to include accented characters. Take the phrase "Hurry up, computer!" which includes the letter *e* with both acute (*é*) and circumflex (*ê*) accents when translated to French. Since these special characters are considered letters, it is possible for capitalization functions to change case appropriately:

```
(clojure.string/upper-case "Dépêchez-vous, l'ordinateur!")
;; -> "DÉPÊCHEZ-VOUS, L'ORDINATEUR!"
```

## See Also

- The `clojure.string` namespace API documentation (*http://bit.ly/clj-string-api*)
- The `java.lang.String` API documentation (*http://bit.ly/javadoc-string*)

# 1.2. Cleaning Up Whitespace in a String

by Ryan Neufeld

## Problem

You need to clean up the whitespace in a string.

## Solution

Use the `clojure.string/trim` function to remove all of the whitespace at the beginning and end of a string:

```
(clojure.string/trim " \tBacon ipsum dolor sit.\n")
;; -> "Bacon ipsum dolor sit."
```

To manage whitespace *inside* a string, you need to get more creative. Use `clojure.string/replace` to fix whitespace inside a string:

```
;; Collapse whitespace into a single space
(clojure.string/replace "Who\t\nput  all this\fwhitespace here?" #"\s+" " ")
;; -> "Who put all this whitespace here?"

;; Replace Windows-style line endings with Unix-style newlines
(clojure.string/replace "Line 1\r\nLine 2" "\r\n" "\n")
;; -> "Line 1\nLine 2"
```

## Discussion

What constitutes whitespace in Clojure? The answer depends on the function: some are more liberal than others, but you can safely assume that a space ( ), tab (`\t`), newline (`\n`), carriage return (`\r`), line feed (`\f`), and vertical tab (`\x0B`) will be treated as whitespace. This set of characters is the set matched by `\s` in Java's regular expression implementation.

Unlike Ruby and other languages that include string manipulation functions in the core namespace, Clojure excludes its `clojure.string` namespace from `clojure.core`, making it unavailable for naked use. A common technique is to require `clojure.string` as a shorthand like `str` or `string` to make code more terse:

```
(require '[clojure.string :as str])
(str/replace "Look Ma, no hands" "hands" "long namespace prefixes")
;; -> "Look Ma, no long namespace prefixes"
```

You might not always want to remove whitespace from both ends of a string. For cases where you want to remove whitespace from just the left- or righthand side of a string, use `clojure.string/triml` or `clojure.string/trimr`, respectively:

```
(clojure.string/triml " Column Header\t")
;; -> "Column Header\t"

(clojure.string/trimr "\t\t* Second-level bullet.\n")
;; -> "\t\t* Second-level bullet."
```

## See Also

- Recipe 1.3, "Building a String from Parts" on page 5

# 1.3. Building a String from Parts

by Ryan Neufeld

## Problem

You have multiple strings, values, or collections that you need to combine into one string.

## Solution

Use the `str` function to concatenate strings and/or values:

```
(str "John" " " "Doe")
;; -> "John Doe"

;; str also works with vars, or any other values
(def first-name "John")
(def last-name "Doe")
(def age 42)

(str last-name ", " first-name " - age: " age)
;; -> "Doe, John - age: 42"
```

Use `apply` with `str` to concatenate a collection of values into a single string:

```
;; To collapse a sequence of characters back into a string
(apply str "ROT13: " [\W \h \y \v \h \f \  \P \n \r \f \n \e])
;; -> "ROT13: Whyvhf Pnrfne"

;; Or, to reconstitute a file from lines (if they already have newlines...)
(def lines ["#! /bin/bash\n", "du -a ./ | sort -n -r\n"])
(apply str lines)
;; -> "#! /bin/bash\ndu -a ./ | sort -n -r\n"
```

## Discussion

Clojure's `str` is like a good Unix tool: it has one job, and it does it well. When provided with one or more arguments, `str` invokes Java's `.toString()` method on its argument, tacking each result onto the next. When provided `nil` or invoked without arguments, `str` will return the identity value for strings, the empty string.

When it comes to string concatenation, Clojure takes a fairly hands-off approach. There is nothing string-specific about `(apply str ...)`. It is merely the higher-order function `apply` being used to emulate calling `str` with a variable number of arguments.

This `apply`:

```
(apply str ["a" "b" "c"])
```

is functionally equivalent to:

```
(str "a" "b" "c")
```

Since Clojure injects little opinion into joining strings, you're free to inject your own with the plethora of manipulating functions Clojure provides. For example, take constructing a comma-separated value (CSV) from a header and a number of rows. This example is particularly well suited for `apply`, as you can prefix the header without having to insert it onto the front of your `rows` collection:

```
;; Constructing a CSV from a header string and vector of rows
(def header "first_name,last_name,employee_number\n")
(def rows ["luke,vanderhart,1","ryan,neufeld,2"])

(apply str header (interpose "\n" rows))
;; -> "first_name,last_name,employee_number\nluke,vanderhart,1\nryan,neufeld,2"
```

`apply` and `interpose` can be a lot of ceremony when you're not doing anything too fancy. It is often easier to use the `clojure.string/join` function for simple string joins. The `join` function takes a collection and an optional separator. With a separator, `join` returns a string with each item of the collection separated by the provided separator. Without, it returns each item squashed together, similar to what `(apply str coll)` would return:

```
(def food-items ["milk" "butter" "flour" "eggs"])
(clojure.string/join ", " food-items)
;; -> "milk, butter, flour, eggs"

(clojure.string/join [1 2 3 4])
;; -> "1234"
```

## See Also

- Recipe 1.6, "Formatting Strings" on page 10

- The clojure.string namespace API documentation (*http://bit.ly/clj-string-api*)
- The java.lang.String API documentation (*http://bit.ly/javadoc-string*)

# 1.4. Treating a String as a Sequence of Characters

by Ryan Neufeld

## Problem

You need to work with the individual characters in a string.

## Solution

Use seq on a string to expose the sequence of characters representing it:

```
(seq "Hello, world!")
;; -> (\H \e \l \l \o \, \space \w \o \r \l \d \!)
```

You don't need to call seq every time you want to get at a string's characters, though. Any function taking a sequence will naturally coerce a string into a sequence of characters:

```
;; Count the occurrences of each character in a string.
(frequencies (clojure.string/lower-case "An adult all about A's"))
;; -> {\space 4, \a 5, \b 1, \d 1, \' 1, \l 3, \n 1, \o 1, \s 1, \t 2, \u 2}

;; Is every letter in a string capitalized?
(defn yelling? [s]
  (every? #(or (not (Character/isLetter %))
               (Character/isUpperCase %))
        s))

(yelling? "LOUD NOISES!")
;; -> true

(yelling? "Take a DEEP breath.")
;; -> false
```

## Discussion

In computer science, "string" means "sequence of characters," and Clojure treats strings exactly as such. Because Clojure strings are sequences under the covers, you may substitute a string anywhere a collection is expected. When you do so, the string will be interpreted as a collection of characters. There's nothing special about (seq string). The seq function is merely returning a seq of the collection of characters that make up the string.

More often than not, after you've done some work on the characters within a string, you'll want to transform that collection back into a string. Use `apply` with `str` on a collection of characters to collapse them into a string:

```
(apply str [\H \e \l \l \o \, \space \w \o \r \l \d \!])
;; -> "Hello, world!"
```

## See Also

- Recipe 1.3, "Building a String from Parts" on page 5
- Recipe 1.5, "Converting Between Characters and Integers" on page 8

# 1.5. Converting Between Characters and Integers

by Ryan Neufeld

## Problem

You need to convert characters to their respective Unicode code points (as integer values), or vice versa.

## Solution

Use the `int` function to convert a character to its integer value:

```
(int \a)
;; -> 97

(int \ø)
;; -> 248

(int \α) ; Greek letter alpha
;; -> 945

(int \u03B1) ; Greek letter alpha (by code point)
;; -> 945

(map int "Hello, world!")
;; -> (72 101 108 108 111 44 32 119 111 114 108 100 33)
```

Use the `char` function to return a character corresponding to the code point specified by the integer:

```
(char 97)
;; -> \a

(char 125)
;; -> \}
```

```
(char 945)
;; -> \α

(reduce #(str %1 (char %2))
        ""
        [115 101 99 114 101 116 32 109 101 115 115 97 103 101 115])
;; -> "secret messages"
```

## Discussion

Clojure inherits the JVM's robust Unicode support. All strings are UTF-16 strings, and all characters are Unicode characters. Conveniently, the first 256 Unicode code points are identical to ASCII, which makes standard ASCII text easy to work with. However, Clojure (like Java) does not actually privilege ASCII in any way; the 1:1 correspondence between characters and integers indicating code points continues all the way up through the Unicode space.

For example, the expression `(map char (range 0x0410 0x042F))` prints out all the Cyrillic capital letters, which happen to lie on that range on the Unicode spectrum:

```
(\А \Б \В \Г \Д \Е \Ж \З \И \Й \К \Л \М \Н \О \П \Р \С \Т \У \Ф
\Х \Ц \Ч \Ш \Щ \Ъ \Ы \Ь \Э \Ю)
```

The `char` and `int` functions are useful primarily for coercing a number into an instance of either `java.lang.Integer` or `java.lang.Character`. Both `Integers` and `Characters` are, ultimately, encoded as numbers, although `Characters` support additional text-related methods and cannot be used in mathematic expressions without first being converted to a true numeric type.

## See Also

- *Unicode Explained* (*http://oreil.ly/unicode-explained*), by Jukka K. Korpela (O'Reilly), for truly comprehensive coverage of how Unicode and internationalization works
- Recipe 1.4, "Treating a String as a Sequence of Characters" on page 7, for details on working with the characters that constitute a string
- Recipe 1.15, "Parsing Numbers" on page 25

## 1.6. Formatting Strings

by Ryan Neufeld

### Problem

You need to insert values into a string, formatting how those values appear in the string.

### Solution

The quickest method for formatting values into a string is the `str` function:

```
(def me {:first-name "Ryan", :favorite-language "Clojure"})
(str "My name is " (:first-name me)
     ", and I really like to program in " (:favorite-language me))
;; -> "My name is Ryan, and I really like to program in Clojure"

(apply str (interpose " " [1 2.000 (/ 3 1) (/ 4 9)]))
;; -> "1 2.0 3 4/9"
```

With `str`, however, values are inserted blindly, appearing in their default `.toString()` appearance. Not only that, but it can sometimes be difficult to look at a `str` form and interpret what the intended output is.

For greater control over how values are printed, use the `format` function:

```
;; Produce a filename with a zero-padded sortable index
(defn filename [name i]
  (format "%03d-%s" i name)) ; ❶

(filename "my-awesome-file.txt" 42)
;; -> "042-my-awesome-file.txt"

;; Create a table using justification
(defn tableify [row]
  (apply format "%-20s | %-20s | %-20s" row)) ; ❷

(def header ["First Name", "Last Name", "Employee ID"])
(def employees [["Ryan", "Neufeld", 2]
                ["Luke", "Vanderhart", 1]])

(->> (concat [header] employees)
     (map tableify)
     (mapv println))
;; *out*
;; First Name           | Last Name            | Employee ID
;; Ryan                 | Neufeld              | 2
;; Luke                 | Vanderhart           | 1
```

❶ The `0` flag indicates to pad a digit (`d`) with zeros (three, in this case).

❷ The `-` flag indicates to left justify the string (`s`), giving it a total minimum width of 20 characters.

## Discussion

When it comes to inserting values into a string, you have two very different options. You can use `str`, which is great for a quick fix but lacks control over how values are presented. Or you can use `format`, which exposes fine-grained control over how values are displayed but requires knowledge of C and Java-style formatting strings. Ultimately, you should use only as much tooling/complexity as is necessary for the task at hand: stick to `str` when the default formatting for a value will suffice, and use `format` when you need more control over how values display.

### Format Strings

The first argument passed to `format` is what is called a *format string*. The syntax for these strings isn't new or unique to Clojure or even Java, but in fact comes from C's `printf` function. Clojure's `format` function uses Java's `String/format`, which implements `printf`-style value substitution.

A format string is a normal string with any number of embedded format specifiers. A format specifier is a placeholder to be replaced by a value later. In its simplest form, this is a `%` followed by a type specifier character; for example, `%d` for an integer (*d* is for digit) or `%f` for a float. Beyond specifiers for strings, integers, and floats, there are specifiers for characters, dates, and numbers of different bases (octal and hexadecimal), to name a few.

What makes these format specifiers special is that you may indicate any number of flags and options between the percent sign and the specifier character. For instance, "`%-10s`" indicates the provided string (`s`) should be left justified (`-`) with a total minimum width of 10. "`%07.3f`" would turn a number into a zero-padded number that was seven characters wide and included three decimal places (just like the numbers used in the Dewey Decimal system):

```
(format "%07.3f" 0.005)
;; -> "000.005" ;; The Dewey Decimal subclass for books on "Computer
;;              ;; programming, programs & data"
```

Visit the API documentation for `java.util.Formatter` (*http://bit.ly/javadoc-formatter*) to learn more about formatting strings.

## See Also

- Recipe 1.3, "Building a String from Parts" on page 5
- Recipe 1.28, "Formatting Dates Using clj-time" on page 48

# 1.7. Searching a String by Pattern

by Ryan Neufeld

## Problem

You need to test a string to see if parts of it match a pattern.

## Solution

To check for the presence of a pattern inside a string, invoke `re-find` with a desired pattern and the string to test. Express the desired pattern using a regular expression literal (like `"foo"` or `"\d+"`):

```
;; Any contiguous groups of numbers
(re-find #"\d+" "I've just finished reading Fahrenheit 451")
;; -> "451"

(re-find #"Bees" "Beads aren't cheap.")
;; -> nil
```

## Discussion

`re-find` is quite handy for quickly testing a string for the presence of a pattern. It takes a regular expression pattern and a string, then returns either the first match of that pattern or `nil`.

If your criterion is more stringent and you require that the *entire* string match a pattern, use `re-matches`. Unlike `re-find`, which matches any portion of a string, `re-matches` matches if and only if the *entire* string matches the pattern:

```
;; In find, #"\w+" is any contiguous word characters
(re-find #"\w+" "my-param")
;; -> "my"

;; But in matches, #"\w+" means "all word characters"
(re-matches #"\w+" "my-param")
;; -> nil

(re-matches #"\w+" "justLetters")
;; -> "justLetters"
```

## See Also

- The API documentation (*http://bit.ly/javadoc-pattern*) for `java.lang.Pattern`, which defines the exact regex syntax supported by Java (and Clojure's regular expression literals)
- Recipe 1.8, "Pulling Values Out of a String Using Regular Expressions" on page 13, for information on extracting values from a string using regular expressions
- Recipe 1.9, "Performing Find and Replace on Strings" on page 15

# 1.8. Pulling Values Out of a String Using Regular Expressions

by Ryan Neufeld

## Problem

You need to extract portions of a string matching a given pattern.

## Solution

Use `re-seq` with a regular expression pattern and a string to retrieve a sequence of successive matches:

```
;; Extract simple words from a sentence
(re-seq #"\w+" "My Favorite Things")
;; -> ("My" "Favorite" "Things")

;; Extract simple 7-digit phone numbers
(re-seq #"\d{3}-\d{4}" "My phone number is 555-1234.")
;; -> ("555-1234")
```

Regular expressions with matching groups (parentheses) will return a vector for each total match:

```
;; Extract all of the Twitter usernames and hashtags in a tweet
(defn mentions [tweet]
  (re-seq #"(@|#)(\w+)" tweet))

(mentions "So long, @earth, and thanks for all the #fish. #goodbyes")
;; -> (["@earth" "@" "earth"] ["#fish" "#" "fish"] ["#goodbyes" "#" "goodbyes"])
```

## Discussion

Provided a simple pattern (one without matching groups), `re-seq` will return a flat sequence of matches. Fully expressing the power of Clojure, this is a lazy sequence.

Calling `re-seq` on a gigantic string will not scan the entire string right away; you're free to consume those values incrementally, or defer evaluation to some other constituent part of your application further down the road.

When given a regular expression containing matching groups, `re-seq` will do something a little different. Don't worry, the resulting sequence is still lazy—but instead of flat strings, its values will be vectors. The first value of the vector will always be the whole match, grouped or not; subsequent values will be the strings captured by matching group parentheses. These captured values will appear in the order in which their opening parentheses appeared, despite any nesting. Take a look at this example:

```
;; Using re to capture and decompose a phone number and its title
(def re-phone-number #"(\w+): \((\d{3})\) (\d{3}-\d{4})")

(re-seq re-phone-number "Home: (919) 555-1234, Work: (191) 555-1234")
;; -> (["Home: (919) 555-1234" "Home" "919" "555-1234"]
;;     ["Work: (191) 555-1234" "Work" "191" "555-1234"])
```

If all you're looking for is a single match from a string, then use `re-find`. It behaves almost identically to `re-seq`, but returns only the first match as a singular value, instead of a sequence of match values.

Apart from `re-seq`, there is another way to iterate over the matches in a string. You *could* do this by repeatedly calling `re-find` on a `re-matcher`, but we don't suggest this approach. Why? Because it isn't very idiomatic Clojure. Mutating a `re-matcher` object with repeated calls to `re-find` is just wrong; it completely violates the principle of pure functions. We highly suggest you prefer `re-seq` over `re-matcher` and `re-find` unless you have a really good reason not to.

## See Also

- Recipe 1.7, "Searching a String by Pattern" on page 12, for testing a string for the presence of a pattern
- Recipe 1.9, "Performing Find and Replace on Strings" on page 15, for information on using regular expressions to find and replace portions of a string
- The API documentation (*http://bit.ly/javadoc-pattern*) for `java.lang.Pattern`, which defines the exact regex syntax supported by Java (and Clojure's regular expression literals)

# 1.9. Performing Find and Replace on Strings

by Ryan Neufeld

## Problem

You need to modify portions of a string that match some well-defined pattern.

## Solution

The versatile `clojure.string/replace` is the function you should reach for when you need to selectively replace portions of a string.

For simple patterns, use `replace` with a normal string as its matcher:

```
(def about-me "My favorite color is green!")
(clojure.string/replace about-me "green" "red")
;; -> "My favorite color is red!"

(defn de-canadianize [s]
  (clojure.string/replace s "ou" "o"))
(de-canadianize (str "Those Canadian neighbours have coloured behaviour"
                     " when it comes to word endings"))
;; -> "Those Canadian neighbors have colored behavior when it comes to word
;;     endings"
```

Plain string replacement will only get you so far. When you need to replace a pattern with some variability to it, you'll need to reach for the big guns: regular expressions. Use Clojure's regular expression literals (`#"..."`) to specify a pattern as a regular expression:

```
(defn linkify-comment
  "Add Markdown-style links for any GitHub issue numbers present in comment"
  [repo comment]
  (clojure.string/replace comment
                          #"#(\d+)"
                          (str "[#$1](https://github.com/" repo "/issues/$1)")))

(linkify-comment "next/big-thing" "As soon as we fix #42 and #1337 we
should be set to release!")
;; -> "As soon as we fix
;;     [#42](https://github.com/next/big-thing/issues/42) and
;;     [#1337](https://github.com/next/big-thing/issues/1337) we
;;     should be set to release!"
```

## Discussion

As far as string functions go, `replace` is one of the more powerful and most complex ones. The majority of this complexity arises from the varying `match` and `replacement` types it can operate with.

When passed a string `match`, `replace` expects a string `replacement`. Any occurrences of `match` in the supplied string will be replaced directly with `replacement`.

When passed a character `match` (such as `\c` or `\n`), `replace` expects a character `replacement`. Like string/string, the character/character mode of `replace` replaces items directly.

When passed a regular expression for a match, `replace` gets much more interesting. One possible `replacement` for a regex match is a string, like in the `linkify-comment` example; this string interprets special character combinations like `$1` or `$2` as variables to be replaced by matching groups in the match. In the `linkify-comment` example, any contiguous digits (`\d+`) following a number sign (`#`) are captured in parentheses and are available as `$1` in the replacement.

When passing a regex `match`, you can also provide a function for replacement instead of a string. In Clojure, the world is your oyster when you can pass a function as an argument. You can capture your replacement in a reusable (and testable) function, pass in different functions depending on the circumstances, or even pass a map that dictates replacements:

```
;; linkify-comment rewritten with linkification as a separate function
(defn linkify [repo [full-match id]]
  (str "[" full-match "](https://github.com/" repo "/issues/" id ")"))

(defn linkify-comment [repo comment]
  (clojure.string/replace comment #"#(\d+)" (partial linkify repo)))
```

If you've not used regular expressions before, then you're in for a treat. Regexes are a powerful tool for modifying strings with unbounded flexibility. As with any powerful new tool, it's easy to overdo it. Because of their terse and compact syntax, it's very easy to produce regexes that are both difficult to interpret and at a high risk ofbeing incorrect. You should use regular expressions sparingly and only if you fully understand their syntax.

Jeffrey Friedl's *Mastering Regular Expressions*, 3rd ed. (*http://oreil.ly/Mastering_RegEx*) (O'Reilly) is a fantastic book for learning and mastering regular expression syntax.

## See Also

- Recipe 1.7, "Searching a String by Pattern" on page 12

- `clojure.string/replace-first`, a function that operates nearly identically to `clojure.string/replace` but only replaces the first occurrence of `match`
- The API documentation (*http://bit.ly/javadoc-pattern*) for `java.lang.Pattern`, which defines the exact regex syntax supported by Java (and Clojure's regular-expression literals)

# 1.10. Splitting a String into Parts

by Ryan Neufeld

## Problem

You need to split a string into a number of parts.

## Solution

Use `clojure.string/split` to tokenize a string into a vector of tokens. `split` takes two arguments, a string to tokenize and a regular expression to split on:

```
(clojure.string/split "HEADER1,HEADER2,HEADER3" #",")
;; -> ["HEADER1" "HEADER2" "HEADER3"]

(clojure.string/split "Spaces   Newlines\n\n" #"\s+")
;; -> ["Spaces" "Newlines"]
```

## Discussion

In addition to just naively splitting on a regular expression, `split` allows you to control how many (or how few) times to split the provided string. You can control this with the optional `limit` argument. The most obvious effect of `limit` is to limit the number of values returned in the resulting collection. That said, `limit` doesn't always work like you would expect, and even the absence of this argument carries a meaning.

Without `limit`, the `split` function will return every possible delimitation but exclude any trailing empty matches:

```
;; Splitting on whitespace without an explicit limit performs an implicit trim
(clojure.string/split "field1    field2 field3   " #"\s+")
;; -> ["field1" "field2" "field3"]
```

If you want absolutely every match, including trailing empty ones, then you can specify `-1` as the limit:

```
;; In CSV parsing an empty match at the end of a line is still a meaningful one
(clojure.string/split "ryan,neufeld," #"," -1)
;; -> ["ryan" "neufeld" ""]
```

Specifying some other positive number as a `limit` will cause `split` to return at maximum `limit` substrings:

```
(def data-delimiters #"[ :-]")

;; No-limit split on any delimiter
(clojure.string/split "2013-04-05 14:39" data-delimiters)
;; -> ["2013" "04" "05" "14" "39"]

;; Limit of 1 - functionally: return this string in a collection
(clojure.string/split "2013-04-05 14:39" data-delimiters 1)
;; -> ["2013-04-05 14:39"]

;; Limit of 2
(clojure.string/split "2013-04-05 14:39" data-delimiters 2)
;; -> ["2013" "04-05 14:39"]

;; Limit of 100
(clojure.string/split "2013-04-05 14:39" data-delimiters 100)
;; -> ["2013" "04" "05" "14" "39"]
```

## See Also

- The `clojure.string` namespace API documentation (*http://bit.ly/clj-string-api*)
- Recipe 1.7, "Searching a String by Pattern" on page 12
- Recipe 1.8, "Pulling Values Out of a String Using Regular Expressions" on page 13

# 1.11. Pluralizing Strings Based on a Quantity

by Ryan Neufeld

## Problem

You need to pluralize a word given some quantity, such as "0 eggs" or "1 chicken."

## Solution

When you need to perform Ruby on Rails–style pluralization, use Roman Scherer's `inflections` (*https://github.com/r0man/inflections-clj*) library.

To follow along with this recipe, start a REPL using `lein-try`:[3]

```
$ lein try inflections
```

3. If you haven't already installed `lein-try`, follow the instructions in "Our Golden Boy, lein-try" on page xv.

Use `inflections.core/pluralize` with a count to attempt to pluralize that word if the count is not one:

```
(require '[inflections.core :as inf])

(inf/pluralize 1 "monkey")
;; -> "1 monkey"

(inf/pluralize 12 "monkey")
;; -> "12 monkeys"
```

If you have a special or nonstandard pluralization, you can provide your own pluralization as an optional third argument to `pluralize`:

```
(inf/pluralize 1 "box" "boxen")
;; -> "1 box"

(inf/pluralize 3 "box" "boxen")
;; -> "3 boxen"
```

## Discussion

When it comes to user-facing text, inflection is key. Humanizing the output of your programs or websites goes a long way to building a trustworthy and professional image. Ruby on Rails (*http://rubyonrails.org*) set the gold standard for friendly and humanized text with its `ActiveSupport::Inflections` class. `Inflections#pluralize` is one such inflection, but `Inflections` is chock-full of cutesy-sounding methods ending in "ize" that change the inflection of strings. `inflections` provides nearly all of these capabilities in a Clojure context.

Two interesting functions in the `inflections` library are `plural` and `singular`. These functions work a bit like the `upper-case` and `lower-case` of pluralization; `plural` transforms words into their plural form, and `singular` coerces words to their singular form. These transformations are based on a number of rules in `inflections.plural`.

You can add your own rules for pluralization with `inflections.core/plural!`:

```
(inf/plural "box")
;; -> "boxes"

;; Words ending in 'ox' pluralize with 'en' (and not 'es')
(inf/plural! #"(ox)(?i)$" "$1en")

(inf/plural "box")
;; -> "boxen"

;; plural is also the basis for pluralize...
(inf/pluralize 2 "box")
;; -> "2 boxen"
```

The library also has support for inflections like `camelize`, `parameterize`, and `ordinalize`:

```
;; Convert "snake_case" to "CamelCase"
(inf/camelize "my_object")
;; -> "MyObject"

;; Clean strings for usage as URL parameters
(inf/parameterize "My most favorite URL!")
;; -> "my-most-favorite-url"

;; Turn numbers into ordinal numbers
(inf/ordinalize 42)
;; -> "42nd"
```

## See Also

- The `inflections-clj` GitHub repository (*https://github.com/r0man/inflections-clj/*) for the most up-to-date listing of inflections available

# 1.12. Converting Between Strings, Symbols, and Keywords

by Colin Jones

## Problem

You have a string, a symbol, or a keyword and you'd like to convert it into a different one of these string-like data types.

## Solution

To convert from a string to a symbol, use the `symbol` function:

```
(symbol "valid?")
;; -> valid?
```

To convert from a symbol to a string, use `str`:

```
(str 'valid?)
;; -> "valid?"
```

When you have a keyword and want a string, you can use `name`, or `str` if you want the leading colon:

```
(name :triumph)
;; -> "triumph"
```

```
;; Or, to include the leading colon:
(str :triumph)
;; -> ":triumph"
```

To convert from a symbol or string to a keyword, use `keyword`:

```
(keyword "fantastic")
;; -> :fantastic

(keyword 'fantastic)
;; -> :fantastic
```

You'll need an intermediate step, through `name`, to go from keyword to symbol:

```
(symbol (name :wonderful))
;; -> wonderful
```

## Discussion

The primary conversion functions here are `str`, `keyword`, and `symbol`—each named for the data type it returns. One of these, `symbol`, is a bit more strict in terms of the input it allows: it must take a string, which is why you need the extra step in the keyword-to-symbol conversion.

There is another class of differences among these types: namely, that keywords and symbols may be namespaced, signified by a slash (/) in the middle. For these kinds of keywords and symbols, the `name` function may or may not be sufficient to convert to a string, depending on your use case:

```
;; If you only want the name part of a keyword
(name :user/valid?)
;; -> "valid?"

;; If you only want the namespace
(namespace :user/valid?)
;; -> "user"
```

Very often, you actually want both parts. You could collect them separately and concatenate the strings with a / in the middle, but there's an easier way. Java has a rich set of performant methods for dealing with immutable strings. You can take the leading-colon string and lop off the first character with `java.lang.String.substring(int)`:

```
(str :user/valid?)
;; -> ":user/valid?"

(.substring (str :user/valid?) 1)
;; -> "user/valid?"
```

See the `java.lang.String` API documentation (*http://bit.ly/javadoc-string*) for more string methods.

You can convert namespaced symbols to keywords just as easily as their non-namespaced counterparts, but again, converting in the other direction (keyword to symbol) takes an extra step:

```
(keyword 'produce/onions)
;; -> :produce/onions

(symbol (.substring (str :produce/onions) 1))
;; -> produce/onions
```

And finally, both the `keyword` and `symbol` functions have two-argument versions that allow you to pass in the namespace and name separately. Sometimes this is nicer—for example, when you already have one or both of the values bound in a `def`, `let`, or other binding:

```
(def shopping-area "bakery")

(keyword shopping-area "bagels")
;; -> :bakery/bagels

(symbol shopping-area "cakes")
;; -> bakery/cakes
```

These three string-like data types are all great for different situations, and how to choose among them is another topic. But it's quite common to need to convert among them, so `keyword`, `symbol`, `str`, `namespace`, and `name` are handy to have in your tool belt.

### See Also

- Recipe 1.5, "Converting Between Characters and Integers" on page 8

## 1.13. Maintaining Accuracy with Extremely Large/Small Numbers

by Ryan Neufeld

### Problem

You need to work precisely with numbers, especially those that are very large or very small, without the imprecision implied by using floating-point representations such as `double` values.

### Solution

First, know that Clojure supports exponents as literal numbers, allowing you to succinctly express large/small numbers:

```
;; Avogadro's number
6.0221413e23
;; -> 6.0221413E23

;; 1 Angstrom in meters
1e-10
;; -> 1.0E-10
```

Integer values passing the upper bound of a size-bounded type (like `long`) will raise an integer overflow error. Use the "quote" versions of numeric operations like `-` or `*` to allow promotion to `Big` types:

```
(* 9999 9999 9999 9999 9999)
;; ArithmeticException integer overflow  clojure.lang.Numbers.throwIntOverflow

(*' 9999 9999 9999 9999 9999)
;; -> 99950009999000049999N
```

## Discussion

Clojure has a number of numeric types: integer and `long`, `double`, and `BigInteger` and `BigDecimal`. The bounded types (`int`, `long`, and `double`) all seamlessly transition as needed while inside the *total* bounds of those types. Exceeding those bounds causes one of two things to happen. For integers, an integer overflow error is raised. For floating-point numbers, the result will become `Infinity`. With integers, you can avoid this error by using quote versions of `+`, `-`, `*`, and `/`. These operations support arbitrary precision and will promote integers to `BigInteger` if necessary.

Floating-point values are a little more tricky. The quote versions of numeric operations won't help here; you'll need to infect your operations with the `BigDecimal` type. In Clojure, the `BigInteger` and `BigDecimal` types are what you would call "contagious." Once a "big" number is introduced to an operation, it infects all of the follow-on results. You *could* do something like multiplying a number by a `BigDecimal` 1, but it's much easier to use the `bigdec` or `bigint` functions to promote a value manually:

```
(* 2 Double/MAX_VALUE)
;; -> Double/POSITIVE_INFINITY

(* 2 (bigdec Double/MAX_VALUE))
;; -> 3.5953862697246314E+308M
```

Contagion doesn't only occur with `Big` types; it also pops up in the integer-to–floating-point boundary. Floating-point numbers are contagious to integers. Arithmetic involving *any* floating-point values will always return a floating-point value.

## See Also

- Recipe 1.14, "Working with Rational Numbers" on page 24, for information on maintaining accuracy when using rational numbers

# 1.14. Working with Rational Numbers

by Ryan Neufeld

## Problem

You need to manipulate fractional numbers with absolute precision.

## Solution

When manipulating integers (or other rationals), you can expect to maintain precision, including recurring fractions like 1/3 (0.333...):

```
(/ 1 3)
;; -> 1/3

(type (/ 1 3))
;; -> clojure.lang.Ratio

(* 3 (/ 1 3))
;; -> 1N
```

Use `rationalize` on `doubles` to coerce them to rationals to avoid losing precision:

```
(+ (/ 1 3) 0.3)
;; -> 0.6333333333333333

(rationalize 0.3)
;; -> 3/10

(+ (/ 1 3) (rationalize 0.3))
;; -> 19/30
```

## Discussion

Clojure does its best to help you retain accuracy when working with numbers, especially integers. When dividing integers, Clojure maintains accuracy by expressing the quotient as an accurate ratio of integers instead of a lossy `double`. This accuracy isn't without a cost, though; operations on rational numbers are much slower than operations on simpler types. As is discussed in Recipe 1.13, "Maintaining Accuracy with Extremely Large/Small Numbers" on page 22, accuracy is always a trade-off for performance, and is something you need to consider given the problem at hand.

When operating on both doubles and rationals at the same time, care is advised; on account of the way type contagion works in Clojure, performing an operation over both types will cause the rational number to be coerced to a double. This transition isn't necessarily inaccurate for a single operation, but the change in type introduces the possibility for inaccuracy to creep in.

To maintain accuracy when working with doubles, use the rationalize function. This function returns the rational value of any number. Calling rationalize on any values that might possibly be doubles will allow you to maintain absolute accuracy (at the cost of performance).

## See Also

- Recipe 1.13, "Maintaining Accuracy with Extremely Large/Small Numbers" on page 22

# 1.15. Parsing Numbers

by Ryan Neufeld

## Problem

You need to parse numbers out of strings.

## Solution

For "normal"-sized large or precise numbers, use Integer/parseInt or Double/parseDouble to parse them:

```
(Integer/parseInt "-42")
;; -> -42

(Double/parseDouble "3.14")
;; -> 3.14
```

## Discussion

What is a "normal"-sized number? For Integer/parseInt, normal is anything below Integer/MAX_VALUE (2147483647); and for Double/parseDouble, it's anything below Double/MAX_VALUE (around 1.79 × 10^308).functions

When the numbers you are parsing are either abnormally large or abnormally precise, you'll need to parse them with BigInteger or BigDecimal to avoid losing precision.

The versatile `bigint` and `bigdec` functions can coerce strings (or any other numerical types, for that matter) into infinite-precision containers:

```
(bigdec "3.1415926535897932384626433832795028841971")
;; -> 3.1415926535897932384626433832795028841971M

(bigint "122333444455555666666777777788888888999999999")
;; -> 122333444455555666666777777788888888999999999N
```

## See Also

- The API documentation for `Integer/parseInt` (*http://bit.ly/javadoc-parseInt*) and `Double/parseDouble` (*http://bit.ly/javadoc-parseDouble*)

# 1.16. Truncating and Rounding Numbers

by Ryan Neufeld

## Problem

You need to truncate or round a decimal number to a lower-precision number.

## Solution

If the integer portion of a number is all you are concerned with, use `int` to coerce the number to an integer. Of course, this completely discards any decimal places without performing any rounding:

```
(int 2.0001)
;; -> 2

(int 2.999999999)
;; -> 2
```

If you still value some level of precision, then rounding is probably what you're after. You can use `Math/round` to perform simple rounding:

```
(Math/round 2.0001)
;; -> 2

(Math/round 2.999)
;; -> 3

;; This is equivalent to:
(int (+ 2.99 0.5))
;; -> 3
```

If you want to perform an unbalanced rounding, such as unconditionally "rounding up" or "rounding down," then you should use `Math/ceil` or `Math/floor`, respectively:

```
(Math/ceil 2.0001)
;; -> 3.0

(Math/floor 2.999)
;; -> 2.0
```

You'll notice these functions return decimal numbers. Wrap calls to `ceil` or `floor` in `int` to return an integer.

## Discussion

One of the simplest ways to "round" numbers is truncation. `int` will do this for you, coercing floating-point numbers to integers by simply chopping off any trailing decimal places. This isn't necessarily mathematically correct, but it is certainly convenient if it is accurate enough for the problem at hand.

`Math/round` is the next step up in rounding technology. As with many other primitive manipulation functions in Clojure, the language prefers *not* to reinvent the wheel. `Math/round` is a Java function that rounds by adding 1/2 to a number before dropping decimal places similarly to `int`.

For more advanced rounding, such as controlling the number of decimal places or complex rounding modes, you may need to resort to using the `with-precision` function. You likely already know `BigDecimal` numbers are backed by Java classes, but you might not have known that Java exposes a number of knobs for tweaking `BigDecimal` calculations; `with-precision` exposes these knobs.

`with-precision` is a macro that accepts a `BigDecimal` precision mode and any number of expressions, executing those expressions in a `BigDecimal` context tuned to that precision. So what does precision look like? Well, it's a little strange. The most basic precision is simply a positive integer "scale" value. This value specifies the number of decimal places to work with. More complex precisions involve a `:rounding` value, specified as a key/value pair like `:rounding FLOOR` (this *is* a macro of course, so why not?). When not specified, the default rounding mode is `HALF_UP`, but any of the values `CEILING`, `FLOOR`, `HALF_UP`, `HALF_DOWN`, `HALF_EVEN`, `UP`, `DOWN`, or `UNNECESSARY` are allowed (see the `RoundingMode` documentation (*http://bit.ly/javadoc-rounding-mode*) for more detailed descriptions of each mode):

```
(with-precision 3 (/ 7M 9))
;; -> 0.778M

(with-precision 1 (/ 7M 9))
;; -> 0.8M
```

```
(with-precision 1 :rounding FLOOR (/ 7M 9))
;; -> 0.7M
```

One notable "gotcha" with `with-precision` is that it only changes the behavior of `BigDecimal` arithmetic, leaving regular arithmetic unchanged. You'll have to introduce `BigDecimal` values into your expressions with literal values (`3M`), or by means of the `bigdec` function:

```
(with-precision 3 (/ 1 3))
;; -> 1/3

(with-precision 3 (/ (bigdec 1) 3))
;; -> 0.333M
```

## See Also

- Recipe 1.13, "Maintaining Accuracy with Extremely Large/Small Numbers" on page 22, for more information on `BigDecimal`, specifically type contagion
- Recipe 1.17, "Performing Fuzzy Comparison" on page 28

# 1.17. Performing Fuzzy Comparison

by Ryan Neufeld

## Problem

You need to test for equality with some tolerance for minute differences. This is especially a problem when comparing floating-point numbers, which are susceptible to "drift" through repeated operations.

## Solution

Clojure has no built-in functions for fault-tolerant equality, or "fuzzy comparison," as it is often called. It's trivial to implement your own `fuzzy=` function:

```
(defn fuzzy= [tolerance x y]
  (let [diff (Math/abs (- x y))]
    (< diff tolerance)))

(fuzzy= 0.01 10 10.000000000001)
;; -> true

(fuzzy= 0.01 10 10.1)
;; -> false
```

## Discussion

`fuzzy=` works like most other fuzzy comparison algorithms do: first it finds the absolute difference between the two operands; and second, it tests whether that difference falls beneath the given tolerance. Of course, there's nothing dictating that the tolerance needs to be some minute fractional number. If you were comparing large numbers and wanted to ignore variations under a thousand, you could set the tolerance to `1000`.

Even with `fuzzy=`, you still need to take care when comparing floating-point values, especially for values differing by numbers *very close* to your tolerance. At differences bordering the supplied tolerance, you may find the results a bit strange:

```
(- 0.22 0.23)
;; -> -0.010000000000000009

(- 0.23 0.24)
;; -> -0.009999999999999981
```

As odd as this is, this isn't unexpected. The IEEE 754 specification for floating-point values is a purposefully limited format, a trade-off between accuracy and performance. If absolute precision is what you're after, then you should be using `BigDecimal` or `BigInt`. See Recipe 1.13, "Maintaining Accuracy with Extremely Large/Small Numbers" on page 22, for more information on those two types.

The `fuzzy=` function, as written, has a number of interesting side effects. First and foremost, having tolerance as the first argument makes it use `partial` to produce partially applied equals functions tuned to a specific tolerance:

```
(def equal-within-ten? (partial fuzzy= 10))

(equal-within-ten? 100 109)
;; -> true

(equal-within-ten? 100 110)
;; -> false
```

What if you wanted to sort using fuzzy comparison? The `sort` function takes as an optional argument a predicate or comparator. Let's write a function `fuzzy-comparator` that returns a comparator with a given tolerance:

```
(defn fuzzy-comparator [tolerance]
  (fn [x y]
    (if (fuzzy= tolerance x y) ; ❶
      0
      (compare x y)))) ; ❷

(sort (fuzzy-comparator 10) [100 11 150 10 9])
;; -> (11 10 9 100 150) ; 100 and 150 have moved, but not 11, 10, and 9
```

❶ If the two values being compared are within `tolerance` of each other, return `0` to indicate they are equal.

❷ Otherwise, fall back to normal `compare`.

## See Also

- The Wikipedia article on IEEE floating point (*http://bit.ly/ieee-floating-point*)
- Recipe 1.13, "Maintaining Accuracy with Extremely Large/Small Numbers" on page 22
- Recipe 1.16, "Truncating and Rounding Numbers" on page 26

# 1.18. Performing Trigonometry

by Ryan Neufeld

## Problem

You need to implement mathematical functions that require trigonometry.

## Solution

All of the trigonometric functions are accessible via `java.lang.Math` (*http://bit.ly/javadoc-math*), which is available as `Math`. Use them like you would any other namespaced function:

```
;; Calculating sin(a + b). The formula for this is
;; sin(a + b) = sin a * cos b + sin b cos a
(defn sin-plus [a b]
  (+ (* (Math/sin a) (Math/cos b))
     (* (Math/sin b) (Math/cos a))))

(sin-plus 0.1 0.3)
;; -> 0.38941834230865047
```

Trigonometric functions operate on values measured in radians. If you have values measured in degrees, such as latitude or longitude, then you'll need to convert them to radians first. Use `Math/toRadians` to convert degrees to radians:

```
;; Calculating the distance in kilometers between two points on Earth
(def earth-radius 6371.009)

(defn degrees->radians [point]
  (mapv #(Math/toRadians %) point))

(defn distance-between
```

```
  "Calculate the distance in km between two points on Earth. Each
   point is a pair of degrees latitude and longitude, in that order."
  ([p1 p2] (distance-between p1 p2 earth-radius))
  ([p1 p2 radius]
     (let [[lat1 long1] (degrees->radians p1)
           [lat2 long2] (degrees->radians p2)]
       (* radius
          (Math/acos (+ (* (Math/sin lat1) (Math/sin lat2))
                        (* (Math/cos lat1)
                           (Math/cos lat2)
                           (Math/cos (- long1 long2))))))))))

(distance-between [49.2000 -98.1000] [35.9939, -78.8989])
;; -> 2139.42827188432
```

## Discussion

It may be surprising to some that Clojure doesn't have its own internal math namespace, but why reinvent the wheel? Despite its tainted reputation, Java can perform, especially when it comes to math. Clojure's Java interop forms and typing sugar make doing math using `java.lang.Math` almost pleasant.

`java.lang.Math` isn't only for trigonometry. It also contains a number of functions useful for dealing with exponentiation, logarithms, and roots. A full list of methods is available in the `java.lang.Math` javadoc (*http://bit.ly/javadoc-math*).

## See Also

- Recipe 8.5, "Alleviating Performance Problems with Type Hinting" on page 360, for tips on improving performance

# 1.19. Inputting and Outputting Integers with Different Bases

by Ryan Neufeld

## Problem

You need to enter numbers into a Clojure REPL or code in a different base (such as hexadecimal or binary).

## Solution

Specify the base or *radix* of a literal number by prefixing it with the radix number (e.g., 2, 16, etc.) and the letter `r`. Any base from 2 to 36 is valid (there *are*, of course, 10 digits and 26 letters available):

```
2r101010
;; -> 42

3r1120
;; -> 42

16r2A
;; -> 42

36rABUNCH
;; -> 624567473
```

To output integers, use the Java method `Integer/toString`:

```
(Integer/toString 13 2)
;; -> "1101"

(Integer/toString 42 16)
;; -> "2a"

(Integer/toString 35 36)
;; -> "z"
```

## Discussion

Unlike the ordering of most Clojure functions, this method takes an integer first and the optional base second, making it hard to partially apply without wrapping it in another function. You can write a small wrapper around `Integer/toString` to accomplish this:

```
(defn to-base [radix n]
  (Integer/toString n radix))

(def base-two (partial to-base 2))

(base-two 9001)
;; -> "10001100101001"
```

## See Also

- Recipe 1.6, "Formatting Strings" on page 10, for information on `format` (the `o` and `x` specifiers print integers in octal and hexadecimal, respectively)
- Recipe 1.15, "Parsing Numbers" on page 25

# 1.20. Calculating Statistics on Collections of Numbers

by Ryan Neufeld and Jean Niklas L'orange

## Problem

You need to calculate simple statistics like mean, median, mode, and standard deviation on a collection of numbers.

## Solution

Find the *mean* (average) of a collection by dividing its total by the `count` of the collection:

```
(defn mean [coll]
  (let [sum (apply + coll)
        count (count coll)]
    (if (pos? count)
      (/ sum count)
      0)))

(mean [1 2 3 4])
;; -> 5/2

(mean [1 1.6 7.4 10])
;; -> 5.0

(mean [])
;; -> 0
```

Find the *median* (middle value) of a collection by sorting its values and getting its middle value. There are, of course, special considerations for collections of even length. In these cases, the median is considering the mean of the *two* middle values:

```
(defn median [coll]
  (let [sorted (sort coll)
        cnt (count sorted)
        halfway (int (/ cnt 2))]
    (if (odd? cnt)
      (nth sorted halfway) ; ❶
      (let [bottom (dec halfway)
            bottom-val (nth sorted bottom)
            top-val (nth sorted halfway)]
        (mean [bottom-val top-val]))))) ; ❷

(median [5 2 4 1 3])
;; -> 3

(median [7 0 2 3])
;; -> 5/2  ; The average of 2 and 3.
```

❶ In the case that `coll` has an odd number of items, simply retrieve that item with `nth`.

❷ When `coll` has an even number of items, find the index for the other central value (`bottom`), and take the mean of the top and bottom values.

Find the *mode* (most frequently occurring value) of a collection by using `frequencies` to tally occurrences. Then massage that tally to retrieve the discrete list of modes:

```
(defn mode [coll]
  (let [freqs (frequencies coll)
        occurrences (group-by second freqs)
        modes (last (sort occurrences))
        modes (->> modes
                   second
                   (map first))]
     modes))

(mode [:alan :bob :alan :greg])
;; -> (:alan)

(mode [:smith :carpenter :doe :smith :doe])
;; -> (:smith :doe)
```

### Standard deviation

Find the sample *standard deviation* by completing the following steps:

1. For each value in the collection, subtract the `mean` from the value and multiply that result by itself.
2. Then, sum up all those values.
3. Divide the result by the number of values *minus one.*
4. Finally, take the square root of the previous result:

```
(defn standard-deviation [coll]
  (let [avg (mean coll)
        squares (for [x coll]
                  (let [x-avg (- x avg)]
                    (* x-avg x-avg)))
        total (count coll)]
    (-> (/ (apply + squares)
           (- total 1))
        (Math/sqrt))))

(standard-deviation [4 5 2 9 5 7 4 5 4])
;; -> 2.0
```

```
(standard-deviation [4 5 5 4 4 2 2 6])
;; -> 1.4142135623730951
```

## Discussion

Both mean and median are fairly easy to reproduce in Clojure, but mode requires a bit more effort. mode is a little different than mean or median in that it generally only makes sense for nonnumeric data. Calculating the modes of a collection is a little more involved and ultimately requires a good deal of processing compared to its numeric cousins.

Here is a breakdown of how mode works:

```
(defn mode [coll]
  (let [freqs (frequencies coll)                 ; ❶
        occurrences (group-by second freqs) ; ❷
        modes (last (sort occurrences))     ; ❸
        modes (->> modes                    ; ❹
                   second
                   (map first))]
    modes))
```

❶ frequencies returns a map that tallies the number of times each value in coll occurs. This would be something like {:a 1 :b 2}.

❷ group-by with second inverts the freqs map, turning keys into values and merging duplicates into groups. This would turn {:a 1 :b 1} into {1 [[:a 1] [:b 1]]}.

❸ The list of occurrences is now sortable. The last pair in the sorted list will be the modes, or most frequently occurring values.

❹ The final step is processing the raw mode pairs into discrete values. Taking second turns [2 [[:alan 2]]] into [[:alan 2]], and (map first) turns that into (:alan).

The standard deviation measures how much, on average, the individual values in a population deviate from the mean: the higher the standard deviation is, the farther away the individual values will be (on average). standard-deviation is a bit more mathematical than mean, median, and mode. Follow along the execution of this function step by step:

```
(defn standard-deviation [coll]
  (let [avg (mean coll)                   ; ❶
        squares (for [x coll]             ; ❷
                  (let [x-avg (- x avg)]
                    (* x-avg x-avg)))
        total (count coll)]
    (-> (/ (apply + squares)              ; ❸
```

```
             (- total 1))
          (Math/sqrt))))
```

❶ Calculate the mean of the collection.

❷ For each value, calculate the square of the difference between the value and the mean.

❸ Finally, calculate the *sample* standard deviation by taking the square root of the sum of squares over population size minus one.

If you have the complete population, you can compute the *population* standard deviation by dividing by `total` instead of `(- total 1)`.

## See Also

- The Wikipedia article on standard deviation (*http://bit.ly/wiki-std-dev*) for more information on standard deviation and what it can be used for

# 1.21. Performing Bitwise Operations

by Ryan Neufeld

## Problem

You need to perform bitwise operations on numbers.

## Solution

Bitwise operations aren't quite as commonly used in high-level languages (like Clojure) as they are in systems languages like C or C++, but the techniques learned in those systems languages can still be useful. Clojure exposes a number of bitwise operations in its core namespace, all prefixed with `bit-`. One place bitwise operations really shine is in compressing a large number of binary flags into a single value:

```
;; Modeling a subset of Unix filesystem flags in a single integer
(def fs-flags [:owner-read :owner-write
               :group-read :group-write
               :global-read :global-write])

;; Fold flags into a map of flag->bit
(def bitmap (zipmap fs-flags
                    (map (partial bit-shift-left 1) (range))))
;; -> {:owner-read 1, :owner-write 2, :group-read 4, ...}
```

```
(defn permissions-int [& flags]
  (reduce bit-or 0 (map bitmap flags)))

(def owner-only (permissions-int :owner-read :owner-write))
(Integer/toBinaryString owner-only)
;; -> "11"

(def read-only (permissions-int :owner-read :group-read :global-read))
(Integer/toBinaryString read-only)
;; -> "10101"

(defn able-to? [permissions flag]
  (not= 0 (bit-and permissions (bitmap flag))))

(able-to? read-only :global-read)  ;; -> true
(able-to? read-only :global-write) ;; -> false
```

## Discussion

Clojure provides a full complement of bitwise operations in its core library. This includes the logic operations *and* and *or*, their negations, and shifts, to name a few. When working with bitwise operations, it can often be necessary to view the binary representation of an integer. Java's `Integer/toBinaryString` can conveniently print out a binary representation of a number.

Interestingly enough, core also includes a `bit-set` and a `bit-test`. These two operations set or test an individual bit position in an integer. Instead of working in multiples of two, as is necessary for operations like `bit-and`, you can operate by the *index* of the flag you're interested in. This drastically simplifies the preceding example:

```
;; Modeling a subset of Unix filesystem flags in a single integer
(def fs-flags [:owner-read :owner-write
               :group-read :group-write
               :global-read :global-write])

(def bitmap (zipmap fs-flags
                    (map #(.indexOf fs-flags %) fs-flags)))

(def no-permissions 0)
(def owner-read (bit-set no-permissions (:owner-read bitmap)))

(Integer/toBinaryString owner-read)
;; -> "1"

;; Granting global permissions...
(def anything (reduce #(bit-set %1 (bitmap %2)) no-permissions fs-flags))
(Integer/toBinaryString anything)
;; -> "111111"
```

## See Also

- Recipe 8.6, "Fast Math with Primitive Java Arrays" on page 363

# 1.22. Generating Random Numbers

by Ryan Neufeld

## Problem

You need to generate a random number.

## Solution

Clojure makes available a number of pseudorandom number generating functions for your disposal.

For generating random floating-point numbers from `0.0` up to (but not including) `1.0`, use `rand`:

```
(rand)
;; -> 0.0249306187447903

(rand)
;; -> 0.9242089829055088
```

For generating random integers, use `rand-int`:

```
;; Emulating a six-sided die
(defn roll-d6 []
  (inc (rand-int 6)))

(roll-d6)
;; -> 1

(roll-d6)
;; -> 3
```

## Discussion

In addition to generating a number from `0.0` to `1.0`, `rand` also accepts an optional argument that specifies the exclusive maximum value. For example, `(rand 5)` would return a floating-point number ranging from `0.0` (inclusive) to `5.0` (exclusive).

`(rand-int 5)`, on the other hand, would return a random *integer* between `0` (inclusive) and `5` (exclusive). At first blush, `rand-int` might seem like an ideal way to select a random element from a vector or list. This is a lot of ceremony, though. Use `rand-nth` instead to get a random element from any sequential collection (i.e., the collection responds to `nth`):

```
(rand-nth [1 2 3])
;; -> 1

(rand-nth '(:a :b :c))
;; -> :c
```

This won't work for sets or hash maps, however. If you want to retrieve a random element from a nonsequential collection like a set, use `seq` to transform that collection into a sequence before calling `rand-nth` on it:

```
(rand-nth (seq #{:heads :tails}))
;; -> :heads
```

If you're trying to randomly sort a collection, use `shuffle` to receive a random permutation of your collection:

```
(shuffle [1 2 3 4 5 6])
;; -> [3 1 4 5 2 6]
```

## See Also

- The API documentation (*http://bit.ly/javadoc-random*) for `java.util.Random`
- Recipe 10.3, "Thoroughly Testing by Randomizing Inputs" on page 413

# 1.23. Working with Currency

by Ryan Neufeld

## Problem

You need to manipulate values that represent currency.

## Solution

Use the Money (*https://github.com/clojurewerkz/money*) library for representing, manipulating, and storing values in monetary units.

To follow along with this recipe, add `[clojurewerkz/money "1.4.0"]` to your project's dependencies, or start a REPL using `lein-try`:

```
$ lein try clojurewerkz/money
```

The `clojurewerkz.money.amounts` namespace contains functions for creating, modifying, and comparing units of currency:

```
(require '[clojurewerkz.money.amounts    :as ma])
(require '[clojurewerkz.money.currencies :as mc])

;; $2.00 in USD
(def two (ma/amount-of mc/USD 2))
two
;; -> #<Money USD 2.00>


(ma/plus two two)
;; -> #<Money USD 4.00>

(ma/minus two two)
;; -> #<Money USD 0.00>

(ma/< two (ma/amount-of mc/USD 2.01))
;; -> true

(ma/total [two two two two])
;; -> #<Money USD 8.00>
```

## Discussion

Working with currency is serious business. Never trust built-in numerical types with handling currency, especially floating-point values. These types are simply not meant to capture and manipulate currency with the semantics and precision required. In particular, floating-point values of the IEEE 754 standard carry a certain imprecision by design:

```
(- 0.23 0.24)
;; -> -0.009999999999999981
```

You should always use a library custom-tailored for dealing with money. The Money library wraps the trusted and battle-tested Java library Joda-Money. Money provides a large amount of functionality beyond arithmetic, including rounding and currency conversion:

```
(ma/round (ma/amount-of mc/USD 3.14) 0 :down)
;; -> #<Money USD 3.00>

(ma/convert-to (ma/amount-of mc/CAD 152.34) mc/USD 1.01696 :down)
;; -> #<Money USD 154.92>
```

The `round` function takes four arguments. The first three are an amount of currency, a scale factor, and a rounding mode. The scaling factor is a somewhat peculiar argument. It might be familiar to you if you've ever done scaling with `BigDecimal`, which shares identical factors. A scale of `-1` scales to the tens place, `0` scales to the ones place, and so on and so forth. Further details can be found in the javadoc for the `rounded` (*http://bit.ly/joda-money-rounded-src*) method of Joda-Money's `Money` class. The final argument is a rounding mode, of which there are quite a few. `:ceiling` and `:floor` round toward positive or negative infinity. `:up` and `:down` round toward or away from zero. Finally `:half-up`, `:half-down`, and `:half-even` round toward the nearest neighbor, preferring up, down, or the most even neighbor.

`clojurewerkz.money.amounts/convert-to` is a much less complicated function. `convert-to` takes an amount of currency, a target currency, a conversion factor, and a rounding mode. Money doesn't provide its own conversion factor, since conversion rates change so often, so you'll need to seek out a reputable source for them. Unfortunately, we can't help you with this one.

Money also provides support for a number of different persistence and serialization mediums, including Cheshire (*https://github.com/dakrone/cheshire*) for converting to/from JSON and Monger (*http://clojuremongodb.info/*) for persisting currency values to MongoDB.

### See Also

- Recipe 1.13, "Maintaining Accuracy with Extremely Large/Small Numbers" on page 22, and Recipe 1.16, "Truncating and Rounding Numbers" on page 26

## 1.24. Generating Unique IDs

by Ryan Neufeld

### Problem

You need to generate a unique ID.

### Solution

Use Java's `java.util.UUID/randomUUID` to generate a universally unique ID (UUID):

```
(java.util.UUID/randomUUID)
;; -> #uuid "5358e6e3-7f81-40f0-84e5-750e29e6ee05"

(java.util.UUID/randomUUID)
;; -> #uuid "a6f92a6f-f736-468f-9e26-f392852825f4"
```

### Discussion

Oftentimes when building systems, you want to assign unique IDs to objects and records. IDs are usually simple integers that monotonically increase with time. This isn't without its problems, though.

You can't mingle IDs of objects from different origins; and worse, they reveal information about the amount and input volume of your data.

This is where UUIDs come in. UUIDs, or universally unique identifiers, are 128-bit random numbers almost certainly unique across the entire universe. A bold claim, of course—see RFC 4122 (*http://bit.ly/rfc4122*) for more detailed information on UUIDs, how they're generated, and the math behind them.

You may have noticed Clojure prints UUIDs with a `#uuid` in front of them. This is a reader literal tag. It acts as a shortcut for the Clojure reader to read and initialize UUID objects. Reader literals are a lot like string or number literals like `"Hi"` or `42`, but they can capture more complex data types.

This makes it possible for formats like edn (*https://github.com/edn-format/edn*) (extensible data notation) to communicate in a common lingo about things like UUIDs without resorting to string interning and accompanying custom parsing logic.

## Sequential IDs

One thing you will lose with the move from sequential IDs to UUIDs is the implicit sortability of a chronologically increasing number. What if you could generate UUIDs that were both unique *and* sortable? Datomic does something similar with its `datomic.api/squuid` function.

This approximation of Datomic's `squuid` splits and reassembles a random UUID, using `bit-or` to merge the current time with the most significant 32 bits of the UUID. The two halves of the UUID are then reassembled using the `java.util.UUID.` constructor, yielding UUIDs that increase sequentially over time:

```
(def first (squuid))
first
;; -> #uuid "527bf210-dfae-4c73-8b7a-302d3b511f41"

(def second (squuid))
second
;; -> #uuid "527bf219-65f0-4241-a165-c5c541cb98ea"

(def third (squuid))
third
;; -> #uuid "527bf232-42b2-44bc-8dd7-ddae2abfcb87"

(sort [first second third])
;; -> (#uuid "527bf210-dfae-4c73-8b7a-302d3b511f41"
;;     #uuid "527bf219-65f0-4241-a165-c5c541cb98ea"
;;     #uuid "527bf232-42b2-44bc-8dd7-ddae2abfcb87")
```

## See Also

- Recipe 1.21, "Performing Bitwise Operations" on page 36
- Recipe 1.26, "Representing Dates as Literals" on page 44, for information on `#inst`, another example of a reader literal, for dates
- The `java.util.UUID` API documentation (*http://bit.ly/javadoc-uuid*)

# 1.25. Obtaining the Current Date and Time

by Ryan Neufeld

## Problem

You need to obtain the current date or time.

## Solution

Use Java's `java.util.Date` (*http://bit.ly/javadoc-date*) constructor to create a `Date` instance representing the present time and date:

```
(defn now []
  (java.util.Date.))

(now)
;; -> #inst "2013-04-06T14:33:45.740-00:00"

;; A few seconds later...
(now)
;; -> #inst "2013-04-06T14:33:51.234-00:00"
```

If you're more interested in the current Unix timestamp, use `System/currentTimeMillis`:

```
(System/currentTimeMillis)
;; -> 1365260110635

(System/currentTimeMillis)
;; -> 1365260157013
```

## Discussion

It doesn't make much sense for Clojure to reimplement or wrap the JVM's backing time and date functionality. As such, the norm is to use Clojure's Java interop forms to instantiate a `Date` object representing "now."

`#inst "2013-04-06T14:33:51.234-00:00"` doesn't look very much like Java, does it? That's because Clojure's "instant" reader literal uses `java.util.Date` as its backing implementation. You can learn more about the `#inst` reader literal in Recipe 1.26, "Representing Dates as Literals" on page 44.

Using `System/currentTimeMillis` can be useful for performing a one-off benchmark, but given the high-quality tools out there that do this already, `currentTimeMillis` is of limited utility; you may want to try Hugo Duncan's Criterium (*https://github.com/hugoduncan/criterium*) library if benchmarking is what you're after. Additionally, you shouldn't try to use `currentTimeMillis` as some sort of unique value—UUIDs do a much better job of this.

If you decide you would rather use `clj-time` (*https://github.com/clj-time/clj-time*) to work with dates, it provides the function `clj-time.core/now` to get the current `DateTime`:

```
(require '[clj-time.core :as timec])

(timec/now)
;; -> #<DateTime 2013-04-06T14:35:15.453Z>
```

Use `clj-time.local/local-now` to retrieve a `DateTime` instance for the present scoped to your machine's local time zone:

```
(require '[clj-time.local :as timel])

(timel/local-now)
;; -> #<DateTime 2013-04-06T09:35:20.141-05:00>
```

## See Also

- Recipe 1.24, "Generating Unique IDs" on page 41, to learn how to generate universally unique IDs
- Recipe 1.26, "Representing Dates as Literals" on page 44, for more information on the `#inst` reader literal

# 1.26. Representing Dates as Literals

by Ryan Neufeld

## Problem

You need to represent instances of time in a readable and serializable form.

## Solution

Use Clojure's `#inst` literals in source to represent fixed points in time:

```
(def ryans-birthday #inst "1987-02-18T18:00:00.000-00:00")

(println ryans-birthday)
;; *out*
;; #inst "1987-02-18T18:00:00.000-00:00"
```

When communicating with other Clojure processes (or anything else that speaks edn (*https://github.com/edn-format/edn*)), use `clojure.edn/read` to reify instant literal strings into `Date` objects:

```
;; A faux communication channel that "receives" edn strings
(require 'clojure.edn)
(import '[java.io PushbackReader StringReader])

(defn remote-server-receive-date []
  (-> "#inst \"1987-02-18T18:00:00.000-00:00\""
      (StringReader.)
      (PushbackReader.)))

(clojure.edn/read (remote-server-receive-date))
;; -> #inst "1987-02-18T18:00:00.000-00:00"
```

In the preceding example, `remote-server-receive-date` emulates a communication channel upon which you may receive edn data.

## Discussion

Since Clojure 1.4, instants in time have been represented via the `#inst` reader literal. This means dates are no longer represented by code that must be evaluated, but instead have a textual representation that is both consistent and serializable. This standard allows any process capable of communicating in extensible data notation to speak clearly about instants of time. See the edn implementations list (*http://bit.ly/edn-impls*) for a list of languages that speak edn; the list includes Clojure, Ruby, and JavaScript so far, with many more implementations in the works.

### clojure.core/read Versus clojure.edn/read

While it may *seem* convenient to read strings using Clojure's built-in reader (`clojure.core/read`), it is *never* safe to parse input from an untrusted source using this reader. If you need to receive simple Clojure data from an external source, it is best to use the edn reader (`clojure.edn/read`).

`clojure.core/read` isn't safe because it was only designed for reading Clojure data and strings from trusted sources (such as the source files you write). `clojure.edn/read` is designed specifically for use as part of a communication channel, and as such is built with security in mind.

It's also possible to vary how the reader evaluates `#inst` literals by changing the binding of `*data-readers*`. By varying the binding of `*data-readers*`, it is possible to read `#inst` literals as `java.util.Calendar` (*http://bit.ly/javadoc-calendar*) or `java.sql.Timestamp` (*http://bit.ly/javadoc-timestamp*), if you so desire:

```
(def instant "#inst \"1987-02-18T18:00:00.000-00:00\"")

(binding [*data-readers* {'inst clojure.instant/read-instant-calendar}]
  (class (read-string instant)))
;; -> java.util.GregorianCalendar

(binding [*data-readers* {'inst clojure.instant/read-instant-timestamp}]
  (class (read-string instant)))
;; -> java.sql.Timestamp
```

## See Also

- Recipe 1.24, "Generating Unique IDs" on page 41, for another example of a reader literal included with Clojure

# 1.27. Parsing Dates and Times Using clj-time

by Ryan Neufeld

## Problem

You need to parse dates from a string.

## Solution

Working directly with Java's date and time classes is like pulling teeth. We suggest using `clj-time` (*https://github.com/clj-time/clj-time*), a Clojure wrapper over the excellent Joda-Time library (*http://bit.ly/joda-time*).

Before starting, add `[clj-time "0.6.0"]` to your project's dependencies or start a REPL using `lein-try`:

```
$ lein try clj-time
```

Use `clj-time.format/formatter` to create custom date/time representations capable of parsing candidate strings. Use the `clj-time.format/parse` function with those formatters to parse strings into `DateTime` objects:

```
(require '[clj-time.format :as tf])

;; To parse dates like "02/18/87"
(def government-forms-date (tf/formatter "MM/dd/yy"))

(tf/parse government-forms-date "02/18/87")
;; -> #<DateTime 1987-02-18T00:00:00.000Z>

(def wonky-format (tf/formatter "HH:mm:ss:SS' on 'yyyy-MM-dd"))
;; -> #'user/wonky-format

(tf/parse wonky-format "16:13:49:06 on 2013-04-06")
;; -> #<DateTime 2013-04-06T16:13:49.060Z>
```

## Discussion

The `formatter` function is a powerful little function that takes a date/time format string and returns an object capable of parsing date/time strings in that format. This format string can include any number of symbols representing portions of a time or date. Some example symbols include year ("yy" or "yyyy"), day ("dd"), or even a literal string like `"on"`. The full list of these symbols is available in the Joda-Time `DateTimeFormat` (*http://bit.ly/joda-time-dtf-doc*) javadoc.

More often than not, the dates and times you're parsing may be strange, but not so strange that no one has seen them before. For this, `clj-time` includes a large number of built-in formatters. Use `clj-time.format/show-formatters` to print out a list of built-in formats and a sample date/time in each format. Once you've picked a suitable format, use `clj-time.format/formatters` with its keyword to receive the appropriate `DateTimeFormatter`.

By default, `formatter` always parses strings into `DateTime` objects with a UTC time zone. `formatter` optionally takes a time zone as its second argument. You can use `clj-time.core/time-zone-for-offset` or `clj-time.core/time-zone-for-id` to receive a `DateTimeZone` object to pass to `formatter`.

## See Also

- Recipe 1.28, "Formatting Dates Using clj-time" on page 48, for information on how to use formatters to unparse strings
- The official API documentation (*http://bit.ly/javadoc-simple-date-format*) for Java's simple date formatter

# 1.28. Formatting Dates Using clj-time

by Ryan Neufeld

## Problem

You need to print dates or times in a particular format.

## Solution

While it is possible to format Java date–like instances (`Date`, `Calendar`, and `Timestamp`) with `clojure.core/format`, you should use `clj-time` (*https://github.com/clj-time/clj-time*) to format dates.

Before starting, add `[clj-time "0.6.0"]` to your project's dependencies or start a REPL using `lein-try`:

```
$ lein try clj-time
```

To output a date/time as a string, use `clj-time.format/unparse` with a `DateTimeFormatter`. There are a number of built-in formatters available via `clj-time.format/formatters`, or you can build your own with `clj-time.format/formatter`:

```
(require '[clj-time.format :as tf])
(require '[clj-time.core :as t])

(tf/unparse (tf/formatters :date) (t/now))
;; -> "2013-04-06"

(def my-format (tf/formatter "MMM d, yyyy 'at' hh:mm"))
(tf/unparse my-format (t/now))
;; -> "Apr 6, 2013 at 04:54"
```

## Discussion

It is certainly possible to format pure Java dates and times; however, in our experience, it isn't worth the hassle—the syntax is ugly, and the workflow is verbose. `clj-time` and its backing library Joda-Time have a track record for making it easy to work with dates and times on the JVM.

The `formatter` function is quite the gem. Not only does it produce a "format" capable of printing or `unparse`ing a date, but it is also capable of parsing strings back into dates. In other words, `DateTimeFormatter` is capable of round-tripping from string to `Date` and back again. Much of how `formatter` and `formatters` work is covered in Recipe 1.27, "Parsing Dates and Times Using clj-time" on page 46.

One format symbol used less frequently in parsing is the textual day of the week (i.e., "Tuesday" or "Tue"). Use "E" in your format string to output the abbreviated day of the week, and "EEEE" for the full-length day of the week:

```
(def abbr-day (tf/formatter "E"))
(def full-day (tf/formatter "EEEE"))

(tf/unparse abbr-day (t/now))
;; -> "Mon"
(tf/unparse full-day (t/now))
;; -> "Monday"
```

If you need to format native Java date/time instances, you can use the functions in the `clj-time.coerce` namespace to coerce any number of Java date/time instances into Joda-Time instances:

```
(require '[clj-time.coerce :as tc])

(tc/from-date (java.util.Date.))
;; -> #<DateTime 2013-04-06T17:03:16.872Z>
```

Similarly, you can use `clj-time.coerce` to coerce instances from Joda-Time instances into other formats:

```
(tc/to-date (t/now))
;; -> #inst "2013-04-06T17:03:57.239-00:00"

(tc/to-long (t/now))
;; -> 1365267761585
```

## See Also

- The `clj-time` project page (*https://github.com/clj-time/clj-time*) on GitHub
- Recipe 1.27, "Parsing Dates and Times Using clj-time" on page 46, for more detailed information on `formatter` and `formatters`
- The official API documentation (*http://bit.ly/javadoc-simple-date-format*) for Java's simple date formatter

# 1.29. Comparing Dates

by Ryan Neufeld

## Problem

You need to compare one date to another, or you need to sort a sequence of dates.

## Solution

You can compare Java Dates using the compare function:

```
(defn now [] (java.util.Date.))
(def one-second-ago (now))
(Thread/sleep 1000)

;; Now is greater than (1) one second ago.
(compare (now) one-second-ago)
;; -> 1

;; One second ago is less than (-1) now.
(compare one-second-ago (now))
;; -> -1

;; "Equal" manifests as 0.
(compare one-second-ago one-second-ago)
;; -> 0
```

## Discussion

Why not just compare dates using Clojure's built-in comparison operators (<=, >, etc.)? The problem with these operators is that they utilize clojure.lang.Numbers and attempt to coerce their arguments to numerical types.

Since regular comparison won't work, it's necessary to use the compare function. The compare function takes two arguments and returns a number indicating that the first argument was either less than (-1), equal to (0), or greater than (+1) the second argument.

Clojure's sort functions use compare under the hood, so no extra work is required to sort a collection of dates:

```
(def occurrences
  [#inst "2013-04-06T17:40:57.688-00:00"
   #inst "2002-12-25T00:40:57.688-00:00"
   #inst "2025-12-25T11:23:31.123-00:00"])

(sort occurrences)
;; -> (#inst "2002-12-25T00:40:57.688-00:00"
;;     #inst "2013-04-06T17:40:57.688-00:00"
;;     #inst "2025-12-25T11:23:31.123-00:00")
```

If you've been doing more complex work with dates and times and have Joda-Time objects in hand, then all of this still applies. If you wish to compare Joda-Time objects to Java time objects, however, you will have to coerce them to one uniform type using the functions in clj-time.coerce.

## See Also

- Recipe 2.24, "Comparing and Sorting Values" on page 107

# 1.30. Calculating the Length of a Time Interval

by Ryan Neufeld

## Problem

You need to calculate the difference between two points in time.

## Solution

Since Java date and time classes have poor support for time zones and leap years, use the `clj-time` (*https://github.com/clj-time/clj-time*) library for calculating the length of a time interval.

Before starting, add `[clj-time "0.6.0"]` to your project's dependencies or start a REPL using `lein-try`:

```
$ lein try clj-time
```

Use `interval` along with the numerous `in-<unit>` helper functions in the `clj-time.core` namespace to calculate the difference between times:

```
(require '[clj-time.core :as t])

;; The first step is to capture two dates as an interval
(def since-april-first
  (t/interval (t/date-time 2013 04 01) (t/now)))

;; dt is the interval between April Fools Day, 2013 and today
since-april-first
;; -> #<Interval 2013-04-01T00:00:00.000Z/2013-04-06T20:06:30.507Z>

(t/in-days since-april-first)
;; -> 5

;; Years since the Moon landing
(t/in-years (t/interval (t/date-time 1969 07 20) (t/now)))
;; -> 43

;; Days from Feb. 28 to March 1 in 2012 (a leap year)
(t/in-days (t/interval (t/date-time 2012 02 28)
                       (t/date-time 2012 03 01)))
;; -> 2

;; And in a non-leap year
```

```
(t/in-days (t/interval (t/date-time 2013 02 28)
                       (t/date-time 2013 03 01)))
;; -> 1
```

## Discussion

Calculating the length of an interval is one of the more complex operations you can perform with times. Time on Earth is a complex beast, complicated by constructs like leap time and time zones; `clj-time` (*https://github.com/clj-time/clj-time*) is the only library we're aware of that is capable of wrangling this complexity.

The `clj-time.core/interval` function takes two dates and returns a representation of that discrete interval of time. From there, the `clj-time.core` namespace includes a myriad of `in-<unit>` functions that can present that time interval in different units. These helpers run the gamut in scale from `in-msecs` to `in-years`, covering nearly every scale useful for nonspecialized applications.

One area `clj-time` lacks support is for leap seconds. Joda-Time's official FAQ (*http://bit.ly/joda-time-faq*) explains why the feature is missing. We're not aware of any Clojure library that *can* reason about time at this granularity. If this concerns you, then you're likely one of few people even capable of doing it right. Good luck to you.

## See Also


- Recipe 1.29, "Comparing Dates" on page 49
- Recipe 1.31, "Generating Ranges of Dates and Times" on page 52
- Recipe 1.33, "Retrieving Dates Relative to One Another" on page 57


# 1.31. Generating Ranges of Dates and Times

by Ryan Neufeld

## Problem

You need to generate a lazy sequence covering a range of dates and/or times.

## Solution

This problem has no easy solution in Java, nor does it have one in Clojure—third-party libraries included. It is possible to use `clj-time` (*https://github.com/clj-time/clj-time*) to get close, though. By composing `clj-time`'s `Interval` and `periodic-seq` functionality, you can create a function `time-range` that mimics `range`'s capabilities, but for `DateTimes`:

```
(require '[clj-time.core :as time])
(require '[clj-time.periodic :as time-period])

(defn time-range
  "Return a lazy sequence of DateTimes from start to end, incremented
  by 'step' units of time."
  [start end step]
  (let [inf-range (time-period/periodic-seq start step)
        below-end? (fn [t] (time/within? (time/interval start end)
                                         t))]
    (take-while below-end? inf-range)))
```

This is how you can use the `time-range` function:

```
(def months-of-the-year (time-range (time/date-time 2012 01)
                                    (time/date-time 2013 01)
                                    (time/months 1)))

;; months-of-the-year is an unrealized lazy sequence
(realized? months-of-the-year)
;; -> false

(count months-of-the-year)
;; -> 12

;; now realized
(realized? months-of-the-year)
;; -> true
```

## Discussion

While there is no ready-made, out-of-the-box `time-range` solution in Clojure, it is trivial to construct such a function with purely lazy semantics. The basis for our lazy `time-range` function is an infinite sequence of values with a fixed starting time:

```
(defn time-range
  "Return a lazy sequence of DateTimes from start to end, incremented
  by 'step' units of time."
  [start end step]
  (let [inf-range (time-period/periodic-seq start step)          ; ❶
        below-end? (fn [t] (time/within? (time/interval start end) ; ❷
                                         t))]
    (take-while below-end? inf-range)))                          ; ❸
```

❶ Acquire a lazy infinite sequence.

❷ Create a predicate to terminate the sequence.

❸ Modify the infinite sequence to terminate when `below-end?` fails (lazily, of course).

Invoking `periodic-seq` with `start` and `step` returns an infinite lazy sequence of values beginning at `start`, each subsequent value one `step` later than the last.

Having a lazy infinite sequence is one thing, but we need a lazy way to *stop* acquiring values when `end` is reached. The `below-end?` function created in `let` uses `clj-time.core/interval` to construct an interval from `start` to `end` and `clj-time.core/within?` to test if a time `t` falls within that interval. This function is passed as the predicate to `take-while`, which will lazily consume values until `below-end?` fails.

All together, `time-range` returns a lazy sequence of `DateTime` objects that stretches from a start time to an end time, stepped appropriately by the provided `step` value.

Imagine trying to build something similar in a language without first-class laziness.

## See Also


- Recipe 1.29, "Comparing Dates" on page 49
- Recipe 1.30, "Calculating the Length of a Time Interval" on page 51
- Recipe 1.32, "Generating Ranges of Dates and Times Using Native Java Types" on page 54, for an alternative that uses only native types
- Recipe 1.33, "Retrieving Dates Relative to One Another" on page 57


# 1.32. Generating Ranges of Dates and Times Using Native Java Types

by Tom Hicks

## Problem

You would like to generate a lazy sequence of dates (or times) beginning with a specific date and time. Further, unlike in Recipe 1.31, "Generating Ranges of Dates and Times" on page 52, you would like to do this using only built-in types.

## Solution

You can use Java's `java.util.GregorianCalendar` (*http://bit.ly/javadoc-gregorian*) class coupled with Clojure's `repeatedly` function to generate a lazy sequence of Gregorian calendar dates. You can then use `java.text.SimpleDateFormat` (*http://bit.ly/javadoc-simple-date-format*) to format the dates, with a huge variety of output formats available.

This example creates an infinite lazy sequence of Gregorian calendar dates,[4] beginning on January 1, 1970 and each spanning a single day. The core `take` and `drop` functions are then used to select the last two days of February (be careful not to evaluate the infinite sequence itself in the REPL):

```
(def daily-from-epoch
  (let [start-date (java.util.GregorianCalendar. 1970 0 0 0 0) ]
    (repeatedly
      (fn []
        (.add start-date java.util.Calendar/DAY_OF_YEAR 1)
        (.clone start-date)))))

(take 2 (drop 57 daily-from-epoch))
;; -> (#inst "1970-02-27T00:00:00.000-07:00"
;;     #inst "1970-02-28T00:00:00.000-07:00")
```

## Discussion

Clojure has no date type of its own; by default, it relies on its ability to easily interoperate with Java (but see the `clj-time` library for alternatives to Java's date, time, and calendar classes).

This solution is based on the core `repeatedly` function, which creates a lazy sequence by repeatedly calling the argument function it is given and returning a sequence of the function's results. Because you do not provide the optional, limiting argument to `repeatedly`, the result sequences produced are infinite. Consequently, in the REPL environment, you must be careful to evaluate your result sequences in contexts (such as `take` and `drop`) that limit the values produced.

Since the function given to `repeatedly` is a function of no arguments, it is presumed to achieve its goals by side effects (making it an impure function). Here, the impurity occurs as the argument function creates a Gregorian calendar date and repeatedly increments it by a single `java.util.Calendar` (*http://bit.ly/javadoc-calendar*) day unit. For each call of the function, it returns a copy of the Gregorian calendar object (to avoid mysterious and unintended side effects, it is advisable to avoid returning the mutated object directly).

The date values in the result sequence are of type `java.util.GregorianCalendar`, but the `print` function of the REPL displays them as an `#inst` reader literal. You can verify that the sequence elements are Gregorian calendar objects by mapping the `class` (or `type`) function onto the sequence:

4. "Gregorian" is the formal name for the style of calendar we all know and love. Read more on Wikipedia (*http://bit.ly/gregorian-calendar*).

```
(def end-of-feb (take 2 (drop 57 daily-from-epoch)))
(map class end-of-feb)
;; -> (java.util.GregorianCalendar java.util.GregorianCalendar)
```

You can generalize the solution to a function that takes a starting year argument but defaults to some convenient year if the argument is not provided:

```
(defn daily-from-year [& [start-year]]
  (let [start-date (java.util.GregorianCalendar. (or start-year 1970)
                                                  0 0 0 0)]
    (repeatedly
      (fn []
        (.add start-date java.util.Calendar/DAY_OF_YEAR 1)
        (.clone start-date) ))))

(take 3 (daily-from-year 1999))
;; -> (#inst "1999-01-01T00:00:00.000-07:00"
;;     #inst "1999-01-02T00:00:00.000-07:00"
;;     #inst "1999-01-03T00:00:00.000-07:00")

(take 2 (daily-from-year))
;; -> (#inst "1970-01-01T00:00:00.000-07:00"
;;     #inst "1970-01-02T00:00:00.000-07:00")
```

Using the `java.text.SimpleDateFormat` class, you can then format the dates in a wide variety of different formats:

```
(def end-of-days (take 3 (drop 353 (daily-from-year 2012))))
(def cal-format (java.text.SimpleDateFormat. "EEE M/d/yyyy"))
(def iso8601-format (java.text.SimpleDateFormat. "yyyy-MM-dd'T'HH:mm:ss'Z'"))

(map #(.format cal-format (.getTime %)) end-of-days)
;; -> ("Wed 12/19/2012" "Thu 12/20/2012" "Fri 12/21/2012")

(map #(.format iso8601-format (.getTime %)) end-of-days)
;; -> ("2012-12-19T00:00:00Z" "2012-12-20T00:00:00Z" "2012-12-21T00:00:00Z")
```

To put it all together, create a function that generates an infinite lazy sequence of formatted Gregorian date strings. For convenience, the function takes optional starting year and date format string arguments:

```
(defn gregorian-day-seq
  "Return an infinite sequence of formatted Gregorian day strings
  starting on January 1st of the given year (default 1970)"
  [& [start-year date-format]]
  (let [gd-format (java.text.SimpleDateFormat. (or date-format "EEE M/d/yyyy"))
        start-date (java.util.GregorianCalendar. (or start-year 1970) 0 0 0 0)]
    (repeatedly
      (fn []
        (.add start-date java.util.Calendar/DAY_OF_YEAR 1)
        (.format gd-format (.getTime start-date)) ))))
```

To test the function, select the last Sunday of the year by finding all of the Sundays in a year:

```
(def y2k (take 366 (gregorian-day-seq 2000)))
(last (filter #(.startsWith % "Sun") y2k))
;; -> "Sun 12/31/2000"
```

## See Also

- Recipe 1.25, "Obtaining the Current Date and Time" on page 43, for information on using `java.util.Date` from Clojure
- Recipe 1.26, "Representing Dates as Literals" on page 44, to learn about Clojure's `#inst` reader literal for date/times
- Recipe 1.31, "Generating Ranges of Dates and Times" on page 52, for an alternative that utilizes `clj-time`/Joda-Time

# 1.33. Retrieving Dates Relative to One Another

by Ryan Neufeld

## Problem

You need to calculate a time relative to some other time, à la Ruby on Rails' (*http://rubyonrails.org/*) `2.days.from_now`.

## Solution

Because relative time is such a complex beast, we suggest using `clj-time` (*https://github.com/clj-time/clj-time*) for calculating relative dates and times.

Before starting, add `[clj-time "0.6.0"]` to your project's dependencies or start a REPL using `lein-try`:

```
$ lein try clj-time
```

If you've used the Ruby on Rails framework, then you're likely accustomed to statements like `1.day.from_now`, `3.days.ago`, or `some_date - 2.years`. You'll be pleased to know that `clj-time` exposes similar functionality:

```
(require '[clj-time.core :as t])

;; 1.day.from_now (it's April 6 at the time of this writing)
(-> 1
    t/days
    t/from-now)
;; -> #<DateTime 2013-04-07T20:36:52.012Z>
```

```
;; 3.days.ago
(-> 3
    t/days
    t/ago)
;; -> #<DateTime 2013-04-03T20:37:06.844Z>
```

The `clj-time.core` functions `from-now` and `ago` are just syntactic sugar over `plus` and `minus`:

```
;; 1.day.from_now
(t/plus (t/now) (t/years 1))
;; -> #<DateTime 2014-04-06T20:41:43.638Z>

;; some_date - 2.years
(def some-date (t/date-time 2053 12 25))
(t/minus some-date (t/years 2))
;; -> #<DateTime 2051-12-25T00:00:00.000Z>
```

## Discussion

Despite how difficult dates and times can sometimes be in Java, `clj-time` manages to expose a joyful syntax for adding to and subtracting from dates.

The functions `plus`, `minus`, `from-now`, and `ago` all take a period of time and adjust a `DateTime` by that amount (be that time "now," as in `from-now` or `ago`, or some provided time).

`clj-time.core` includes a number of useful period helpers ranging from `millis` to `years` that produce a time period at a given scale.

Depending on your use case, it's even possible to arrange operation, time period, and time in such a manner that they almost read like a sentence.

Take `(-> 1 t/years t/from-now)`, for example. In this case, the threading macro `->` threads each value as an argument to the next, producing `(t/from-now (t/years 1))`.

It's up to you to arrange your function calls as you see fit, but know that it is quite possible to produce readable deep-nested calls like this.

## See Also

- Recipe 1.29, "Comparing Dates" on page 49
- Recipe 1.31, "Generating Ranges of Dates and Times" on page 52

# 1.34. Working with Time Zones

by Ryan Neufeld

## Problem

You need to gracefully handle times and dates in a number of time zones.

## Solution

The JVM's built-in time and date classes don't work well with the notion of time zones. For one, `Date` treats every value as UTC, and `Calendar` is cumbersome to work with in Clojure (or Java, for that matter). Use `clj-time` (*https://github.com/clj-time/clj-time*) to properly deal with time zones.

Before starting, add `[clj-time "0.6.0"]` to your project's dependencies or start a REPL using `lein-try`:

```
$ lein try clj-time
```

```
(require '[clj-time.core :as t])

;; My birth-time, in the correct time zone
(def bday (t/from-time-zone (t/date-time 2012 02 18 18)
                            (t/time-zone-for-offset -6)))

bday
;; -> #<DateTime 2012-02-18T18:00:00.000-06:00>

;; What time was it in Brisbane when I was born?
(def australia-bday
  (t/to-time-zone bday (t/time-zone-for-id "Australia/Brisbane")))

australia-bday
;; -> #<DateTime 2012-02-19T10:00:00.000+10:00>

;; Yet they are the same instant in time.
(compare bday australia-bday)
;; -> 0
```

## Discussion

Unlike Java built-ins, `clj-time` knows a lot about time zones. Joda-Time (*http://bit.ly/joda-time*), the library `clj-time` wraps, bundles the internationally recognized `tz` database (*http://bit.ly/tz-info*). This database captures the IDs and time offsets for nearly every location on the planet.

The `tz` database also captures information about daylight saving time. For example, Los Angeles is UTC-08:00 in the winter and UTC-07:00 during the summer. This is accurately reflected when using `clj-time`:

```
(def la-tz (t/time-zone-for-id "America/Los_Angeles"))

;; LA is UTC-08:00 in winter
(t/from-time-zone (t/date-time 2012 01 01) la-tz)
;; -> #<DateTime 2012-01-01T00:00:00.000-08:00>

;; ... and UTC-07:00 in summer
(t/from-time-zone (t/date-time 2012 06 01) la-tz)
;; -> #<DateTime 2012-06-01T00:00:00.000-07:00>
```

The `clj-time.core/from-time-zone` function takes any `DateTime` and modifies its time zone to the desired time zone. This is useful in cases where you receive a date, time, and time zone separately and want to combine them into an accurate `DateTime` instance.

The `clj-time.core/to-time-zone` function has the same signature as `from-time-zone`; it returns a `DateTime` for the exact same point in time, but from the perspective of another time zone. This is useful for presenting time and date information from disparate sources to a user in her preferred time zone.

Sometimes you may only want to deal with machine-local time. The `clj-time.local` namespace provides a number of functions to that end, including `local-now`, for getting a time in the local time zone, and `to-local-date-time`, which shifts the perspective of a time to the local time zone.

## See Also

- Recipe 1.30, "Calculating the Length of a Time Interval" on page 51, and Recipe 1.33, "Retrieving Dates Relative to One Another" on page 57

# 1.35. Converting a Unix Timestamp to a Date

by Steven Proctor

## Problem

You need to get a `Date` object from a Unix timestamp.

## Solution

When dealing with data from outside systems, you'll find that many systems express timestamps in Unix time format. You may encounter this when dealing with certain datastores, parsing out data from timestamps in log files, or working with any number of other systems that have to deal with dates and times across multiple different time zones and cultures.

Fortunately, with Clojure's ability for nice interoperability with Java, you have an easy solution at hand:

```
(defn from-unix-time
  "Return a Java Date object from a Unix time representation expressed
  in whole seconds."
  [unix-time]
  (java.util.Date. unix-time))
```

This is how you can use the `from-unix-time` function:

```
(from-unix-time 1366127520000)
;; -> #inst "2013-04-16T15:52:00.000-00:00"
```

## Discussion

To get a Java `Date` object from a Unix time object, all you need to do is construct a new `java.util.Date` (*http://bit.ly/javadoc-date*) object using Clojure's Java interop functionality.

If you are already using or wish to use the `clj-time` (*https://github.com/clj-time/clj-time*) library, you can use `clj-time` to obtain a `DateTime` object from a Unix timestamp:

```
(require '[clj-time.coerce :as timec])

(defn datetime-from-unix-time
  "Return a DateTime object from a Unix time representation expressed
  in whole seconds."
  [unix-time]
  (timec/from-long unix-time))
```

And using the `datetime-from-unix-time` function, you can see you get a `DateTime` object back with the correct time:

```
(datetime-from-unix-time 1366127520000)
;; -> #<DateTime 2013-04-16T15:52:00.000Z>
```

You may not need to worry about dates and times being expressed as seconds very often, but when you do, isn't it nice to know how easy it can be to get those timestamps into a date format used by the rest of the system?

## See Also

- Recipe 1.25, "Obtaining the Current Date and Time" on page 43
- Recipe 1.36, "Converting a Date to a Unix Timestamp" on page 62

# 1.36. Converting a Date to a Unix Timestamp

by Steven Proctor

## Problem

You need to get a Unix timestamp representation for a `Date` object.

## Solution

Many systems express timestamps in Unix time format, and when you have to interact with these systems, you have to give them date and time information in the format they desire.

Fortunately, with Clojure's ability for nice interoperability with Java, you have an easy solution at hand:

```
(defn to-unix-time
  "Returns a Unix time representation expressed in whole seconds
   given a java.util.Date."
  [date]
  (.getTime date))
```

This is how you can use the `to-unix-time` function:

```
(def date (read-string "#inst \"2013-04-16T15:52:00.000-00:00\""))
;; -> #'user/date

(to-unix-time date)
;; -> 1366127520000
```

## Discussion

When you have a `java.util.Date` (*http://bit.ly/javadoc-date*) object, you can use the Java interop provided by Clojure as an easy way to get the time represented as a Unix time. Java's `Date` objects have a method called `getTime` that returns the date as a Unix time.

If you are already using or wish to use the `clj-time` (*https://github.com/clj-time/clj-time*) library, you can use `clj-time` to obtain a Unix time–formatted `DateTime` object if you have a `DateTime` object:

```
(require '[clj-time.coerce :as timec])

(defn datetime-to-unix-time
  "Returns a Unix time representation expressed in whole seconds
   given a DateTime."
  [datetime]
  (timec/to-long datetime))
```

And using the `datetime-to-unix-time` function, you can see you get a Unix time format for a `DateTime` object:

```
(def datetime (clj-time.core/date-time 2013 04 16 15 52))
;; #'user/datetime

(datetime-to-unix-time datetime)
;; 1366127520000
```

Thanks to `clj-time.coerce`, all that is needed is to use the function `to-long` to get a Joda-Time `DateTime` object into a Unix time format.

Your system may never need to interact with other systems that expect timestamps expressed in Unix time, but if you are designing a system that does, Clojure makes it very easy to express a `Date` or `DateTime` in Unix time format.

## See Also


- Recipe 1.25, "Obtaining the Current Date and Time" on page 43
- Recipe 1.35, "Converting a Unix Timestamp to a Date" on page 60

# CHAPTER 2
# Composite Data

## 2.0. Introduction

Now that we've got primitives out of the way, we need to start doing something with them. Single atomic values are great and all, but things get much more interesting when we start globbing them all together. As you'll see soon enough, data manipulation is one of Clojure's strong suits.

What makes Clojure so good at manipulating collections? It comes down to three things: *immutability*, *persistence*, and the *sequence abstraction*. Every one of Clojure's built-in collection types has these properties and is thus unified in its API's appearance and behavior.

As the great Alan J. Perlis (an early computer science pioneer) put it:

> It is better to have 100 functions operate on one data structure than to have 10 functions operate on 10 data structures.

This chapter introduces Clojure collections and where/how to use them. Finally, we wrap things up by showing you how to build your own feature-complete types that look and behave just like the rest of Clojure's collections by leveraging Clojure's capacity for interface polymorphism.

### Immutability

Immutability means that a Clojure data structure, once created, can never change. You can only "modify" an immutable data structure by creating a *new* data structure that is a copy of the old, with the desired changes in place.

Immutability also means that Clojure data structures, however deeply nested, are simple *values*, just like the number `3` or the character `\z`. It doesn't make sense to speak of "changing" the value of 3— it just is. If you "change" it by, say, incrementing it, you don't modify 3 itself. Instead, you end up with an entirely new and different value, 4. Clojure extends this notion of value to all data structures. In Clojure, any action that in another language would perform any kind of update on a data structure will instead return an entirely new one. You can continue to pass around and use both the old and the new versions with confidence, knowing that nothing you can do will cause any unintended changes elsewhere in your program.

This feature is extremely important in concurrent and parallel programming, where unexpected mutation is the source of a large class of bugs. With immutable data, any number of threads can read from the same data without any worrying about locks or race conditions—it's always safe to read something that can't change. "Clone" operations are not only free, but unnecessary.

## Persistence

But, you may ask, how can that possibly be efficient? Surely it is impractical to do a full copy of an object every time you need to add something?

Yes, it would be, except for the feature of persistence. Persistence means that Clojure's data structures, although logically immutable, can still share pieces of their internal structure for efficiency in both time and space. Essentially, updated versions of immutable data only need to store the deltas from pervious versions, rather than doing a full deep copy.

To make it performant, all of this uses some extremely clever algorithms, of course. See the book *Purely Functional Data Structures* by Chris Okasaki (Cambridge University Press) for a detailed description of how they work.

## The Sequence Abstraction

From vectors, maps, sets, and lists to strings and streams, every last one of Clojure's collections behaves in a similar, predictable fashion. They are simple tools for a more civilized age. This is on account of Clojure's sequence abstraction.

The array of collection-manipulating functions in Clojure are all implemented in terms of one simple abstraction: every collection can be treated as a sequence of values. By implementing `first`, `rest`, and `cons`, any data structure—even ones you build yourself—can participate in the `ISeq` interface.

Then, you can use Clojure's huge library of functions that can operate on sequences, with *any* of the data structures. All of functional programming's most beloved functions (`map`, `reduce`, `filter`, etc.) will work interchangeably on any data structure. In essence, the sequence abstraction allows all the expressiveness of traditional list-based LISP programming without forcing you to actually use lists. Instead, use whatever type is most efficient for the task, knowing that you can consume them all in the same way when it makes sense to do so.

## 2.1. Creating a List

by Luke VanderHart

### Problem

You want to create a list data structure in your source code.

### Solution

There are two basic ways to specifically construct a list (a `clojure.lang.PersistentList`).

You can use parentheses in combination with a single quote to indicate that the list should only be read as a data structure, not immediately evaluated:

```
'(1 :2 "3")
;; -> (1 :2 "3")
```

Or, more commonly, you can use the `list` function, which takes a variadic number of arguments and constructs a list from them:

```
(list 1 :2 "3")
;; -> (1 :2 "3")
```

### Discussion

Typically, between these two approaches, using the `list` function is the better choice. The problem with constructing quoted lists is that the quote also prevents evaluation of everything *inside* the list, which means that symbols will be returned as literal symbols, instead of resolving variables or calling functions. `list`, however, will evaluate its arguments in the normal way before constructing the list and is usually what is desired for nonmacro code:

```
(def x 2)

'(1 x)
;; -> (1 x)

(list 1 x)
;; -> (1 2)
```

That said, `'()` is the idiomatic way to create an empty list—it is more terse, and the concern about evaluating its contents is irrelevant when it's empty.

> **Lists Versus Vectors**
>
> Clojure includes both list and vector types. Both are sequential data structures. However, for most purposes, vectors are a better fit and are more commonly used in idiomatic Clojure.
>
> There are a couple of reasons for this. Vectors have a cleaner literal syntax than lists and are just as space-efficient and performant. In addition, vectors support near-constant lookup time by index ($O(\log_{32} n)$), as opposed to lists, which require linear time ($O(n)$).
>
> In general, the only reason to explicitly choose a list over a vector is if you need a data structure that supports efficient insertions at the beginning, which lists do; vectors are most efficient when appending items to the end.

### See Also


- Recipe 2.2, "Creating a List from an Existing Data Structure" on page 68
- Recipe 2.6, "Creating a Vector" on page 73


## 2.2. Creating a List from an Existing Data Structure

by Luke VanderHart

### Problem

You have an existing sequential data structure that you would like to convert into a list as its concrete data type.

### Solution

The easiest solution is: don't. Having a concrete list provides little or no advantage over simply using the sequence abstraction directly on your existing data, and for large data structures, conversion can be expensive.

If you do know that you need an explicit conversion of the concrete data structure, there are two ways to do it.

First, you could use the `apply` function to call the `list` function, passing it your existing data structure as its arguments:

```
(apply list [1 2 3 4 5])
;; -> (1 2 3 4 5)
```

Alternatively, you could use the `into` function to repeatedly conjoin elements from your original data onto a list. Note, however, that this approach has the effect of reversing the order of the original collection:

```
(into '() [1 2 3 4 5])
;; -> (5 4 3 2 1)
```

## Discussion

These two approaches are both viable choices. However, what actually happens in each case is very different.

When using `apply`, you are actually invoking the `list` function with however many arguments are in the data structure. This may sound strange, particularly if the data structure contains millions of items. What does it mean to invoke a function with a million arguments? How does that even work, given that the JVM limits methods to 255 arguments (see the JVM class file specification (*http://bit.ly/jvm-class-file-format*))?

As it turns out, functions with variadic arguments (such as `list`) are handled in a somewhat special way: the argument list is passed in as a sequence. `apply` knows this and passes this sequence view of the original structure directly through to the receiving function. This is why it works; there is never actually a JVM method invocation with a million arguments.

`into` works quite differently: it takes two arguments, the first being a data structure and the second being a sequence. It then repeatedly conjoins items from the sequence onto the data structure provided using the `conj` function (discussed in greater detail elsewhere). This is why the sequence is reversed; items are always pulled from the front of the sequence, but `conj` on a list *prepends* the element being added. Therefore, the first element in the input sequence will end up being the last item in the list, and so on.

So why ever choose `into` over `apply`, given that it reverses the order? Speed. `into` utilizes Clojure *transients*, which provide a considerable performance improvement. On the author's machine, converting a million-item vector to a list using `apply` took an average of 750 milliseconds, while using `into` took about half that time, for an average of 350 milliseconds. Of course, the list was in reverse order, and reversing either the input or the output negates the speed advantage. In the end, `into` is only advantageous in situations where a reversed order is acceptable.

## See Also


- Recipe 2.1, "Creating a List" on page 67

# 2.3. "Adding" an Item to a List

by Luke VanderHart

## Problem

You want to add an item to a list; or, putting it in functional terms, you want to derive from an existing list a new list that contains an additional item.

## Solution

Use the `conj` function. `conj` is used to add an item or items to a logical collection and is polymorphic, meaning it works on multiple concrete data types, including lists:

```
(conj (list 1 2 3) 4)
;; -> (4 1 2 3)
```

You can also add multiple items at once:

```
(conj (list 1 2 3) 4 5)
;; -> (5 4 1 2 3)
```

## Discussion

The behavior of `conj` may vary slightly depending on the concrete type. It always "adds" an item to an immutable collection by returning a new collection containing the new item, but may add the item to different places in the collection depending on what is most efficient for the particular type.

In the case of lists, `conj` will always add the item at the *beginning* of the list, since a linked list data structure supports constant-time insertion only at the beginning.

### conj Versus cons

If you are familiar with Common Lisp or Scheme, you were probably expecting to see the `cons` function used, instead of `conj`. Clojure does have a `cons` function, but it has a slightly different purpose.

While `conj` will return a new concrete `clojure.lang.PersistentList` (when used on a list), `cons` will always construct a new *sequence*, where the item added is the *first* and the collection is the *rest*.

This distinction is subtle, especially since a `clojure.lang.PersistentList` and a sequence constructed using `cons` are both types of persistent linked lists, algorithmically speaking.

The best way to think about it is that `conj` is a concrete *data structure* operation, which will not change the concrete type of the data structure it is applied to, while `cons` is a *sequence* operation and only guarantees that it will return a sequence: in fact, it returns a cons cell (`clojure.lang.Cons`) that implements the sequence interface, no matter what type of *seq*-able collection you gave it to start with.

Unlike `conj`, `cons` is also guaranteed to return a sequence with the item prepended to the beginning no matter what the collection type is.

## See Also

- Recipe 2.7, "“Adding” an Item to a Vector" on page 74

# 2.4. "Removing" an Item from a List

by Luke VanderHart

## Problem

You want to obtain a list without a particular item in it, removing an item from the original list.

## Solution

Removing the first item from a list is easily accomplished using one of two functions, `rest` or `pop`. Both work identically when used on a nonempty list:

```
(pop '(1 2 3))
;; -> (2 3)

(rest '(1 2 3))
;; -> (2 3)
```

## Discussion

`rest` is actually a sequence function, used to obtain the tail of a sequence. Since Clojure lists implement the sequence interface directly, using `rest` on a list will always return another (possibly empty) list.

`pop` is similar to `conj` in that it operates on concrete data structures rather than the sequence interface. Like `conj`, it is polymorphic; also like `conj`, the position it removes the item from depends on what's most efficient for the concrete type.

When used on an empty list, the behavior does differ; pop will throw an exception, while rest will return an empty list:

```
(pop '())
;; -> IllegalStateException Can't pop empty list ...

(rest '())
;; -> ()
```

Lists do not support removing items except at the first position. If you need to remove an item in the middle or at the end of a list, you'll have to do so using the sequence manipulation functions, then convert the result back into a concrete list (if you absolutely need it to be a list, for some reason).

## See Also

- Recipe 2.8, ""Removing" an Item from a Vector" on page 75

# 2.5. Testing for a List

by Steve Miner

## Problem

You want to test if a value is a list.

## Solution

The `list?` function may seem like the obvious choice, but in most cases, it's better to use the more general `seq?` function as your test.

## Discussion

The `list?` function specifically tests if the argument implements `clojure.lang.IPersistentList`, but in most cases, you really want to know if the value is a *seq* (implements `clojure.lang.ISeq`), which is a more general abstraction than a list.

Not everything that prints as a *list* (in parentheses) actually satisfies the `list?` test. In practice, you'll often receive `Cons` and `LazySeq` values when manipulating lists. By focusing on the fundamental *seq* abstraction, you don't need to worry about the details of those concrete implementations:

```
;; A list constructed via list satisfies both list? and seq?
(list? (list 1 2 3))
;; -> true
(seq? (list 1 2 3))
```

```
;; -> true

;; cons, however *looks* like a list, but is actually a Cons
(list? (cons 1 '(2 3)))
;; -> false
(type (cons 1 '(2 3)))
;; -> clojure.lang.Cons
(seq? (cons 1 '(2 3)))
;; -> true

;; range's lazy return value is a seq, but not a list
(list? (range 3))
;; -> false
(seq? (range 3))
;; -> true
(type (range 3))
;; -> clojure.lang.LazySeq
```

It's almost always better to use `seq?` instead of `list?`.

## See Also


- Recipe 2.1, "Creating a List" on page 67
- Recipe 2.3, ""Adding" an Item to a List" on page 70
- Recipe 2.26, "Determining if a Collection Holds One of Several Values" on page 113


# 2.6. Creating a Vector

by Luke VanderHart

## Problem

You want to create a vector data structure, either as a literal or from an existing data structure.

## Solution

By far, the easiest way to create a vector is using the literal vector notation of square brackets. However, it is also possible to use the `vector` function, which creates a vector of its arguments:

```
[1 :2 "3"]
;; -> [1 :2 "3"]

(vector 1 :2 "3")
;; -> [1 :2 "3"]
```

To construct a vector from an existing data structure, you can use the `vec` function, which takes any collection and returns a vector containing the same items:

```
(vec '(1 :2 "3"))
;; -> [1 :2 "3"]
```

Alternatively, you can use the `into` function, which takes two collections and repeatedly invokes `conj` on the first with items from the second:

```
(into [] '(1 :2 "3"))
;; -> [1 :2 "3"]
```

## Discussion

There is rarely any reason to use the `vector` function over the literal vector syntax. Unlike lists, vectors are not evaluated as function calls (or anything else) in Clojure, so quoting is not a concern as it is with list literals.

Oddly enough, when constructing a vector from an existing collection, using the `into` approach is currently about 30% more performant on large collections compared to `vec` due to its use of transients to speed things up. If you're converting large collections and speed matters, consider using `into`. Otherwise, `vec` is usually more readable.

## See Also


- Recipe 2.1, "Creating a List" on page 67
- Recipe 2.2, "Creating a List from an Existing Data Structure" on page 68


# 2.7. "Adding" an Item to a Vector

by Luke VanderHart

## Problem

You want to add an item to a vector, yielding a new vector containing the item.

## Solution

When used on a vector, the `conj` function returns a vector with one or more items appended to the end:

```
(conj [1 2 3] 4)
;; -> [1 2 3 4]

(conj [1 2 3] 4 5)
;; -> [1 2 3 4 5]
```

## Discussion

Vectors do not support adding new items anywhere aside from the end. If you need to insert an item in the middle, you will have to use a sequence manipulation function and convert back to a vector (if necessary) when you're done.

Since vectors are associative (mapping integer indexes to values), you can also use the `assoc` function with an index equal to the current length of the vector (one greater than the maximum index) to append an item:

```
(assoc [:a :b :c] 3 :x)
;; -> [:a :b :c :x]
```

However, this approach is somewhat more fragile than `conj`. If the index you provide is too small, you might simply "overwrite" an earlier value in the vector; and if it's greater than the vector's current length, it will throw an `IndexOutOfBoundsException`.

Still, this technique is worth remembering. If you have code that is `assoc`-ing to a vector already, you can use this technique to produce new vectors with updated values.

## See Also

- Recipe 2.3, ""Adding" an Item to a List" on page 70
- Recipe 2.6, "Creating a Vector" on page 73

# 2.8. "Removing" an Item from a Vector

by Luke VanderHart

## Problem

You want to remove an item from a vector, obtaining a new vector without the item.

## Solution

To efficiently remove an item from the end of a vector, use the `pop` function, which takes a vector and returns a new vector without the last item:

```
(pop [1 2 3 4])
;; -> [1 2 3]
```

## Discussion

Although there is no operation designed specifically to remove items from the beginning of a vector, as `pop` does from the end, there *is* a function, `subvec`, that can be used to efficiently *remove* any number of items from the beginning or end of a vector. Given a vector, a start index, and an (optional) end index, it will return a vector from the start (inclusive) to end (exclusive) indexes.

The following example drops a single item from the beginning of a vector. You can use `subvec` like so:

```
(subvec [:a :b :c :d] 1)
;; -> [:b :c :d]
```

Or, to remove items from the beginning and the end of a vector, pass an end index to `subvec` as well:

```
(subvec [:a :b :c :d] 1 3)
;; -> [:b :c]
```

Because `subvec` exploits the internal representation of a vector to create a subvector that shares the internal structure of the original, it is extremely efficient and runs in constant time. It is the only way to efficiently *remove* items from the beginning of a vector.

While it is certainly also possible to use a function like `rest` or `drop` on a vector, these are technically *sequence* operations, not *vector* operations. The value they return is only guaranteed to be a sequence, not a concrete vector, and as such will not support the same features or performance guarantees that vectors do.

Of course, you can convert any sequence back into a concrete vector using `vec` or `into []`, but this can be an expensive operation for large vectors.

## See Also


- Recipe 2.4, ""Removing" an Item from a List" on page 71
- Recipe 2.6, "Creating a Vector" on page 73


# 2.9. Getting the Value at an Index

by Luke VanderHart

## Problem

You have a vector, and you want to retrieve the value the vector contains at a particular location (index).

## Solution

There are several ways to do this.

### Using nth

The nth function, which works on all sequences, is special-cased to provide constant-time performance when used with indexed collections such as vectors:

```
(nth [:a :b :c :d] 2)
;; -> :c
```

If given an index greater than the size of the vector, nth will throw an exception unless you pass it an optional third argument, which will be returned if the provided index is out of bounds:

```
(nth [:a :b :c] 4)
;; -> IndexOutOfBoundsException

(nth [:a :b :c] 4 :not-found)
;; -> :not-found
```

### Using vectors as functions of their indexes

Vectors are themselves functions that when called with an integer argument, will return the value at that index:

```
(def v [:a :b :c])
(v 2)
;; -> :c
```

Using an out-of-range index when invoking a vector as a function will result in an IndexOutOfBoundsException.

### Using get

Because vectors support the associative interface with integer indexes as keys, you can also use the get function to retrieve values by index:

```
(get [:a :b :c] 2)
;; -> :c
```

Unlike nth, when you pass an out-of-range index to get it will return nil, not throw an exception—unless, that is, you provide a default value to be returned if the key (the index, in this case) is not found:

```
(get [:a :b :c] 5)
;; -> :nil

(get [:a :b :c] 5 :not-found)
;; -> :not-found
```

## Discussion

Which technique should you use? All work equally well, but the choice does emphasize the way in which you're looking at your vector. nth focuses on its sequential nature, whereas `get` emphasizes its indexed, associative quality. Using the vector as a function is also consistent with the way all associative collections in Clojure act as functions of their keys.

Ultimately, when making a choice like this, you should consider:

- What would make the code most evident?
- What is the nature of the data in this case? For example, is it most fundamentally a sequence and only coincidentally a vector (implying `nth`), or fundamentally a correlation of values to indexes (implying `get`)?
- What is the failure mode of the proposed technique? For example, would a `nil` return value or an exception be preferable?

## See Also

- Recipe 2.16, "Retrieving Values from a Map" on page 88

# 2.10. Setting the Value at an Index

by Luke VanderHart

## Problem

Given a vector, you would like to obtain a new vector with a different value at a particular index.

## Solution

Use `assoc` to set the value at a particular index:

```
(assoc [:a :b :c ] 1 :x)
;; -> [:a :x :c]
```

`assoc` can also be used to set multiple indexes at the same time, by providing additional index/value pairs:

```
(assoc [:a :b :c ] 1 :x 2 :y)
;; -> [:a :x :y]
```

## Discussion

As you may have noticed, `assoc` is the same function used to set the values of keys in a map. This is because vectors, like maps, are associative and implement the same interface (`clojure.lang.Associative`), which is what `assoc` uses under the hood.

Unlike with maps, however, the keys used when using `assoc` on a vector must be integer indexes within the range of the vector. Attempting to use a noninteger key will cause an `IllegalArgumentException`, and attempting to `assoc` an index greater than the size of the vector will throw an `IndexOutOfBoundsException`.

Note that it *is* possible to `assoc` to an index equal to the current size of the vector (one greater than the maximum index). This will have the result of appending the item to the end.

## See Also


- Recipe 2.7, "“Adding” an Item to a Vector" on page 74
- Recipe 2.18, "Setting Keys in a Map" on page 92


# 2.11. Creating a Set

by Luke VanderHart

## Problem

You want to create an unordered collection of *distinct* objects, which can be tested for membership quickly.

## Solution

Use a set literal to create a set of objects:

```
#{:a :b :c}
;; -> #{:a :c :b}

;; Duplicate elements in set literals are an error
#{:x :y :z :z :z}
;; -> IllegalArgumentException Duplicate key: :y :z ...
```

Use `hash-set` to create a set from arguments:

```
(hash-set :a :b :c)
;; -> #{:a :c :b}

(apply hash-set :a [:b :c])
;; -> #{:a :c :b}
```

Use `set` to create a set from another collection:

```
(set "hello")
;; -> #{\e \h \l \o}
```

Alternatively, use `into` with a set to create a new set:

```
(into #{} [:a :b :c :a])
;; -> #{:a :b :c}

(into #{:a :b} [:b :c :d])
;; -> #{:a :b :c :d}
```

**Set construction performance**

At the time of writing, the `into` technique is about three times faster than `set` for large collections of objects. Use it whenever you're working with large sets where performance is a concern:

```
(def largeseq (doall (range 1e5)))

(time (dotimes [_ 100] (set largeseq)))
;; *out*
;; "Elapsed time: 5594.961 msecs"

(time (dotimes [_ 100] (into #{} largeseq)))
;; *out*
;; "Elapsed time: 1329.66 msecs"
```

Create a sorted set with `sorted-set`:

```
(sorted-set 99 4 32 7)
;; -> #{4 7 32 99}

(into (sorted-set) "the quick brown fox jumps over the lazy dog")
;; -> #{\space \a \b \c \d \e \f \g \h \i \j \k \l \m \n \o \p
;;      \q \r \s \t \u \v \w \x \y \z}
```

## Discussion

Sets are very useful data structures. They are commonly used when you have a collection of values but you are only concerned with the distinct values. Lookup of an element in a set is typically O(1).

The techniques just shown all construct *hash sets*—sets that are unordered and use a hash table as their internal representation.

Clojure also supports creating *sorted sets*, which maintain the order of their elements. Sets created with `sorted-set` keep their elements in ascending order using `compare`. This is useful when treating the set as a seq:

```
(def alphabet (into (sorted-set) "qwertyuiopasdfghjklzxcvbnm"))
(last alphabet)
;; -> \z
(second (disj alphabet \b))
;; -> \c
```

All of the elements in a sorted set must be comparable against one another (e.g., you cannot have a sorted set that contains both strings and numbers). Attempting to add an uncomparable value will result in a runtime error.

Adding or removing objects in a sorted set will always return another sorted set.

If the values you want to store don't have a natural sort order (or you don't want to use their natural ordering), you can specify a custom comparator using `sorted-set-by`. The comparator used to create the set is preserved when adding or removing objects:

```
(def descending-set (sorted-set-by > 1 2 3))

(into descending-set [-1 4])
;; -> #{4 3 2 1 -1}
```

There are some performance trade-offs to consider when choosing between hash sets and sorted sets. Hash sets are based on hash tables, which offer constant time insert and lookup in most cases. However, they do require some degree of memory overhead. Sorted sets, based on a balanced red-black binary tree, are more memory-efficient but slower for lookup and insertion.

## See Also


- Recipe 2.6, "Creating a Vector" on page 73
- Recipe 2.12, "Adding and Removing Items from Sets" on page 81


# 2.12. Adding and Removing Items from Sets

by Luke VanderHart

## Problem

You want to obtain a new set with items added or removed.

## Solution

The `conj` function supports sets, just as it does lists, vectors, and maps. Use it to add an item or items to a set: just pass it the set and any number of items to add:

```
(conj #{:a :b :c} :d)
;; -> #{:a :c :b :d}

(conj #{:a :b :c} :d :e)
;; -> #{:a :c :b :d :e}
```

To remove one or more items, use the `disj` function, which is specific to sets. It takes a set and one or more keys to remove:

```
(disj #{:a :b :c} :b)
;; -> #{:a :c}

(disj #{:a :b :c} :b :c)
;; -> #{:a}
```

## Discussion

Since sets are unordered, there is no concept of "where" items are added or removed; either a set contains an item, or it doesn't.

Note that both `conj` and `disj` return a set of the same concrete type as the original. A hash set will remain a hash set, and a sorted set will remain a sorted set.

Also worth noting is that these operations are simply no-ops if the set already does or does not contain the item being added or removed. `conj` returns the same set if it already contains the item, just as `disj` does if the specified item was already absent.

If you're adding or removing large numbers of items to or from sets, you should also consider using the dedicated set manipulation functions from the `clojure.set` namespace: particularly `clojure.set/union`, which can be used to add the items of multiple sets together, and `clojure.set/difference`, which can be used to obtain a set of items *not* contained in another set. These are typically a far more natural expression of set operations than issuing many calls to `conj` or `disj`, or invoking them with large numbers of arguments.

## See Also

- Recipe 2.3, ""Adding" an Item to a List" on page 70
- Recipe 2.7, ""Adding" an Item to a Vector" on page 74
- Recipe 2.14, "Using Set Operations" on page 84

# 2.13. Testing Set Membership

by Luke VanderHart

## Problem

You want to check if an item is a member of a set.

## Solution

The easiest way to check a single item is with the contains? function, which takes a set and an item and returns true if the item is a member of the set:

```
(contains? #{:red :white :green} :blue)
;; -> false

(contains? #{:red :white :green} :green)
;; -> true
```

The get function also works with sets and does basically the same thing, except instead of returning true or false, it returns the value itself if it is a member, or nil if it is not:

```
(get #{:red :white :green} :blue)
;; -> nil

(get #{:red :white :green} :green)
;; -> :green
```

Finally, sets are also functions. When you invoke them with a single argument, they work just like get, returning the argument if it is a member, and nil otherwise:

```
(def my-set #{:red :white :green})

(my-set :blue)
;; -> nil

(my-set :green)
;; -> :green
```

Note as well that keywords behave in the same manner for sets as they do with maps. Thus, the following is equivalent to having used get:

```
(:blue #{:red :white :green})
;; -> nil

(:green #{:red :white :green})
;; -> :green
```

## Discussion

The choice between contains? and get is mainly an aesthetic one. However, if your set might contain nil as an actual value you care about, you'll definitely need to use contains?, since a nil return from get wouldn't tell you anything in that case.

The ability to use a set as a function is interesting, but it's especially useful when you want to use it as a predicate function on a sequence operation. For example, it's fairly common to want to filter a sequence to only contain items in a set. In this case, using the set itself is both easy and idiomatic:

```
(take 10
  (filter #{1 2 3}
          (repeatedly #(rand-int 10))))
;; -> (2 1 2 3 2 2 1 2 2 1)
```

This snippet first creates an infinite lazy sequence consisting of random numbers between 1 and 10, using `repeatedly` to call `rand-int` (wrapped in an anonymous function) over and over. Then it feeds this sequence through a filter, with a set of the numbers 1–3 as the filter predicate.

The result is another infinite lazy sequence, but containing only members of the predicate set.

This example is contrived. However, using sets as predicate functions is an extremely useful technique that that pops up quite frequently in Clojure projects.

## See Also

- Recipe 2.14, "Using Set Operations" on page 84
- Recipe 2.16, "Retrieving Values from a Map" on page 88

# 2.14. Using Set Operations

by Luke VanderHart

## Problem

You want to perform common operations on sets, such as taking the union, intersection, or difference of two sets, or you want to test if one set is a subset or superset of another.

## Solution

All these functions are available in the `clojure.set` namespace, which is built into Clojure.

`union` takes any number of sets as arguments and returns a set containing their union (i.e., a set containing all the elements from all the sets):

```
(clojure.set/union #{:red :white} #{:white :blue} #{:blue :green})
;; -> #{:white :red :blue :green}
```

`intersection` also takes any number of sets as args and returns their intersection (a set consisting only of the items shared by all the argument sets):

```
(clojure.set/intersection #{:red :white :blue}
                          #{:red :blue :green}
                          #{:yellow :blue :red})
;; -> #{:red :blue}
```

difference takes a set as its first argument and returns it without elements from the sets given in the additional arguments:

```
(clojure.set/difference #{:red :white :blue :yellow}
                        #{:red :blue}
                        #{:white})
;; -> #{:yellow}
```

subset? returns true if and only if the first argument is a subset of the second (that is, if every member of the first set is also a member of the second):

```
(clojure.set/subset? #{:blue :white}
                     #{:red :white :blue})
;; -> true

(clojure.set/subset? #{:blue :black}
                     #{:red :white :blue})
;; -> false
```

superset? works the same way, except it returns true only if the first set is a *superset* of the second.

As you may have noticed, superset? is actually identical to subset?, only with the order of the arguments reversed.

## Discussion

In general, you should try to use these set manipulation functions wherever they are applicable. Sets represent a sizable portion of the data most developers work with day to day, whether they are recognized and explicitly modeled as sets or not.

There are a large number of bugs that can be caused by assumptions regarding the behaviors of collections. In programming, the type of data structure used for a given purpose is actually a *communication*, from the initial writer of the code to future programmers, that tells a number of things about the nature of the collection. Sets are *unordered, unique* collections—they emphasize that the important fact is whether an item is a member of the set, not the order or number of occurrences.

If your data does represent a logical set, then model it using set data structures, and try to think about manipulating it in terms of set operations. In many cases, you will find that this makes your program substantially easier to reason about, and makes it more self-documenting regarding the source and intended use of the data it contains.

## See Also

- Recipe 2.13, "Testing Set Membership" on page 82
- Recipe 2.26, "Determining if a Collection Holds One of Several Values" on page 113

# 2.15. Creating a Map

by Luke VanderHart

## Problem

You want to create an association that maps keys to values. You possibly want to maintain a specific ordering of keys.

## Solution

Use map literals (curly braces) with alternating keys and values to create simple maps:

```
{:name ""
 :class :barbarian
 :race :half-orc
 :level 20
 :skills [:bashing :hacking :smashing]}
```

Keys and values can be any type. Commas may be used to delimit key/value pairs where the structure would be hard to discern at a glance:

```
{1 1, 8 64, 2 4, 9 81}
```

In Clojure, commas are whitespace, which means that they can be used *anywhere* in a form with no effect on the value; it is just one way to make your code easier to read.

Create an empty, unsorted map with a pair of braces: `{}`.

Create specific types of maps with map constructor functions. `array-map`, `hash-map`, and `sorted-map` each return a map of the corresponding type:

```
(array-map)
;; -> {}

(sorted-map :key1 "val1" :key2 "val2")
;; -> {:key1 "val1" :key2 "val2"}
```

If a key occurs multiple times in the argument list, the last value will be that used in the final return map.

Use `sorted-map-by` to create a sorted map using a custom comparator:

```
(sorted-map-by #(< (count %1) (count %2))
               "pigs" 14
               "horses" 2
               "elephants" 1
               "manatees" 3)
;; -> {"pigs" 14, "horses" 2, "manatees" 3, "elephants" 1}
```

## Discussion

Clojure maps can have one of three distinct concrete implementations:

*Array maps*, `clojure.lang.PersistentArrayMap`
: These are backed by a simple array. They are efficient for very small maps, but not for larger sizes.

*Hash maps*, `clojure.lang.PersistentHashMap`
: These are backed by a hash table data structure. Hash tables support near constant-time lookup and insertion, but also require a certain amount of overhead space, using up slightly more heap space.

*Sorted maps*, `clojure.lang.PersistentTreeMap`
: These are backed by a balanced red-black binary tree. They are more space-efficient than hash maps, but have slower insertion and access times.

Array maps are the default implementation for small maps (under 10 entries at the time of writing), and hash maps are the default for larger ones. Sorted maps can only be created by explicitly invoking the `sorted-map` or `sorted-map-by` functions.

Using `assoc` or `conj` on a sorted map will always yield another sorted map. However, `assoc`-ing onto an array map will yield a hash map once it reaches a certain size. The inverse is not true; using `dissoc` on a hash map will not yield an array map, even if it becomes very small.

## See Also

- Recipe 1.29, "Comparing Dates" on page 49, and Recipe 1.17, "Performing Fuzzy Comparison" on page 28, to see more uses for `compare`
- Recipe 2.11, "Creating a Set" on page 79
- Recipe 2.18, "Setting Keys in a Map" on page 92
- Recipe 2.24, "Comparing and Sorting Values" on page 107

# 2.16. Retrieving Values from a Map

by Luke VanderHart

## Problem

You want to retrieve the value stored at a particular key in a map.

## Solution

As with sets, there are several ways to retrieve the value of a key.

The most straightforward way is to use the `get` function, which, given a map and a key, returns the value stored at the key or `nil` if the map does not contain the key:

```
(get {:name "Kvothe" :class "Bard"} :name)
;; -> "Kvothe"

(get {:name "Kvothe" :class "Bard"} :race)
;; -> nil
```

If desired, you can also pass a third argument to be used as the default return value instead of `nil` if a map doesn't contain the key:

```
(get {:name "Kvothe" :class "Bard"} :race "Human")
;; -> "Human"
```

If your map uses keywords as keys, you can use the keyword itself as a function. Keywords implement the `IFn` interface, and when invoked with a map as an argument, they will look themselves up in the map, returning the value if it is present or `nil` if not. You can also pass a second argument that will be used as a default return value in the case of a missing key, just as you can with `get`:

```
(:name {:name "Marcus" :class "Paladin"})
;; -> "Marcus"

(:race {:name "Marcus" :class "Paladin"} "Human")
;; -> "Human"
```

Finally, the third basic way to look up a value in a map is to use the map itself as a function, passing the key to be retrieved as the argument. As with `get` and keyword functions, it is also possible to pass a second argument for use as a default value if the key is not found; otherwise, `nil` is returned:

```
(def character {:name "Brock" :class "Barbarian"})

(character :name)
;; -> "Brock"
```

```
(character :race)
;; -> nil

(character :race "Human")
;; -> "Human"
```

There is a convenience function for looking up items in nested maps: `get-in`. Instead of passing a single key, you can pass a sequence of keys, and they will be successively looked up in a nested structure, as if repeatedly calling `get` on each level of the nested data structure. `nil` is returned if any key is missing:

```
(get-in {:name "Marcus" :weapon {:type :greatsword :damage "2d6"}}
        [:weapon :damage])
;; -> "2d6"

(get-in {:name "Marcus"}
        [:weapon :damage])
;; -> nil
```

`get-in` also takes an optional default value, which will be returned if *any* key in the nested hierarchy is missing:

```
(get-in {:name "Marcus"}
        [:weapon :damage]
        "1d2 (fists)")
;; -> "1d2 (fists)"
```

Note that `get-in` works with *any* associative data structure, not just maps. This means that it can be combined to work with, for example, indexes of vectors:

```
(get-in [{:name "Marcus" :class "Paladin"}
         {:name "Kvothe" :class "Bard"}
         {:name "Felter" :class "Druid"}]
        [1 :class])
;; -> "Bard"
```

## Discussion

Which technique of the three discussed is the best to use? All have identical semantics, but in idiomatic Clojure, they convey different implications about the scenario in which they are used.

Typically, keyword-as-a-function lookup is used when maps are being used as "objects" and the keys as "fields"; where the map contains a relatively small, well-known set of keys; and when there is a reasonable expectation that the key will actually be present.

The `get` function and map-as-a-function lookup techniques, on the other hand, are more frequently used with large maps where the set of possible keys is more open-ended. There is less motivation for choosing between these two; the only difference to be aware of is that when the map provided is `nil` for some reason, using it in function position will throw an exception, while applying `get` to `nil` will simply return `nil`.

It is interesting to note, as well, that the ability to use a map itself as a function is not just an arbitrary convenience. In the technical sense of the word "function," maps *are* functions of keys to values. Consider the following function definition and map:

```
(defn square [x] (* x x))
```

```
(def square {1 1, 2 4, 3 9, 4 16, 5 25})
```

Using an invocation of the form `(square 3)`, the caller can actually be *agnostic* as to whether `square` is a "real" function or a map. Of course, the normally defined function has a number of advantages in this case. For one, it has an unlimited domain instead of just the keys enumerated. And the multiplication function is fairly fast, so precomputing results is not a win. But in some cases, for functions that do have a more naturally constrained domain and are more expensive to compute, being able to use a map implementation of a function can be a real boon to performance.

Because all of the different techniques for retrieving values from a map return `nil` if the key is not present, special handling is required if you need to differentiate the case in which a key *does* exist in a map with a value of `nil` from the case in which the key does not exist at all.

The easiest way to do this is to always provide a default value to be returned in the case of a missing key. To be absolutely sure that you can differentiate the default value from any possible value the map might contain, you can use a namespace-qualified keyword (e.g., `::not-found`).

It is also possible to use the `contains?` function, which takes a collection and a key, and returns `true` if and only if the collection has a specific entry for that key (even if the value is `nil`).

### The Meaning of contains?

The exact behavior of the `contains?` function often causes confusion, especially since many other languages have a function with a similar name that does something different.

In Clojure, `contains?` is *not* a search function—it does not inspect a collection to see if the item is present. Rather, it is a *lookup* function, and only works on associative or indexed collections. In other languages, it is often named `containsKey` or similar.

This means it works as one would expect on maps and sets, returning `true` if the specified key is a valid key or member in the collection. But for vectors, it will return `true` only if passed an integer between zero and the maximum index of the vector. And it will throw an exception if used at all with a list or a sequence.

## See Also


- Recipe 2.17, "Retrieving Multiple Keys from a Map Simultaneously" on page 91
- Recipe 2.18, "Setting Keys in a Map" on page 92
- Recipe 2.20, "Treating Maps as Sequences (and Vice Versa)" on page 98


# 2.17. Retrieving Multiple Keys from a Map Simultaneously

by Leonardo Borges

## Problem

You want to retrieve multiple values from a map at one time.

## Solution

Use `vals` and `select-keys` when the order of returned values is not important:

```
;; How many red and green beans are there?
(def beans {:red 10
            :blue 3
            :green 1})

(reduce + (vals (select-keys beans [:red :green])))
;; -> 11
```

Use `juxt` when order matters:

```
;; What are the red and green bean totals?
((juxt :red :green) beans)
;; -> [10 1]
```

## Discussion

`juxt` and the combination of `vals` and `select-keys` are both apt tools for retrieving multiple keys from a map. There are subtleties to their behavior that are important to understand, though.

At first glance, the `juxt` approach seems to be the clear winner of the two. However, it only goes so far: the approach falls apart when any of the keys you wish to retrieve is not a keyword (more specifically, not a *function*). This is because `juxt` merely *juxtaposes* the return values of multiple functions. Since keywords are functions, it's possible to `juxt` them and retrieve a strongly ordered list of values.

If the keys in the `beans` map were strings, it would not be possible to retrieve their values with `juxt`:

```
((juxt "a" "b") beans)
;; -> ClassCastException java.lang.String cannot be cast to clojure.lang.IFn ...
```

`select-keys`, on the other hand, *is* capable of pulling values for any number of arbitrary keys. The `select-keys` function takes a map and a sequence of keys and returns a new map populated with *only* those keys:

```
(def weird-map {"a" 1, {:foo :bar} :baz, 13 31})

(select-keys weird-map
             ["a" {:foo :bar}])
;; -> {{:foo :bar} :baz, "a" 1}

(vals {{:foo :bar} :baz, "a" 1})
;; -> (1 :baz)
```

Since maps are not ordered, it is *not* safe to assume that the ordering of keys and values is identical (even if you stumble upon an example where it is). In cases where you're pulling multiple values from nonkeyword maps, it is probably easiest to wrap that interaction up via `juxt`:

```
(def a-str-then-foo-bar-map
  (juxt #(get % "a")
        #(get % {:foo :bar})))

(a-str-then-foo-bar-map weird-map)
;; -> [1 :baz]
```

You'll avoid weird maps now, won't you?

## See Also

- Recipe 2.16, "Retrieving Values from a Map" on page 88
- Recipe 2.19, "Using Composite Values as Map Keys" on page 96

# 2.18. Setting Keys in a Map

by Luke VanderHart

## Problem

You want to "change" a map by adding, setting, or removing keys.

## Solution

The most basic way to change a map is using the `assoc` function. Given a map and any number of additional key/value pairs as arguments, it will return an updated map containing the respective keys and values:

```
(def villain {:honorific "Dr." :name "Mayhem"})
(assoc villain :occupation "Mad Scientist" :status :at-large)
;; -> {:honorific "Dr.", :name "Mayhem",
;;     :occupation "Mad Scientist", :status :at-large}
```

If used on a map that already contains a key, the `assoc` function will return an updated map with the newly specified value for the key:

```
(def villain {:honorific "Dr.", :name "Mayhem",
              :occupation "Mad Scientist", :status :at-large})
(assoc villain :status :deceased)
;; -> {:honorific "Dr.", :name "Mayhem",
;;     :occupation "Mad Scientist", :status :deceased}
```

To remove keys, use the `dissoc` function. Given a map and any number of keys, it returns a map minus those keys:

```
(def villain {:honorific "Dr.", :name "Mayhem",
              :occupation "Mad Scientist", :status :deceased})
(dissoc villain :occupation :honorific)
;; -> {:name "Mayhem", :status :deceased}
```

## Discussion

It's fairly common to have maps contained in other maps. If it is necessary to update a deeply nested value, nested calls to `assoc` quickly become inconvenient, especially since they need to be "inside-out." Consider the following data structure:

```
(def book {:title "Clojure Cookbook"
           :author {:name "Ryan Neufeld"
                    :residence {:country "USA"}}})
```

If Ryan were to move back to his native land of Canada, fully updating the map representing this book using only `assoc` would look something like the following:

```
(assoc book :author
  (assoc (:author book) :residence
    (assoc (:residence (:author book)) :country "Canada")))
```

Obviously, this is inconvenient and difficult to read.

The `assoc-in` function removes this inconvenience, allowing you to specify a *key path* instead of a sole key. Instead of changing a value one key deep, a *key path* lists a sequence of keys, applied recursively to change a deeply nested value:

```
(assoc-in book
          [:author :residence :country]
          "Canada")
;; -> {:author {:name "Ryan Neufeld"
;;              :residence {:country "Canada"}}
;;              :title "Clojure Cookbook"}
```

The preceding sample first looks up the map associated with the `:residence` key in the nested data structure, then associates `"Canada"` with the `:country` key. Finally, the entire data structure is returned.

What if you needed to *update* a value based on its previous value, instead of just changing it?

Fortunately, Clojure provides `update-in` expressly for this purpose. Instead of taking a new value, `update-in` takes an *update function*. This function is invoked with the value retrieved at *key path* and any trailing arguments passed to `update-in`. It's a peculiar function to wrap your head around at first. Perhaps it is best to illustrate with an example:

```
(def website {:clojure-cookbook {:hits 1236}})

;; Register 101 new hits to the Cookbook website
(update-in website                    ; ❶
           [:clojure-cookbook :hits] ; ❷
           +                          ; ❸
           101)                       ; ❹
;; -> {:clojure-cookbook {:hits 1337}}
```

❶ The map

❷ The key path

❸ The update function, +

❹ Additional arguments to +

`update-in` will also actually create maps for any of the keys in the vector that don't exist. This means it can be used to create structure as well as to update values:

```
(update-in {} [:author :residence] assoc :country "USA")
;; -> {:author {:residence {:country "USA"}}}
```

Even though the starting map is empty, two empty maps are created for the values of the `:author` and `:residence` keys, meaning the `assoc` will be applied to a new, empty map.

### Treating Clojure's State Constructs Like Maps

One other common use case for maps is as the values of one of Clojure's state constructs: *atoms*, *refs*, or *agents*. Clojure maps themselves are immutable values. In a very literal sense, if you "add" a key to a map, it is no longer the same value any more. But sometimes, it is necessary to preserve a logical *identity* for different values across time. That's when to use one of the state management tools.

To update the value of a piece of state (ref, atom, or agent), you invoke its specific state transition function (`alter`, `swap!`, or `send`, respectively). State transition functions share a common form: they take the reference as the first argument, the function to apply to the value as the second argument, and any arguments to the function as additional arguments.

So, for example, to deeply update an item contained in a map referenced by an atom, you can invoke the `swap!` function (the state transition function for atoms), passing it your atom and the `update-in` function, along with the list of keys and the function to use to update the value:

```
(def retail-data (atom {:customers [{:id 123 :name "Luke"}
                                    {:id 321 :name "Ryan"}]
                        :orders [{:sku "Q2M9" :customer 123 :qty 4}
                                 {:sku "43XP" :customer 321 :qty 1}]}))

(swap! retail-data update-in [:orders] conj
       {:sku "9QED" :customer 321 :qty 2})
```

This will add a new order map to the list of orders contained in the map contained in the `retail-data` atom.

Although such triple combos are not terribly common, they illustrate the general consistency of functions that take other functions and arguments, and how they can be combined arbitrarily deeply. In this case, what starts with a single call to `swap!` ends up also updating a map and conjoining to a vector in the same form.

## See Also


- Recipe 2.20, "Treating Maps as Sequences (and Vice Versa)" on page 98
- Recipe 2.22, "Keeping Multiple Values for a Key" on page 102
- Recipe 2.23, "Combining Maps" on page 105

# 2.19. Using Composite Values as Map Keys

by Luke VanderHart

## Problem

You'd like to use a value that isn't a simple primitive type as a lookup key in a map. For example:

- You'd like to use geographic or Cartesian coordinates as map keys.
- You'd like to associate values with functions.

## Solution

Because of its robust identity semantics on composite values, Clojure fully supports using any immutable value as a map key. More importantly, doing so is reasonably efficient.

For example, consider the data structure to represent a chessboard, an 8 × 8 grid where each position can have one of six possible types of piece. Rows are represented by the numbers 1–8, and columns by the letters *a*–*h*.

In Clojure, you can represent this directly as a map:

```
(def chessboard {[:a 5] [:white :king]
                 [:a 4] [:white :pawn]
                 [:d 4] [:black :king]})
```

Moving a piece then requires two operations, `dissoc`-ing the old position for a piece and `assoc`-ing the new position:

```
(defn move
  "Given a map representing a chessboard, move the piece at src
  to dest"
  [board source dest]
  (-> board
      (dissoc source)
      (assoc dest (board source))))

(move chessboard [:a 5] [:a 4])
;; -> {[:d 4] [:black :king]
;;     [:a 4] [:white :king]}
```

As another example of nontraditional map keys, consider the situation where you have a set of functions, and you want to be able to assign them each a "weighting" and multiply the return value by the corresponding weight whenever the function is called.

An easy way to do this is to store the functions and weights in a map, with the functions as keys:

```
(def plus-two (partial + 2))
(def plus-three (partial + 3))
(def weight-map {plus-two 1.0
                 plus-three 0.8})
```

Then you can use a simple wrapper function to apply the functions with the weights applied:

```
(defn apply-weighted
  "Given a weight map, a function, and args, applies the function
  to the args, multiplying the result by the weighting for the
  function. If the weight map does not specify a weight for the
  function, a default of 1.0 is used."
  [weight-map f & args]
  (* (get weight-map f 1.0)
     (apply f args)))

(apply-weighted weight-map plus-two 2)
;; -> 4.0

(apply-weighted weight-map plus-three 1)
;; -> 3.2
```

## Discussion

A more traditional way to model the chess game would be with a two-dimensional array, or, in Clojure's case, with a vector of vectors.

This is certainly a reasonable thing to do, and is (possibly) slightly more performant. However, it is a less clean model of the actual problem domain. It requires a translation, for example, from chess's row/column numbers and letters to zero-indexed indexes. Using a map lets you store the positions directly, in native chess terminology.

Similarly, there are alternative implementations for the function-weighting example. It could be implemented using a cond statement with all the functions and weights enumerated, or by replacing the functions altogether with a protocol method that could then have varying implementations with different weights.

However, storing the functions and weights in a map has the benefit of making it obvious at a glance what the weightings for particular functions are. More importantly, it is possible to store multiple different sets of weights, and switch between different weight schemes dynamically at runtime.

## See Also

- Recipe 2.16, "Retrieving Values from a Map" on page 88, and Recipe 2.18, "Setting Keys in a Map" on page 92

# 2.20. Treating Maps as Sequences (and Vice Versa)

by Luke VanderHart

## Problem

You want to treat the contents of a map as a sequence of entries. Alternatively, you want to convert a sequence of entries back into a map.

## Solution

To obtain a sequence view of a map, simply call `seq` on it. Note that most sequence-processing functions call `seq` on their arguments themselves, so it's usually not necessary to do this explicitly:

```
(seq {:a 1, :b 2, :c 3, :d 4})
;; -> ([:a 1] [:c 3] [:b 2] [:d 4])
```

This creates a sequence of key/value pairs, which you can then process as you would any sequence.

To create a map *from* a sequence, you can exploit the fact that `conj`, when applied to a map, can take a two-element vector as a key/value pair and use it to add the respective key and value on to the map:

```
(def m {:a 1, :b 2})
(conj m [:c 3])
;; -> {:a 1, :b 2, :c 3}
```

Because the `into` function uses repeated applications of `conj` to add items from one sequence onto a collection, this means it can be used to transform a sequence of pairs into a single map:

```
(into {} [[:a 1] [:b 2] [:c 3]])
;; -> {:a 1, :b 2, :c 3}
```

It is also possible to construct a map from *two* sequences: one containing keys and one containing values. This is the purpose of the `zipmap` function. Given two sequences, it will return a single map with keys from the first argument sequence and values from the second:

```
(zipmap [:a :b :c] [1 2 3])
;; -> {:c 3, :b 2, :a 1}
```

If one of the sequences passed to `zipmap` is shorter than the other, the extra values will be ignored, and the output map will only contain entries up to the length of the shortest sequence.

## Discussion

When obtaining a sequence view of a *hash map*, the map entries will be returned in an arbitrary or undefined order. Conveniently, this order (although arbitrary) *is* guaranteed to be consistent if the same map is turned into a sequence multiple times.

When using a *sorted map*, the entries will be returned according to their sort order in the map. For example:

```
(seq (hash-map :a 1, :b 2, :c 3, :d 4))
;; -> ([:a 1] [:c 3] [:b 2] [:d 4])

(seq (sorted-map :a 1, :b 2, :c 3, :d 4))
;; -> ([:a 1] [:b 2] [:c 3] [:d 4])
```

There is another interesting fact about the entry values in this sequence. They are printed as vectors, and they *are* vectors insofar as they implement the full vector interface. However, their concrete type is not actually `clojure.lang.PersistentVector`; rather, they are a different kind of vector called a *map entry*, which not only is a vector but also supports the `clojure.lang.MapEntry` interface.

The `MapEntry` interface provides `key` and `val` functions that can be used to retrieve the key and value of an entry:

```
(def entry (first {:a 1 :b 2}))

(class entry)
;; -> clojure.lang.MapEntry

(key entry)
;; -> :a

(val entry)
;; -> :1
```

These functions should be preferred to using the `first` and `second` functions on map entries when processing maps as sequences, since they preserve the semantic of key/value pairs, making the code easier to read.

## See Also

- Recipe 2.21, "Applying Functions to Maps" on page 100

# 2.21. Applying Functions to Maps

by Luke VanderHart

## Problem

You'd like to apply a transformation function to the keys or the values of a map.

## Solution

Use one of these simple general-purpose functions, modified to suit any needs you have:

```
(defn map-keys
  "Given a map and a function, returns the map resulting from applying
  the function to each key."
  [m f]
  (zipmap (map f (keys m)) (vals m)))

(map-keys {"a" 1 "b" 2} keyword)
;; -> {:b 2, :a 1}

(defn map-vals
  "Given a map and a function, returns the map resulting from applying
  the function to each value."
  [m f]
  (zipmap (keys m) (map f (vals m))))

(map-vals {:a 1, :b 1} inc)
;; -> {:b 2, :a 2}

(defn map-kv
  "Given a map and a function of two arguments, returns the map
  resulting from applying the function to each of its entries. The
  provided function must return a pair (a two-element sequence.)"
  [m f]
  (into {} (map (fn [[k v]] (f k v)) m)))

(map-kv {"a" 1 "b" 1} (fn [k v] [(keyword k) (inc v)]))
;; -> {:a 2, :b 2}
```

## Discussion

`map-keys` and `map-vals` are extremely straightforward. They each start by breaking the map, `m`, down into a sequence of keys and a sequence of values using the `keys` and `vals` functions, which return a sequence of the keys or values of a map, respectively. Then, they use the `map` function to transform either the sequence of keys or the sequence of vals. Finally, the `zipmap` function is used to recombine the key and value sequences into a single map, with the updates in place.

map-kv works a bit differently. It starts by converting the map into a sequence of map entries, then uses map to apply them to an anonymous function that destructures the key and value, and then passes the key and value to the caller-provided function. Finally, it uses into to repeatedly conjoin the resulting pairs onto an empty map, returning a new map consisting of the transformed keys and values.

The following example is identical, but does not use destructuring, so the high-level structure is a bit more clear:

```
(defn map-kv
  [m f]
  (into {} (map (fn [entry]
                  (f (key entry) (val entry)))
                m)))
```

It is easy to see that these three functions are all riffs on the standard map function, applied to map data structures. What about the other staple of functional programming, reduce?

Clojure already has a reduce-kv function built in, which was added in version 1.4.

reduce-kv takes three arguments: a function, an initial value, and an associative collection. The provided function must also take three arguments. reduce-kv reduces the provided collection by first applying the function to the initial value, the first key, and its corresponding value from the map. The resulting value is then reapplied along with the second key and value, the resulting value with the third key and value, and so on.

The following example uses reduce-kv to obtain the sum of all the values in a map:

```
(reduce-kv (fn [agg _ val]
             (+ agg val))
           0
           {:a 1 :b 2 :c 3})
;; -> 6
```

Note that an underscore (_) is used instead of key in the function argument declaration. This is idiomatic in Clojure to name any argument that isn't actually used in the body.

It's also possible to define map-kv using reduce-kv:

```
(defn map-kv
    [m f]
    (reduce-kv (fn [agg k v] (conj agg (f k v))) {} m))
```

which could be used in this example:

```
(map-kv {:one 1 :two 2 :three 3}
        #(vector (-> %1 str (subs 1)) (inc %2)))
;; -> {"one" 2, "three" 4, "two" 3}
```

## See Also

- Recipe 2.20, "Treating Maps as Sequences (and Vice Versa)" on page 98

# 2.22. Keeping Multiple Values for a Key

by Luke VanderHart

## Problem

Normally, maps are strictly one value per key: if you `assoc` an existing key, the old value is replaced. However, sometimes it would be useful to have a map-like interface (a "multimap") capable of storing *multiple values* for the same key.

You would like to create a map-like data structure that implements a multimap-like interface in Clojure.

## Solution

To introduce such a capability on top of normal maps, create and extend a protocol `MultiAssociative` that defines this behavior:

```
(defprotocol MultiAssociative
  "An associative structure that can contain multiple values for a key"
  (insert [m key value] "Insert a value into a MultiAssociative")
  (delete [m key value] "Remove a value from a MultiAssociative")
  (get-all [m key] "Returns a set of all values stored at key in a
                    MultiAssociative. Returns the empty set if there
                    are no values."))

(defn- value-set?
  "Helper predicate that returns true if the value is a set that
  represents multiple values in a MultiAssociative"
  [v]
  (and (set? v) (::multi-value (meta v))))

(defn value-set
  "Given any number of items as arguments, returns a set representing
  multiple values in a MultiAssociative. If there is only one item,
  simply returns the item."
  [& items]
  (if (= 1 (count items))
    (first items)
    (with-meta (set items) {::multi-value true})))

(extend-protocol MultiAssociative
  clojure.lang.Associative
  (insert [this key value]
```

```
    (let [v (get this key)]
      (assoc this key (cond
                        (nil? v) value
                        (value-set? v) (conj v value)
                        :else (value-set v value)))))
  (delete [this key value]
    (let [v (get this key)]
      (if (value-set? v)
        (assoc this key (apply value-set (disj v value)))
        (if (= v value)
          (dissoc this key)
          this))))
  (get-all [this key]
    (let [v (get this key)]
      (cond
       (value-set? v) v
       (nil? v) #{}
       :else #{v}))))
```

and, of course, corresponding unit tests (using `clojure.test`):

```
(require '[clojure.test :refer :all])

(deftest test-insert
  (testing "inserting to a new key"
    (is (= {:k :v} (insert {} :k :v))))
  (testing "inserting to an existing key (single existing item)"
    (let [m (insert {} :k :v1)]
      (is (= {:k #{:v1 :v2}}
             (insert m :k :v2)))))
  (testing "inserting to an existing key (multiple existing items)"
    (let [m (insert (insert {} :k :v1) :k :v2)]
      (is (= {:k #{:v1 :v2 :v3}}
             (insert m :k :v3))))))

(deftest test-delete
  (testing "deleting a non-present key"
    (is (= {:k :v} (delete {:k :v} :nosuch :nada))))
  (testing "deleting a non-present value"
    (is (= {:k :v} (delete {:k :v} :k :nada))))
  (testing "deleting a single value"
    (is (= {} (delete {:k :v} :k :v))))
  (testing "deleting one of two values"
    (let [m (insert (insert {} :k :v1) :k :v2)]
      (is (= {:k :v1} (delete m :k :v2)))))
  (testing "deleting one of several values"
    (let [m (insert (insert (insert {} :k :v1) :k :v2) :k :v3)]
      (is (= {:k #{:v1 :v2}} (delete m :k :v3))))))

(deftest test-get-all
  (testing "get a non-present key"
    (is (= #{} (get-all {} :nosuch))))
  (testing "get a single value"
```

```
    (is (= #{:v} (get-all {:k :v} :k))))
  (testing "get multiple values"
    (is (= #{:v1 :v2} (get-all (insert (insert {} :k :v1) :k :v2) :k)))))

(run-tests)
;; -> {:type :summary, :pass 11, :test 3, :error 0, :fail 0}
```

## Discussion

First, this code defines a protocol to implement the set of functions that comprises the multimap behavior. A protocol is a great choice in this situation: it ties together several methods that perform related operations on the same object, and it allows for multiple concrete implementations.

In this case, there are three methods required to implement the desired functionality. Note that the protocol implementation does *not* override or reimplement any of the core map methods (`assoc`, `dissoc`, etc.). It is only the semantics of the new behavior that differ from those of regular maps. Clojure defines very strong semantics around core functions. Breaking or overriding these expectations is always a bad idea, especially when using a distinct set of functions makes it clear when multimap functionality is being used.

The concrete implementation of `MultiAssociative` extends the protocol to the `clojure.lang.Associative` interface. It would certainly be possible to implement it on something more targeted, such as `IPersistentSet`, but since it only *requires* something associative for the implementation, it's best not to be too specific. Coding against `clojure.lang.Associative` also gives several additional capabilities for free. For example, there is now automatically a "multivector" that can store multiple values at each index (provided they are added using `insert`).

Reading the code, you'll notice that a good deal of the actual logic is devoted to making sure that single values are stored plainly, while multiple values are wrapped in a set. This is maintained both when inserting and when deleting items, requiring the functions to run a check on what type the value is and wrap or unwrap accordingly. Similarly, `get-all` needs to wrap single values in a set before returning, since it specifies that it must return a set.

This is a design decision that has several benefits and trade-offs. The alternative would be to always wrap the values in a set, even single values. This would make the code a bit simpler and would eliminate most of the type checking as well as the wrapping and unwrapping of forms.

However, the simplicity would come with a price. If values (even single values) were *always* wrapped in a set, the map being used as a multimap would not be easily usable via the normal map functions. It would contain a lot of odd-looking single-item sets, and if anything were added to it using `assoc`, it would be incompatible with future uses of `insert` on that key.

In essence, the wrapping and unwrapping is to allow any map to be usable via both the standard `Associative` *and* the `MultiAssociative` interfaces, without requiring the user to keep track of which "kind" of a map it is. Values inserted using `assoc` can be read with `get-all`, and values inserted using `insert` can be removed with `dissoc`. All expectations regarding normal maps should hold. In the case of a normal `get` on a key with multiple values, a set containing multiple items will be returned. This is probably what the user would expect upon inspecting the data.

There is one more feature of this code that deserves commentary: the use of `::multi-value` metadata on the sets used to store multiple values, applied and tested using the `value-set` and `value-set?` functions.

This is to handle the edge case where the intended *value* for a key is itself a set. The code needs a way to disambiguate between sets it creates in order to manage multiple keys for a value and sets that are simply values provided by users.

This is accomplished by placing metadata on sets created to contain values. A namespace-scoped keyword is used to ensure that it will not collide with any possible existing metadata on values provided by the user. Then, all the code has to do is check if a set has the `::multi-value` metadata to know whether it's a set containing values, or is itself a value.

### See Also

- Recipe 3.10, "Extending a Built-In Type" on page 147

## 2.23. Combining Maps

by Tom Hicks

### Problem

You have two or more maps you wish to combine to produce a single map.

### Solution

Use `merge` to combine two or more maps with no keys in common:

```
(def arizona-bird-counts {:cactus-wren 8})
(def florida-bird-counts {:gull 20 :pelican 14})
```

```
(merge florida-bird-counts arizona-bird-counts)
;; -> {:pelican 14, :cactus-wren 8, :gull 20}
```

Use `merge-with` when you want more explicit control of the merge strategy for keys that exist in more than one map:

```
(def florida-bird-counts    {:gull 20 :pelican 1 :egret 4})
(def california-bird-counts {:gull 12 :pelican 4 :jay 3})

;; Merge values with + to get their totals
(merge-with + california-bird-counts florida-bird-counts)
;; -> {:pelican 5, :egret 4, :gull 32, :jay 3}
```

## Discussion

In both `merge` and `merge-with`, maps are combined from left to right, returning a new immutable map as a result. This functions much like a "left fold." `merge` is the simpler function of the pair, always returning the last value it sees for every key.

When mappings for the same key exist in more than one map, the latter mapping is used in the result. This can be useful, for example, when you receive new totals throughout the day, but only for values that have changed:

```
;; Favorite ice cream flavor votes throughout the day
(def votes-am {:vanilla 3 :chocolate 5})
(def votes-pm {:vanilla 4 :neapoliton 2})
(merge votes-am votes-pm)
;; -> {:vanilla 4, :chocolate 5, :neapoliton 2}
```

`merge-with` facilitates powerful recipes for map combination by allowing you to control *how* values are merged. You can imagine `merge-with` as `reduce` for maps with common keys. The first argument to `merge-with` is a merge function that will be invoked for each pair of duplicated values.

With careful choice of map value types, `merge-with` provides some concise solutions to common problems. For example, by merging with `clojure.set/intersection`, you can find the intersection of "like" and "dislike" sets in a team of programmers:

```
(def Alice {:loves #{:clojure :lisp :scheme} :hates #{:fortran :c :c++}})
(def Bob   {:loves #{:clojure :scheme}       :hates #{:c :c++ :algol}})
(def Ted   {:loves #{:clojure :lisp :scheme} :hates #{:algol :basic :c
                                                       :c++ :fortran}})

(merge-with clojure.set/intersection Alice Bob Ted)
;; -> {:loves #{:scheme :clojure}, :hates #{:c :c++}}
```

It is also possible to merge nested maps by creating a recursive merge function:

```
(defn deep-merge
  [& maps]
  (apply merge-with deep-merge maps))
```

```
(deep-merge {:foo {:bar {:baz 1}}}
            {:foo {:bar {:qux 42}}})
;; -> {:foo {:bar {:qux 42, :baz 1}}}
```

As you saw in the previous examples, `merge-with` is a versatile tool: we used + to add values of the same key, `clojure.set/intersection` to find shared values of multiple sets, and a recursive function `deep-merge` to recursively merge nested maps. `merge-with` is a very powerful function, indeed.

## See Also


- Recipe 2.18, "Setting Keys in a Map" on page 92
- Recipe 2.22, "Keeping Multiple Values for a Key" on page 102


# 2.24. Comparing and Sorting Values

by Luke VanderHart

## Problem

You want to compare two values according to some comparison function, or you want to sort a collection by comparing all the items in it.

## Solution

Use the `clojure.core/compare` function to compare two items. They must be comparable with respect to each other. For example, a `double` can be compared to a ratio because they're both numbers, but a string can't be compared to a vector.

`compare` returns a negative number if the first argument is less than the second, zero if it is logically equal, and a positive number if it is greater:

```
(compare 5 2)
;; -> 1

(compare 0.5 1)
;; -> -1

(compare (/ 1 4) 0.25)
;; -> 0

(compare "brewer" "aardvark")
;; -> 1
```

To sort an entire collection, pass it to the `clojure.core/sort` function. `sort` applies `compare` as needed and returns a sorted sequence.

For example, the following code breaks down a string into a sequence of characters (`sort` calls `seq` on its argument), then sorts them. The result is concatenated back to a string, for better readability:

```
(apply str (sort "The quick brown fox jumped over the lazy dog"))
;; -> "        Tabcddeeeefghhijklmnoooopqrrtuuvwxyz"
```

As seen previously, many of Clojure's data types have a *natural* comparison order, which is what `compare` uses. For example, numbers, dates, and strings all sort as one would expect, from low to high, based on the well-understood and accepted inherent ordering between them.

If you want to sort a data type that does not have a natural ordering, or if you want to override the natural sort (such as sorting a set from high to low), you are not limited to using the built-in comparator function. `sort` allows you to specify a custom comparison function that can perform any operation you like to determine the relative ordering between two items. This function must take two arguments. It can return values like `compare` does (that is, a positive integer, a negative integer, or zero). Alternatively, it can return a Boolean value (i.e., a *predicate* function). The predicate function should return `true` if and only if the first argument should be sorted before the second argument.

This means that you can pass regular Clojure predicates to `sort`:

```
(sort > [1 4 3 2])
;; -> (4 3 2 1)

(sort > [1 4 3 2])
;; -> (1 2 3 4)
```

Or, you can write your own arbitrary comparator. For example, the custom comparator used in the next example cares only about the length of a string, not the contents of it; strings will be sorted as equal if they have the same number of characters, whatever those characters are:

```
(sort #(< (count %1) (count %2)) ["z" "yy" "zzz" "a" "bb" "ccc"])
;; -> ("z" "a" "yy" "bb" "zzz" "ccc")
```

## Discussion

Under the hood, Clojure uses Java's built-in sort mechanism. Java uses a slightly modified merge sort algorithm that is highly performant for the vast majority of cases. It requires $n \log(n)$ comparisons in the worst case and performs at near $O(n)$ when the input is largely sorted already.

The sort is also *stable*, meaning that if two items are equal in terms of the comparator function being used, their relative ordering will remain unchanged after sorting.

Although you can use any predicate as a comparison function or write your own comparison function that returns a positive/negative/zero integer, the actual function must behave properly in order to work. Specifically, it must:

*Have a consistent total order for all the members being sorted*
: If `x` is sorted before `y`, and `y` is sorted before `z`, then `x` must *always* be sorted before `z`. In other words, there must always be a single fully deterministic sort order for a given collection and comparator, without any contradictions or inconsistencies caused by the comparison function.

*Be consistent with the .equals method and Clojure's = function*
: If two items are logically equal, then that must be reflected in the comparison function. When using the integer return values, the function ought to return `0`. When using a predicate function, `(pred x y)` and `(pred y x)` should return the same thing in the case where `x` and `y` are equal.

*Have no side effects*
: The comparison function may be called an arbitrary number of times as the sort is evaluated.

### Comparators and the JVM

Clojure fully participates in Java's comparison and sorting mechanisms. All Clojure objects that have a natural order implement `java.lang.Comparable` (*http://bit.ly/javadoc-comparable*) and implement the `compareTo` method.

More importantly, every Clojure function actually implements the `java.util.Comparator` (*http://bit.ly/javadoc-comparator*) interface. This means that you can pass a Clojure function to any Java method that requires an instance of `java.util.Comparator`, and it will invoke the function with two arguments. This is what allows you to pass arbitrary Clojure functions as the comparator to `sort`. The function object itself is actually being used as a Java comparator, and invoking the Java `.compare` method on a Clojure function will actually call it, passing it the two values being compared as two arguments.

Because predicate functions (those returning a Boolean value) do not map exactly to the positive/negative/zero integer return values expected from a `java.util.Comparator`, Clojure itself handles the logical mapping between them. If a function used as a comparator (that is, `(pred x y)`) returns `true`, the implementation will return `-1`, indicating that `x` is less than `y` in the given sort. If not, it will invoke the function again with the arguments reversed. If `(pred x y)` and `(pred y x)` are both `false`, it is assumed that the objects are equal, and the implementation returns `0`. Otherwise, it presumes `x` is greater than `y` and returns `1`.

### sort-by

Sometimes, you want to sort a collection not by the values themselves, but by some derivative function of the values. For example, say you have the following data, and you'd like to sort alphabetically by name. Unfortunately, maps don't have a natural sort, so you'll need to tell Clojure how to sort the data:

```
(def people [{:name "Luke"   :role :author}
             {:name "Ryan"   :role :author}
             {:name "John"   :role :reviewer}
             {:name "Travis" :role :reviewer}
             {:name "Tom"    :role :reviewer}
             {:name "Meghan" :role :editor}])
```

One option would be to use a custom comparator, which extracts the `:name` key and then invokes `compare` on it:

```
(sort #(compare (:name %1) (:name %2)) people)
;; -> ({:name "John", :role :reviewer}
;;     {:name "Luke", :role :author}
;;     {:name "Meghan", :role :editor}
;;     {:name "Ryan", :role :author}
;;     {:name "Tom", :role :reviewer}
;;     {:name "Travis", :role :reviewer})
```

However, there's an easier way. The `sort-by` function works the same as `sort`, but takes an additional function `keyfn` as an argument to apply to the elements before sorting them. Instead of sorting on the elements themselves, it sorts the result of applying `keyfn` to the elements.

So, passing in `:name` as the `keyfn` (as discussed in Recipe 2.16, "Retrieving Values from a Map" on page 88, keywords are functions that look themselves up in a map), you can call:

```
(sort-by :name people)
;;-> ({:name "John", :role :reviewer}
;;     {:name "Luke", :role :author}
;;     {:name "Meghan", :role :editor}
;;     {:name "Ryan", :role :author}
;;     {:name "Tom", :role :reviewer}
;;     {:name "Travis", :role :reviewer})
```

Like `sort`, `sort-by` also takes an optional comparator function that it will use to compare the values extracted by the `keyfn`.

For another example, the following expression uses the `str` function as a `keyfn` to sort the numbers from 1 to 20 not on their numeric value, but lexographically as strings (meaning that "2" is greater than "10," etc.). It also demonstrates using a custom comparator to specify the results in *descending* order:

```
;; Descending lexographic order
(sort-by str #(* -1 (compare %1 %2)) (range 1 20))
;; -> (9 8 7 6 5 4 3 2 19 18 17 16 15 14 13 12 11 10 1)
```

#### Natural sort of data structures

Some compositive data structures can also be compared if they implement `Comparable`, are of the same type, and contain comparable values. The comparison order is implementation dependent. For example, by default, vectors are compared first by their length, then by the result of applying `compare` to their first value, then to their second value if the first is equal, etc.:

```
(sort [[2 1] [1] [1 2] [1 1 1] [2]])
;; -> ([1] [2] [1 2] [2 1] [1 1 1])
```

Some data structures are not comparable. For example, the fact that a set is defined to be unordered means that a meaningful greater-than/less-than comparison is not possible in the general case, so no comparison is provided.

## See Also

- The API documentation for `java.lang.Comparable` (*http://bit.ly/javadoc-comparable*)
- The API documentation for `java.util.Comparator` (*http://bit.ly/javadoc-comparator*)
- Recipe 1.17, "Performing Fuzzy Comparison" on page 28
- Recipe 1.29, "Comparing Dates" on page 49

# 2.25. Removing Duplicate Elements from a Collection

by John Cromartie

## Problem

You have a sequence of elements and you want to remove any duplicates, while possibly preserving the order of elements.

## Solution

When the sequence of elements you're working with is of a bounded, reasonable size, use `set` to coerce the collection into a hash set containing only distinct values:

```
(set [:a :a :g :a :b :g])
;; -> #{:a :b :g}
```

When the sequence is infinite, or you wish to maintain ordering, use `distinct` to return a lazy sequence of unique values in a collection in the order they appear:

```
(distinct [:a :a :g :a :b :g])
;; -> (:a :g :b)
```

## Discussion

There are a number of trade-offs between these two approaches. For starters, `set` consumes the entire sequence to produce a new set collection. Because of this, `set` cannot be used to filter an infinite sequence. `distinct`, on the other hand, is designed for consuming lazy sequences. The value of `distinct` is a lazy view or projection over another sequence, yielding new values the first time they appear:

```
(defn rand-int-seq
  "Returns an infinite sequence of ints from [0, n)"
  [n]
  (repeatedly #(rand-int n)))

;; Taking the set of an infinite sequence will *never* return:
;; (set (rand-int-seq 10)) ; don't do it!

;; However, if you limit the seq, set will work
(set (take 10 (rand-int-seq 10)))
;; -> #{0 1 2 3 4 7 8 9}

;; distinct works no matter what
(take 10 (distinct (rand-int-seq 10)))
;; -> (8 3 4 6 0 5 9 7 1 2)
```

Since `distinct` produces new values as it sees them, it *does* maintain ordering. `set`, on the other hand, returns an unordered set.

If `distinct` is both ordered and lazy over sequences of any length, what is the advantage of `set`? Speed. Using `distinct` is by far the slowest option; simply calling `set` is about two times faster.

## See Also

- Recipe 2.11, "Creating a Set" on page 79

# 2.26. Determining if a Collection Holds One of Several Values

by John Touron

## Problem

You have a collection and you want to determine if it holds one of several possible values.

## Solution

Use `some`, along with a set:

```
(some #{1 2} (range 10))
;; -> 1

(some #{10} (range 10))
;; -> nil
```

## Discussion

Since sets can act like functions, they can be used as predicates to test whether the argument is a member of the set. This idiom will test each item in a collection, returning either the first match or `nil` if a match couldn't be found. However, a problem arises when `nil` or `false` is a member of the set you're using to test a collection with. Consider the following:

```
(if (some #{nil} [1 2 nil 3])
  ::found
  ::not-found)
;; -> :user/not-found

(if (some #{false} [1 2 false 3])
  ::found
  ::not-found)
;; -> :user/not-found
```

Because the `some` function returns the *value* returned from the predicate function, not just `true` or `false`, using it with sets that contain `nil` or `false` probably isn't what you want—it will return `nil` or `false` if the item actually *is* in the set. The simplest solution is to test for `nil` or `false` separately, using the `nil?` or `false?` predicate functions built into Clojure:

```
(if (some nil? [nil false])
  ::found
  ::not-found)
;; -> :user/found
```

```
(if (some false? [nil false])
  ::found
  ::not-found)
;; -> :user/found
```

Or, to test both at once:

```
(if (some #(or (false? %)
               (nil? %))
      [nil false])
  ::found
  ::not-found)
;; -> :user/found
```

## See Also

- Recipe 2.13, "Testing Set Membership" on page 82
- Recipe 2.16, "Retrieving Values from a Map" on page 88

# 2.27. Implementing Custom Data Structures: Red-Black Trees—Part I

by Leonardo Borges

## Problem

You want to implement a data structure in Clojure with very specific performance characteristics.

For example, you need fast, efficient in-memory searches across a large, random, and ever-changing dataset.

## Solution

After identifying that Clojure's core data structures are not appropriate for your domain, your first step is to determine what data structure *is* appropriate.

For the purpose of this recipe, assume you are trying to choose and implement a data structure appropriate for fast in-memory search of a large, random, and ever-changing dataset. At first, a binary search tree (BST) seems like a good solution. A BST is most efficient over a sorted dataset, however. Adding and removing large amounts of data may unbalance a BST and degenerate its performance to that of a linked list.

Red-black trees (RBTs) are similar to BSTs, but are self-balancing. This would be an appropriate data structure for the dataset in question.

The next step is to implement the data structure itself. The implementation of RBTs relies on pattern matching. Use `core.match` (*https://github.com/clojure/core.match*) to simplify the implementation of an RBT. Add `[org.clojure/core.match "0.2.0"]` to your project's dependencies, or start a REPL with `lein-try`:

```
$ lein try org.clojure/core.match
```

First, implement the core of an RBT, the `balance` and `insert-val` functions. By using `core.match`, it is possible to succinctly express the required behaviors based on the shape of the tree:

```
(require '[clojure.core.match :refer [match]])

(defn balance
  "Ensures the given subtree stays balanced by rearranging black nodes
  that have at least one red child and one red grandchild"
  [tree]
  (match [tree]
         [(:or ;; Left child red with left red grandchild
               [:black [:red [:red a x b] y c] z d]
               ;; Left child red with right red grandchild
               [:black [:red a x [:red b y c]] z d]
               ;; Right child red with left red grandchild
               [:black a x [:red [:red b y c] z d]]
               ;; Right child red with right red grandchild
               [:black a x [:red b y [:red c z d]]])] [:red [:black a x b]
                                                             y
                                                             [:black c z d]]
               :else tree))

(defn insert-val
  "Inserts x in tree.
  Returns a node with x and no children if tree is nil.

  Returned tree is balanced. See also `balance`"
  [tree x]
  (let [ins (fn ins [tree]
              (match tree
                     nil [:red nil x nil]
                     [color a y b] (cond
                                    (< x y) (balance [color (ins a) y b])
                                    (> x y) (balance [color a y (ins b)])
                                    :else tree)))
        [_ a y b] (ins tree)]
    [:black a y b]))
```

With insertion and balance out of the way, the only remaining function to implement is a `find-val` function for testing if a value is present in an RBT. The easiest way to do this is by breaking down individual tree nodes with `match` and recursively scanning for the desired value:

```
(defn find-val
  "Finds value x in tree"
  [tree x]
  (match tree
         nil nil
         [_ a y b] (cond
                     (< x y) (recur a x)
                     (> x y) (recur b x)
                     :else x)))
```

With all of this in place, it is now possible to create and query an RBT:

```
(def rb-tree (reduce insert-val nil (range 4)))

rb-tree
;; -> [:black [:black nil 0 nil] 1 [:black nil 2 [:red nil 3 nil]]]

(find-val rb-tree 2)
;; -> 2

(find-val rb-tree 100)
;; -> nil
```

## Discussion

For anyone who has ever had to implement a red-black tree—or at least attended a class in computer science where the algorithm was taught—the implementation of `balance` might seem extremely short. The reason for this is threefold:

- Our red-black tree is persistent: operations on it, such as insert and balance, are not destructive.
- `balance` and `find-val` use `core.match` to codify logic as patterns to match.
- Nodes are represented as vectors.

The two latter points are related, as you'll see shortly.

Conveniently enough, `core.match` allows us to match on the shape and values of a data structure and perform structural binding at the same time. For example, the following tries to match `a-vector` against two clauses:

```
(def a-vector [1 2 3])

(match a-vector
       [_ y] (str "Got y: " y)
       [_ _ z] (str "Got z: " z))
;; -> "Got z: 3"
```

The first clause matches a two-element vector, whereas the second matches a three-element vector. Given that `a-vector` has exactly three elements, it matches the second clause. In the expression that follows, named values (such as `z`) are bound to the positions they match.

This is why it was convenient to represent nodes as vectors—it makes pattern matching against them a breeze:

```
(def rb-node [:red nil 3 [:black nil 4 nil]])

(match rb-node
       [:red left value right]   (str "Red node with value: " value)
       [:black left value right] (str "Black node with value: " value))
;; -> "Red node with value: 3"
```

Assuming this new custom data structure meets your performance criteria, what is left? (You are benchmarking all of your custom data structures, right?) Unlike built-in data structures, this custom data structure doesn't work with core functions such as `map` and `filter`.

In the second part of this recipe, Recipe 2.28, "Implementing Custom Data Structures: Red-Black Trees—Part II" on page 117, we'll rectify this situation by participating in the core sequence abstraction.

## See Also

- The second part of this recipe, Recipe 2.28, "Implementing Custom Data Structures: Red-Black Trees—Part II" on page 117, where we add sequence functionality to our RBT.
- Red-black trees on Wikipedia (*http://bit.ly/wiki-rbt*) for a more traditional take on this interesting data structure.
- For the functional approach used in this recipe, the book *Purely Functional Data Structures* (*http://bit.ly/pure-fds*) by Chris Okasaki (Cambridge University Press) is an excellent source. It deals with how to efficiently implement data structures in a functional setting. The author chose to use ML and Haskell, but the concepts are transferable to Clojure, as demonstrated previously.

# 2.28. Implementing Custom Data Structures: Red-Black Trees—Part II

by Ryan Neufeld; originally submitted by Leonardo Borges

## Problem

You want to use Clojure's core sequence functions (`conj`, `map`, `filter`, etc.) with your custom data structure.

## Solution

In part one of this recipe (Recipe 2.27, "Implementing Custom Data Structures: Red-Black Trees—Part I" on page 114), you implemented all the functions necessary for creating an efficient red-black tree. What's missing is participation in Clojure's sequence abstraction.

The most important part of participating in sequence abstraction is the ability to expose values of a data structure sequentially. The built-in `tree-seq` is well suited for this task. One extra step is needed, however; `tree-seq` returns a sequence of nodes, not values.

Here's the final `rb-tree->seq` function:

```
(defn- rb-tree->tree-seq
  "Return a seq of all nodes in an red-black tree."
  [rb-tree]
  (tree-seq sequential? (fn [[_ left _ right]]
                          (remove nil? [left right]))
            rb-tree))

(defn rb-tree->seq
  "Convert a red-black tree to a seq of its values."
  [rb-tree]
  (map (fn [[_ _ val _]] val) (rb-tree->tree-seq rb-tree)))

(rb-tree->seq (-> nil
                  (insert-val 5)
                  (insert-val 2)))
;; -> (5 2)
```

Since RBTs most closely resemble sets, they should adhere well to the `IPersistent Set` interface. Extend the `IPersistentSet` and `IFn` protocols to a new `RedBlackTree` type, implementing all of the necessary functions. It's also wise to implement the multimethod `print-method` for `RedBlackTree`, as the default implementation will fail for `RedBlackTree` as implemented:

```
(deftype RedBlackTree [tree]
  clojure.lang.IPersistentSet
  (cons [self v] (RedBlackTree. (insert-val tree v)))
  (empty [self] (RedBlackTree. nil))
  (equiv [self o] (if (instance? RedBlackTree o)
                    (= tree (.tree o))
                    false))
  (seq [this] (if tree (rb-tree->seq tree)))
  (get [this n] (find-val tree n))
  (contains [this n] (boolean (get this n)))
  ;; (disjoin [this n] ...) ;; Omitted due to complexity
  clojure.lang.IFn
  (invoke [this n] (get this n))
  Object
  (toString [this] (pr-str this)))
```

```
(defmethod print-method RedBlackTree [o ^java.io.Writer w]
  (.write w (str "#rbt " (pr-str (.tree o)))))
```

disjoin and the corresponding remove-val functions are left as exercises for the reader.

It is now possible to use a RedBlackTree instance like any other collection—in particular, instances act like sets:

```
(into (->RedBlackTree nil) (range 2))
;; -> #rbt [:black nil 0 [:red nil 1 nil]]

(def to-ten (into (->RedBlackTree nil) (range 10)))

(seq to-ten)
;; -> (3 1 0 2 5 4 7 6 8 9)

(get to-ten 9)
;; -> 9

(contains? to-ten 9)
;; -> true

(to-ten 9)
;; -> 9

(map inc to-ten)
;; -> (4 2 1 3 6 5 8 7 9 10)
```

## Discussion

In the end, it doesn't take a lot to participate in the sequence abstraction. By implementing a small handful of interface functions, the red-black tree implementation from Recipe 2.27, "Implementing Custom Data Structures: Red-Black Trees—Part I" on page 114, can participate in an array of sequence-oriented functions: `map`, `filter`, `reduce`, you name it.

At its essence, `clojure.lang.IPersistentSet` is an abstraction of what it means to represent a mathematical set structure; this matches a tree data structure well. A set isn't a list or sequence, though. So how is `RedBlackTree` then said to be participating in the sequence abstraction?

In Clojure, types extending the `clojure.lang.ISeq` interface are true *sequences*, represented as a logical list of head and tail. While `IPersistentSet` does not inherit from

ISeq, it does share a common ancestry with it. Both interfaces extend clojure.lang.IPersistentCollection and its parent clojure.lang.Seqable. As luck would have it,[1] sequence functions rely on collections being Seqable, not ISeq. Since RedBlackTree can be read as a sequence, it is Seqable and can be operated on by all of the sequence functions you know and love.

Most of the functions in the IPersistentSet interface are self-explanatory, but some deserve further explanation. The function cons is a historical name for constructing a new list by appending a value to an existing list. seq is intended to produce a sequence from a collection, or nil if empty:

*IPersistentSet.java*:

```
public interface IPersistentSet extends IPersistentCollection, Counted {
  public IPersistentSet disjoin(Object key);
  public boolean contains(Object key);
  public Object get(Object key);
}
```

*IPersistentCollection.java*:

```
public interface IPersistentCollection extends Seqable {
  int count();
  IPersistentCollection cons(Object o);
  IPersistentCollection empty();
  boolean equiv(Object o);
}
```

*Seqable.java*:

```
public interface Seqable {
  ISeq seq();
}
```

The most challenging part of any Seqable implementation is actually making a sequence out of the underlying data structure. This would be particularly challenging if you needed to write your own lazy tree-traversal algorithms, but luckily Clojure has a built-in function, tree-seq, that does precisely this. By leveraging tree-seq to produce a sequence of nodes, it is trivial to write an rb-tree->seq conversion function that lazily traverses a RedBlackTree, yielding node values as it goes.

tree-seq accepts three arguments:

branch?
: A conditional that returns true if a node is a branch (not a leaf node). For RedBlackTree, sequential? is an adequate check, as every node is a vector.

1. Actually, as design would have it.

`children`
: A function that returns all of the children for a given node.

`root`
: The node to begin traversal on.

`tree-seq` performs a depth-first traversal of trees. Given how red-black trees are represented, this will *not* be an ordered traversal.

With a sequence conversion function in hand, it is easy enough to write the `seq` function. Similarly, `cons` and `empty` are a breeze—simply utilize the existing tree functions. Equality testing can be a bit more difficult, however.

For the sake of simplicity, we chose to implement equality (`equiv`) between *only* `RedBlackTree` instances. Further, the implementation compares a sorted sequence of their elements. In this case, `equiv` is answering the question, "Do these trees have the same values?" and not the question, "Are these the same trees?" It's an important distinction, one you'll need to consider carefully when implementing your own data structures.

As discussed in Recipe 2.26, "Determining if a Collection Holds One of Several Values" on page 113, one of the big bonuses of sets is their ability to be invoked just like any other function. It's easy enough to provide this ability to `RedBlackTrees` too. By implementing the single-arity `invoke` function of the `clojure.lang.IFn` interface, `RedBlackTrees` can be invoked like any other function (or set, for that matter):

```
(some (rbt [2 3 5 7]) [6])
;; -> nil

((rbt (range 10)) 3)
;; -> 3
```

Even with the full `IPersistentSet` interface implemented, there are still a number of conveniences `RedBlackTree` is lacking. For one, you need to use the kludgy `/→RedBlackTree` or `RedBlackTree.` functions to create a new `RedBlackTree` and add values to it manually. By convention, many built-in collections provide convenience functions for populating them (aside from literal tags like `[]` or `{}`, of course).

It's easy enough to mirror `vec` and `vector` for `RedBlackTrees`:

```
(defn rbt
 "Create a new RedBlackTree with the contents of coll."
 [coll]
 (into (->RedBlackTree nil) coll))

(defn red-black-tree
```

```
  "Creates a new RedBlackTree containing the args."
  [& args]
  (rbt args))

(rbt (range 3))
;; -> #rbt [:black [:black nil 0 nil] 1 [:black nil 2 nil]]

(red-black-tree 7 42)
;; -> #rbt [:black nil 7 [:red nil 42 nil]]
```

You may also have noticed printing is not a concern of the sequence abstraction, although it is certainly an important consideration to make for developing developer- and machine-friendly data structures. There are two types of printing in Clojure: `toString` and `pr`-based printing. The `toString` function is intended for printing human-readable values at the REPL, while the `pr` family of functions are meant (more or less) to be readable by the Clojure reader.

To provide our own readable representation of RBT, we must implement `print-method` (the heart of `pr`) for the `RedBlackTree` type. By writing in a "tagged literal" format (e.g., `#rbt`), it is possible to configure the reader to ingest and hydrate written values as first-class objects:

```
(require '[clojure.edn :as edn])

;; Recall ...
(defmethod print-method RedBlackTree [o ^java.io.Writer w]
  (.write w (str "#rbt " (pr-str (.tree o)))))

(def rbt-string (pr-str (rbt [1 4 2])))
rbt-string
;; -> "#rbt [:black [:black nil 1 nil] 2 [:black nil 4 nil]]"

(edn/read-string rbt-string)
;; -> RuntimeException No reader function for tag rbt ...

(edn/read-string {:readers {'rbt ->RedBlackTree}}
                 rbt-string)
;; -> #rbt [:black [:black nil 1 nil] 2 [:black nil 4 nil]]
```

## See Also

- The first part of this recipe, Recipe 2.27, "Implementing Custom Data Structures: Red-Black Trees—Part I" on page 114, where we define the initial red-black tree implementation
- Recipe 4.14, "Reading and Writing Clojure Data" on page 190, and Recipe 4.17, "Handling Unknown Tagged Literals When Reading Clojure Data" on page 198, for more information on reading Clojure data

CHAPTER 3

# General Computing

## 3.0. Introduction

There's a saying in business that no organization operates in a vacuum. The same applies to Clojure. For all the cool tools and techniques Clojure offers, there are still a number of activities and techniques that for whatever reason aren't always on the direct path to shipping software. Some might call them academic, or incidental complexity, but for the time being, we call them life.

This chapter covers some of the topics about Clojure development that don't quite fill chapters on their own. Topics like:

- How do I use Clojure's development ecosystem?
- How do abstract concepts (such as polymorphism) apply to Clojure?
- What is logic programming, and when might I want to use it?

## 3.1. Running a Minimal Clojure REPL

by John Cromartie

### Problem

You want to play with a Clojure REPL but you don't want to install additional tools.

### Solution

Obtain the Clojure Java archive (JAR) file by downloading and unzipping a release from *http://clojure.org/downloads*. Using a terminal, navigate to where you extracted the JAR, and start a Clojure REPL:

```
$ java -cp "clojure-1.5.1.jar" clojure.main
```

You are now running an interactive Clojure REPL (read-eval-print loop). Type an expression and hit Enter to evaluate it. Press Ctrl-D to exit.

## Discussion

The fact that Clojure on the JVM is encapsulated in a simple JAR file has some great benefits. For one, it means that Clojure is never really installed. It's just a dependency, like any other Java library. You can easily swap out one version of Clojure for another by replacing a single file.

Let's dissect the `java` invocation here a bit. First, we set the Java classpath to include Clojure (and only Clojure, in this example):

```
-cp "clojure-1.5.1.jar"
```

A full explanation of the classpath is beyond the scope of this recipe, but suffice it to say thatit is a list of places where Java should look to load classes. A full discussion of classpaths on the JVM can be found at *http://bit.ly/docs-classpaths*. In the final part of the invocation, we specify the class that Java should load and execute the `main` method:

```
clojure.main
```

Yes, `clojure.main` is really a Java class. The reason this doesn't *look* like a typical Java invocation is because Clojure namespaces, which are compiled to classes, do not conventionally use capitalized names like Java classes do.

This is the absolute bare-minimum Clojure environment and is all you need to run Clojure code on any system with Java installed. Of course, for regular use and development, you will most certainly want a more feature-rich solution like Leiningen.

In some cases, however, hand-tuning a Java invocation may be the best way to integrate Clojure into your environment. This is particularly useful on servers where deploying a simple JAR file is trivial compared to installing more complex packages.

## See Also

- The Leiningen (*http://leiningen.org/*) website
- Recipe 3.6, "Running Programs from the Command Line" on page 132

# 3.2. Interactive Documentation

by John Cromartie

## Problem

From a REPL, you want to read documentation for a function.

## Solution

Print the documentation for a function at the REPL with the `doc` macro:

```
user=> (doc conj)
 -------------------------
clojure.core/conj
([coll x] [coll x & xs])
  conj[oin]. Returns a new collection with the xs
    'added'. (conj nil item) returns (item).  The 'addition' may
    happen at different 'places' depending on the concrete type.
```

Print the source code for a function at the REPL with the `source` macro:

```
user=> (source reverse)
(defn reverse
  "Returns a seq of the items in coll in reverse order. Not lazy."
  {:added "1.0"
   :static true}
  [coll]
    (reduce1 conj () coll))
```

Find functions with documentation matching a given regular expression using `find-doc`:

```
user=> (find-doc #"defmacro")
 -------------------------
clojure.core/definline
([name & decl])
Macro
  Experimental - like defmacro, except defines a named function whose
  body is the expansion, calls to which may be expanded inline as if
  it were a macro. Cannot be used with variadic (&) args.
 -------------------------
clojure.core/defmacro
([name doc-string? attr-map? [params*] body]
 [name doc-string? attr-map? ([params*] body) + attr-map?])
Macro
  Like defn, but the resulting function name is declared as a
  macro and will be used as a macro by the compiler when it is
  called.
```

## Discussion

Clojure supports inline documentation of functions (more about that later), along with other metadata, which allows you to introspect things like documentation any time you want. The doc and source macros are just convenience functions for the REPL.

You can peek under the hood at almost everything in Clojure at any time. The next example may be a bit mind-expanding if you're not used to this level of introspection at runtime:

```
user=> (source source)
(defmacro source
  "Prints the source code for the given symbol, if it can find it.
  This requires that the symbol resolve to a Var defined in a
  namespace for which the .clj is in the classpath.

  Example: (source filter)"
  [n]
  `(println (or (source-fn '~n) (str "Source not found"))))
```

Keeping in mind that source was defined in the clojure.repl namespace, we can peek at how exactly it retrieves the source by evaluating (source clojure.repl/source-fn).

In most REPL implementations, clojure.repl macros like source and doc are only referred into the user namespace. This means as soon as you switch into another namespace, the unqualified clojure.repl macros will no longer be available. You can get around this by namespacing the macros (clojure.repl/doc instead of doc,) or, for extended use, by use-ing the namespace:

```
user=> (ns foo)
foo=> (doc +)
CompilerException java.lang.RuntimeException: Unable to resolve symbol: doc
in this context, compiling:(NO_SOURCE_PATH:1:1)

foo=> (use 'clojure.repl)
nil

foo=> (doc +)
 -------------------------
clojure.core/+
([] [x] [x y] [x y & more])
  Returns the sum of nums. (+) returns 0. Does not auto-promote
  longs, will throw on overflow. See also: +'
```

Exploring Clojure in this way is a great way to learn about core functions and advanced Clojure programming techniques. The clojure.core namespace is chock-full of high-quality and high-performance code at your fingertips.

## See Also

- The `clojure.repl` API documentation (*http://bit.ly/clj-repl-doc*)
- Recipe 3.3, "Exploring Namespaces" on page 127

# 3.3. Exploring Namespaces

by John Cromartie

## Problem

You want to know what namespaces are loaded and what public vars are available inside them.

## Solution

Use `loaded-libs` to obtain the set of currently loaded namespaces. For example, from a REPL:

```
user=> (pprint (loaded-libs))
#{clojure.core.protocols clojure.instant clojure.java.browse
  clojure.java.io clojure.java.javadoc clojure.java.shell clojure.main
  clojure.pprint clojure.repl clojure.string clojure.uuid clojure.walk}
```

Use `dir` from a REPL to print the public vars in a namespace:

```
user=> (dir clojure.instant)
parse-timestamp
read-instant-calendar
read-instant-date
read-instant-timestamp
validated
```

Use `ns-publics` to obtain a mapping of symbols to public vars in a namespace:

```
(ns-publics 'clojure.instant)
;; -> {read-instant-calendar #'clojure.instant/read-instant-calendar,
;;      read-instant-timestamp #'clojure.instant/read-instant-timestamp,
;;      validated #'clojure.instant/validated,
;;      read-instant-date #'clojure.instant/read-instant-date,
;;      parse-timestamp #'clojure.instant/parse-timestamp}
```

## Discussion

Namespaces in Clojure are dynamic mappings of symbols to vars. A namespace is not available until it is required by something else; for example, when starting a REPL or as a dependency in an `ns` declaration. Nothing is known about available Clojure libraries and namespaces until runtime, which is in contrast to typical Java development (where most everything about a package is known at compile time).

The downside of this dynamic nature is that you need to at least know which namespaces to load in order to explore them.

## See Also

- The `clojure.repl` API documentation (*http://bit.ly/clj-repl-doc*)
- Recipe 3.2, "Interactive Documentation" on page 125

# 3.4. Trying a Library Without Explicit Dependencies

by Mark Whelan

## Problem

You want to try a library in the REPL without having to modify your project's dependencies or create a new project.

## Solution

Use Ryan Neufeld's `lein-try` to launch the REPL. Library dependencies will be met automatically.

To gain this capability, first make sure you are using Leiningen 2.1.3 or later. Then edit your *~/.lein/profiles.clj* file, adding `[lein-try "0.4.1"]` to the `:plugins` vector of the `:user` profile:

```
{:user {:plugins [[lein-try "0.4.1"]]}}
```

Now you can experience nearly instant gratification with the library of your choice:

```
$ lein try clj-time
Retrieving clj-time/clj-time/0.6.0/clj-time-0.6.0.pom from clojars
Retrieving clj-time/clj-time/0.6.0/clj-time-0.6.0.jar from clojars
nREPL server started on port 58981 on host 127.0.0.1
REPL-y 0.2.1
Clojure 1.5.1
    Docs: (doc function-name-here)
          (find-doc "part-of-name-here")
  Source: (source function-name-here)
 Javadoc: (javadoc java-object-or-class-here)
    Exit: Control+D or (exit) or (quit)

user=>
```

## Discussion

Notice that we did not have to give a version number for the library in the example. `lein-try` will automatically grab the most recent released version.

Of course, you can specify a library version if you like. Just add the version number after the library name:

```
$ lein try clj-time 0.5.1
#...
user=>
```

For a quick view of usage options, invoke **`lein help try`**:

```
$ lein help try
Launch REPL with specified dependencies available.

  Usage:

    lein try [io.rkn/conformity "0.2.1"] [com.datomic/datomic-free "0.8.4020.26"]
    lein try io.rkn/conformity 0.2.1
    lein try io.rkn/conformity # This uses the most recent version

  NOTE: lein-try does not require []

Arguments: ([& args])
```

As befits a Clojure tool, `lein-try` is an elegant way to make a task less laborious. Use it to summon powerful libraries from the Net at your whim, without having to set them up, and enjoy a wizardly satisfaction from the sudden confluence of new abilities.

## See Also

- The official list of Leiningen plug-ins (*http://bit.ly/lein-plugins*)
- "Our Golden Boy, lein-try" on page xv

# 3.5. Running Clojure Programs

by John Cromartie

## Problem

You want to run a program with a single entry point from Clojure source code.

## Solution

Run a file full of Clojure expressions by passing the filename as an argument to `clojure.main`.

To follow along with this recipe, you can download a version of *clojure.jar* at *http://clojure.org/downloads.*

For example, given a file *my_clojure_program.clj* with the contents:

```
(println "Hi.")
```

invoke the `java` command with *my_clojure_program.clj* as the final argument:

```
$ java -cp clojure.jar clojure.main my_clojure_program.clj
Hi.
```

In a more structured project, you'll probably have files organized in a *src/* folder. For example, given a file *src/com/example/my_program.clj*:

```
(ns com.example.my-program)

(defn -main [& args]
  (println "Hey!"))
```

to load and run the `-main` function, specify the desired namespace with the `-m/--main` option and add *src* to the classpath list (via `-cp`):

```
$ java -cp clojure.jar:src clojure.main --main com.example.my-program
Hey!
```

## Discussion

Although you will spend most of your time evaluating Clojure code in a REPL, it is sometimes useful to be able to either run a simple "script" full of Clojure expressions or run a more structured Clojure application with a `-main` entry point.

In either case, you have access to any extra command-line arguments passed after the script name or the main namespace name.

For example, let's say you have written the following program, in a file called *hello.clj*:

```
(defn greet
  [name]
  (str "Hello, " name "!"))

(doseq [name *command-line-args*]
  (println (greet name)))
```

Invoking this Clojure program directly will yield predictable output:

```
$ java -cp clojure.jar clojure.main hello.clj Alice Bob
Hello, Alice!
Hello, Bob!
```

This simple script has the side effect of printing output when it is loaded. Most Clojure code is not organized this way.

As you will typically want to keep your code in well-organized namespaces, you can provide an entry point through a namespace with a `-main` function. This allows you to avoid side effects while loading, and you can even tweak and invoke your `-main` function from the REPL just like any other function during interactive development.

Let's say you've moved your `greet` function into a `foo.util` namespace, and your project is structured something like this:

```
./src/foo/util.clj
./src/foo.clj
```

Your `foo` namespace requires the `foo.util` namespace and provides a `-main` function, like so:

```
(ns foo
  (:require foo.util))

(defn -main
  [& args]
  (doseq [name args]
    (println (foo.util/greet name))))
```

When you invoke Clojure with `foo.core` as the "main" namespace, it calls the `-main` function with the provided command-line arguments:

```
$ java -cp clojure.jar:src clojure.main --main foo Alice Bob
Hello, Alice!
Hello, Bob!
```

You'll also note the addition of `:src` to the `-cp` option. This indicates to Java that the classpath for execution not only includes *clojure.jar*, but also the contents of the *src/* directory on disk.

## See Also

- Recipe 3.6, "Running Programs from the Command Line" on page 132, to learn how to run Leiningen projects from the command line
- Recipe 3.7, "Parsing Command-Line Arguments" on page 134, to learn how to cleanly expose multiple options and flags in your command-line applications

# 3.6. Running Programs from the Command Line

by Ryan Neufeld

## Problem

You want to invoke your Clojure application from the command line.

## Solution

In any Leiningen project, use the **`lein run`** command to invoke your application from the command line. To follow along with this recipe, create a new Leiningen project:

```
$ lein new my-cli
```

Configure which namespace will be the entry point to your application by adding a `:main` key to the project's *project.clj* file:

```
(defproject my-cli "0.1.0-SNAPSHOT"
  :description "FIXME: write description"
  :url "http://example.com/FIXME"
  :license {:name "Eclipse Public License"
            :url "http://www.eclipse.org/legal/epl-v10.html"}
  :dependencies [[org.clojure/clojure "1.5.1"]]
  :main my-cli.core)
```

Finally, add a `-main` function to the namespace configured in *project.clj*:

```
(ns my-cli.core)

(defn -main [& args]
  (println "My CLI received arguments:" args))
```

Now, invoke **`lein run`** to run your application:

```
$ lein run
My CLI received arguments: nil

$ lein run 1 :foo "bar"
My CLI received arguments: (1 :foo bar)
```

## Discussion

As it turns out, invoking your application from the command line couldn't be easier. Leiningen's `run` command quickly and easily connects your application to the command line with little fuss. In its base form, `lein run` will invoke the `-main` function of whatever namespace you have specified as `:main` in your project's *project.clj* file. For example, setting `:main my-cli.core` will invoke `my-cli.core/-main`. Alternatively, you may omit implementing `-main` and provide `:main` with the fully qualified name of a function (e.g., `my.cli.core/alt-main`); this function will be invoked instead of `-main`.

While the printed arguments in the preceding solution *look* like Clojure data, they are in fact regular strings. For simple arguments, you may choose to parse these strings yourself; otherwise, we suggest using the `tools.cli` (*https://github.com/clojure/tools.cli*) library. See Recipe 3.7, "Parsing Command-Line Arguments" on page 134, for more information on `tools.cli`.

Although a project can only have one default `:main` entry point, you can invoke other functions from the command line by setting the `-m` option to a namespace or function. If you set `-m` to a namespace (e.g., `my-cli.core`), the `-main` function of that namespace will be invoked. If you provide `-m` with the fully qualified name of a function (e.g., `my-cli.core/alt-main`), that function will be invoked. There's no requirement that this function be prefixed with a `-` (indicating it is a Java method); it simply must accept a variable number of arguments (as `-main` normally does).

For example, you can add a function `add-main` to `my.cli/core`:

```
(ns my-cli.core)

(defn -main [& args]
  (println "My CLI received arguments:" args))

(defn add-main [& args]
  (->> (map #(Integer/parseInt %) args)
       (reduce + 0)
       (println "The sum is:")))
```

then invoke it from the command line with the command **`lein run -m my-cli.core/add-main`**:

```
$ lein run -m my-cli.core/add-main 1 2 3
The sum is: 6
```

## See Also

- Recipe 3.5, "Running Clojure Programs" on page 129, to learn how to run plain Clojure files with **`java`**
- Recipe 3.7, "Parsing Command-Line Arguments" on page 134, to learn how to parse command-line arguments using `tools.cli`
- Recipe 8.2, "Packaging a Project into a JAR File" on page 347, to learn how to package an application as an executable JAR
- Recipe 8.4, "Running an Application as a Daemon" on page 354, to learn how to daemonize applications

# 3.7. Parsing Command-Line Arguments

by Ryan Neufeld; originally submitted by Nicolas Bessi

## Problem

You want to write command-line tools in Clojure that can parse input arguments.

## Solution

Use the `tools.cli` (*https://github.com/clojure/tools.cli*) library.

Before starting, add `[org.clojure/tools.cli "0.2.4"]` to your project's dependencies, or start a REPL using `lein-try`:

```
$ lein try org.clojure/tools.cli
```

Use the `clojure.tools.cli/cli` function in your project's `-main` function entry point to parse command-line arguments:[1]

```
(require '[clojure.tools.cli :refer [cli]])

(defn -main [& args]
  (let [[opts args banner] (cli args
                                ["-h" "--help" "Print this help"
                                 :default false :flag true])]
    (when (:help opts)
      (println banner))))

;; Simulate entry into -main at the command line
(-main "-h")
;; *out*
;; Usage:
;;
;;  Switches                 Default  Desc
;;  --------                 -------  ----
;;  -h, --no-help, --help    false    Print this help
```

## Discussion

Clojure's `tools.cli` is a simple library, with only one function, `cli`, and a slim data-oriented API for specifying how arguments should be parsed. Handily enough, there isn't much special about this function: an arguments vector and specifications go in, and a map of parsed options, variadic arguments, and a help banner come out. It's really the epitome of good, composable functional programming.

1. Since `tools.cli` is so cool, this example can run entirely at the REPL.

To configure how options are parsed, pass any number of spec vectors after the `args` list. To specify a `:port` parameter, for example, you would provide the spec `["-p" "--port"]`. The `"-p"` isn't strictly necessary, but it is customary to provide a single-letter shortcut for command-line options (especially long ones). In the returned `opts` map, the text of the last option name will be interned to a keyword (less the `--`). For example, `"--port"` would become `:port`, and `"--super-long-option"` would become `:super-long-option`.

If you're a polite command-line application developer, you'll also include a description for each of your options. Specify this as an optional string following the final argument name:

```
["-p" "--port" "The incoming port the application will listen on."]
```

Everything after the argument name and description will be interpreted as options in key/value pairs. `tools.cli` provides the following options:

`:default`
: The default value returned in the absence of user input. Without specifying, the default of `:default` is `nil`.

`:flag`
: If truthy (not `false` or `nil`), indicates an argument behaves like a flag or switch. This argument will *not* take any value as its input.

`:parse-fn`
: The function used to parse an argument's value. This can be used to turn string values into integers, floats, or other data types.

`:assoc-fn`
: The function used to combine multiple values for a single argument.

Here's a complete example:

```
(def app-specs [["-n" "--count" :default 5
                                :parse-fn #(Integer. %)
                                :assoc-fn max]
                ["-v" "--verbose" :flag true
                                  :default true]])

(first (apply cli ["-n" "2" "-n" "50"] app-specs))
;; -> {:count 50, :verbose true}

(first (apply cli ["--no-verbose"] app-specs))
;; -> {:count 5, :verbose false}
```

When writing flag options, a useful shortcut is to omit the `:flag` option and add a `"[no-]"` prefix to the argument's name. `cli` will interpret this argument spec as including `:flag true` without you having to specify it as such:

```
["-v" "--[no-]verbose" :default true]
```

One thing the `tools.cli` library *doesn't* provide is a hook into the application container's launch life cycle. It is your responsibility to add a `cli` call to your `-main` function and know when to print the help banner. A general pattern for use is to capture the results of `cli` in a `let` block and determine if help needs to be printed. This is also useful for ensuring the validity of arguments (especially since there is no `:required` option):

```
(def required-opts #{:port})

(defn missing-required?
  "Returns true if opts is missing any of the required-opts"
  [opts]
  (not-every? opts required-opts))

(defn -main [& args]
  (let [[opts args banner] (cli args
                                ["-h" "--help" "Print this help"
                                 :default false :flag true]
                                ["-p" "--port" :parse-fn #(Integer. %)])]
    (when (or (:help opts)
              (missing-required? opts))
      (println banner))))
```

As with many applications, you may want to accept a variable number of arguments; for example, a list of filenames. In most cases, you don't need to do anything special to capture these arguments—just supply them after any other options. These variadic arguments will be returned as the second item in `cli`'s returned vector:

```
(second (apply cli ["-n" "5" "foo.txt" "bar.txt"] app-specs))
;; -> ["foo.txt" "bar.txt"]
```

If your variadic arguments look like flags, however, you'll need another trick. Use `--` as an argument to indicate to `cli` that everything that follows is a variadic argument. This is useful if you're invoking another program with the options originally passed to your program:

```
(second (apply cli ["-n" "5" "--port" "80"] app-specs))
;; -> Exception '--port' is not a valid argument ...

(second (apply cli ["-n" "5" "--" "--port" "80"] app-specs))
;; -> ["--port" "80"]
```

Once you've finished toying with your application's option parsing at the REPL, you'll probably want to try invoking options via **`lein run`**. Just like your application needs to use `--` to indicate arguments to pass on to subsequent programs, so too must you use `--` to indicate to **`lein run`** which arguments are for your program and which are for it:

```
# If app-specs were rigged up to a project...
$ lein run -- -n 5 --no-verbose
```

## See Also

- Recipe 3.6, "Running Programs from the Command Line" on page 132, to learn more about invoking applications from the command line
- Recipe 4.1, "Writing to STDOUT and STDERR" on page 167, to learn about input and output streams
- Recipe 8.2, "Packaging a Project into a JAR File" on page 347, to learn how to package an application as an executable JAR file
- For building *ncurses*-style applications, see `clojure-lanterna` (*http://bit.ly/clj-lanterna*), a wrapper around the Lanterna terminal output library

# 3.8. Creating Custom Project Templates

by Travis Vachon

## Problem

You regularly create new, similar projects and want an easy way to generate customized boilerplate. Or, you work on an open source project and want to give users an easy way to get started with your software.

## Solution

Leiningen templates give Clojure programmers an easy way to automatically generate customized project boilerplate with a single shell command. We'll explore them by creating a template for a simple web service.

First, generate a new template with **`lein new template cookbook-sample-template-<github_user>`**. Replace `<github_user>` with your own GitHub username—you'll be publishing this template to Clojars, and it will need a unique name. In the examples, we'll use `clojure-cookbook` as our GitHub username:

```
$ lein new template cookbook-sample-template-clojure-cookbook
Generating fresh 'lein new' template project.

$ cd cookbook-sample-template-clojure-cookbook
```

Create a new project file template with the following contents in *src/leiningen/new/<project-name>/project.clj*.

```
(defproject {{ns-name}} "0.1.0"
  :description "FIXME: write description"
  :url "http://example.com/FIXME"
  :license {:name "Eclipse Public License"
```

```
           :url "http://www.eclipse.org/legal/epl-v10.html"}
  :dependencies [[org.clojure/clojure "1.5.1"]])
```

Since you are creating a template for a web service and you'll want Clojure's `ring` and `ring-jetty-adapter` to be available by default, add them to the `:dependencies` section:

```
  :dependencies [[org.clojure/clojure "1.5.1"]
                 [ring "1.1.8"]
                 [ring/ring-jetty-adapter "1.2.0"]]
```

Next, open the template definition (*src/leiningen/new/<project-name>.clj*) and add `project.clj` to the list of files to be generated. Add `sanitize-ns` to the namespace's `:require` directive to expose a sanitized namespace string:

```
(ns leiningen.new.cookbook-sample-template-clojure-cookbook
  (:require [leiningen.new.templates :refer [renderer
                                              name-to-path
                                              ->files
                                              sanitize-ns]]
            [leiningen.core.main :as main])) ; ❶

(def render (renderer "cookbook-sample-template-clojure-cookbook"))

(defn cookbook-sample-template-clojure-cookbook
  "FIXME: write documentation"
  [name]
  (let [data {:name name
              :ns-name (sanitize-ns name)                     ; ❷
              :sanitized (name-to-path name)}]
    (->files data
             ["project.clj" (render "project.clj" data)]      ; ❸
             ["src/{{sanitized}}/foo.clj" (render "foo.clj" data)])))
```

❶ Add `sanitize-ns` to the `:require` declaration.

❷ Expose `:ns-name` as the sanitized `name`.

❸ Add *project.clj* to the list of files in the template.

A good template gives users a basic skeleton on which to build. Create a new file at *src/leiningen/new/<project-name>/site.clj* with some bare-bones web server logic:

```
(ns {{ns-name}}.site
    "My website! It will rock!"
    (:require [ring.adapter.jetty :refer [run-jetty]]))

(defn handler [request]
  {:status 200
   :headers {"Content-Type" "text/html"}
   :body "Hello World"})

(defn -main []
  (run-jetty handler {:port 3000}))
```

Back in the template's *project.clj* file, add a key/value for the `:main` option to indicate `my-website.site` is the core runnable namespace for the project:

```
:main {{ns-name}}.site
```

Go back to your template definition (*<project-name>.clj*) and change both `foo.clj` references to `site.clj`. Delete the *src/leiningen/new/<project-name>/foo.clj* file as well:

```
;; ...
["src/{{sanitized}}/site.clj" (render "site.clj" data)])))
```

To test the template locally, change directories to the root of your template project and run:

```
$ lein install
$ lein new cookbook-sample-template-clojure-cookbook my-first-website --snapshot
$ cd my-first-website
$ lein run
# ... Leiningen noisily fetching dependencies ...
2013-08-22 16:41:43.337:INFO:oejs.Server:jetty-7.6.8.v20121106
2013-08-22 16:41:43.379:
  INFO:oejs.AbstractConnector:Started SelectChannelConnector@0.0.0.0:3000
```

If `lein` prints an error about not being able to find your template, you should make sure you're using the latest version with **`lein upgrade`**.

To make the template available to other users, you'll need to publish it to Clojars. First, open up the template project's *project.clj* and change the version to a release version—by default `lein` will only use non-SNAPSHOT templates:

```
(defproject cookbook-sample-template-clojure-cookbook/lein-template "0.1.0"
;; ...
```

Next, visit clojars.org to create a Clojars account and then deploy from the template project root:

```
$ lein deploy clojars
```

Other users can now create projects using your template name as the first argument to **`lein new`**. Leiningen will automatically fetch your project template from Clojars:

```
$ lein new cookbook-sample-template-clojure-cookbook my-second-website
```

## Discussion

Leiningen uses Clojars as a well-known source of templates. When you pass a template name to `lein new`, it first looks for that template by name in the local Maven repository. If it doesn't find it there, it will look for an appropriately named template on *http://clojars.org*. If it finds one, it will download the template and use it to create the new project. The result is an almost magic-seeming project creation interface that lends itself extremely well to getting Clojure programmers going with new technology very quickly.

Once a project template has been downloaded, Leiningen will use *src/leiningen/new/<project-name>.clj* to create a new project. This file can be customized extensively to create sophisticated templates that match your needs. We'll review this file and talk about some of the tools available to the template developer.

We first declare a namespace that matches the template name and require some useful functions provided by Leiningen for template development: `leiningen.new.templates` contains a variety of other functions you may find useful and is worth reviewing before you develop your own templates—problems you encounter during development may already be solved by the library. In this case, `name-to-path` and `sanitize-ns` will help us create strings that we'll substitute into file templates in a number of places:

```
(ns leiningen.new.cookbook-sample-template-clojure-cookbook
  (:require [leiningen.new.templates :refer [renderer
                                             name-to-path
                                             ->files
                                             sanitize-ns]]))
```

A new project is generated by loading a set of mustache (*http://mustache.github.io/*) template files and rendering them in the context of a named set of strings. The `renderer` function creates a function that looks for mustache templates in a place determined by the name of your template. In this case it will look for templates in *src/leiningen/new/cookbook_sample_template_clojure_cookbook/*:

```
(def render (renderer "cookbook-sample-template-clojure-cookbook"))
```

Continuing the spirit of convention over configuration, Leiningen will search this namespace for a function with the same name as your template. You may execute arbitrary Clojure code in this function, which means you can make project generation arbitrarily sophisticated:

```
(defn cookbook-sample-template-clojure-cookbook
  "FIXME: write documentation"
  [name]
```

This is the data our renderer will use to create your new project files from the templates your provide. In this case, we give our templates access to the project name, the namespace that will result from that name, and a sanitized path based on that name:

```
  (let [data {:name name
              :ns-name (sanitize-ns name)
              :sanitized (name-to-path name)}]
```

Finally, we pass the `->files` (pronounced "to files") function a list of filename/content tuples. The filename determines where in the new project a file will end up. Content is generated using the `render` function we defined earlier. `render` accepts a relative path to the template file and the key/value map we created:

```
(->files data
         ["project.clj" (render "project.clj" data)]
         ["src/{{sanitized}}/site.clj" (render "site.clj" data)])))
```

Mustache templates are very simple, implementing nothing more than simple key substitution. For example, the following snippet is used to generate the `ns` statement for our new project's main file, *site.clj*:

```
(ns {{ns-name}}.site
    "My website! It will rock!"
    (:require [ring.adapter.jetty :refer [run-jetty]]))
```

Leiningen templates are a powerful tool for saving Clojure developers from the drudgery of project setup. More importantly, they are an invaluable tool for open source developers to showcase their projects and make it incredibly easy for potential users to get started with an unfamiliar piece of software. If you've been developing Clojure for a while, or even if you've just started, it's well worth your time to take templates for a spin today!"

## See Also

- The Leiningen template documentation (*http://bit.ly/lein-templates*)
- The source of the `leiningen.new.templates` (*http://bit.ly/lein-templates-clj*) namespace
- `mustache` templates (*http://mustache.github.io/*)

# 3.9. Building Functions with Polymorphic Behavior

by Ryan Neufeld; originally submitted by David McNeil

## Problem

You want to create functions whose behavior varies based upon the arguments passed to them. For example, you want to develop a set of flexible geometry functions.

## Solution

The easiest way to implement runtime polymorphism is via hand-rolled, map-based dispatch using functions like `cond` or `condp`:

```
(defn area
  "Calculate the area of a shape"
  [shape]
  (condp = (:type shape)
    :triangle  (* (:base shape) (:height shape) (/ 1 2))
    :rectangle (* (:length shape) (:width shape))))
```

```
(area {:type :triangle :base 2 :height 4})
;; -> 4N

(area {:type :rectangle :length 2 :width 4})
;; -> 8
```

This approach is a little raw, though: `area` ties together dispatch and multiple shapes' area implementations, all under one function. Use the `defmulti` and `defmethod` macros to define a multimethod, which will separate dispatch from implementation and introduce a measure of extensibility:

```
(defmulti area
  "Calculate the area of a shape"
  :type)

(defmethod area :rectangle [shape]
  (* (:length shape) (:width shape)))

(area {:type :rectangle :length 2 :width 4})
;; -> 8

;; Trying to get the area of a new shape...
(area {:type :circle :radius 1})
;; -> IllegalArgumentException No method in multimethod 'area' for
;;    dispatch value: :circle ...

(defmethod area :circle [shape]
  (* (. Math PI) (:radius shape) (:radius shape)))

(area {:type :circle :radius 1})
;; -> 3.141592653589793
```

Better, but things start to fall apart if you want to add new geometric functions like `perimeter`. With multimethods you'll need to repeat dispatch logic for each function and write a combinatorial explosion of implementations to suit. It would be better if these functions and their implementations could be grouped and written together.

Use Clojure's *protocol* facilities to define a protocol interface and extend it with concrete implementations:

```
;; Define the "shape" of a Shape object
(defprotocol Shape
  (area [s] "Calculate the area of a shape")
  (perimeter [s] "Calculate the perimeter of a shape"))

;; Define a concrete Shape, the Rectangle
(defrecord Rectangle [length width]
  Shape
  (area [this] (* length width))
  (perimeter [this] (+ (* 2 length)
                       (* 2 width))))
```

```
(->Rectangle 2 4)
;; -> #user.Rectangle{:length 2, :width 4}

(area (->Rectangle 2 4))
;; -> 8
```

## Discussion

As you've seen in this recipe, there are a multitude of different ways to implement polymorphism in Clojure. While the preceding example settled on protocols as a method for implementing polymorphism, there are no hard and fast rules about which technique to use. Each approach has its own unique set of trade-offs that need to be considered when introducing polymorphism.

The first approach considered was simple map-based polymorphism using `condp`. In retrospect, it's not the right choice for building a geometry library in Clojure, but that is not to say it is without its uses. This approach is best used in the small (*http://bit.ly/wiki-its*): you could use `cond` to prototype early iterations of a protocol at the REPL, or in places where you aren't defining new types.

It's important to note that there are techniques beyond `cond` for implementing map-based dispatch. One such technique is a dispatch map, generally implemented as a map of keys to functions.

Next up are multimethods. Unlike `cond`-based polymorphism, multimethods separate dispatch from implementation. On account of this, they can be extended after their creation. Multimethods are defined using the `defmulti` macro, which behaves similarly to `defn` but specifies a dispatch function instead of an implementation.

Let's break down the `defmulti` declaration for a rather simple multimethod, the `area` function:

```
(defmulti area ;                          ❶
  "Calculate the area of a shape" ; ❷
  :type) ;                                ❸
```

❶ The function name for this multimethod

❷ A docstring describing the function

❸ The dispatch function

Using the keyword `:type` as a dispatch function doesn't do justice to the flexibility of multimethods: they're capable of much more. Multimethods allow you to perform arbitrarily complex introspection of the arguments they are invoked with.

When choosing a map lookup like `:type` for a dispatch function, you also imply the *arity* of the function (the number of arguments it accepts). Since keywords act as a function on one argument (a map), `area` is a single-arity function. Other functions will imply different arities. A common pattern with multimethods is to use an anonymous function to make the intended arity of a multimethod more explicit:

```
(defmulti ingest-message
  "Ingest a message into an application"
  (fn [app message] ;          ❶
    (:priority message)) ; ❷
  :default :low) ;          ❸
```

❶ `ingest-messages` accepts two arguments, an app and a message.

❷ `message` will be processed differently depending on its priority.

❸ In the absence of a `:priority` key on `message`, the default priority will be `:low`. Without specifying, the default dispatch value is `:default`.

```
(defmethod ingest-message :low [app message]
  (println (str "Ingesting message " message ", eventually...")))

(defmethod ingest-message :high [app message]
  (println (str "Ingesting message " message ", now.")))

(ingest-message {} {:type :stats :value [1 2 3]})
;; *out*
;; Ingesting message {:type :stats :value [1 2 3]}, eventually...

(ingest-message {} {:type :heartbeat :priority :high})
;; *out*
;; Ingesting message {:type :heartbeat, :priority :high}, now.
```

In all of the examples so far, we've always dispatched on a single value. Multimethods also support something called *multiple dispatch*, whereby a function can be dispatched upon any number of factors.

By returning a vector rather than a single value in our dispatch, we can make more dynamic decisions:

```
(defmulti convert
  "Convert a thing from one type to another"
  (fn [request thing]
    [(:input-format request) (:output-format request)])) ; ❶

(require 'clojure.edn)
(defmethod convert [:edn-string :clojure] ;                ❷
  [_ str]
  (clojure.edn/read-string str))

(require 'clojure.data.json)
(defmethod convert [:clojure :json] ;                      ❸
  [_ thing]
  (clojure.data.json/write-str thing))
```

```
(convert {:input-format :edn-string
          :output-format :clojure}
         "{:foo :bar}")
;; -> {:foo :bar}

(convert {:input-format :clojure
          :output-format :json}
         {:foo [:bar :baz]})
;; -> "{\"foo\":[\"bar\",\"baz\"]}"
```

❶ The `convert` multimethod dispatches on input *and* output format.

❷ An implementation of `convert` that converts from edn strings to Clojure data.

❸ Similarly, an implementation that converts from Clojure data to JSON.

All this power comes at a cost, however; because multimethods are so dynamic, they can be quite slow. Further, there is no good way to group sets of related multimethods into an all-or-nothing package.[2] If speed or implementing a complete interface is among your chief concerns, then you will likely be better served by protocols.

Clojure's protocol feature provides extensible polymorphism with fast dispatch akin to Java's interfaces, with one notable difference from multimethods: protocols can only perform single dispatch (based on type).

Protocols are defined using the `defprotocol` macro, which accepts a name, an optional docstring, and any number of named method signatures. A method signature is made up of a few parts: the name, at least one type signature, and an optional docstring. The first argument of any type signature is always the object itself—Clojure dispatches on the type of this argument. Perhaps an example would be the easiest way to dig into `defprotocol`'s syntax:

```
(defprotocol Frobnozzle
  "Basic methods for any Frobnozzle"
  (blint [this x] "Blint the frobnozzle with x") ;                        ❶
  (crand [this f] [this f x] (str "Crand a frobnozzle with another " ; ❷
                                  "optionally incorporating x")))
```

❶ A function, `blint`, with a single additional argument, `x`

❷ A multi-arity function, `crand`, that takes an optional `x` argument

Once a protocol is defined, there are numerous ways to provide an implementation for it. `deftype`, `defrecord`, and `reify` all define a protocol implementation while creating an object. The `deftype` and `defrecord` forms create new named types, while `reify`

2. That is to say, you cannot force a multimethod to implement all of the required methods when extending behavior to its own type.

creates an anonymous type. Each form is used by indicating the protocol being extended, followed by concrete implementations of each of that protocol's methods:

```
;; deftype has a similar syntax, but is not really applicable for an
;; immutable shape
(defrecord Square [length]
  Shape ;                                  ❶
  (area [this] (* length length)) ;        ❷
  (perimeter [this] (* 4 length))
  ;                                        ❸
  )

(perimeter (->Square 1))
;; -> 4

;; Calculate the area of a parallelogram without defining a record
(area
  (let [b 2
        h 3]
    (reify Shape
      (area [this] (* b h))
      (perimeter [this] (* 2 (+ b h))))))
;; -> 6
```

❶ Indicate the protocol being implemented.

❷ Implement all of its methods.

❸ Repeat steps one and two for any remaining protocols you wish to implement.

### The Difference Between a Type and a Record

Types and records share a very similar syntax, so it can be hard to understand how each should be used.

Chas Emerick explained it best in an appendix to *Clojure Programming* (O'Reilly):

> Is your class modeling a domain value—thus benefiting from hash map–like functionality and semantics? Use `defrecord`.
>
> Do you need to define mutable fields? Use `deftype`.

There you have it.

For implementing protocols on existing types, you will want to use the `extend` family of built-in functions (`extend`, `extend-type`, and `extend-protocol`). Instead of creating a new type, these functions define implementations for existing types.

## See Also

- The official documentation for multimethods and hierarchies (*http://clojure.org/multimethods*), which covers multimethods in depth. This document also covers hierarchies as they relate to multimethods, a feature not covered in this recipe.
- The official documentation for protocols (*http://clojure.org/protocols*), which covers protocols in depth, including information on how protocols relate to interfaces.
- Recipe 2.28, "Implementing Custom Data Structures: Red-Black Trees—Part II" on page 117, for a concrete example of implementing a protocol.
- Recipe 3.10, "Extending a Built-In Type" on page 147, for examples of using `extend` and its convenience macros `extend-type` and `extend-protocol`.

# 3.10. Extending a Built-In Type

by David McNeil

## Problem

You need to extend one of the built-in types with your own functions.

## Solution

Suppose you would like to add domain-specific functions to the core `java.lang.String` type. In this example, you will add a `first-name` and a `last-name` function to `String`.

Define a protocol with the functions you need. The protocol declares the signature of the functions:

```
(defprotocol Person
  "Represents the name of a person."
  (first-name [person])
  (last-name [person]))
```

Extend the type to the `java.lang.String` class:

```
(extend-type String
  Person
  (first-name [s] (first (clojure.string/split s #" ")))
  (last-name [s] (second (clojure.string/split s #" "))))
```

Now you can invoke your functions on strings:

```
(first-name "john")
;; -> "john"
```

```
(last-name "john smith")
;; -> "smith"
```

## Discussion

Why use protocols when multimethods already exist? For one, speed: protocols dispatch only on the type of their first parameter. Further, protocols allow you to group and name an extension. This makes it much easier to reason about what a group of functions confer about a type and ensures a proper, full implementation.

It is good practice to only extend a protocol to a type if you are the author of either the protocol or the type. This will avoid cases where you violate the assumptions of the original author(s).

If you already had functions to use, then it would make sense to use `extend` instead of the `extend-type` form:

```
(defn first-word [s]
  (first (clojure.string/split s #" ")))

(defn second-word [s]
  (second (clojure.string/split s #" ")))

(extend String
  Person
  {:first-name first-word
   :last-name second-word})
```

## See Also

- An excellent explanation (*http://bit.ly/protocols-explanation*) of why protocols exist as it relates to the "Expression Problem" by Jörg W Mittag on StackOverflow

# 3.11. Decoupling Consumers and Producers with core.async

by Daemian Mack

## Problem

You want to decouple your program's consumers and producers by introducing explicit queues between them.

For example, if you are building a web dashboard that fetches Twitter messages, this application must both persist these events to a database and publish them via server-sent events (SSE) to a browser.

## Solution

Introducing explicit queues between components allows them to communicate asynchronously, making them simpler to manage independently and freeing up computational resources.

Use the `core.async` (*https://github.com/clojure/core.async*) library to introduce and coordinate asynchronous channels.

To follow along with this recipe, start a REPL using `lein-try`:

```
$ lein try org.clojure/core.async
```

Consider the following passage illustrating a synchronous approach:

```
(defn database-consumer
  "Accept messages and persist them to a database."
  [msg]
  (println (format "database-consumer received message %s" msg)))

(defn sse-consumer
  "Accept messages and pass them to web browsers via SSE."
  [msg]
  (println (format "sse-consumer received message %s" msg)))

(defn messages
  "Fetch messages from Twitter."
  []
  (range 4))

(defn message-producer
  "Produce messages and deliver them to consumers."
  [& consumers]
  (doseq [msg (messages)
          consumer consumers]
    (consumer msg)))

(message-producer database-consumer sse-consumer)
;; *out*
;; database-consumer received message 0
;; sse-consumer received message 0
;; database-consumer received message 1
;; sse-consumer received message 1
;; database-consumer received message 2
;; sse-consumer received message 2
;; database-consumer received message 3
;; sse-consumer received message 3
```

Each message received is passed directly to each consumer of `message-producer`. As implemented, this approach is rather brittle; any slow consumer could cause the entire pipeline to grind to a halt.

To make processing asynchronous, introduce explicit queues with `clojure.core.async/chan`. Perform work asynchronously by wrapping it in one of `core.async`'s `clojure.core.async/go` forms:

```
(require '[clojure.core.async :refer [chan sliding-buffer go
                                       go-loop timeout >! <!]])

(defn database-consumer
  "Accept messages and persist them to a database."
  []
  (let [in (chan (sliding-buffer 64))]
    (go-loop [data (<! in)]
             (when data
               (println (format "database-consumer received data %s" data))
               (recur (<! in))))
    in))

(defn sse-consumer
  "Accept messages and pass them to web browsers via SSE."
  []
  (let [in (chan (sliding-buffer 64))]
    (go-loop [data (<! in)]
             (when data
               (println (format "sse-consumer received data %s" data))
               (recur (<! in))))
    in))

(defn messages
  "Fetch messages from Twitter."
  []
  (range 4))

(defn producer
  "Produce messages and deliver them to consumers."
  [& channels]
  (go
   (doseq [msg (messages)
           out  channels]
     (<! (timeout 100))
     (>! out msg))))

(producer (database-consumer) (sse-consumer))
;; *out*
;; database-consumer received data 0
;; sse-consumer received data 0
;; database-consumer received data 1
;; sse-consumer received data 1
;; database-consumer received data 2
;; sse-consumer received data 2
;; database-consumer received data 3
;; sse-consumer received data 3
```

## Discussion

> There comes a time in all good programs when components or subsystems must stop communicating directly with one another.
>
> — Rich Hickey
> *Clojure core.async Channels*

This code is larger than the original implementation. What has this afforded us?

The original approach was rigid. It offered no control over consumer latency and was therefore extremely vulnerable to lag. By buffering communication over channels and doing work asynchronously, we've created service boundaries around producers and consumers, allowing them to operate as independently as possible.

Let's examine one of the new consumers in depth to understand how it has changed.

Instead of receiving messages via function invocation, consumers now draw messages from a buffered channel. Where a consumer (e.g., `database-consumer`) used to consume a single message at a time, it now uses a `go-loop` to continuously consume messages from its producer.

In traditional callback-oriented code, accomplishing something like this would require splitting logic out across numerous functions, introducing "callback hell." One of the benefits of `core.async` is that it lets you write code inline, in a more straightforward style:

```
(defn database-consumer
  "Accept messages and persist them to a database."
  []
  (let [in (chan (sliding-buffer 64))] ; ❶
    (go-loop [data (<! in)]           ; ❷
             (when data               ; ❸
               (println (format "database-consumer received data %s" data))
               (recur (<! in))))      ; ❹
    in))
```

❶ Here the channel is given a buffer of size 64. The `sliding-buffer` variant dictates that if this channel accumulates more than 64 unread values, older values will start "falling off" the end, trading off historical completeness in favor of recency. Using `dropping-buffer` instead would optimize in the opposite direction.

❷ `go-loop` is the `core.async` equivalent to looping via something like `while true`. This `go-loop` reads its initial value by "taking" (`<!`) from the input channel (`in`).

❸ Because channels return `nil` when closed, as long as we can read `data` from them, we know we have work to do.

❹ To `recur` the `go-loop` to the beginning, take the next value from the channel and invoke `recur` with it.

Because the `go-loop` block is asynchronous, the take call (`<!`) parks until a value is placed on the channel. The remainder of the `go-loop` block—here, the `println` call—is pending. Since the channel is returned as the `database-consumer` function's value, other parts of the system—namely, the producer—are free to write to the channel while the take waits. The first value written to the channel will satisfy that read call, allowing the rest of the `go-loop` block to continue.

This consumer is now asynchronous, reading values until the channel closes. Since the channel is buffered, we now have some measure of control over the system's resiliency. For example, buffers allow a consumer to lag behind a producer by a specified amount.

Fewer changes are required to make `producer` asynchronous:

```
(defn producer
  [& channels]
  (go
   (doseq [msg (messages)
           out  channels] ; ❶
     (<! (timeout 100))   ; ❷
     (>! out item))))     ; ❸
```

❶ For each message and channel...

❷ Take from a `timeout` channel to simulate a short pause for effect...

❸ And put a message onto the channel with `>!`.

Although the operations are asynchronous, they still occur serially. Using unbuffered consumer channels would mean that if one of the consumers took from the channel too slowly, the pipeline would stall; the producer would not be able to put further values onto the channels.

## See Also

- `core.async` has more advanced facilities for layout and coordination of channels. For more details, see the `core.async` overview (*http://bit.ly/core-async-doc*).
- Recipe 5.8, "Using ZeroMQ Concurrently" on page 242, to see how to use `core.async` to communicate over ZeroMQ.

# 3.12. Making a Parser for Clojure Expressions Using core.match

by Chris Frisz

## Problem

You want to parse Clojure expressions, say, from the input to a macro, into a different representation (like maps).

For this example, consider a heavily simplified version of Clojure that consists of the following expression types:

- A variable represented by a valid Clojure symbol
- An `fn` expression that accepts a single argument and whose body is also a valid expression
- An application of a valid expression in the language to another valid expression

You can represent this language by the following grammar:

```
Expr = var
     | (fn [var] Expr)
     | (Expr Expr)
```

## Solution

Use `core.match` to pattern match over the input and return the expression represented as maps of maps.

Before starting, add `[org.clojure/core.match "0.2.0"]` to your project's dependencies, or start a REPL using `lein-try`:

```
$ lein try org.clojure/core.match
```

Now, codify the language's grammar using `clojure.core.match/match`:

```
(require '[clojure.core.match :refer (match)])

(defn simple-clojure-parser
  [expr]
  (match [expr]
    [(var :guard symbol?)] {:variable var}
    [(['fn [arg] body] :seq)] {:closure
                               {:arg arg
                                :body (simple-clojure-parser body)}}
    [([operator operand] :seq)] {:application
                                 {:operator (simple-clojure-parser operator)
                                  :operand (simple-clojure-parser operand)}}
    :else (throw (Exception. (str "invalid expression: " expr)))))

(simple-clojure-parser 'a)
;; -> {:variable a}

(simple-clojure-parser '(fn [x] x))
;; -> {:closure {:arg x, :body {:variable x}}}
```

```
(simple-clojure-parser '((fn [x] x) a))
;; -> {:application
;;     {:operator {:closure {:arg x, :body {:variable x}}}
;;      :operand {:variable a}}}

;; fn expression can only have one argument!
(simple-clojure-parser '(fn [x y] x))
;; -> Exception invalid expression: (fn [x y] x) ...
```

## Discussion

A `match` statement in `core.match` is made up of two basic parts. The first part is a vector of vars to be matched. In our example, this is `[expr]`. This vector isn't limited to a single entry—it can contain as many items to match as you would like. The next part is a variable list of question/answer pairs. A *question* is a vector representing the *shape* the vars vector must take. As with `cond`, an *answer* is what will be returned should a var satisfy a question.

Questions take a variety of forms in `core.match`. Here are explanations of the preceding samples:

- The first match pattern, `[(var :guard symbol?)]`, matches the variable case of our syntax, binding the matched expression to `var`. The special `:guard` form applies the predicate `symbol?` to `var`, only returning the answer if `symbol?` returns `true`.
- The second pattern, `[(['fn [arg] body] :seq)]`, matches the `fn` case.[3] Note the special `([...] :seq)` syntax for matching over lists, used here to represent an `fn` expression. Also notice that to match on the literal `fn`, it had to be quoted in the match pattern. Interestingly, since the `body` expression should also be accepted by this parser, it makes a self-recursive call, `(simple-clojure-parser body)`, in the righthand side of the match pattern.
- For the third `:application` pattern, the parser again matches on a list using the `([...] :seq)` syntax. As in the body of the `fn` expression, both the `operator` and `operand` expressions should be accepted by the parser, so it makes a recursive call for each one.

  Finally, the parser throws an exception if the given expression doesn't match any of the three accepted patterns. This gives a somewhat more helpful error message if you accidentally hand the parser a malformed expression.

3. The match pattern for `fn` could (and should) include a guard on the `arg` to ensure that it's a symbol, but that's elided here for brevity.

Writing your parser this way gives you succinct code that closely resembles the target input. Alternatively, you could write it using conditional expressions (`if` or `cond`) and explicitly destructure the input. To illustrate the difference in length and clarity of the code, consider this function that only parses the `fn` expressions of the Clojure subset:

```
(defn parse-fn
  [expr]
  (if (and (list? expr)
           (= (count expr) 3)
           (= (nth expr 0) 'fn)
           (vector? (nth expr 1))
           (= (count (nth expr 1)) 1))
    {:closure {:arg (nth (nth expr 1) 0)
               :body (simple-clojure-parser (nth expr 2))}}
    (throw (Exception. (str "unexpected non-fn expression: " expr)))))
```

Notice how much more code this version needed in order to express the same properties about an `fn` expression? Not only did the non-`match` version require more code, but the `if` test doesn't resemble the structure of the expression the way the `match` pattern does. Further, `match` binds the matched input to the variable names in the match pattern automatically, saving you from having to `let`-bind them yourself or repeatedly write the same list access code (as shown with `(nth expr)` in `parse-fn` above). Needless to say, the `match` is much easier to read and maintain.

## See Also

- The `core.match` wiki's Overview page (*http://bit.ly/clj-core-match*) for a broader view over all of the library's capabilities

# 3.13. Querying Hierarchical Graphs with core.logic

by Ryan Senior

## Problem

You have a graph-like hierarchical data structure, serialized as a flat list of nodes, that you want to query. For example, you have a graph of movie metadata represented as entity-attribute-value triples. Writing this code with the standard `seq` functions has proven to be too tedious and error prone.

## Solution

The `core.logic` library is a Clojure implementation of the miniKanren domain-specific language (DSL) for logic programming. Its declarative style is well suited for querying flattened hierarchical data.

To follow along with this recipe, start a REPL using `lein-try`:

```
$ lein try org.clojure/core.logic
```

The first thing you need is a dataset to query. Consider, for example, that you have represented a graph of movie metadata as a list of tuples:

```
(def movie-graph
  [;; The "Newmarket Films" studio
   [:a1 :type :FilmStudio]
   [:a1 :name "Newmarket Films"]
   [:a1 :filmsCollection :a2]

   ;; Collection of films made by Newmarket Films
   [:a2 :type :FilmCollection]
   [:a2 :film :a3]
   [:a2 :film :a6]

   ;; The movie "Memento"
   [:a3 :type :Film]
   [:a3 :name "Memento"]
   [:a3 :cast :a4]

   ;; Connects the film to its cast (actors/director/producer etc.)
   [:a4 :type :FilmCast]
   [:a4 :director :a5]

   ;; The director of "Memento"
   [:a5 :type :Person]
   [:a5 :name "Christopher Nolan"]

   ;; The movie "The Usual Suspects"
   [:a6 :type :Film]
   [:a6 :filmName "The Usual Suspects"]
   [:a6 :cast :a7]

   ;; Connects the film to its cast (actors/director/producer etc.)
   [:a7 :type :FilmCast]
   [:a7 :director :a8]

   ;; The director of "The Usual Suspects"
   [:a8 :type :Person]
   [:a8 :name "Bryan Singer"]])
```

With all of this data in hand, how would you go about querying it? In an imperative model, you would likely arduously "connect the dots" from node to node using filters, maps, and conditionals.[4] With `core.logic`, however, it is possible to connect these dots using declarative logic statements.

4. Oh my!

For example, to answer the question, "Which directors have made movies at a given studio?" create a number of dots (*logic variables*) using `clojure.core.logic/fresh` and connect (*ground*) them using `clojure.core.logic/membero`. Finally, invoke `clojure.core.logic/run*` to obtain all of the possible solutions:

```
(require '[clojure.core.logic :as cl])

(defn directors-at
  "Find all of the directors that have directed at a given studio"
  [graph studio-name]
  (cl/run* [director-name]
    (cl/fresh [studio film-coll film cast director]
      ;; Relate the original studio-name to a film collection
      (cl/membero [studio :name studio-name] graph)
      (cl/membero [studio :type :FilmStudio] graph)
      (cl/membero [studio :filmsCollection film-coll] graph)

      ;; Relate any film collections to their individual films
      (cl/membero [film-coll :type :FilmCollection] graph)
      (cl/membero [film-coll :film film] graph)

      ;; Then from film to cast members
      (cl/membero [film :type :Film] graph)
      (cl/membero [film :cast cast] graph)

      ;; Grounding to cast members of type :director
      (cl/membero [cast :type :FilmCast] graph)
      (cl/membero [cast :director director] graph)

      ;; Finally, attach to the director-name
      (cl/membero [director :type :Person] graph)
      (cl/membero [director :name director-name] graph))))

(directors-at movie-graph "Newmarket Films")
;; -> ("Christopher Nolan" "Bryan Singer")
```

## Discussion

miniKanren is a domain-specific language written in Scheme, intended to give many of the benefits of a logic programming language (such as Prolog) from within Scheme. David Nolen created an implementation of miniKanren for Clojure, with a focus on performance. One of the benefits of logic programming languages is their very declarative style. By using `core.logic`, we are able to say *what* we are looking for in the graph without saying *how* `core.logic` should go about finding it.

In general, all `core.logic` queries begin with one of the library's `run` macros, with `clojure.core.logic/run` returning a finite number of solutions and `clojure.core.logic/run*` returning *all* of the solutions.

The first argument to the run macro is the *goal*, a variable used to store the result of the query. In the preceding solution, this was the director-name variable. The rest is the body of the core.logic program. A program is made up of *logic variables* (created using clojure.core.logic/fresh) grounded to values or constrained by logic statements.

run is a clue that our programming paradigm is changing to logic programming. In a core.logic program, *unification* is used rather than traditional variable assignment and seqential expression evaluation. Unification uses substitution of values for variables in an attempt to make two expressions syntactically identical. Statements in a core.logic program can appear in any order. For example, you can use clojure.core.logic/== to unify 1 and q:

```
(cl/run 1 [q]
  (cl/== 1 q))
;; -> (1)

(cl/run 1 [q]
  (cl/== q 1))
;; -> (1)
```

core.logic is also able to unify the contents of lists and vectors, finding the right substitution to make both expressions the same:

```
(cl/run 1 [q]
  (cl/== [1 2 3]
         [1 2 q]))
;; -> (3)

(cl/run 1 [q]
  (cl/== ["foo" "bar" "baz"]
         [q     "bar" "baz"]))
;; -> ("foo")
```

Technically speaking, unification is a relation, relating the first form with the second form. This is a kind of puzzle for core.logic to solve. In the previous example, q is a logic variable, and core.logic is charged with binding a value to q such that the left and the right sides of the unification (the clojure.core.logic/== relation) are syntactically identical. When there is no binding that satisfies the puzzle, no solution exists:

```
;; There is no way a single value is both 1 AND 2
(cl/run 1 [q]
  (cl/== 1 q)
  (cl/== 2 q))
;; -> ()
```

fresh is one way to create more logic variables:

```
(cl/run 1 [q]
  (cl/fresh [x y z]
    (cl/== x 1)
    (cl/== y 2)
```

```
    (cl/== z 3)
    (cl/== q [x y z])))
;; -> ([1 2 3])
```

Just as `clojure.core.logic/==` is a relation between two forms, `clojure.core.logic/membero` is a relation between an element in a list and the list itself:

```
(cl/run 1 [q]
  (cl/membero q [1]))
;; -> (1)

(cl/run 1 [q]
  (cl/membero 1 q))
;; -> ((1 . _0))
```

The first example is asking for any member of the list `[1]`, which happens to only be `1`. The second example is the opposite, asking for any list where `1` is a member. The dot notation indicates an improper tail with `_0` in it. This means `1` could be in a list by itself, or it could be followed by any other sequence of numbers, strings, lists, etc. `_0` is an unbound variable, since there was no further restriction on the list other than `1` being an element.

`clojure.core.logic/run*` is a macro that asks for all possible solutions. Asking for all of the lists that contain a `1` will not terminate.

Unification can peek inside structures with `clojure.core.logic/membero` as well:

```
(cl/run 1 [q]
  (cl/membero [1 q 3] [[1 2 3] [4 5 6] [7 8 9]]))
;; -> (2)
```

Logic variables live for the duration of the program, making it possible to use the same logic variable in multiple statements:

```
(let [seq-a [["foo" 1 2] ["bar" 3 4] ["baz" 5 6]]
      seq-b [["foo" 9 8] ["bar" 7 6] ["baz" 5 4]]]
  (cl/run 1 [q]
    (cl/fresh [first-item middle-item last-a last-b]
      (cl/membero [first-item middle-item last-a] seq-a)
      (cl/membero [first-item middle-item last-b] seq-b)
      (cl/== q [last-a last-b]))))
;; -> ([6 4])
```

The previous example does not specify `first-item`, only that it should be the same for `seq-a` and `seq-b`. `core.logic` uses the data provided to bind values to the variable that satisfy the constraints. The same is true with `middle-item`.

Building up from this, we can traverse the graph described in the solution:

```
(cl/run 1 [director-name]
  (cl/fresh [studio film-coll film cast director]
    (cl/membero [studio :name "Newmarket Films"] graph)
    (cl/membero [studio :type :FilmStudio] graph)
    (cl/membero [studio :filmsCollection film-coll] graph)

    (cl/membero [film-coll :type :FilmCollection] graph)
    (cl/membero [film-coll :film film] graph)

    (cl/membero [film :type :Film] graph)
    (cl/membero [film :cast cast] graph)

    (cl/membero [cast :type :FilmCast] graph)
    (cl/membero [cast :director director] graph)

    (cl/membero [director :type :Person] graph)
    (cl/membero [director :name director-name] graph)))
;; -> ("Christopher Nolan")
```

There is one minor difference between the preceding code and the original solution: rather than using `clojure.core.logic/run*`, asking for all solutions, `clojure.core.logic/run 1` was used. The program has multiple answers to the query for a director at Newmarket Films. Asking for more answers will return more with no other code change.

Slight modifications to the preceding query can significantly change the results. Swapping `"Newmarket Films"` for a new fresh variable will return all directors, for all studios. A macro could also be created to reduce some of the code duplication if desired.

One benefit of the relational solution to this problem is being able to generate a graph from the values:

```
(first
  (cl/run 1 [graph]
    (cl/fresh [studio film-coll film cast director]
      (cl/membero [studio :name "Newmarket Films"] graph)
      (cl/membero [studio :type :FilmStudio] graph)
      (cl/membero [studio :filmsCollection film-coll] graph)

      (cl/membero [film-coll :type :FilmCollection] graph)
      (cl/membero [film-coll :film film] graph)

      (cl/membero [film :type :Film] graph)
      (cl/membero [film :cast cast] graph)

      (cl/membero [cast :type :FilmCast] graph)
      (cl/membero [cast :director director] graph)
```

```
      (cl/membero [director :type :Person] graph)
      (cl/membero [director :name "Baz"] graph))))
;; -> ([_0 :name "Newmarket Films"]
;;     [_0 :type :FilmStudio]
;;     [_0 :filmsCollection _1]
;;     ...)
```

For small graphs, membero is fast enough. Larger graphs will experience performance problems as core.logic will traverse the list many times to find the elements. Using clojure.core.logic/to-stream with some basic indexing can greatly improve the query performance.

## See Also

- *The Reasoned Schemer*, by Daniel P. Friedman, William E. Byrd, and Oleg Kiselyov (MIT Press)
- The core.logic wiki (*http://bit.ly/core-logic-wiki*)
- The miniKanren website (*http://minikanren.org/*)
- The core.logic repository (*https://github.com/clojure/core.logic*) for examples of using clojure.core.logic/to-stream
- core.match (*https://github.com/clojure/core.match*), a (nonunification) matching library with some similar ideas, described briefly in Recipe 3.12, "Making a Parser for Clojure Expressions Using core.match" on page 152

# 3.14. Playing a Nursery Rhyme

by Chris Ford

## Problem

You want to code a nursery rhyme to inspire your children to take up programming.

## Solution

Use Overtone (*https://github.com/overtone/overtone*) to bring the song to life.

Before starting, add [overtone "0.8.1"] to your project's dependencies or start a REPL using lein-try:[5]

```
$ lein try overtone
```

5. There are some additional installation concerns if you are running Overtone on Linux. See the Overtone wiki (*http://bit.ly/overtone-install*) for more detailed installation instructions.

To start, define the melody for an old children's song:

```
(require '[overtone.live :as overtone])

(defn note [timing pitch] {:time timing :pitch pitch})

(def melody
  (let [pitches
         [0 0 0 1 2
          ; Row, row, row your boat,
          2 1 2 3 4
          ; Gently down the stream,
          7 7 7 4 4 4 2 2 2 0 0 0
          ; (take 4 (repeat "merrily"))
          4 3 2 1 0]
          ; Life is but a dream!
        durations
         [1 1 2/3 1/3 1
          2/3 1/3 2/3 1/3 2
          1/3 1/3 1/3 1/3 1/3 1/3 1/3 1/3 1/3 1/3 1/3 1/3
          2/3 1/3 2/3 1/3 2]
        times (reductions + 0 durations)]
      (map note times pitches)))

melody
;; -> ({:time 0, :pitch 0}   ; Row,
;;     {:time 1, :pitch 0}   ; row,
;;     {:time 2, :pitch 0}   ; row
;;     {:time 8/3, :pitch 1} ; your
;;     {:time 3N, :pitch 2}  ; boat
;;     ...)
```

Convert the piece into a specific key by transforming each note's pitch using a function that represents the key:

```
(defn where [k f notes] (map #(update-in % [k] f) notes))

(defn scale [intervals] (fn [degree] (apply + (take degree intervals))))
(def major (scale [2 2 1 2 2 2 1]))

(defn from [n] (partial + n))
(def A (from 69))

(->> melody
  (where :pitch (comp A major)))
;; -> ({:time 0, :pitch 69} ; Row,
;;     {:time 1, :pitch 69} ; row,
;;     ...)
```

Convert the piece into a specific tempo by transforming each note's time using a function that represents the tempo:

```
(defn bpm [beats] (fn [beat] (/ (* beat 60 1000) beats)))

(->> melody
  (where :time (comp (from (overtone/now)) (bpm 90))))
;; -> ({:time 1383316072169, :pitch 0}
;;     {:time 4149948218507/3, :pitch 0}
;;     ...)
```

Now, define an instrument and use it to play the melody. The following example synthesized instrument is a simple sine wave, whose amplitude and duration are controlled by an envelope:

```
(require '[overtone.live :refer [definst line sin-osc FREE midi->hz at]])

(definst beep [freq 440]
  (let [envelope (line 1 0 0.5 :action FREE)]
    (* envelope (sin-osc freq))))

(defn play [notes]
  (doseq [{ms :time midi :pitch} notes]
    (at ms (beep (midi->hz midi)))))

;; Make sure your speakers are on...
(->> melody
  (where :pitch (comp A major))
  (where :time (comp (from (overtone/now)) (bpm 90)))
  play)
;; -> <music playing on your speakers>
```

If your nursery rhyme is a round, like "Row, Row, Row Your Boat," you can use it to accompany itself:

```
(defn round [beats notes]
  (concat notes (->> notes (where :time (from beats)))))

(->> melody
  (round 4)
  (where :pitch (comp A major))
  (where :time (comp (from (overtone/now)) (bpm 90)))
  play)
```

## Discussion

A *note* is a sound of a particular pitch that occurs at a particular time. A *song* is a series of notes. We can therefore simply represent music in Clojure as a sequence of time/pitch pairs.

This representation is structurally very similar to Western music notation, where each dot on a stave has a time and a pitch determined by its horizontal and vertical position. But unlike traditional music notation, the Clojure representation can be manipulated by functional programming techniques.

Pieces of Western music, like "Row, Row, Row Your Boat," aren't composed of arbitrary pitches. Within a given melody, the notes are typically confined to a subset of all possible pitches called a *scale*.

The approach taken here is to express the pitches by integers denoting where they appear in the scale, called *degrees*. So, for example, degree `0` signifies the first pitch of the scale, and degree `4` signifies the fifth pitch of the scale.

This simplifies the description of the melody, because we don't have to worry about inadvertently specifying pitches that are outside our chosen scale. It also allows us to vary our chosen scale without having to rewrite the melody.

To work with degrees, we need a function that translates a degree into the actual pitch. Since "Row, Row, Row Your Boat" is in a major scale, we need a function that represents such a scale.

We use the observation that in a major scale, there is a regular pattern of double and single spaces between adjacent pitches (known to musicians as tones and semitones). We define a function called `major` that accepts a degree and outputs the number of semitones it represents.

Our pitches still aren't quite right, because they're relative to the lowest note of the piece. We need to establish a musical reference point that we will use to interpret our degrees.

Concert A is conventionally used as a reference point by orchestras, so we'll use it as our musical zero. In other words, we will put "Row, Row, Row Your Boat" into A major. Now a degree of `0` means A.

Note that we can simply compose together our functions for major and for A to arrive at a composite A major function.

We need to do a similar transformation for time. Each note's time is expressed in *beats*, but we need it to be in milliseconds. We use the current system time as our temporal reference point, meaning that the piece will start from now (and not the start of the Unix epoch).

"Row, Row, Row Your Boat" is a round, meaning it harmonizes if sung as an accompaniment to itself, offset by a particular number of beats. As an extra flourish, we produce a second version of the melody that starts four beats after the first.

We encourage you to experiment with the tune, perhaps by varying the speed or using a different key (as a hint, a minor key has the following pattern of tones and semitones: `[2 1 2 2 1 2 2]`).

We also encourage you to think about how this approach to modeling a series of events can be applied to other domains. The idea of expressing a time series as a sequence and then applying transformations across that series is a simple, flexible, and composable way of describing a problem.

Music is a wonderful and moving thing. It's also incredibly well suited to being modeled in a functional programming language. We hope your children agree.

## See Also

- Overtone (*https://github.com/overtone/overtone*), a music environment for Clojure

CHAPTER 4

# Local I/O

## 4.0. Introduction

We've done a lot of work in the last few chapters, but clearly, the rubber has to meet the road somewhere. How did we get all of this data *into* our Clojure programs, and more importantly, how do we get it *out*? This chapter is all about input and output to a local computer—the primary place where most applications' data hits the road, so to speak.

There are a variety of modes and mediums for communicating with a local machine. What do we communicate with, in what way, and in what format? It's a little like the classic board game Clue: was it plain text, in the console, with command-line arguments; or Clojure data, in a file, as configuration data? In this chapter we'll explore files, formats, and applications of both GUI and console flavors, to name a few topics.

While it isn't possible for us to enumerate every possible combination, it is our hope that this chapter will give you a strong idea of what is possible. Handily enough, most good solutions in Clojure *compose*; you should have little trouble sticking together any number of recipes in this chapter to suit your needs.

## 4.1. Writing to STDOUT and STDERR

by Alan Busby

### Problem

You want to write to `STDOUT` and `STDERR`.

### Solution

By default, the `print` and `println` functions will print content passed to them to `STDOUT`:

```
(println "This text will be printed to STDOUT.")
;; *out*
;; This text will be printed to STDOUT.

(do
  (print "a")
  (print "b"))
;; *out*
;; ab
```

Change the binding of `*out*` to `*err*` to print to `STDERR` instead of `STDOUT`:

```
(binding [*out* *err*]
  (println "Blew up!"))
;; *err*
;; Blew up!\n
```

## Discussion

In Clojure, the dynamic binding vars `*out*` and `*err*` are bound to your application environment's built-in `STDOUT` and `STDERR` streams, respectively.

All of the printing functions in Clojure, such as `print` and `println`, utilize the `*out*` binding as the destination to write to. Consequently, you can rebind that var to `*err*` (using `binding`) to change the destination of print messages from `STDOUT` to `STDERR`. Other printing functions include `pr`, `prn`, `printf`, and a handful of others.

The bound value of `*out*` is not restricted to operating system streams; `*out*` can be *any* stream-like object. This makes print functions powerful tools. They can be used to write to files, sockets, or any other pipes you desire. The built-in function `clojure.java.io/writer` is a versatile constructor for output streams:

```
;; Create a writer to file foo.txt and print to it.
(def foo-file (clojure.java.io/writer "foo.txt"))
(binding [*out* foo-file]
  (println "Foo, bar."))

;; Nothing is printed to *out*.

;; And of course, close the file.
(.close foo-file)
```

## See Also

- `pr`'s documentation (*http://bit.ly/clojure-pr*) and source (*http://bit.ly/clojure-pr-source*) to get a better idea of how `*out*`-based printing works
- `clojure.java.io/writer`'s documentation (*http://bit.ly/java-io-writer*) for more information on creating writers

# 4.2. Reading a Single Keystroke from the Console

by John Jacobsen

## Problem

Console input via `stdin` is normally buffered by lines; you want to read a single, unbuffered keystroke from the console.

## Solution

Use `ConsoleReader` from the JLine library (*https://github.com/jline/jline2*), a Java library for handling console input.

JLine is similar to BSD editline and GNU readline. To follow along with this recipe, create a new library using the command **`lein new keystroke`**. Inside *project.clj*, add `[jline "2.11"]` to the `:dependencies` vector.

Inside the *src/keystroke/core.clj* file, use `ConsoleReader` to read characters from the terminal:

```
(ns keystroke.core
  (:import [jline.console ConsoleReader]))

(defn show-keystroke []
  (print "Enter a keystroke: ")
  (flush)
  (let [cr (ConsoleReader.)
        keyint (.readCharacter cr)]
    (println (format "Got %d ('%c')!" keyint (char keyint)))))
```

## Discussion

As in most languages, console I/O in Java is buffered; `flush` writes the initial prompt to the standard output stream. However, input is buffered as well by default. The JLine library provides a `ConsoleReader` object whose `readCharacter` method lets you avoid the input buffering. Beware, however, of testing `show-keystroke` at the REPL:

```
$ lein repl
user=> (require '[keystroke.core :refer [show-keystroke]])
user=> (show-keystroke)
Enter a keystroke:
;; HANGS!
```

In order to connect the console's input correctly to the REPL, use **`lein trampoline repl`** (the `<r>` here means the user types the letter `r`):

```
$ lein trampoline repl
user=> (require '[keystroke.core :refer [show-keystroke]])
```

```
user=> (show-keystroke)
Enter a keystroke: <r>Got 114 ('r')!
nil
user=>
```

`lein trampoline` is necessary because, by default, a Leiningen REPL actually runs the REPL and its associated console I/O in a separate JVM process from your application code. Using the `trampoline` option forces Leiningen to run your code in the same process as the REPL, "trampolining" control back and forth. Normally this is invisible, but it is a problem when running code that itself is attempting to use the console directly.

When running your program outside the REPL (as you typically would be, with a command-line application written in Clojure), this is not an issue.

## See Also

- If you want a richer terminal-based interface similar to what the C *curses* library provides, the `clojure-lanterna` (*http://bit.ly/clj-lanterna*) library may be a good place to start.

# 4.3. Executing System Commands

by Mark Whelan and Ryan Neufeld

## Problem

You want to send a command to the underlying operating system and get its output.

## Solution

Use the `clj-commons-exec` library to run shell commands on your local system.

To follow along, start a REPL using `lein-try`:

```
$ lein try org.clojars.hozumi/clj-commons-exec "1.0.6"
```

Invoking the `clj-commons-exec/exec` function with a command will return a promise, eventually delivering a map of the command's output, exit status, and any errors that occurred (available via the `:out`, `:exit`, and `:err` keys, respectively):

```
(require '[clj-commons-exec :as exec])

(def p (exec/sh ["date"]))

(deref p)
;; -> {:exit 0, :out "Sun Dec  1 19:43:49 EST 2013\n", :err nil}
```

If your command requires options or arguments, simply append them to the command vector as strings:

```
@(exec/sh ["ls" "-l" "/etc/passwd"])
;; -> {:exit 0
;;     :out "-rw-r--r--  1 root  wheel  4962 May 27 07:54 /etc/passwd\n"
;;     :err nil}

@(exec/sh ["ls" "-l" "nosuchfile"])
;; -> {:exit 1
;;     :out nil
;;     :err "ls: nosuchfile: No such file or directory\n"
;;     :exception #<ExecuteException ... Process exited with an error: 1 ...)>}
```

## Discussion

Up until this point, we've neglected to mention that functionality equivalent to `exec/sh` already exists in Clojure proper (as `clojure.java.shell/sh`). Now that the cat is out of the bag, it must be asked: why use a library over a built-in? Simple: `clj-commons-exec` is a functional veneer over the excellent Apache Commons Exec (*http://bit.ly/commons-exec*) library, providing capabilities like *piping* not available in `clojure.java.sh`.

To pipe data through multiple commands, use the `clj-commons-exec/sh-pipe` function. Just as with regular Unix pipes, pairs of commands will have their `STDOUT` and `STDIN` streams bound to each other. The API of `sh-pipe` is nearly identically to that of `sh`, the only notable exception being that you will pass more than one command to `sh-pipe`. The return value of `sh-pipe` is a list of promises that fulfill as each subcommand completes execution:

```
(def results (exec/sh-pipe ["cat"] ["wc" "-w"] {:in "Hello, world!"}))

results
;; -> (#<core$promise$reify__6310@71eed8d: {:exit 0, :out nil, :err nil}>
;;     #<core$promise$reify__6310@7f7dc7a1: {:exit 0,
;;                                           :out "       2\n",
;;                                           :err nil}>)

@(last results)
;; -> {:exit 0, :out "       2\n", :err nil}
```

Like any reasonable shell-process library, `clj-commons-exec` allows you to configure the environment in which your commands execute. To control the execution environment of either `sh` or `sh-pipe`, specify options in a map as the final argument to either function. The `:dir` option controls the path on which a command executes:

```
(println (:out @(exec/sh ["ls"] {:dir "/"})))
;; *out*
Applications
```

```
Library
# ...
usr
var
```

The `:env` and `:add-env` options control the environment variables available to the executing command. `:add-env` appends variables to the existing set of environment variables, while `:env` replaces the existing set with a completely new one. Each option is a map of variable names to values, like `{"USER" "jeff"}`:

```
@(exec/sh ["printenv" "HOME"])
;; -> {:exit 0, :out "/Users/ryan\n", :err nil}

@(exec/sh ["printenv" "HOME"] {:env {}})
;; -> {:exit 1, :out nil, :err nil, :exception #<ExecuteException ..)>}

@(exec/sh ["printenv" "HOME"] {:env {"HOME" "/Users/jeff"}})
;; -> {:exit 0, :out "/Users/jeff\n", :err nil}
```

There are a number of other options available in `sh` and `sh-pipe`:

`:watchdog`
: The time in number of seconds to wait for a command to finish executing before terminating it

`:shutdown`
: A flag indicating that subprocesses should be destroyed when the VM exits

`:as-success` *and* `:as-successes`
: An integer or sequence of integers that will be considered successful exit codes, respectively

`:result-handler-fn`
: A custom function to be used to handle results

If you initiate long-running subprocesses inside of a `-main` function, your application will hang until those processes complete. If this isn't desirable, forcibly terminate your application by invoking `(System/exit)` directly at the end of your `-main` function. Additionally, set the option `:shutdown` to `true` for any subprocesses to ensure you leave your system tidy and free of rogue processes.

To check if a subprocess has returned without waiting for it to finish, invoke the `realized?` function on the promise returned by `sh` (this is especially useful for monitoring the progress of the sequence of promises returned by `sh-pipe`):

```
;; Any old long-running command
(def p (exec/sh ["sleep" "5"]))
```

```
(realized? p)
;; -> false

;; A few seconds later...
(realized? p)
;; -> true
```

## See Also

- If you don't need piping or `clj-common-execs` advanced features, consider using `clojure.java.shell` (*http://bit.ly/clj-java-shell-api*)

# 4.4. Accessing Resource Files

by John Jacobsen, with help from John Cromartie and Alex Petrov

## Problem

You want to include a resource file from the classpath in your Clojure project.

## Solution

Place resource files in the *resources/* directory at the top level of your Leiningen project. To follow along with this recipe, create a new project with the command **`lein new people`**.

For example, suppose you have a file *resources/people.edn* with the following contents:

```
[{:first-name "John", :last-name "McCarthy", :language "Lisp"}
 {:first-name "Guido", :last-name "Van Rossum", :language "Python"}
 {:first-name "Rich", :last-name "Hickey", :language "Clojure"}]
```

Pass the name of the file (relative to the *resources* directory) to the `clojure.java.io/resource` function to obtain an instance of `java.io.File`, which you can then read as you please (for example, using the `slurp` function):

```
(require '[clojure.java.io :as io]
         '[clojure.edn :as edn])

(->> "people.edn"
     io/resource
     slurp
     edn/read-string
     (map :language))
;; -> ("Lisp" "Python" "Clojure")
```

## Discussion

Resources are commonly used to store any kind of file that is logically a part of your application, but is not code.

Resources are loaded via the Java classpath, just like Clojure code is. Leiningen puts the *resources/* directory on the classpath automatically whenever it starts a Java process, and when packaged, the contents of *resources/* are copied to the root of any emitted JAR files.

You can also specify an alternative (or additional) resource directory using the `:resources-paths` key in your *project.clj*:

```
:resource-paths ["my-resources" "src/other-resources"]
```

Using classpath-based resources is very convenient, but it does have its drawbacks.

Be aware that in the context of a web application, any change to resources is likely to require a full redeployment, because they are included wholesale in the JAR or WAR file that will be deployed. Typically, this means it's best to use resources only for items that really are completely static. For example, though it's possible to place your application's configuration files in the *resources/* directory and load them from there, to do so is really to make them part of your application's source code, which rather defeats the purpose. You may wish to load that kind of (relatively) frequently changing resource in a known filesystem location and load from there instead, rather than using the classpath.

Also, there are sometimes additional reasons to *not* serve from the classpath. For example, consider static images on a website. If you place them in your web application's classpath, then they will be served by your application server container (Jetty, Tomcat, JBoss, etc.). Typically, these applications are optimized for serving dynamic HTML resources, not larger binary blobs. Serving larger static files is often more suited to the *HTTP server* level of your architecture than the *application server* level, and should be delegated to Apache, Nginx, or whatever other HTTP server you're using. Or, you might even want to split them off and serve them via a separate mechanism entirely, such as a content delivery network (CDN). In either case, it is difficult to set up the HTTP server or CDN to introspect resources *inside* of your application's JAR file—it's usually better to store them elsewhere, from the start.

## See Also

- The Leiningen `sample.project.clj` (*http://bit.ly/lein-sample*), which includes a more detailed description of how the `:resource-paths` option works
- Recipe 4.14, "Reading and Writing Clojure Data" on page 190

# 4.5. Copying Files

by Stefan Karlsson

## Problem

You need to copy a file on your local filesystem.

## Solution

Invoke `clojure.java.io/copy`, passing it the source and destination files:

```
(clojure.java.io/copy
  (clojure.java.io/file "./file-to-copy.txt")
  (clojure.java.io/file "./my-new-copy.txt"))
;; -> nil
```

If the input file is not found, a `java.io.FileNotFoundException` will be thrown:

```
(clojure.java.io/copy
  (clojure.java.io/file "./file-do-not-exist.txt")
  (clojure.java.io/file "./my-new-copy.txt"))
;; -> java.io.FileNotFoundException
```

The input argument to `copy` doesn't have to be a file; it can be an `InputStream`, a `Reader`, a byte array, or a string. This makes it easier to copy the data you are working with directly to the output file:

```
(clojure.java.io/copy "some text" (clojure.java.io/file "./str-test.txt"))
;; -> nil
```

If required, an encoding can be specified by the `:encoding` option:

```
(clojure.java.io/copy "some text"
                      (clojure.java.io/file "./str-test.txt")
                      :encoding "UTF-8")
```

## Discussion

Note that if the file already exists, it will be overwritten. If that is not what you want, you can put together a "safe" copy function that will catch any exceptions and optionally overwrite:

```
(defn safe-copy [source-path destination-path & opts]
  (let [source (clojure.java.io/file source-path)
        destination (clojure.java.io/file destination-path)
        options (merge {:overwrite false} (apply hash-map opts))] ; ❶
    (if (and (.exists source)                                     ; ❷
             (or (:overwrite options)
                 (= false (.exists destination))))
```

```
      (try
        (= nil (clojure.java.io/copy source destination))       ; ❸
        (catch Exception e (str "exception: " (.getMessage e))))
      false)))

(safe-copy "./file-to-copy.txt" "./my-new-copy.txt")
;; -> true
(safe-copy "./file-to-copy.txt" "./my-new-copy.txt")
;; -> false
(safe-copy "./file-to-copy.txt" "./my-new-copy.txt" :overwrite true)
;; -> true
```

The `safe-copy` function takes the source and destination file paths to copy from and to. It also takes a number of key/value pairs as options.

❶ These options are then merged with the default values. In this example, there is only one option, `:overwrite`, but with this structure for optional arguments, you can easily add your own (such as `:encoding` if needed).

❷ After the options have been processed, the function checks whether the destination file exists, and if so, if it should be overwritten. If all is OK, it will then perform the `copy` inside a `try-catch` body.

❸ Note the equality check against `nil` for when the file is copied. If you add this, you will always get a Boolean value from the function. This makes the function more convenient to use, since you can then conditionally check whether the operation succeed or not.

You can also use `clojure.java.io/copy` with a `java.io.Reader` and a `java.io.Writer`, as well as with streams:

```
(with-open [reader (clojure.java.io/reader "file-to-copy.txt")
            writer (clojure.java.io/writer "my-new-copy.txt")]
  (clojure.java.io/copy reader writer))
```

The same efficiency considerations that apply to reading and writing to a file in regard to selecting input and output sources from `File`, `Reader`, `Writer`, or streams should be applied to `copy`. See Recipe 4.9, "Reading and Writing Text Files" on page 181, for more information.

By default, a buffer size of 1,024 bytes is used when calling `copy`. That is the amount of data that will be read from the source and written to the destination in one pass. This is done until the complete source has been copied. The buffer size used can be changed with the `:buffer-size` option. Keeping this number low would cause more file access operations but would keep less data in memory. On the other hand, increasing the buffer size will lower the number of file accesses but will require more data to be loaded into memory.

## See Also

- `clojure.java.io`'s API documentation (*http://bit.ly/clj-java-io-api*)

# 4.6. Deleting Files or Directories

by Stefan Karlsson

## Problem

You need to delete a file from your local filesystem.

## Solution

Use `clojure.java.io/delete-file` to delete the file:

```
(clojure.java.io/delete-file "./file-to-delete.txt")
;; -> true
```

If you're trying to delete a file that does not exist, a `java.io.IOException` will be thrown:

```
(clojure.java.io/delete-file "./file-that-does-not-exist.txt")
;; -> java.io.IOException: Couldn't delete
```

If you do not want `delete-file` to throw exceptions when the given file could not be deleted for whatever reason, you can add the `silently` flag set to `true` to the arguments:

```
(clojure.java.io/delete-file "./file-that-does-not-exist.txt" true)
;; -> true
```

## Discussion

For times when you want to do some custom handling of the eventual exceptions thrown, you should put the call to `delete-file` inside a `try-catch` body:

```
(try
  (clojure.java.io/delete-file "./file-that-does-not-exist.txt")
  (catch Exception e (str "exception: " (.getMessage e))))
;; -> "exception: Couldn't delete ./file-that-does-not-exist.txt"
```

`java.io.File` has an `.exists` property that simply gives you a Boolean answer as to whether a file exists or not. You can put this property together with a `try-catch` body to get a "safe" delete utility function. This function will first check to see if the file with the path from the argument exists before trying to delete it:

```
(defn safe-delete [file-path]
  (if (.exists (clojure.java.io/file file-path))
    (try
      (clojure.java.io/delete-file file-path)
```

```
      (catch Exception e (str "exception: " (.getMessage e))))
    false))

(safe-delete "./file-that-does-not-exist.txt")
;; -> false
(safe-delete "./file-to-delete.txt")
;; -> true
```

The `clojure.java.io/delete-file` function can also be used to delete directories. Directories must be empty for the deletion to be successful, so any utility function you make to delete a directory must first delete all files in the given directory:

```
(clojure.java.io/delete-file "./dir-to-delete")
;; -> false

(defn delete-directory [directory-path]
  (let [directory-contents (file-seq (clojure.java.io/file directory-path))
        files-to-delete (filter #(.isFile %) directory-contents)]
    (doseq [file files-to-delete]
      (safe-delete (.getPath file)))
    (safe-delete directory-path)))

(delete-directory "./dir-to-delete")
;; -> true
```

The `delete-directory` function will get a `file-seq` with the contents of the given path. It will then filter to only get the files of that directory. The next step is to delete all the files, and then finish up by deleting the directory itself. Note the call to `doall`. If you do not call `doall`, the deletion of the files would be lazy and then the files would still exist when the call to delete the actual directory was made, so that call would fail.

## See Also

- `clojure.java.io`'s API documentation (*http://bit.ly/clj-java-io-api*)
- Recipe 4.7, "Listing Files in a Directory" on page 178, for more details on using a `file-seq` to get the files from a directory

# 4.7. Listing Files in a Directory

by Ryan Neufeld and Stefan Karlsson

## Problem

Given a directory, you want to access the files inside.

## Solution

Call the built-in `file-seq` function.

To follow along with this recipe, create some sample files and folders using these commands (on Linux or Mac):

```
$ mkdir -p next-gen
$ touch next-gen/picard.jpg next-gen/locutus.bmp next-gen/data.txt
```

`file-seq` returns a lazy sequence of `java.io.File` objects:

```
(def tng-dir (file-seq (clojure.java.io/file "./next-gen")))

tng-dir
;; -> (#<File ./next-gen>
;;     #<File ./next-gen/picard.jpg>
;;     #<File ./next-gen/locutus.bmp>
;;     #<File ./next-gen/data.txt>)
```

## Discussion

Sequences are one of Clojure's more powerful abstractions; treating a directory hierarchy as a sequence allows you to leverage functions like `map` and `filter` to manipulate files and directories.

Consider, for example, the case where you would like to select only files in a directory hierarchy (and not directories). You can define such a function by taking a sequence of files and directories and filtering them by the `.isFile` property of `java.io.File` objects:

```
(defn only-files
  "Filter a sequence of files/directories by the .isFile property of
  java.io.File"
  [file-s]
  (filter #(.isFile %) file-s))

(only-files tng-dir)
;; -> (#<File ./next-gen/data.txt>
;;     #<File ./next-gen/locutus.bmp>
;;     #<File ./next-gen/picard.jpg>)
```

What if you want to display the string names of all those files? Define a `names` function to map the `.getName` property over a sequence of files, combining `only-files` and `names` to get a list of filenames in a directory:

```
(defn names
  "Return the .getName property of a sequence of files"
  [file-s]
  (map #(.getName %) file-s))
```

```
(-> tng-dir
    only-files
    names)
;; -> ("data.txt" "locutus.bmp" "picard.jpg")
```

## See Also

- The documentation for the `File` class (*http://bit.ly/javadoc-file*) for a complete list of properties and methods available on `File` objects.
- Combine these techniques with utility libraries like Google Guava's `Files` class (*http://bit.ly/guava-files*) or Apache Commons `FilenameUtils` class (*http://bit.ly/commons-io-filename-utils*) to exert even greater leverage over the file sequence abstraction.

# 4.8. Memory Mapping a File

by Alan Busby

## Problem

You want to use memory mapping to access a large file as though it were fully loaded into memory, without actually loading the whole thing.

## Solution

Use the `clj-mmap` (*https://github.com/thebusby/clj-mmap*) library, which wraps the memory-mapping functionality provided by Java's NIO (New I/O) library.

Before starting, add `[clj-mmap "1.1.2"]` to your project's dependencies or start a REPL using `lein-try`:

```
$ lein try clj-mmap
```

To read the first and last *N* bytes of UTF-8 encoded text file, use the `get-bytes` function:

```
(require '[clj-mmap :as mmap])

(with-open [file (mmap/get-mmap "/path/to/file/file.txt")]
  (let [n-bytes       10
        file-size     (.size file)
        first-n-bytes (mmap/get-bytes file 0 n-bytes)
        last-n-bytes  (mmap/get-bytes file (- file-size n-bytes) n-bytes)]
    [(String. first-n-bytes "UTF-8")
     (String. last-n-bytes  "UTF-8")]))
```

To overwrite the first *N* bytes of a text file, call `put-bytes`:

```
(with-open [file (mmap/get-mmap "/path/to/file/file.txt")]
  (let [bytes-to-write (.getBytes "New text goes here" "UTF-8")
        file-size      (.size file)]
    (if (> file-size
           (alength bytes-to-write))
      (mmap/put-bytes file bytes-to-write 0))))
```

## Discussion

Memory mapping, or *mmap* per the POSIX standard, is a method of leveraging the operating system's virtual memory to perform file I/O. By mapping the file into the applications memory space, copying between buffers is reduced, and I/O performance is increased.

Memory-mapped files are especially useful when working with large files, structured binary data, or text files where Java's `String` overhead may be unwelcome.

While Clojure makes it simple to work with Java's NIO primitives directly, NIO makes working with files larger than 2 GB especially difficult. `clj-mmap` wraps this complexity, but it doesn't expose all the features that NIO does. The NIO Java API is still available via interop, should it be needed.

## See Also

- The `mmap` Wikipedia article (*http://bit.ly/wiki-mmap*)
- The `clj-mmap` GitHub repository (*https://github.com/thebusby/clj-mmap*)

# 4.9. Reading and Writing Text Files

by Stefan Karlsson

## Problem

You need to read or write a text file to the local filesystem.

## Solution

Write a string to a file with the built-in `spit` function:

```
(spit "stuff.txt" "my stuff")
```

Read the contents of a file with the built-in `slurp` function:

```
(slurp "stuff.txt")
;; -> "all my stuff"
```

If required, an encoding can be specified with the `:encoding` option:

```
(slurp "stuff.txt" :encoding "UTF-8")
;; -> "all my stuff"
```

Append data to an existing file using the `:append true` option to `spit`:

```
(spit "stuff.txt" "even more stuff" :append true)
```

To read a file line by line, instead of loading the entire contents into memory at once, use a `java.io.Reader` together with the `line-seq` function:

```
(with-open [r (clojure.java.io/reader "stuff.txt")]
  (doseq [line (line-seq r)]
    (println line)))
```

To write a large amount of data to a file without realizing it all as a string, use a `java.io.Writer`:

```
(with-open [w (clojure.java.io/writer "stuff.txt")]
  (doseq [line some-large-seq-of-strings]
    (.write w line)
    (.newLine w)))
```

## Discussion

When using `:append`, text will be appended to the end of the file. Use newlines at the end of each line by appending `"\n"` to the string to be printed. All lines in a text file should end with a newline, including the last one:

```
(defn spitn
  "Append to file with newline"
  [path text]
  (spit path (str text "\n") :append true)
```

When used with strings, `spit` and `slurp` deal with the entire contents of a file at a time and close the file after reading or writing. If you need to read or write a lot of data, it is more efficient (in terms of both memory and time) to use a streaming API such as `java.io.Reader` or `java.io.Writer`, since they do not require realizing the contents of the file in memory.

When using writers and streams, however, it is important to flush any writes to the underlying stream in order to ensure your data is actually written and resources are cleaned up. The `with-open` macro flushes and closes the stream specified in its binding after executing its body.

Be especially aware that any lazy sequences based on a stream will throw an error if the underlying stream is closed before the sequence is realized. Even when using `with-open`, it is possible to return an unrealized lazy sequence; the `with-open` macro has no way of knowing that the stream is still needed and so will close it anyway, leaving a sequence that cannot be realized.

Generally, it is best to not let lazy sequences based on streams escape the scope in which the stream is open. If you do, you must be extremely careful to ensure that the resources required for the realization of a lazy sequence are still open as long as the sequence has any readers. Typically, the latter approach involves manually tracking which streams are still open rather than relying on a `try/finally` or `with-open` block.

## See Also

- Recipe 4.14, "Reading and Writing Clojure Data" on page 190
- The documentation for `java.io.Reader` (*http://bit.ly/javadoc-reader*) and `java.io.Writer` (*http://bit.ly/javadoc-writer*)

# 4.10. Using Temporary Files

by Alan Busby

## Problem

You want to use a temporary file on the local filesystem.

## Solution

Use the static method `createTempFile` of Java's built-in `java.io.File` class to create a temporary file in the default temporary-file directory of the JVM, with the provided prefix and suffix:

```
(def my-temp-file (java.io.File/createTempFile "filename" ".txt"))
```

You can then write to the temporary file like you would to any other instance of `java.io.File`:

```
(with-open [file (clojure.java.io/writer my-temp-file)]
  (binding [*out* file]
    (println "Example output.")))
```

## Discussion

Temporary files are often quite useful to interact with other programs that prefer a file-based API. Using `createTempFile` is important to ensure that temporary files are placed in an appropriate location on the filesystem, which can differ based on the operating system being used.

To get the full path and filename for the created temporary file:

```
(.getAbsolutePath my-temp-file)
```

You can use the `File.deleteOnExit` method to mark the temporary file to be deleted automatically when the JVM exits:

```
(.deleteOnExit my-temp-file)
```

Note that the file is not actually deleted until the JVM terminates and may not be deleted if the process crashes or exits abnormally. It is good practice to delete temporary files immediately when they are no longer being used:

```
(.delete my-temp-file)
```

## See Also

- The `java.io.File` API documentation (*http://bit.ly/javadoc-file*)

# 4.11. Reading and Writing Files at Arbitrary Positions

by John Jacobsen

## Problem

You want to read data from a file, or write data to it, at various locations rather than sequentially.

## Solution

To open a (potentially very large) file for random access, use Java's `RandomAccessFile`. `seek` to the location you desire, then use the various `write` methods to write data at that location.

For example, to make a 1 GB file filled with zeros except the integer 1,234 at the end:

```
(import '[java.io RandomAccessFile])

(doto (RandomAccessFile. "/tmp/longfile" "rw")
  (.seek (* 1000 1000 1000))
  (.writeInt 1234)
  (.close))
```

Getting the `length` of a "normal" Java file object shows that the file is the correct size:

```
(require '[clojure.java.io :refer [file]])
(.length (file "/tmp/longfile"))

;; -> 1000000004
```

(You can also call `length` on a `RandomAccessFile` directly.)

Reading a value back from the proper location in Clojure is quite similar to writing. Again, `seek` a `RandomAccessFile`. Then use the appropriate `read` method:

```
(let [raf (RandomAccessFile. "/tmp/longfile" "r")
      _ (.seek raf (* 1000 1000 1000))
      result (.readInt raf)]
  (.close raf)
  result)

;; -> 1234
```

## Discussion

Files written in this way are populated by zeros by default and may be treated as "sparse files" by the JVM implementation and the underlying operating system, leading to extra efficiency in reading and writing.

Examining the file we created using the Unix od program to do a hex dump from the command line shows that the file consists of zeros with our `1234` at the end:

```
$ od -Ad -tx4 /tmp/longfile
0000000          00000000        00000000        00000000        00000000
*
1000000000          d2040000
1000000004
```

At byte offset 1000000000 can be seen the value `d2040000`, which is the hex representation of a big-endian integer with the value 1,234. (Java integers are big-endian by default. This means that the highest-order bytes are stored at the lowest addresses.)

## See Also

- Recipe 4.14, "Reading and Writing Clojure Data" on page 190, for information on reading entire files
- The `java.io.RandomAccessFile` (*http://bit.ly/javadoc-raf*) API documentation
- The Unix od (*http://bit.ly/wiki-od*) command

# 4.12. Parallelizing File Processing

by Edmund Jackson

## Problem

You want to transform a text file line by line, but using all cores and without loading it into memory.

## Solution

A quick win using `pmap` over a sequence returned by `line-seq`:

```
(require ['clojure.java.io :as 'jio])

(defn pmap-file
  "Process input-file in parallel, applying processing-fn to each row
  outputting into output-file"
  [processing-fn input-file output-file]
  (with-open [rdr (jio/reader input-file)
              wtr (jio/writer output-file)]
    (let [lines (line-seq rdr)]
      (dorun
       (map #(.write wtr %)
            (pmap processing-fn lines))))))

;; Example of calling this
(def accumulator (atom 0))

(defn- example-row-fn
  "Trivial example"
  [row-string]
  (str row-string "," (swap! accumulator inc) "\n"))

;; Call it
(pmap-file example-row-fn "input.txt" "output.txt")
```

## Discussion

The key functions used in this example (beyond basic Clojure constructs like `map` or `dorun`) are `line-seq` and `pmap`.

`line-seq`, given an instance of `java.io.BufferedReader` (which `clojure.java.io/reader` returns), will return a lazy sequence of strings. Each string is a line in the input file. What constitutes a newline for the purposes of line splitting is determined by the `line.separator` JVM option, which will be set in a platform-specific way. Specifically, it will be a carriage return character followed by a line feed character in Windows, and a single newline character in Unix-derived systems such as Linux or Mac OS X.

`pmap` functions identically to `map` and applies a function to each item in a sequence, returning a lazy sequence of return values. The difference is that as it applies the mapping function, it does so in a separate thread for each item in the collection (up to a certain fixed number of threads related to the number of CPUs on your system). Threads realizing the sequence will block if the values are not ready yet.

`pmap` can yield substantial performance improvements by distributing work across multiple CPU cores and performing it concurrently, but it isn't a magic bullet. Specifically, it incurs a certain amount of coordination overhead to schedule the multithreaded operations. Typically, it gives the most benefit when performing very heavyweight operations, where the mapping function is so computationally expensive that it makes the coordination overhead worth it. For simple functions that complete very quickly (such as basic operations on primitives), the coordination overhead is likely to be much larger than any performance gains, and `pmap` will actually be much slower than `map` in that case.

The idea is to use `pmap` to map over the sequence of file rows in parallel. However, you then need to pass each processed row through `(map #(.write wtr %) ...)` in order to ensure the rows are written one at a time (put the `write` in the processing function to see what happens otherwise). Finally, as these are lazy sequences, you need to realize their side effects before exiting the `with-open` block or the file will be closed by the time you wish to evaluate them. This is accomplished by calling `dorun`.

There are a couple of caveats here. Firstly, although the row ordering of the output file will match that of the input, the execution order is not guaranteed. Secondly, the process will become I/O-bound quite quickly as all the writes happen on one thread, so you may not get the speedup you expect unless the processing function is substantial. Finally, `pmap` is not perfectly efficient at allocating work, so the degree of speedup you see might not correspond exactly to the number of processors on your system, as you might expect.

Another drawback to the `pmap` approach is that the actual reading of the file is serialized, using a single `java.io.Reader`. Considerable gains can still be realized if the processing task is expensive compared to reading, but in lightweight tasks the bottleneck is likely to be reading the file itself, in which case parallelizing the processing work will give little to no gains in terms of total runtime (or even make it worse).

## See Also

- Recipe 4.13, "Parallelizing File Processing with Reducers" on page 187, for a similar approach that parallelizes reading the file itself using memory mapping (as well as using Clojure reducers for greater efficiency)

# 4.13. Parallelizing File Processing with Reducers

by Edmund Jackson

## Problem

You want to use Clojure's reducers on a file to realize parallel processing without loading the file into memory.

## Solution

Use the Iota (*https://github.com/thebusby/iota*) library in conjunction with the `filter`, `map`, and `fold` functions from the Clojure Reducers library in the `clojure.core.reducers` namespace. To follow along with this recipe, add `[iota "1.1.1"]` to your project's dependencies, or start a REPL with `lein-try`:

```
$ lein try iota
```

To count the words in a very large file, for example:

```
(require '[iota                  :as io]
         '[clojure.core.reducers :as r]
         '[clojure.string        :as str])


;; Word-counting functions
(defn count-map
  "Returns a map of words to occurence count in the given string"
  [s]
  (reduce (fn [m w] (update-in m [w] (fnil (partial inc) 0)))
          {}
          (str/split s #" ")))

(defn add-maps
  "Returns a map where each key is the sum of vals of that key in m1 and m2."
  ([] {}) ;; Necessary base case for use as combiner in fold
  ([m1 m2]
     (reduce (fn [m [k v]] (update-in m [k] (fnil (partial + v) 0))) m1 m2)))


;; Main file processing
(defn keyword-count
  "Returns a map of the word counts"
  [filename]
  (->> (iota/seq filename)
       (r/filter identity)
       (r/map count-map)
       (r/fold add-maps)))
```

## Discussion

The Iota library creates sequences from files on the local filesystem. Unlike the purely sequential lazy sequences produced from something like `file-seq`, the sequences returned by Iota are optimized for use with Clojure's Reducers library, which uses the Java Fork/Join work-stealing framework[1] under the hood to provide efficient parallel processing.

1. For more information, see the Java tutorial (*http://bit.ly/forkjoin-tut*) on Fork/Join and work stealing.

The `keyword-count` function first creates a reducible sequence of lines in the file and filters out blank lines (using the `identity` function to eliminate `nil` values from the sequence). Then it applies the `count-map` function in parallel, and finally aggregates the results by folding with the `add-maps` function.

`r/filter` and `r/map` function exactly the same as their non-Reducer counterparts; the only difference is one of performance, and how the Reducers library is able to break down and combine operations. They also return reducible sequences that can be utilized efficiently by other operations from the Reducers library.

`r/fold` is the core function of the Reducers library, and in its basic form it is functionally very similar to the built-in `reduce` function. Given a function and a reducible collection, it returns a value that is the result of applying the folding function to each item in the collection and an accumulator value.

Unlike with normal `reduce`, however, there is no guaranteed execution order, which is why `fold` doesn't take a single starting value as an argument. It wouldn't make sense, given that the computation can "start" in several places at once, concurrently. This means that the function passed to `fold` (when passed a single function) must also be capable of taking *zero* arguments—the result of the no-arg invocation of the provided function will be used as the seed value for each branch of the computation.

If you need more flexibility than this provides, `fold` allows you to specify both a `reduce` function and a `combine` function, as separate arguments. Exactly what these do is inextricably tied to how Reducers themselves work, so a full explanation is beyond the scope of this recipe. See the API documentation for the `fold` function (*http://bit.ly/reducers-fold-doc*) and the links on the Reducers page (*http://clojure.org/reducers*) on Clojure's website for more information.

### About Reducers

Reducers is a parallel execution framework for extremely efficient parallel processing. A full explanation of how reducers work is beyond the scope of this recipe (see the blog post (*http://bit.ly/reducers-post*) introducing reducers on the Clojure website for a comprehensive treatment).

In short, however, reducers provide performance by two means:

1. They can compose operations. Wherever logically possible, the reducers framework will collapse composable operations into a single operation. For example, the preceding code performs a `filter` and then a `map`. Clojure's standard `filter` and `map` would realize an intermediate sequence: `filter` would produce a sequence that would then be fed to `map`. The reducer versions, however, can compose themselves (if possible) to produce a single `map+filter` operation that can be applied in one shot.

2. They exploit the internal tree-like data structures of the data being reduced. Regular sequences are inherently sequential (no surprise), and because their performant operation is to pull items from the beginning one at a time, it's difficult to efficiently distribute work across their members. However, Reducers is aware of the internal structure of Clojure's persistent data structures and can leverage that to efficiently distribute worker processes across the data.

Under the hood, Iota uses the Java NIO libraries to provide a *memory-mapped* view of the file being processed that provides efficient random access. Iota is also aware of the Reducers framework, and Iota sequences are structured in such a way that Reducers can effectively distribute worker processes across them.

## See Also

- The Iota GitHub repository (*https://github.com/thebusby/iota*)
- NIO's documentation (*http://bit.ly/javadoc-nio*)

# 4.14. Reading and Writing Clojure Data

by John Cromartie

## Problem

You need to store and retrieve Clojure data structures on disk.

## Solution

Use `pr-str` and `spit` to serialize small amounts of data:

```
(spit "data.clj" (pr-str [:a :b :c]))
```

Use `read-string` and `slurp` to read small amounts of data:

```
(read-string (slurp "data.clj"))
;; -> [:a :b :c]
```

Use `pr` to efficiently write large data structures to a stream:

```
(with-open [w (clojure.java.io/writer "data.clj")]
  (binding [*out* w]
    (pr large-data-structure)))
```

Use `read` to efficiently read large data structures from a stream:

```
(with-open [r (java.io.PushbackReader. (clojure.java.io/reader "data.clj"))]
  (binding [*read-eval* false]
    (read r)))
```

## Discussion

The fact that code is data in Clojure and that you have runtime access to the same reader the language uses to load source code from files makes this a relatively simple task. However, while this is often a good way to persist data to disk, you should be aware of a few issues.

### Reading, Security, and edn

The `read` function is only appropriate for reading data from *trusted* sources. This is because the Clojure reader is neither designed nor guaranteed to be safe or free from side effects. Binding `*read-eval*` to `false` is just a small safeguard. If you need to read Clojure data structures from *untrusted* sources (i.e., anything you did not write yourself), then see the `clojure.edn` library.

edn (extensible data notation) is a specification of Clojure's data structure serialization format with multiple implementations, so it can be used as a transport and persistence format and consumed from programs written in any language, much like XML or JSON. The `clojure.edn` library is edn's implementation for Clojure.

It works much the same as the Clojure reader and writer; however, it provides additional security guarantees that the Clojure reader does not, and should always be used for any external or untrusted input.

The simple case of `slurp` and `spit` becomes unusable when the data is very large, because it creates a very large string in memory all at once. For instance, serializing one million random numbers (created with `rand`) results in an 18 MB file and consumes much more memory than that while reading or writing:

```
(spit "data.clj" (pr-str (repeatedly 1e6 rand)))
;; -> OutOfMemoryError Java heap space ...
```

But, if you know you are only dealing with a small amount of data, this approach is perfectly suitable. It is a good way to load configuration data and other types of simple structures.

Reading and writing from streams is far more efficient because it buffers input and output, dealing with data a few bytes at a time.[2]

In addition to reading and writing a single data structure in a file, you can also append additional data structures to the same file and read them back as a sequence later:

2. See Recipe 4.9, "Reading and Writing Text Files" on page 181, for notes on managing streams.

```
(spit "data.clj" (prn-str [1 2 3]))
(spit "data.clj" (prn-str [:a :b :c]) :append true)
;; data.clj now contains two serialized structures
```

This is useful for appending small amounts of data to a file over time, such as for an event or transaction log.

However `read-string` will not suffice for reading multiple objects from a single string. To read a series of objects from a stream, you must continue to call `read` until it has reached the end:

```
(defn- read-one
  [r]
  (try
    (read r)
    (catch java.lang.RuntimeException e
      (if (= "EOF while reading" (.getMessage e))
        ::EOF
        (throw e)))))

(defn read-seq-from-file
  "Reads a sequence of top-level objects in file at path."
  [path]
  (with-open [r (java.io.PushbackReader. (clojure.java.io/reader path))]
    (binding [*read-eval* false]
      (doall (take-while #(not= ::EOF %) (repeatedly #(read-one r)))))))
```

## See Also

- Recipe 4.4, "Accessing Resource Files" on page 173
- Recipe 4.15, "Using edn for Configuration Files" on page 192
- Recipe 4.17, "Handling Unknown Tagged Literals When Reading Clojure Data" on page 198

# 4.15. Using edn for Configuration Files

by Luke VanderHart

## Problem

You want to configure your application using Clojure-like data literals.

## Solution

Use Clojure data structures stored in edn files to define a map that contains configuration items you care about.

For example, the edn configuration of an application that needs to know its own hostname and connection info for a relational database might look something like this:

```
{:hostname "localhost"
 :database {:host "my.db.server"
            :port 5432
            :name "my-app"
            :user "root"
            :password "s00p3rs3cr3t"}}
```

The basic function to read this data into a Clojure map is trivial using the edn reader:

```
(require '[clojure.edn :as edn])

(defn load-config
  "Given a filename, load & return a config file"
  [filename]
  (edn/read-string (slurp filename)))
```

Invoking the newly defined `load-config` function will now return a configuration map that you can pass around and use in your application as you would any other map.

## Discussion

As can be seen from the preceding code, the basic process for obtaining a map containing configuration data is extremely trivial. A more interesting question is what to do with the config map once you have it, and there are two general schools of thought regarding the answer.

The first option prioritizes ease of development by making the configuration map ambiently available throughout the entire application. Usually this involves setting a global var to contain the configuration.

However, this is problematic for a number of reasons. First, it becomes more difficult to override the default configuration file in alternate contexts, such as tests, or when running two differently configured systems in the same JVM. (This can be worked around by using thread-local bindings, but this can lead to messy code fairly rapidly.)

More importantly, using a global configuration means that any function that reads the config (most functions, in a sizable application) *cannot be pure*. In Clojure, that is a lot to give up. One of the main benefits of pure Clojure code is its local transparency; the behavior of a function can be determined solely by looking at its arguments and its code. If every function reads a global variable, however, this becomes much more difficult.

The alternative is to explicitly pass around the config everywhere it is needed, like you would every other argument. Since a config file is usually supplied at application start, the config is usually established in the `-main` function and passed wherever else it is needed.

This sounds painful, and indeed it can be somewhat annoying to pass an extra argument to every function. Doing so, however, lends the code a large degree of self-documentation; it becomes extremely evident what parts of the application rely on the config and what parts do not. It also makes it more straightforward to modify the config at runtime or supply an alternative config in testing scenarios.

#### Using multiple config files

A common pattern when configuring an application is to have a number of different classes of configuration items. Some config fields are more or less constants, and don't vary between instances of the application in the same environment. These are often committed to source control along with the application's source code.

Other config items are fairly constant, but can't be checked into source control due to security concerns. Examples of this include database passwords or secure API tokens, and ideally these are put into a separate config file. Still other configuration fields (such as IP addresses) will often be completely different for every instance of a deployed application, and the desire is to specify those separately from the more constant config fields.

A useful technique to handle this heterogeneity is to use multiple configuration files, each handling a different type of concern, and then merge them into a single configuration map before passing it on to the application. This typically uses a simple `deep-merge` function:

```
(defn deep-merge
  "Deep merge two maps"
  [& values]
  (if (every? map? values)
    (apply merge-with deep-merge values)
    (last values)))
```

This will merge two maps, merging values as well if they are all maps. If the values are not all maps, the second one "wins" and is used in the resulting map.

Then, you can rewrite the config loader to accept multiple config files, and merge them together:

```
(defn load-config
  [& filenames]
  (reduce deep-merge (map (comp edn/read-string slurp)
                          filenames)))
```

Using this approach on two separate edn config files, *config-public.edn* and *config-private.edn*, yields a merged map.

*config-public.edn*:

```
{:hostname "localhost"
 :database {:host "my.db.server"
            :port 5432
            :name "my-app"
            :user "root"}}
```

*config-private.edn*:

```
{:database {:password "s3cr3t"}}
```

```
(load-config "config-public.edn" "config-private.edn")
;; -> {:hostname "localhost", :database {:password "s3cr3t",
;;     :host "my.db.server", :port 5432, :name "my-app", :user "root"}}
```

Be aware that any values present in both configuration files will be overridden by the "rightmost" file passed to `load-config`.

### Different configurations for different environments

If your system runs in multiple environments, you may want to vary your configuration based on the current running environment. For example, you may want to connect to a local database while developing your system, but a production database when running your system in production.

You can use Leiningen's *profiles* feature to achieve this end. By providing different `:resource-paths` options for each profile in your project's configuration, you can vary which configuration file is read per environment:[3]

```
(defproject my-great-app "0.1.0-SNAPSHOT"
  {;; ...
  :profiles {:dev {:resource-paths ["resources/dev"]}
             :prod {:resource-paths ["resources/prod"]}}})
```

With a project configuration similar to the previous one, you can then create two different configurations with the same base filename, *resources/dev/config.edn* and *resources/prod/config.edn*:

*resource/dev/config.edn*:

```
{:database-host "localhost"}
```

*resources/prod/config.edn*:

```
{:database-host "production.example.com"}
```

If you're following along on your own, add the `load-config` function to one of your project's namespaces:

3. To follow along, create your own project with **`lein new my-great-app`**.

```
(ns my-great-app.core
  (:require [clojure.edn :as edn]))

(defn load-config
    "Given a filename, load & return a config file"
    [filename]
    (edn/read-string  (slurp filename)))
```

Now, the configuration your application loads will depend on which profile your project is running in:

```
# "dev" is one of Leiningen's default profiles
$ lein repl
user=> (require '[my-great-app.core :refer [load-config]])
user=> (load-config (clojure.java.io/resource "config.edn"))
{:database-host "localhost"}
user=> (exit)

$ lein trampoline with-profile prod repl
user=> (require '[my-great-app.core :refer [load-config]])
user=> (load-config (clojure.java.io/resource "config.edn"))
{:database-host "production.example.com"}
```

## See Also


- Recipe 4.4, "Accessing Resource Files" on page 173
- Recipe 4.16, "Emitting Records as edn Values" on page 196
- Recipe 4.17, "Handling Unknown Tagged Literals When Reading Clojure Data" on page 198

- The Leiningen profiles tutorial (*http://bit.ly/lein-profiles-tut*)

# 4.16. Emitting Records as edn Values

by Steve Miner

## Problem

You want to use Clojure records as edn values, but the edn format doesn't support records.

## Solution

You can use the `tagged` library to read and print records as edn tagged literal values.

Before starting, add `[com.velisco/tagged "0.3.0"]` to your project's dependencies or start a REPL using `lein-try`:

```
$ lein try com.velisco/tagged
```

To extend Clojure's built-in `print-method` multimethod to print a record in a "tagged" format, extend `print-method` for that record with the `miner.tagged/pr-tagged-record-on` helper function:

```
(require '[miner.tagged :as tag])

(defrecord SimpleRecord [a])

(def forty-two (->SimpleRecord 42))

(pr-str forty-two)
;; -> "#user.SimpleRecord{:a 42}" ;; Sadly, not a proper edn value

(defmethod print-method user.SimpleRecord [this w]
  (tag/pr-tagged-record-on this w))

(pr-str forty-two)
;; -> "#user/SimpleRecord {:a 42}"
```

At this point, you can round-trip your records between `pr-str` and `miner.tagged/read-string` using the edn tagged literal format:

```
(tag/read-string (pr-str forty-two))
;; -> #user/SimpleRecord {:a 42}

(= forty-two
   (tag/read-string (pr-str forty-two)))
;; -> true
```

The edn reader still doesn't understand how to parse these tagged values, though. To enable this behavior, use `miner.tagged/tagged-default-reader` as the `:default` option when reading values with `edn`:

```
(require '[clojure.edn :as edn])

(edn/read-string {:default tag/tagged-default-reader}
                 (pr-str {:my-record forty-two}))
;; -> {:my-record #user/SimpleRecord {:a 42}}
```

## Discussion

The edn format is great—it covers a useful subset of the Clojure data types and makes high-fidelity data transfer a breeze. Unfortunately, it doesn't support records. This is easy enough to rectify, however; edn is an extensible format by name. We just need to provide tag-style printing (`#tag <value>`) and an appropriate reader. The `tagged` library makes both of these tasks quite easy.

As seen in the preceding samples, Clojure's default printed value for records is close to, but not quite the tagged format edn expects.

Where Clojure prints `"#user.SimpleRecord{:a 42}"` for a `SimpleRecord`, what is really needed for edn is a tag-style string like `""#user/SimpleRecord {:a 42}"`. The `miner.tagged/pr-tagged-record-on` function understands how to write records in this format (to a `java.io.Writer`). By extending Clojure's `print-method` multimethod with this function, you ensure Clojure always prints a record in a tagged format.

For reading these values back in, you need to tell the edn reader how to parse your new record tags. By design, the `tagged` library provides a `miner.tagged/tagged-default-reader` function that can be used to extend edn to read your record tags. When the edn reader can't parse a tag, it attempts to use a function specified by its `:default` option to rehydrate tags. By providing `tagged-default-reader` as this `:default` option, you allow the edn reader to properly interpret your tagged record values.

## See Also

- Recipe 4.17, "Handling Unknown Tagged Literals When Reading Clojure Data" on page 198, for more information on the `:default` option
- edn: extensible data notation (*https://github.com/edn-format/edn*) on GitHub

# 4.17. Handling Unknown Tagged Literals When Reading Clojure Data

by Steve Miner

## Problem

You want to read Clojure data (in an edn format) that may contain unknown tagged literals.

## Solution

Use the `:default` option of either `clojure.edn/read` or `clojure.edn/read-string`:

```
(require 'clojure.edn)

(defrecord TaggedValue [tag value])

(defn read-preserving-unknown-tags [s]
  (clojure.edn/read-string {:default ->TaggedValue} s))

(read-preserving-unknown-tags "#my.example/unknown 42")
;; -> #user.TaggedValue{:tag my.example/unknown, :value 42}
```

## Discussion

The edn format defines a print representation for a significant subset of Clojure data types and offers extensibility through tagged literals. The best way to read edn data is to use `clojure.edn/read` or `clojure.edn/read-string`. These functions consume edn-formatted data from a stream or string, respectively, and return hydrated Clojure data.

Both functions take an `opts` map, which allows you to control several options when reading. For tags you know about ahead of time, you can define custom readers by supplying a `:readers` map. This map can also be used to override the behavior of built-in types as defined by `clojure.core/default-data-readers`:

```
;; Creating a custom reader
(clojure.edn/read-string {:readers {'inc-this inc}}
                         "#inc-this 1")
;; -> 2

;; Overriding a built-in reader
;; Before..
(clojure.edn/read-string "#inst \"2013-06-08T01:00:00Z\"")
;; -> #inst "2013-06-08T01:00:00.000-00:00"

;; And after...
(clojure.edn/read-string {:readers {'inst str}}
                         "#inst \"2013-06-08T01:00:00Z\"")
;; -> "2013-06-08T01:00:00Z"
```

The `:default` option, as explored in the solution, is ideal for handling unknown tags. Whenever an unknown tag and value are encountered, the function you provide will be called with two arguments, the tag and its value.

When a `:default` is not provided to `read`, reading an unknown tag will throw a `RuntimeException`:

```
(clojure.edn/read-string "#blow-up boom")
;; -> RuntimeException No reader function for tag blow-up ...
```

For most applications, reading an unknown tag **is** an error, so an exception would be appropriate. However, it may sometimes be useful to preserve the "unknowns," perhaps for another stage of processing.

It's trivial to leverage the factory function defined by `defrecord` to capture the unknown reader literal. The order of the arguments for the factory of `TaggedValue` conveniently matches the specification of the `:default` data reader.

The `TaggedValue` record preserves the essential information for later use. Since all of the inbound information has been preserved, you can even print the value again in the original tagged literal format:

```
(defmethod print-method TaggedValue [this ^java.io.Writer w]
   (.write w "#")
   (print-method (:tag this) w)
   (.write w " ")
   (print-method (:value this) w))

;; Now, the TaggedValue will `pr` as the original tagged literal
(read-preserving-unknown-tags "#my.example/unknown 42")
;; -> #my.example/unknown 42
```

### clojure.core/read

The edn reader hasn't always existed, you know. It used to be that if you wanted to read Clojure data, you would use one of the two built-in reader functions, `clojure.core/read` and `clojure.core/read-string`. The purpose of these two functions is to read code or data from *trusted sources.*

Because these functions can execute code,[4] you should *never* (ever) use the `clojure.core` readers to read from untrusted sources. This means user data, remote servers (even your own), or pretty much anywhere else for that matter. (We're being a little extreme, of course, but we want you to be safe.)

In the event that you *do* have a safe environment and absolutely need to evaluate some code, then by all means use the `clojure.core` readers. These readers do have a different interface for setting options than `clojure.edn` readers, though; instead of passing an `opts`, you'll need to change various dynamic bindings to adjust the reader's behavior. For example, the `*default-data-reader-fn*` determines how the core functions deal with unknown tags. See also `*data-readers*` and `*read-eval*` (*http://clojure.github.io/tools.reader/*) for more information. That said, for reading data, it's generally better to use the edn variants.[5]

## See Also

- edn: extensible data notation (*https://github.com/edn-format/edn*) on GitHub
- Recipe 4.14, "Reading and Writing Clojure Data" on page 190, and Recipe 4.16, "Emitting Records as edn Values" on page 196

4. This is actually a feature—they're functions used by the language to, well, execute code.

5. The Clojure mailing list thread "ANN: NEVER use clojure.core/read or read-string for reading untrusted data" (*http://bit.ly/read-unsafe*) talks more about the vulnerabilities with `clojure.core` readers.

# 4.18. Reading Properties from a File

by Tobias Bayer

## Problem

You need to read a property file and access its key/value pairs.

## Solution

The most straightforward way is to use the built-in `java.util.Properties` (*http://bit.ly/javadoc-properties*) class via Java interop. `java.util.Properties` implements `java.util.Map`, which can be easily consumed from Clojure, just like any other map.

Here is an example property file to load, *fruitcolors.properties*:

```
banana=yellow
grannysmith=green
```

Populating an instance of `Properties` from a file is straightforward, using its `load` method and passing in an instance of `java.io.Reader` obtained using the `clojure.java.io` namespace:

```
(require '[clojure.java.io :refer (reader)])

(def props (java.util.Properties.))

(.load props (reader "fruitcolors.properties"))
;; -> nil

props
;; -> {"banana" "yellow", "grannysmith" "green"}
```

Instead of using the built-in `Properties` API via interop, you could also use the `propertea` library for simpler, more idiomatic Clojure access to property files.

Include the `[propertea "1.2.3"]` dependency in your *project.clj* file, or start a REPL using `lein-try`:

```
$ lein try propertea 1.2.3
```

Then read the property file and access its key/value pairs:

```
(require '[propertea.core :refer (read-properties)])

(def props (read-properties "fruitcolors.properties"))

props
;; -> {:grannysmith "green", :banana "yellow"}
```

```
(props :banana)
;; -> "yellow"
```

## Discussion

Although using `java.util.Properties` directly is more straightforward and doesn't require the addition of a dependency, `propertea` does provide some convenience. It returns an actual immutable Clojure map, instead of just a `java.util.Map`. Although both are perfectly usable from Clojure, an immutable map is probably preferable if you intend to do any further manipulation or updates on it.

More importantly, `propertea` converts all string keys into keywords, which are more commonly used than strings as the keys of maps in Clojure.

Additionally, `propertea` has several other features, such as the capability to parse values into numbers or Booleans, and providing default values.

By default, `propertea`'s `read-properties` function treats all property values as strings. Consider the following property file with an integer and Boolean key:

```
intkey=42
booleankey=true
```

You can force these properties to be parsed into their respective types by supplying lists for the `:parse-int` and `:parse-boolean` options:

```
(def props (read-properties "other.properties"
                            :parse-int [:intkey]
                            :parse-boolean [:booleankey]))

(props :intkey)
;; -> 42

(class (props :intkey))
;; -> java.lang.Integer

(props :booleankey)
;; -> true

(class (props :booleankey))
;; -> java.lang.Boolean
```

Sometimes the property file might not contain a key/value pair, and you might want to set a reasonable default value in this case:

```
(def props (read-properties "other.properties" :default [:otherkey "awesome"]))

(props :otherkey)
;; -> "awesome"
```

You can also be strict on required properties. If an expected property is missing in your property file, you can throw an exception:

```
(def props (read-properties "other.properties" :required [:otherkey]))
;; -> java.lang.RuntimeException: (:otherkey) are required ...
```

## See Also

- The `propertea` GitHub repository (*https://github.com/jaycfields/propertea*)
- The `Properties` API documentation (*http://bit.ly/javadoc-properties*)

# 4.19. Reading and Writing Binary Files

by John Jacobsen

## Problem

You need to read or write some binary data.

## Solution

Use Java's `BufferedInputStream`, `BufferedOutputStream`, and `ByteBuffer` classes to work directly with binary data.

## Discussion

While reading and writing text files (e.g., via `slurp` and `spit`) is easy in pure Clojure, writing binary data requires a little more Java interop.

Clojure's `output-stream` wraps the `BufferedOutputStream` Java object. `BufferedOutputStream` has a `write` method that accepts Java byte arrays. The following writes 1,000 zeros (bytes) to */tmp/zeros*:

```
(require '[clojure.java.io :refer [file output-stream input-stream]])

(with-open [out (output-stream (file "/tmp/zeros"))]
  (.write out (byte-array 1000)))
```

To read the bytes in again, use the corresponding `input-stream` function, which wraps `BufferedInputStream`:

```
(with-open [in (input-stream (file "/tmp/zeros"))]
  (let [buf (byte-array 1000)
        n (.read in buf)]
    (println "Read" n "bytes.")))

;;=> Read 1000 bytes.
```

Writing zeros and reading in fixed-length blocks is obviously not very interesting. We want to prepare our byte array with some actual content. A common way to prepare byte arrays is to use a `ByteBuffer`, filling it with data from various types. Let's assume we want to write "strings" in the following format:

1. A version number (byte; `66` in our example)
2. A string length (big-endian `int`)
3. The bytes for the string (in this case, "hello world")

The following function will "pack" the bytes into an array using an intermediate `ByteBuffer`:

```
(import '[java.nio ByteBuffer])

(defn prepare-string [strdata]
  (let [strlen (count strdata)
        version 66
        buflen (+ 1 4 (count strdata))
        bb (ByteBuffer/allocate buflen)
        buf (byte-array buflen)]
    (doto bb
      (.put (.byteValue version))
      (.putInt (.intValue strlen))
      (.put (.getBytes strdata))
      (.flip)         ;; Prepare bb for reading
      (.get buf))
    buf))

(prepare-string "hello world")
;;=> #<byte[] [B@5ccab0e8>
(into [] (prepare-string "hello world"))
;;=> [66 0 0 0 11 104 101 108 108 111 32 119 111 114 108 100]
```

Writing data in this format is then as simple as:

```
(with-open [out (output-stream "/tmp/mystring")]
  (.write out (prepare-string "hello world")))
```

To get the data back, `ByteBuffer` provides a way of unpacking multiple types out of a stream (array) of bytes:

```
(defn unpack-buf [n buf]
  (let [bb (ByteBuffer/allocate n)]
    (.put bb buf 0 n)                    ;; Fill ByteBuffer with array contents
    (.flip bb)                           ;; Prepare for reading
    (let [version (.get bb 0)]
      (.position bb 1)                   ;; Skip version byte
      (let [buflen (.getInt bb)
            strbytes (byte-array buflen)] ;; Prepare buffer to hold string
                                         ;; data...
```

```
        (.get bb strbytes)                ;; ... and read it.
        [version buflen (apply str (map char strbytes))]))))


(with-open [in (input-stream "/tmp/mystring")]
  (let [buf (byte-array 1024)
        n (.read in buf)]
    (unpack-buf n buf)))

;=> [66 11 "hello world"]
```

Note that for both writing and reading, the `flip` operation on the `ByteBuffer` resets the position to the beginning of the buffer to prepare it for reading and writing, respectively.

## See Also

- For more details on `ByteBuffer`, which plays a key role in Java's NIO library, see the Java NIO documentation (*http://bit.ly/javadoc-nio*) or *Java NIO* by Ron Hitchens (O'Reilly).
- The Clojure library `bytebuffer` (*https://github.com/geoffsalmon/bytebuffer*) provides a thin, more idiomatic wrapper for `ByteBuffer` operations.
- The more recent Buffy library (*https://github.com/clojurewerkz/buffy*) provides a wrapper over the related Netty `ByteBuffers`.
- Finally, the Gloss library (*https://github.com/ztellman/gloss*) provides a DSL for reading and writing binary streams of data (whether file-based or network-based).

# 4.20. Reading and Writing CSV Data

by Jason Whitlark

## Problem

You need to read or write CSV data.

## Solution

Use `clojure.data.csv/read-csv` to lazily read CSV data from a `String` or `java.io.Reader`:

```
(clojure.data.csv/read-csv "this,is\na,test" )
;; -> (["this" "is"] ["a" "test"])

(with-open [in-file (clojure.java.io/reader "in-file.csv")]
  (doall
```

```
    (clojure.data.csv/read-csv in-file)))
;; -> (["this" "is"] ["a" "test"])
```

Use `clojure.data.csv/write-csv` to write CSV data to a `java.io.Writer`:

```
(with-open [out-file (clojure.java.io/writer "out.csv")]
           (clojure.data.csv/write-csv out-file [["this" "is"] ["a" "test"]]))
;; -> nil
```

## Discussion

The `clojure.data.csv` library makes it easy to work with CSV. You need to remember that `read-csv` is lazy; if you want to force it to read data immediately, you'll need to wrap the call to `read-csv` in `doall`.

When reading, you can change the separator and quote delimiters, which default to \ and \", respectively. You must specify the delimiters using chars, not strings, though:

```
(csv/read-csv "this$-is $-\na$test" :separator \$ :quote \-)
;; -> (["this" "is $"] ["a" "test"])
```

When writing, as with `read-csv`, you can configure the separator, quote, and newline (between `:lf` (default) and `:cr+lf`), as well as the `quote?` predicate function, which takes a collection and returns `true` or `false` to indicate if the string representation needs to be quoted:

```
(with-open [out-file (clojure.java.io/writer "out.csv")]
           (clojure.data.csv/write-csv out-file [["this" "is"] ["a" "test"]]
                                       :separator \$ :quote \-))
;; -> nil
```

To capture CSV output as a string, use `with-out-str` and write to `*out*`:

```
(with-out-str (csv/write-csv *out* [["this" "is"] ["a" "test"]]))
;; -> "this,is\na,test\n"
```

## See Also

- The `clojure.data.csv` GitHub repository (*https://github.com/clojure/data.csv*)

# 4.21. Reading and Writing Compressed Files

by John Cromartie

## Problem

You want to read or write a file compressed with gzip (i.e., a *.gz* file).

## Solution

Wrap a normal input stream with `java.util.zip.GZIPInputStream` (*http://bit.ly/javadoc-gzip-input*) to get uncompressed data:

```
(with-open [in (java.util.zip.GZIPInputStream.
                (clojure.java.io/input-stream
                 "file.txt.gz"))]
  (slurp in))
```

Wrap a normal output stream with `java.util.zip.GZIPOutputStream` (*http://bit.ly/javadoc-gzip-output*) to compress data as it is written:

```
(with-open [w (-> "output.gz"
                  clojure.java.io/output-stream
                  java.util.zip.GZIPOutputStream.
                  clojure.java.io/writer)]
  (binding [*out* w]
    (println "This will be compressed on disk.")))
```

## Discussion

gzip, based on the DEFLATE algorithm, is a common compression format on Unix-like systems and is used extensively for compression on the Web. It is a good choice for compressing text in particular and can result in huge reductions for source code, or Clojure or JSON data.

Many of Clojure's I/O functions will accept any type of Java stream. The `GZIPInputStream` simply wraps any other input stream and attempts to decompress the original stream. The output variant behaves similarly.

By wrapping a normal input stream, as returned by `clojure.java.io/input-stream`, you can pass it to `slurp` or `line-seq` (or any other function that takes an input stream) and easily read the entire decompressed contents.

You can also leverage this technique to read a large compressed file line by line, or to read back Clojure forms written with `pr` or `pr-str`. You can also decompress data in a similar way from any other kind of stream; for example, one backed by a network socket or a byte array.

By binding an output stream to `*out*`, we can use `println`, `pr`, etc. to output small amounts of data at a time to the stream, which will be compressed on disk when the stream is closed.

A nearly identical approach can be used for writing data in the ZIP compression format, using the `java.util.zip.ZipInputStream` (*http://bit.ly/javadoc-zip-input*) and `java.util.zip.ZipOutputStream` (*http://bit.ly/javadoc-zip-output*) classes.

## See Also

- Recipe 4.14, "Reading and Writing Clojure Data" on page 190, for information on reading Clojure data from files on disk
- The `GZIPInputStream` API documentation (*http://bit.ly/javadoc-gzip-input*)

# 4.22. Working with XML Data

by Stefan Karlsson

## Problem

You need to read or write XML data.

## Solution

Pass a file to `clojure.xml/parse` to get a Clojure map representing the structure of an XML file.

For example, to read the following file:

```
<simple>
  <item id="1">First</item>
  <item id="2">Second</item>
</simple>
```

use `clojure.xml/parse`:

```
(require '[clojure.xml :as xml])
(clojure.xml/parse (clojure.java.io/file "simple.xml"))
;; -> {:tag :simple, :attrs nil, :content [
;;     {:tag :item, :attrs {:id "1"}, :content ["First"]}
;;     {:tag :item, :attrs {:id "2"}, :content ["Second"]}]}
```

If you want to read an XML file as a sequence of nodes, pass the XML map to the `xml-seq` function from the `clojure.core` namespace:

```
(xml/xml-seq (clojure.xml/parse (clojure.java.io/file "simple.xml")))
```

`xml-seq` returns a tree sequence of nodes; that is, a sequence of each node, starting at the root and then doing a depth-first walk of the rest of the document.

To write an XML file, pass an XML structure map to `clojure.xml/emit`. `emit` spits the XML to the currently bound output stream (`*out*`), so to write to a file, either bind `*out*` to the file's output stream or capture the output stream to a string with the `with-out-str` macro, which you can then `spit` to a file:

```
(spit "test.xml" (with-out-str (clojure.xml/emit simple-xml-map)))
```

## Discussion

You can work with your XML data just as you would with any other map. Here is an example of a function that, given an `id` and a file, will parse the file for nodes with an attribute `id` that is equal to the argument:

```
(defn get-with-id [id xml-file]
  (for [node (xml-seq (clojure.xml/parse xml-file))
        :when (= (get-in node [:attrs :id]) id)]
    (:content node)))

(get-with-id "2" simple-xml)

;; -> (["Second"])
```

To modify XML, just use the normal map manipulation functions on the Clojure data representation.

If you are going to work a lot with your XML structure, you might consider using a *zipper*. A zipper is a purely functional data structure useful for navigating and modifying tree-like structures (such as XML) in a convenient and efficient way.

Zippers are a deep topic, and a full discussion is beyond the scope of this recipe, but see the documentation for the `clojure.data.zip` library (*http://clojure.github.io/data.zip/*) for explanation and examples of how to use them effectively with XML.

## See Also

- Recipe 4.9, "Reading and Writing Text Files" on page 181
- The `clojure.zip` (*http://bit.ly/clj-zip-api*) namespace API documentation

# 4.23. Reading and Writing JSON Data

by Stefan Karlsson

## Problem

You need to read or write JSON data.

## Solution

Use the `clojure.data.json/read-str` function to read a string of JSON as Clojure data:

```
(require '[clojure.data.json :as json])
```

```
(json/read-str "[{\"name\":\"Stefan\",\"age\":32}]")
;; -> [{"name" "Stefan", "age" 32}]
```

To write data back to JSON, use the `clojure.data.json/write-str` function with the original Clojure data:

```
(json/write-str [{"name" "Stefan", "age" 32}])
;; -> "[{\"name\":\"Stefan\",\"age\":32}]"
```

## Discussion

Beyond reading and writing strings, `clojure.data.json` also provides the `read` and `write` functions to work with `java.io.Reader` and `java.io.Writer` objects, respectively. With the exception of their `reader`/`writer` parameters, these two functions share the same parameters and options as their string brethren:

```
(with-open [writer (clojure.java.io/writer "foo.json")]
  (json/write [{:foo "bar"}] writer))

(with-open [reader (clojure.java.io/reader "foo.json")]
  (json/read reader))
;; -> [{"foo" "bar"}]
```

By virtue of JavaScript's simpler types, JSON notation has a much lower fidelity than Clojure data. As such, you may find you want to tweak the way keys or values are interpreted.

One common example of this is converting JSON's string-only keys to proper Clojure keywords. You can apply a function to each processed key by using the `:key-fn` option:

```
;; Modifying keys on read

(json/read-str "{\"name\": \"Stefan\"}")
;; -> {"name" "Stefan"}

(json/read-str "{\"name\": \"Stefan\"}" :key-fn keyword)
;; -> {:name "Stefan"}

;; Modifying keys on write

(json/write-str {:name "Stefan"})
;; -> "{\"name\":\"Stefan\"}"

(json/write-str {:name "Stefan"} :key-fn str)
;; -> "{\":name\":\"Stefan\"}" ; Note the extra \:
```

You may also want to control how values are interpreted. Use the `:value-fn` option to specify how values are read/written. The function you provide will be invoked with two arguments, a key and its value:

```
;; Properly read UUID values
(defn str->uuid [key value]
  (if (= key :uuid)
    (java.util.UUID/fromString value)
    value))

(clojure.data.json/read-str
  "{\"name\": \"Stefan\", \"uuid\": \"51674ca0-eadc-4a5b-b9fb-67b05d5a71b7\"}"
  :key-fn keyword
  :value-fn str->uuid)
;; -> {:name "Stefan", :uuid #uuid "51674ca0-eadc-4a5b-b9fb-67b05d5a71b7"}

;; And similarly, write UUID values
(defn uuid->str [key value]
  (if (= key :uuid)
    (str value)
    value))

(clojure.data.json/write-str
  {:name "Stefan", :uuid #uuid "51674ca0-eadc-4a5b-b9fb-67b05d5a71b7"}
        :value-fn uuid->str)
;; -> "{\"name\":\"Stefan\",\"uuid\":\"51674ca0-eadc-4a5b-b9fb-67b05d5a71b7\"}"
```

As you may have inferred, when you provide both a `:key-fn` and a `:value-fn`, the value function will always be called after the key function.

It might go without saying, but the `:key-fn` and `:value-fn` options can also be used with the `write` and `read` functions.

## See Also

- Recipe 4.14, "Reading and Writing Clojure Data" on page 190, for information on reading/writing edn (Clojure) data.
- The API documentation (*http://bit.ly/data-json-doc*) for `clojure.data.json` for more information on reads/writes. Options not covered in this recipe include `:eof-error?`, `:eof-value`, and `:bigdec` on `read`, and `:escape-unicode` and `:escape-slash` on `write`.

# 4.24. Generating PDF Files

by Dmitri Sotnikov

## Problem

You need to generate a PDF from some data.

For example, you have a sequence of maps, such as those returned by a `clojure.java.jdbc` query, and you need to generate a PDF report.

## Solution

Use the `clj-pdf` library to create the report.

Before starting, add `[clj-pdf "1.11.6"]` to your project's dependencies or start a REPL using `lein-try`:

```
$ lein try clj-pdf
```

For the purpose of illustration, imagine we want to render a vector containing the following employee records:

```
(def employees
 [{:country "Germany",
   :place "Nuremberg",
   :occupation "Engineer",
   :name "Neil Chetty"}
  {:country "Germany",
   :place "Ulm",
   :occupation "Engineer",
   :name "Vera Ellison"}])
```

Create a template for rendering each record using the `clj-pdf.core/template` macro:

```
(require '[clj-pdf.core :as pdf])

(def employee-template
 (pdf/template
   [:paragraph
    [:heading (.toUpperCase $name)]
    [:chunk {:style :bold} "occupation: "] $occupation "\n"
    [:chunk {:style :bold} "place: "] $place "\n"
    [:chunk {:style :bold} "country: "] $country
    [:spacer]]))

(employee-template employees)
;; -> ([:paragraph [:heading "NEIL CHETTY"]
;;       [:chunk {:style :bold} "occupation: "] "Engineer" "\n"
;;       [:chunk {:style :bold} "place: "] "Nuremberg" "\n"
;;       [:chunk {:style :bold} "country: "] "Germany" [:spacer]]
;;      [:paragraph [:heading "VERA ELLISON"]
;;       [:chunk {:style :bold} "occupation: "] "Engineer" "\n"
;;       [:chunk {:style :bold} "place: "] "Ulm" "\n"
;;       [:chunk {:style :bold} "country: "] "Germany"
;;       [:spacer]])
```

Use `clj-pdf.core/pdf` to create the PDF using the template and data from above:

```
(pdf/pdf [{:title "Employee Table"}
          (employee-template employees)]
         "employees.pdf")
```

You'll find an *employees.pdf* file in the directory where you ran your project/REPL—it looks something like Figure 4-1.

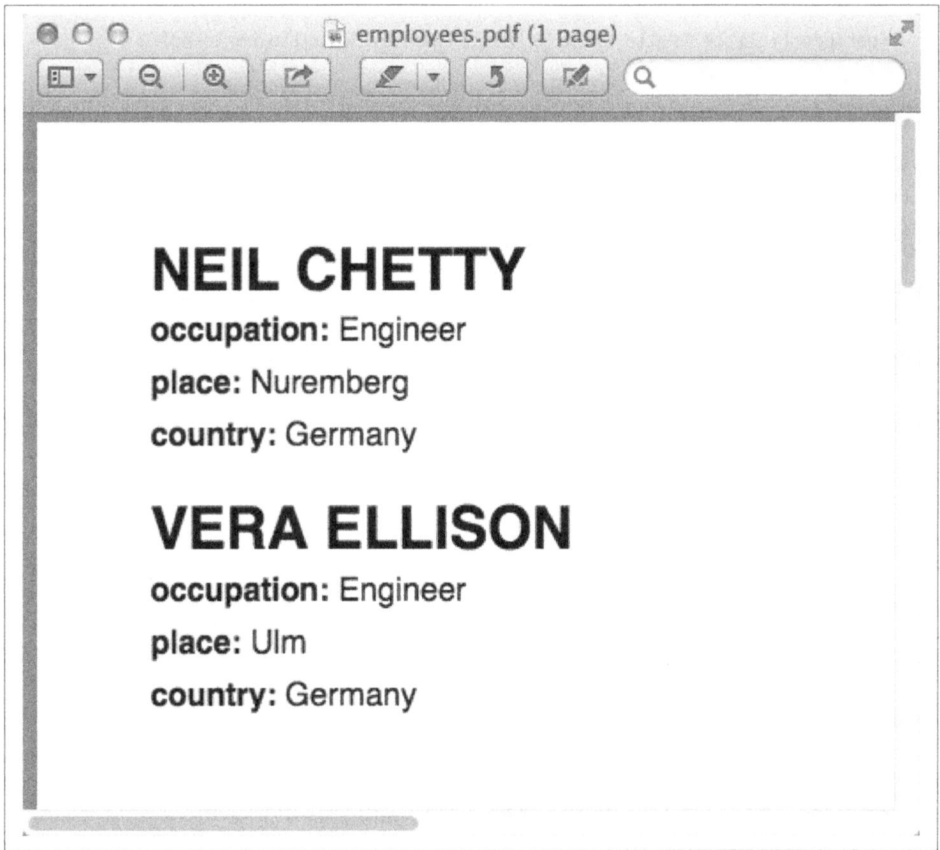


*Figure 4-1. employees.pdf*

## Discussion

The `clj-pdf` library is built on top of the iText and JFreeChart libraries. The templating syntax is inspired by the popular Hiccup HTML templating engine.

In a template, `$` is used to indicate places where dynamic content will be substituted. When populating a template from a map, each substitution anchor (`$name`) is populated with the value of the corresponding keyword key in the map (the value of the `:name` key).

Beyond substituting simple values, it is also possible to perform further processing on those values. The `:heading` portion of the `employee-template` does precisely this by calling `(.toUpperCase $name)`. In `clj-pdf`, a document is represented by a vector containing a map of metadata followed by the content. The content can in turn consist of strings, vectors, or collections of vectors.

A *very* simple PDF:

```
(pdf/pdf [{:title "Hello World"} "Hello, World."] "hello-world.pdf")
```

Under the hood, collections of content are automatically expanded:

```
;; This *collection* of paragraphs...
(pdf [{} [[:paragraph "foo"] [:paragraph "bar"]]] "document.pdf")

;; is equivalent to these *individual* paragraphs
(pdf [{} [:paragraph "foo"] [:paragraph "bar"]] "document.pdf")
```

Apart from plain strings, each content element is represented as a vector. The first element of this vector is a keyword type, and everything that follows is the content itself. Some types `clj-pdf` includes are `:paragraph`, `:phrase`, `:list`, and `:table`:

```
[:heading "Lorem Ipsum"]
[:line]
[:list "first item"
       "second item"
       "third item"]
[:paragraph "I'm a paragraph"]
[:phrase "some text here"]
[:table
   ["foo" "bar" "baz"]
   ["foo1" "bar1" "baz1"]
   ["foo2" "bar2" "baz2"]]
```

Some elements accept optional styling metadata. You can provide this style information as a map immediately following the type parameter (the second item in the vector):

```
[:paragraph {:style :bold} "this text is bold"]

[:chunk {:style :bold
         :size 18
         :family :helvetica
         :color [0 234 123]}
 "some large green text"]
```

The contents of an element can consist of other elements (like an HTML document), and any style applied to a parent element will be inherited by the child elements:

```
[:paragraph "some content"]

[:paragraph {:style :bold}
 "Some bold text"
 [:phrase [:chunk "even more"] "bold text"]]
```

As with Cascading Style Sheets (CSS), child elements can augment or override their parents' styles by specifying their own styles:

```
[:paragraph
 {:style :bold}
 "Bold words"
 [:phrase {:color [0 255 221]} "Bold AND teal!"]]
```

Images can be embedded in the document using the `:image` element. Image content can be one of `java.net.URL`, `java.awt.Image`, a byte array, a Base64 string, or a string representing a URL or a file:

```
[:image "my-image.jpg"]
[:image "http://clojure.org/space/showimage/clojure-icon.gif"]
```

Images larger than the page margins will automatically be scaled to fit.

## See Also

- For more information on using `clj-pdf`, including a complete list of element types and charting capabilities, see the `clj-pdf` GitHub repository (*https://github.com/yogthos/clj-pdf*)

# 4.25. Making a GUI Window with Scrollable Text

by John Jacobsen; originally submitted by John Walker

## Problem

You want to create and display a GUI window.

## Solution

Though Java's Swing library is the most common way to make Java GUIs (at least on the desktop), the Seesaw library, which wraps Swing and provides a more idiomatic and functional interface, is the best tool for creating GUIs with Clojure.

To follow along with this recipe, start a REPL using `lein-try`:

```
$ lein try seesaw
```

Swing implements a "programmable look and feel": the appearance of various widgets and their behavior can be modified, though it is common to set this to match the platform one is on, for the sake of maximum usability. Setting the native look and feel is accomplished in Seesaw with the `native!` function:

```
(require '[seesaw.core :refer [native! frame show! config!
                               pack! text scrollable]])
```

```
(native!)
;; -> nil
```

To create your window object, use `frame` (which, under the covers, makes a `JFrame` Swing object):

```
(frame :title "Lyrical Clojure" :content "Hello World")
;; -> #<JFrame$Tag$a79ba523 seesaw.core.proxy$javax.swing.JFrame$Tag$a79ba523
;;     [frame0,0,22,0x0,invalid,hidden,layout=java.awt.BorderLayout,
;;     title=Lyrical Clojure,resizable,normal,
;;     defaultCloseOperation=HIDE_ON_CLOSE,
;;     rootPane=javax.swing.JRootPane[,0,0,0x0,invalid,
;;     layout=javax.swing.JRootPane$RootLayout,
;;     alignmentX=0.0,alignmentY=0.0,border=,flags=16777673,maximumSize=,
;;     minimumSize=,preferredSize=],rootPaneCheckingEnabled=true]>
```

Although a frame has been created, nothing appears. In order to actually display the frame (as seen in Figure 4-2), use `show!`:

```
(def f (frame :title "Lyrical Clojure"))

(show! f)
;; -> #<JFrame$Tag$a79ba523 [...]>
```

*Figure 4-2. A simple window*

## Discussion

Having created the window, you can set its size, add content, and add scroll bars, as follows.

### Adding content

You can change properties of the frame using `config!`:

```
(config! f :content "Actual content!")
;; -> #<JFrame$Tag$a79ba523 [...]>
```

The result is shown in Figure 4-3.

*Figure 4-3. A window with basic content*

### Sizing the window

You can specify the size of the window at the time of creation:

```
(def f (frame :title "Lyrical Clojure" :width 300 :height 150))
;; -> #<JFrame$Tag$a79ba523 [...]>
```

However, it is common to instead call `pack!` on the resulting frame object; this assigns width and height properties according to its content:

```
(-> f pack! show!)
;; -> #<JFrame$Tag$a79ba523 [...]>
```

### Adding scrollable content

Now add some text, in the form of an excerpt from the sonnets of Shakespeare, to your window:

```
(def sonnet-text (->> "http://www.gutenberg.org/cache/epub/1041/pg1041.txt"
                      slurp
                      (drop 20000)
                      (take 4000)
                      (apply str)))
```

This content is too big to fit in the current window (see Figure 4-4):

```
(config! f :content sonnet-text)
;; -> #<JFrame$Tag$a79ba523 [...]>
```

*Figure 4-4. A window with more text than space*

Normally, one would call `pack!` again to adjust the window size to the new content. However, the content will not fit comfortably on most screens, so set the size explicitly and add scroll bars, as seen in Figure 4-5:

```
(.setSize f 400 400)
(config! f :content (scrollable (text :multi-line? true
                                      :text sonnet-text
                                      :editable? false)))
```

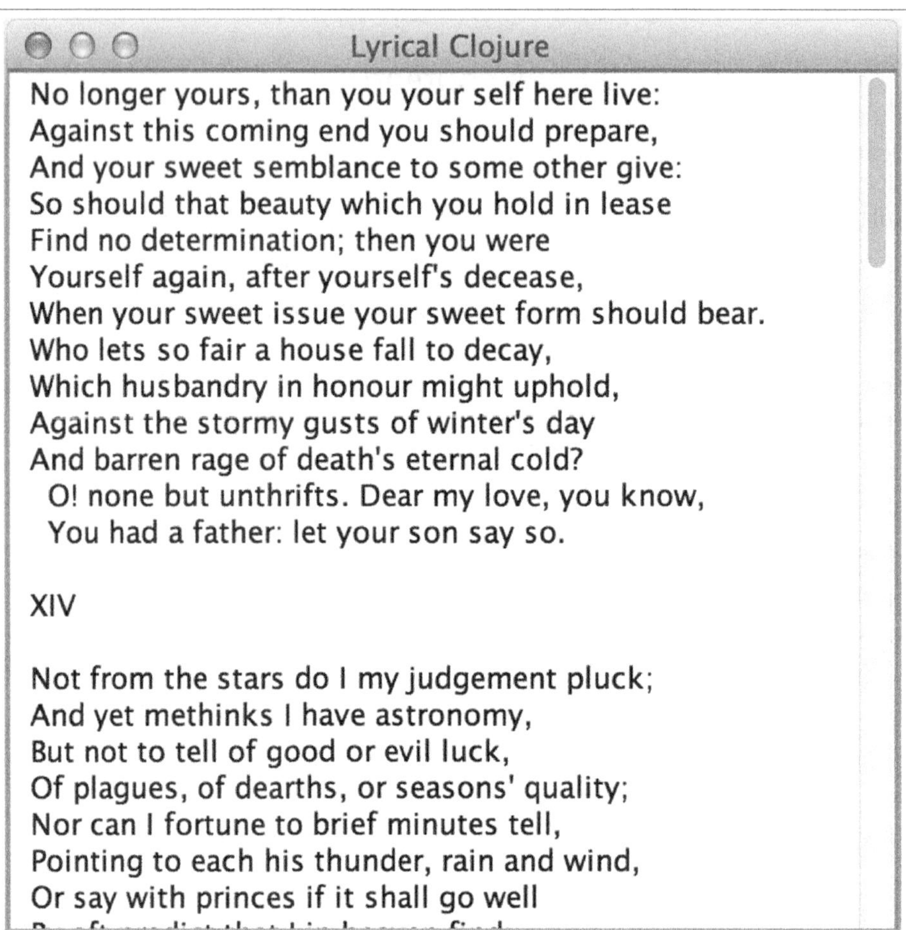


*Figure 4-5. A larger window with a scroll bar*

The `:multi-line?` option to the `text` function selects `JTextArea` as the underlying object, rather than `JTextField` (`JTextArea` is used for multiline text; `JTextField` is for single-line text fields). `:editable?` specifies that you don't want to allow users to edit the text (since it is, perhaps, doubtful that they would improve upon Shakespeare's original).

Like most of the Seesaw functions that create widgets, there are several more options to `text`, which are best learned about by studying the API documentation (*http://bit.ly/cc-seesaw*).

As is always the case in Clojure, the Seesaw library functions return Java objects, which can be operated upon directly using Java methods; for example, our use of the `.setSize` method of the `JFrame` object returned by `frame`. This interoperability provides great power but comes at the cost of a somewhat higher burden on programmers, who must navigate not only the Seesaw API but, frequently, some aspects of the underlying Swing API as well.

Seesaw supports a wide variety of GUI tasks—creation of menus, display of text and images, scroll bars, radio buttons, checkboxes, multipaned windows, drag-and-drop, and much more. In addition to the dozen or so books that have been written about Swing, one could easily write an entire book on Seesaw. This recipe merely serves as a starting point for further investigation of the Seesaw library.

## See Also

- The Seesaw GitHub repository (*https://github.com/daveray/seesaw*)
- *Java Swing*, 2nd ed. (O'Reilly), by Marc Loy *et al.*

# CHAPTER 5
# Network I/O and Web Services

## 5.0. Introduction

More and more these days, it seems like every system we build has to talk to something, somewhere.[1] We'd hardly be doing anything if we didn't actually talk with some other computers over some kind of network.

This chapter covers all of the normal remote communication modes you would expect —HTTP, TCP, UDP, and the like—as well as some relative newcomers[2] like message-oriented architectures.

## 5.1. Making HTTP Requests

by John Cromartie

### Problem

You want to make a simple HTTP GET or POST request.

### Solution

Use `slurp` to make simple HTTP GET requests:

```
(slurp "http://example.com")
;; -> "<!doctype html>\n<html>\n<head>\n    <title>Example Domain</title> ...
```

1. In fact, "There's Just No Getting around It: You're Building a Distributed System" (*http://bit.ly/no-getting-around*).

2. As Australian songwriter Peter Allen so aptly put it: "Everything old is new again."

Use the `clj-http` library to make GET, POST, and other requests with specific parameters or headers, to handle redirects and other special circumstances, or to get specific details about the response.

To follow along, add `[clj-http "0.7.7"]` to your project's dependencies, or use `lein-try` to start a REPL:

```
$ lein try clj-http
```

Use `clj-http.client/get` to make GET requests:

```
(require '[clj-http.client :as http])

(:status (http/get "http://clojure.org"))
;; -> 200

(-> (http/get "http://clojure.org")
    :headers
    (get "server"))
;; -> "nginx"

(-> (http/get "http://www.amazon.com/")
    :cookies
    keys)
;; -> ("session-id" "session-id-time" "x-wl-uid" "skin")
```

Parameters can be included in both GET and POST requests. Use `clj-http.client/post` to make POST requests:

```
(http/get "http://google.com/" {:query-params {:q "clojure"}})
;; -> {:status 200 ...}

(http/post "http://example.com" {:form-params {:username "joecoder"
                                               :password "il0v3clojure"}})
;; -> {:status 200 ...}
```

You can even use the `:multipart` option to upload files, as from an HTML form via a web browser.

## Discussion

`slurp` works to make HTTP GET requests because its arguments are passed to `clojure.java.io/reader`, which in turn correctly handles opening URL strings. This is totally sufficient for issuing a quick HTTP GET to a well-behaved URL. Unfortunately, this is where `slurp`'s usefulness ends. Among other limitations, it will not behave correctly for responses with HTTP redirects.

`clj-http` is an extremely flexible Clojure wrapper around the very robust Apache HttpComponents library (*https://hc.apache.org/*). Its features include convenient functions for other HTTP verbs like PUT and DELETE; for reading and sending cookies, headers, and other request metadata; for reading and writing data using streams, files, or byte arrays; and lots more. Refer to the GitHub repository (*https://github.com/dakrone/clj-http*) to learn about the huge variety of options available and to see many more examples.

If you're building production systems that rely on external services, you may want to consider wrapping HTTP calls in Netflix's Hystrix (*https://github.com/Netflix/Hystrix*) library to make your application more fault-tolerant and resilient. Hystrix provides Clojure bindings (*http://bit.ly/hystrix-clj*) that you can use to wrap network calls and more easily manage complex failure scenarios involving external services.

## See Also

- `clj-http`'s GitHub repository (*https://github.com/dakrone/clj-http*).
- For information on making asynchronous HTTP calls, see Recipe 5.2, "Performing Asynchronous HTTP Requests" on page 223.
- When building production systems that interact with external services, consider Hystrix (*https://github.com/Netflix/Hystrix*) and its Clojure bindings (*http://bit.ly/hystrix-clj*) to wrangle complex failure scenarios.

# 5.2. Performing Asynchronous HTTP Requests

by Alan Busby and Ryan Neufeld

## Problem

You want to perform asynchronous HTTP requests.

## Solution

Use HTTP Kit (*http://http-kit.org/*), a highly performant, event-driven HTTP client/server library.

Before starting, add `[http-kit "2.1.12"]` to your project's dependencies, or follow along in a REPL using `lein-try`:

```
$ lein try http-kit
```

Use any of `org.httpkit.client`'s HTTP verb functions to perform asynchronous HTTP requests. In their base form, these functions return a promise that you can await with `deref` or the `@` reader shorthand:

```
(require '[org.httpkit.client :as http])

(def response (http/get "http://example.com"))
```

```
;; Some time later...

(:status @response)
;; -> 200

;; Or, using deref to specify a timeout length in milliseconds and
;; a value
(deref response 2000 nil)
;; -> {:opts {:url "http://example.com", :method :get}
;;     :body "..."
;;     :headers {:content-type "text/html", :content-length "1270" ...}
;;     :status 200}
```

## Discussion

The bulk of time spent performing HTTP requests is establishing the connection and awaiting the server's response. Asynchronous requests enable your application to continue working while awaiting the delivery of data.

In this vein, HTTP Kit provides both a highly concurrent web server and a powerful HTTP client. It offers both callbacks and promises for asynchronous requests, as well as persistent connections and alternate SSL engines for dealing with unsigned SSL certificates.

The `org.httpkit.client` namespace defines asynchronous versions of numerous HTTP methods, including `get`, `delete`, `head`, `post`, `put`, `options`, and `patch`. Each of these verbs derives from `org.httpkit.client/request`, which defines a common interface. An asynchronous request of a given method is made, and a promise is returned. Upon completion of the request, the promise will be fulfilled with the results/response.

All `request` functions accept an optional map of options where you can specify keys like `:query-params`, `:post-params`, or `:headers`. Functions also allow specifying a callback function to be called upon request completion:

```
(http/get "http://example.com"
          {:timeout 1000 ;; ms
                 :query-params {:search "value"}}
          (fn [{:keys [status headers body error]}]
            (if error
              (binding [*out* *err*]
                (println "Failed with, " error))
              (println body))))
;; -> #<core$promise$reify__6310@582e6c93: :pending>
;; *out*
;; <html>
;; <head>
;;   <title>Example Domain</title>
;; ...
```

## See Also

- See Recipe 5.1, "Making HTTP Requests" on page 221, for details on making normal, nonasynchronous HTTP requests.
- HTTP Kit is heavily inspired by the API of `clj-http` (*https://github.com/dakrone/clj-http*); see Recipe 5.1, "Making HTTP Requests" on page 221, for more information on the library.

# 5.3. Sending a Ping Request

by Jason Webb

## Problem

You want to ping an IP address to check availability.

## Solution

Use the `java.net.InetAddress` class to test if the address `isReachable`:

```
(.isReachable (java.net.InetAddress/getByName "oreilly.com") 5000)
;; -> true
```

## Discussion

Using `isReachable` works great if the correct permissions can be obtained. On a typical Unix-like implementation, you will need to start your Clojure instance with `sudo` to get an actual ICMP ping sent. Otherwise, a standard connection will be attempted on port 7, which in most cases will be blocked by a firewall. More information can be found in the javadoc (*http://bit.ly/javadoc-isReachable*).

A common need when pinging another machine is to time the ping. You can wrap an `.isReachable` invocation in a function `timed-ping` to return timing values with every ping:

```
(defn timed-ping
  "Time an .isReachable ping to a given domain"
  [domain timeout]
  (let [addr (java.net.InetAddress/getByName domain)
        start (. System (nanoTime))
        result (.isReachable addr timeout)
        total (/ (double (- (. System (nanoTime)) start)) 1000000.0)]
    {:time total
     :result result}))
```

```
(timed-ping "oreilly.com" 5000)
;; -> {:time 88.07, :result true}
```

## See Also

- InetAddress/isReachable documentation (*http://bit.ly/javadoc-isReachable*)

# 5.4. Retrieving and Parsing RSS Data

by Osbert Feng

## Problem

You need to parse RSS data.

## Solution

Use the `feedparser-clj` library to parse RSS data.

Before starting, add `[org.clojars.scsibug/feedparser-clj "0.4.0"]` to your project's dependencies, or follow along in a REPL using `lein-try`:

```
$ lein try org.clojars.scsibug/feedparser-clj
```

Invoke `feedparser-clj.core/parse-feed` with the URI of an RSS feed to retrieve that feed and parse it into Clojure data:

```
(require '[feedparser-clj.core :as rss])

(rss/parse-feed (str "https://github.com/clojure-cookbook/clojure-cookbook/"
                     "commits/master.atom"))
;; -> {:authors [...]
;;     :entries [{:link "LINK" :title "TITLE" :contents "CONTENT"} ...]
;;      ...}
```

You can also invoke `parse-feed` with a `java.io.InputStream` to read from a file or other location:

```
(with-open [writer (clojure.java.io/writer "master.atom")]
  (spit writer
        (slurp (str "https://github.com/clojure-cookbook/clojure-cookbook/"
                    "commits/master.atom"))))

(with-open [stream (clojure.java.io/input-stream "master.atom")]
  (rss/parse-feed stream))
;; -> {:authors [...]
;;     :entries [{:link "LINK" :title "TITLE" :contents "CONTENT"} ...]
;;     ...}
```

## Discussion

`feedparser-clj` is a wrapper around the Java ROME library that is capable of processing a variety formats of RSS and Atom feeds. `feedparser-clj.core/parse-feed` returns a Clojure map that closely mimics the underlying XML feed.

Most of the time, what you care about will be under the `:entries` key, which contains an array of maps corresponding to each RSS entry.

Some RSS feeds will have `<link rel="next">` elements that indicate that the returned list is incomplete and more entries can be retrieved by following the link. A lazy list of these RSS entries can be generated:

```
(defn next-uri
  "Return the rel=next href in a feed."
  [feed]
  (-> feed
      :entry-links
      (->> (filter #(= (:rel %) "next")))
      first
      :href))


(defn lazy-stream
  "Return a lazy stream of RSS entries."
  [uri]
   (let [raw-response (rss/parse-feed uri)]
      (lazy-cat (:entries raw-response)
         (if-let [nxt (next-uri raw-response)]
            (lazy-stream nxt)))))
```

To verify that lazy loading is happening, logging or tracing can be added to `lazy-stream`, but it is also easy to confirm that you can retrieve more entries than are present in a single fetch:

```
(def youtube-feed "http://gdata.youtube.com/feeds/api/videos")

(count (rss/parse-feed youtube-feed))
;; -> 15

(count (take 50 (lazy-stream youtube-feed)))
;; -> 50
```

Be careful when evaluating a lazy sequence in a REPL, since it will attempt to print the entire sequence. Use `take` to only realize part of the sequence.

## See Also

- Recipe 4.22, "Working with XML Data" on page 208, for more information on reading and writing XML data like RSS feeds
- Recipe 5.1, "Making HTTP Requests" on page 221

# 5.5. Sending Email

by Ryan Neufeld

## Problem

You need to send emails from inside a Clojure application.

## Solution

Use `postal`, a thin wrapper over the JavaMail package, to send email messages.

To follow along with this recipe, start a REPL using `lein-try`:

```
$ lein try com.draines/postal
```

Send a message by invoking the `postal.core/send-message` function with two maps, the first containing connection details and the second containing message details. For example, to send an email message to yourself via a Gmail account:

```
(require '[postal.core :refer [send-message]])

;; Replace the following with your own credentials
(def email "<<your gmail address>")
(def pass "<your gmail password>")

(def conn {:host "smtp.gmail.com"
           :ssl true
           :user email
           :pass pass})

(send-message conn {:from email
                    :to email
                    :subject "A message, from the past"
                    :body "Hi there, me!"})
;; -> {:error :SUCCESS, :code 0, :message "messages sent"}
```

If all is well, you should receive an email from yourself shortly thereafter.

## Discussion

With the venerable JavaMail at its core, there isn't much `postal` leaves for you to worry about. Even Gmail's oft-maligned authentication setup can be tackled with a single `:ssl` key. While we might normally suggest giving the native Java API a try for simple email delivery, we prefer `postal` because it presents an API oriented around data rather than objects.

One of the places data orientation really shines is in specifying connection details. The first argument to the `send-message` function is a (versatile) map of connection details. Valid connection details are:

`:host`
: Hostname of the desired SMTP server. Optional if running locally.

`:port`
: Port of SMTP server. Numerous contextual defaults exist, including `465` when `:ssl` is set or `25` when `:tls` is set.

`:user`
: Username to authenticate with (if authenticating).

`:pass`
: Password to authenticate with (if authenticating).

`:ssl`
: Enables SSL encryption if value is truthy.

`:tls`
: Enables TLS encryption if value is truthy.

When provided *no* connection details—either by omitting the first argument or passing `nil`—`postal` will attempt to route email through a local sendmail (*http://bit.ly/wiki-sendmail*) instance.

Since Amazon's Simple Email Service (SES) can operate over SMTP, it is possible to use `postal` to send email via Amazon's infrastructure.

Similar to connection details, messages themselves are represented as simple maps of data. The full complement of standard headers are supported as message keys:

- Sender options
  - `:from`

— `:reply-to`

- Recipient options
  — `:to`
  — `:cc`
  — `:bcc`
- Content options
  — `:subject`
  — `:body`
- Metadata options
  — `:date`
  — `:message-id`
  — `:user-agent`

Options specified beyond these will be attached to the message as ancillary headers.

When specifying recipients on the `:to`, `:cc`, or `:bcc` keys, values may be either a single address or a sequence of addresses:

```
{:to "joe@example.com"
 :cc ["joe@example.com", "jim@example.com", "jeff@example.com"]
 :bcc "archive@example.com"}
```

A message's body can be specified as either a string or a sequence of *part* maps. While the former delivers a simple plain-text email, the latter will deliver a multipart *MIME* message. MIME (Multipurpose Internet Mail Extensions) is the standard that allows email messages to contain attachments or other rich content, such as HTML.

A part map is made up of two values: `:type` and `:content`. For message body parts, `:type` is the MIME type of the content, and `:content` is the textual representation of said content. For example, to create a message with both plain text and HTML representations of the content:

```
:body [:alternative
       {:type "text/plain"
        :content "You just won the lottery!"}
       {:type "text/html"
        :content "<html>
                    <body>
                      <p>You just <b>won</b> the lottery!</p>
                    </body>
                  </html>"}]
```

You'll notice the first "part" in the preceding body was not, in fact, a part map, but the keyword `:alternative`. Messages are normally sent in "mixed" mode, indicating to an email client that each part constitutes a piece of the whole message. Messages of the `:alternative` type, however, inform a client that each part represents the entire message, albeit in differing formats.

If you need to send complicated multipart messages and require a high level of control over message creation, you should use the raw JavaMail API to construct messages.

For attachments, the `:type` parameter behaves a little differently, controlling whether the attachment resides inline (`:inline`) or as an attachment (`:attachment`). The contents of an attachment are specified by providing a `File` object for the `:content` key. An attachment's content type and name are generally inferred from the `File` object, but they may be overridden via the `:content-type` and `:file-name` keys, respectively.

For example, forwarding all of your closest friends a picture of your cat might look something like this:

```
:body [{:type "text/plain"
        :content "Hey folks,\n\nCheck out these pictures of my cat!"}
       {:type :inline
        :content (File. "/tmp/lester-flying-photoshop")
        :content-type "image/jpeg"
        :file-name "lester-flying.jpeg"}
       {:type :attachment
        :content (File. "/tmp/lester-upside-down.jpeg")}]
```

## See Also

- `postal`'s GitHub repository (*https://github.com/drewr/postal*)
- JavaMail's API documentation (*http://bit.ly/javamail-api-doc*)

# 5.6. Communicating over Queues Using RabbitMQ

by Ryan Neufeld; originally submitted by Michael Klishin

## Problem

You want to communicate between a number of applications using a queueing broker such as RabbitMQ (*http://rabbitmq.com*).

## Solution

Use Langohr (*http://clojurerabbitmq.info*), a small RabbitMQ client, to communicate with RabbitMQ.

Before starting, add `[com.novemberain/langohr "1.6.0"]` to your project's dependencies, or follow along in a REPL using `lein-try`:

```
$ lein try com.novemberain/langohr
```

In order to follow along with this recipe, you need to have RabbitMQ installed and running (*http://bit.ly/rmq-download*).

Once installed, start a standalone RabbitMQ server with the command **`rabbitmq-server`**:

```
$ rabbitmq-server
```

Prior to performing any operations against RabbitMQ, you must connect to a server and open a communication channel. A channel is the medium over which you can produce and consume messages:

```
(require 'langohr.core
         'langohr.channel)

;; Connect to local RabbitMQ cluster node on localhost:5672
(def conn (langohr.core/connect {:hostname "localhost"}))

;; Open a channel against the connection
(def ch (langohr.channel/open conn))
```

In RabbitMQ, messages are published to *exchanges*, routed to *queues* via a *binding*, then finally consumed by consumers. There are a number of different exchange types that vary the semantics of delivery; the most basic exchange type is *direct*, which routes messages based on their *routing key*.

To construct a pipeline between producer and consumer, start by invoking `langohr.queue/declare` to create a queue with the desired name:

```
(require '[langohr.queue :as lq])

(def resize-queue "imaging.resize")

(lq/declare ch resize-queue)
;; -> {:queue "imaging.resize",
;;     :consumer-count 0,
;;     :message_count 0,
;;     :consumer_count 0,
;;     :message-count 0}
```

By default, RabbitMQ creates a binding between the empty exchange (an empty string) and each queue. You can now publish a message to the `"imaging.resize"` queue by invoking `langohr.basic/publish` with the channel, direct exchange, routing key (your queue name), and a message:

```
(lb/publish ch "" resize-queue "hello.jpg")
```

To consume messages from a queue synchronously, invoke `langohr.basic/get` with the channel and queue name:

```
(def hello-msg (lb/get ch resize-queue))

hello-msg
;; -> [{:routing-key "imaging.resize", :headers nil ...} #<byte[] [B@2b195c88>]

(String. (last hello-msg) "UTF-8")
;; -> "hello.jpg"
```

To consume messages asynchronously as they appear, use `langohr.consumers/subscribe` to subscribe to a queue. The handler function you provide to `subscribe` will be called for each message published to the queue:

```
(require '[langohr.consumers :as lc])

(defn resize-image-handler
  "Spawn a resize process for each resize message received"
  [ch metadata ^bytes payload]
  (let [filename (String. payload "UTF-8")]
    (println (format "Resizing file %s" filename))))

;; Subscribe to the queue with the handler function
(def tag (lc/subscribe ch resize-queue resize-image-handler))

;; The return value of subscribe is a subscription tag
tag
;; -> "amq.ctag-7hsNsSqLDEEoES5AkIC6XQ"

(lb/publish ch "" resize-queue "hello-again.jpg")
;; *out*
;; Resizing file hello-again.jpg

;; Unsubscribe resize-image-handler via the tag value
(lb/cancel ch tag)
```

## Discussion

At this point, you've round-tripped a few messages to RabbitMQ, but you've barely scratched the surface of what Langohr and RabbitMQ are capable of. Langohr is a small RabbitMQ client wrapping the Java RabbitMQ library that supports AMQP 0-9-1 and RabbitMQ extensions of AMQP, and provides an HTTP API client.

AMQP 0-9-1, and by extension, Langohr, centers around a few main concepts: *exchanges*, *queues*, and *bindings*.

### Exchanges

An exchange is very much like a post office: when a message is published to an exchange, the exchange will route the message to one or more queues. How those messages are routed to queues is dependent on both the exchange type and the bindings between the exchange/queues.

There are multiple exchange types, each with its own routing semantics—see Table 5-1. Custom exchange types can be created to deal with sophisticated routing scenarios (e.g., routing based on content or geolocation data) or just for convenience.

*Table 5-1. Built-in exchange types*

| Name | Behavior | Predeclared exchange |
|---|---|---|
| Direct | 1:1, routed based on routing key | `""` |
| Fanout | 1:N, ignoring routing key | `"amq.fanout"` |
| Topic | 1:N, taking routing key into consideration | `"amq.topic"` |
| Headers | 1:1, taking into consideration any number of headers | `"amq.match"` |

To declare one of the built-in exchanges, use one of `langohr.exchange/fanout`, `langohr.exchange/topic`, `langohr.exchange/direct`, or `langohr.exchange/headers`. Each of these functions exposes the relevant options for that exchange type, ultimately invoking `langohr.exchange/declare`:

```
(require '[langohr.exchange :as le])

;; Create a fanout exchange for image processing completion
(le/fanout ch "imaging.complete")
```

Exchanges have several attributes associated with them:

- Name
- Type (direct, fanout, topic, headers, or some custom type)
- Durability (should it survive broker restarts?)
- Whether the exchange is autodeleted when no longer used
- Custom metadata (sometimes known as `x-arguments`)

Using `langohr.exchange/declare` directly, you can customize these attributes to create your own types of exchanges.

### Queues

A queue is like a mailbox in a post office. The `langohr.queue/declare` function creates named queues. Apart from the name, this function accepts a number of keyword arguments that vary the characteristics of the queue, including whether it is `:durable`, `:exclusive`, or `:auto-delete`. Other arguments can be specified in an `:arguments` value:

```
(lq/declare ch "imaging.transcode" :durable true)
;; -> {:queue "imaging.transcode", ...}
```

Queues with unique names can be generated using the `langohr.queue/declare-server-named` function. This functions similarly to `langohr.queue/declare`, but without a name argument:

```
(lq/declare-server-named ch)
;; -> "amq.gen-FcFv8JD9K8-4NuT8kC3jKA"
```

Unlike exchanges, queues in RabbitMQ are all of the same type.

### Bindings

As you saw in the solution, a direct exchange has an implicit binding between the default exchange and every queue, by name. In the wild, however, queues are usually bound to exchanges explicitly. You can create your own bindings by invoking `langohr.queue/bind` with a channel, queue name, and exchange name:

```
;; Create a unique completion queue...
(def completion-queue (lq/declare-server-named ch))

;; and bind it to the imaging.complete fanout
(lq/bind ch completion-queue "imaging.complete")
```

### Publishing

Messages are published to an exchange using the `langohr.basic/publish` function. This function takes three primary arguments (beyond channel):

*The name of an exchange*
: Either a user-made exchange such as `"imaging.complete"`, or a built-in like `"amq.fanout"` or `""`

*A routing key*
: Used by the exchange to perform type-specific routing of messages to queue(s)

*A message*
: A string body for the message to be delivered to the queue

As optional arguments, `publish` allows users to specify a plethora of message headers as keyword arguments. For the full list, see the docstring for the `publish` function.

### Consuming

Having declared a number of queues, there are two ways to consume messages from them:

- Pull, using `langohr.basic/get`
- Push, using `langohr.consumers/subscribe`

In the Push API, you make a synchronous invocation of the `get` function to retrieve a single message from a queue. The return value of `get` is a tuple of metadata map and a body. The body payload, as returned, is an array of bytes—for plain-text messages you can use the string constructor (`String.`) to intern those bytes to a string. Since `String` byte arrays are encoded using UTF-8, it is important to invoke the `String` constructor with an encoding option of `"UTF-8"`:

```
(lb/publish ch "" resize-queue "hello.jpg")
(let [[_ body] (lb/get ch resize-queue)]
  (String. body "UTF-8"))
;; -> "hello.jpg"
```

When no messages are present on a queue, `get` will return `nil`.

In the Pull API, you subscribe to a queue using `langohr.consumers/subscribe`, providing a message handler function that will be invoked for each message the queue receives. This function will be invoked with three arguments: a channel, metadata, and the body bytes:

```
;; A run-of-the-mill handler function
(defn resize-image-handler
  "Spawn a resize process for each resize message received"
  [ch metadata ^bytes payload]
  (let [filename (String. payload "UTF-8")]
    (println (format "Resizing file %s" filename))))
```

`subscribe` is a nonblocking call, and upon completion will return a tag string that can be used to later cancel the subscription using `langohr.consumers/cancel`.

The `subscribe` function also allows you to specify a large number of queue life cycle functions, documented at length in the `langohr.consumers/create-default` docstring.

### Acknowledgment

Consumed messages need to be acknowledged. That can happen automatically (RabbitMQ will consider a message acknowledged as soon as it sends it to a consumer) or manually.

When a message is acknowledged, it is removed from the queue. If a channel closes unexpectedly before a delivery is acknowledged, it will be automatically requeued by

RabbitMQ. Note that these acknowledgments have application-specific semantics and help ensure that messages are processed properly.

With manual acknowledgment, it is application's responsibility to either acknowledge or reject a delivery. This is done with `langohr.basic/ack` and `langohr.basic/nack`, respectively, each of which takes a metadata attribute called `delivery-tag` (the delivery ID). To enable manual acknowledgments, pass `:auto-ack false` to `langohr.consumers/subscribe`:

```
(defn manual-ack-handler
  "Spawn a resize process for each resize message received"
  [ch {:keys [delivery-tag]} ^bytes payload]
  (try
    (String. payload "UTF-8")
    ;; Do some work, then acknowledge the message
    (lb/ack ch delivery-tag)
    (catch Throwable t
      ;; Reject message
      (lb/nack ch delivery-tag))))

(lc/subscribe ch resize-queue manual-ack-handler :auto-ack false)
```

Note that if you requeue a message with just one consumer on it, it will be redelivered immediately.

It is also possible to control how many messages will be pushed to the client before it must receive an ack for at least one of them. This is known as the *prefetch setting* and is set using `langohr.basic/qos`. This setting applies across an entire channel:

```
;; Prefetch a dozen messages
(lb/qos ch 12)
```

RabbitMQ queues can also be mirrored between cluster nodes for high availability, have a bounded length or expiration period for messages, and more. To learn more, see RabbitMQ and Langohr documentation sites.

## See Also

- The Langohr documentation (*http://clojurerabbitmq.info*)
- Langohr's API reference (*http://bit.ly/langohr-docs*)
- The RabbitMQ tutorials (*http://bit.ly/rmq-getting-started*)
- If you need low-level access to RabbitMQ, you may want to investigate using Clojure's Java interop to interact with the RabbitMQ Java client (*http://bit.ly/rmq-java-client*), the library upon which Langohr is based.

# 5.7. Communicating with Embedded Devices via MQTT

By Sandeep Nangia

## Problem

You want to communicate with embedded devices (think "Internet of things") using a publish/subscribe model.

## Solution

Use Machine Head (*https://github.com/clojurewerkz/machine_head*), a Clojure library that enables machine-to-machine (M2M) communication via the MQTT (*http://mqtt.org/*) protocol. The protocol requires an existing MQTT broker with which all devices (or machines) will communicate by publishing messages or subscribing to messages on specific topics. You can use the Mosquitto (*http://mosquitto.org/*) broker with its test installation at *tcp://test.mosquitto.org:1883* (of course, you need a functional Internet connection on your machine).

To follow along with this recipe, launch a REPL using `lein-try`:

```
$ lein try clojurewerkz/machine_head
```

To start, create a simple `connect-and-subscribe` function that listens to a topic and prints messages it receives:

```
(require '[clojurewerkz.machine-head.client :as mh])

(defn message-handler [topic meta payload]
  (let [p (apply str (map char payload))]
    (println "received " p "on topic " topic)))

(defn connect-and-subscribe [broker-addr topics subscriberid]
  (let [qos-levels (vec (repeat (count topics) 2)) ;; All at qos 2
        conn-sub (mh/connect broker-addr subscriberid)]
    (if (mh/connected? conn-sub)
      (do
        (mh/subscribe conn-sub topics message-handler {:qos qos-levels})
        conn-sub)))) ;; Return conn-sub for later mh/disconnect...

(def subscriberid (mh/generate-id))
;; or use a unique id
;; (def subscriberid "SNSubscriber01")

(connect-and-subscribe "tcp://test.mosquitto.org:1883"
                       ["SNControlNetwork/Florida/device1"] subscriberid)
```

Open another terminal window and start a second `lein-try` REPL session. Use the following code to publish messages to the broker. Note that subscriber must be connected already so as not to lose incoming messages:

```
(require '[clojurewerkz.machine-head.client :as mh])

(defn connect-and-publish [broker-addr client-id topic]
  (let [qos 2
        retained false
        conn  (mh/connect broker-addr client-id)]
    (if (mh/connected? conn)
      (do (dotimes [n 5]
            (let [payload (str "msg" n)]
              (mh/publish conn topic payload qos retained)
              (println "published " payload)))
          (mh/disconnect conn)))))

(def pubclientid (mh/generate-id))
pubclientid
;; -> "ryan.1384135173618"

(connect-and-publish "tcp://test.mosquitto.org:1883" pubclientid
                     "SNControlNetwork/Florida/device1")
;; *out* of publish REPL
;; published  msg0
;; published  msg1
;; published  msg2
;; published  msg3
;; published  msg4
;; *out* of client REPL
;; received  msg0 on topic  SNControlNetwork/Florida/device1
;; received  msg1 on topic  SNControlNetwork/Florida/device1
;; received  msg2 on topic  SNControlNetwork/Florida/device1
;; received  msg3 on topic  SNControlNetwork/Florida/device1
;; received  msg4 on topic  SNControlNetwork/Florida/device1
```

## Discussion

MQTT (*http://mqtt.org*) is an open, lightweight publish/subscribe messaging protocol. It is useful for connections where bandwidth is at a premium and/or connections are unreliable. While the AMQP protocol excels at various scenarios for business messaging, MQTT is usually the choice for smaller payloads and last-mile connectivity because it is simple to implement in hardware. The MQTT protocol has the following properties that make it good for constrained networks:

- Designed for devices with limited resources, like battery-operated 8-bit controllers.
- Internally compresses into bitwise headers and variable-length fields. The smallest possible packet size is a mere two bytes.

- No polling required. Implements asynchronous bidirectional push delivery of messages.
- Supports always-connected and sometimes-connected models.
- Tested with low-bandwidth networks like VSAT and GPRS.

The protocol defines three possible Quality of Service (QoS) values: `0`, `1`, and `2`, corresponding to fire-and-forget, at-least-once, and exactly-once qualities of service. QoS parameters `1` and `2` require persistent storage on the client so as to save the message until an acknowledgment arrives. In the preceding recipe, the default persistence implementation provided by the library is used.

MQTT also has a concept of retention of messages. If you were to set `retained` to `true` in the `connect-and-publish` function, the broker would remember the last known retained message on the topic. When the subscriber connects, it is given the last message (for which `retained` was `true`) by the broker and does not have to wait to receive the first message.

WebSphere and RabbitMQ (*http://bit.ly/rmq-mqtt*) also implement MQTT and can be used instead of Mosquitto. While the preceding code used the Mosquitto test broker (*tcp://test.mosquitto.org:1883*), you can install your own Mosquitto broker using the MQTT installation instructions (*http://bit.ly/mosquitto-broker*).

The topics are usually defined with the separator `/` defining hierarchies. As an example, the sensor devices of a particular domain, `SNControl`, might be publishing their values to `SNControl/Florida/device1`, `SNControl/Florida/device2`, and so on. Meanwhile, the devices in domain `RKNControl` might publish their values to `RKNControl/Washington/device1`, for example. Naming the topics in this way helps in subscribing to multiple topics based on wildcards.

This is how wildcards are used:

`/`
: Used as a separator.

`+`
: The single-level wildcard and can appear anywhere in the string.

`#`
: A multilevel wildcard and needs to appear at the end of the string.

For example, these subscriptions are possible:

`SNControl/#`
: Any device under `SNControl/Florida` (e.g., `SNControl/Florida/device1/sensor1` and `SNControl/Florida/device1/sensor2`) and `SNControl/California/device1` will match.

`SNControl/+/device1`
: Any `device1` in states under domain `SNControl` will match(e.g., `SNControl/Florida/device1` and `SNControl/California/device1`).

`SNControl/+/+/sensor1`
: Any `sensor1` in states under domain `SNControl` will match (e.g., `SNControl/Florida/device1/sensor1` and `SNControl/Florida/device2/sensor1`).

In the preceding code, the `connect-and-subscribe` method uses the callback handler `message-handler` to process incoming messages arriving from the broker. In the `connect-and-subscribe` method, the `connect` method from the Machine Head library is invoked by providing it the broker address and client ID (generated using `generate-id`, or some other unique ID). Then it checks that the connection has been established using the `connected?` method. The `subscribe` method is invoked with the connection, a vector of topics to subscribe to, a message handler, and a `:qos` option. The subscriber then waits for some time and disconnects using the `disconnect` method.

The `connect-and-publish` method calls the method `connect`, which accepts the broker address and client ID and returns the connection `conn`. Then it checks if the connection is successful with the `connected?` method and invokes the `publish` method to publish messages (a few times) to the broker. The `publish` method accepts as parameters the connection, topic string, payload, QoS value, and `retained`. The QoS value of `2` corresponds to exactly-once delivery. The `retained` value of `false` instructs the broker not to retain messages. Finally, the `disconnect` method disconnects from the broker.

While the preceding code fragment just prints the incoming messages, you could potentially use the messages in some other way (e.g., triggering some actions based on an alarm that the code has received).

## See Also

- The MQTT protocol website (*http://mqtt.org/*)
- The documentation (*http://clojuremqtt.info/*) of the Machine Head (*https://github.com/clojurewerkz/machine_head*) library
- The Eclipse Paho library (*http://www.eclipse.org/paho/*), the Java library that Machine Head uses under the hood to communicate using MQTT
- Mosquitto (*http://mosquitto.org/*), an open source message broker that implements the MQTT protocol

- *Building Smarter Planet Solutions with MQTT and IBM WebSphere MQ Telemetry* (*http://bit.ly/mqtt-paper*) (IBM Redbooks), by Valerie Lampkin *et al.*, for a more detailed explanation of MQTT
- The TED talk (*http://bit.ly/inno-begins-at-home*) by Andy Stanford-Clark, one of the inventors of MQTT—a humorous and informative session on how MQTT can be used

# 5.8. Using ZeroMQ Concurrently

by Kevin J. Lynagh

## Problem

You want to use ZeroMQ concurrently, but ZeroMQ sockets are not thread-safe. You *could* manually set up mutual exclusion via locks or other Java concurrency primitives, but you'd rather use a simpler method.

## Solution

Use the `zmq-async` (*https://github.com/lynaghk/zmq-async*) library to simplify concurrent usage of ZeroMQ via `core.async`.

In order to follow along with this recipe, your system should have ZeroMQ 3.2 installed.

If you're on a Mac and have the Homebrew (*http://brew.sh*) package manager installed, use this command to install it:

```
$ brew install zeromq
```

Or, if you are on Ubuntu:

```
$ apt-get install libzmq3
```

Otherwise, visit ØMQ's downloads page (*http://bit.ly/zmq-intro*).

Before starting, add `[com.keminglabs/zmq-async "0.1.0"]` to your project's dependencies, or follow along in a REPL using `lein-try`:

```
$ lein try com.keminglabs/zmq-async
```

Here's a simple ping-pong between two asynchronous `go` blocks in `core.async`, communicating via a ZeroMQ in-process socket:

```
(require '[com.keminglabs.zmq-async.core :refer [register-socket!]]
         '[clojure.core.async :refer [>! <! go chan sliding-buffer close!]])

(def addr "inproc://ping-pong")
```

```
(def server-in  (chan (sliding-buffer 64)))
(def server-out (chan (sliding-buffer 64)))
(def client-in  (chan (sliding-buffer 64)))
(def client-out (chan (sliding-buffer 64)))

(register-socket! {:in server-in
                   :out server-out
                   :socket-type :rep
                   :configurator (fn [socket] (.bind socket addr))})

(register-socket! {:in client-in
                   :out client-out
                    :socket-type :req
                   :configurator (fn [socket] (.connect socket addr))})

(do
  ;; A simple server worker that waits for incoming requests and
  ;; responds with "pong"
  (go
    (dotimes [_ 3]
      (println (String. (<! server-out)))
      (>! server-in "pong"))
    (close! server-in))

  ;; A simple client worker that sends a "ping" request and awaits
  ;;  a response
  (go
    (dotimes [_ 3]
      (>! client-in "ping")
      (println (String. (<! client-out))))
    (close! client-in)))
;; *out*
;; ping
;; pong
;; ping
;; pong
;; ping
;; pong
```

## Discussion

ZeroMQ is a message-oriented socket system that supports many communication styles (request/reply, pub/sub, etc.) on top of many transport layers (intra-process, inter-process, inter-machine via TCP, etc.) with bindings to many languages. ZeroMQ sockets are a great substrate upon which to build service-oriented architectures. ZeroMQ sockets have less overhead than HTTP and are architecturally more flexible, supporting publish/subscribe, fanout, and other topologies in addition to request/reply.

However, ZeroMQ sockets are not thread-safe—concurrent usage typically requires explicit locking or dedicated threads and queues. The `zmq-async` library handles all of that for you, creating ZeroMQ sockets on your behalf and giving you access to them via thread-safe `core.async` channels.

The `zmq-async` library provides one function, `com.keminglabs.zmq-async.core/register-socket!`, which associates a ZeroMQ socket with either one or two `core.async` channels: `:in` (to which you can write strings or byte arrays) and `:out` (from which you can read byte arrays). Writing a Clojure collection of strings and/or byte arrays to a channel using `>!` sends a multipart message. Received multipart messages are placed on `core.async` channels. Reading these messages with `<!` will yield a vector of byte arrays.

To simulate two asynchronous processes interacting over ZeroMQ, the preceding sample uses two `go` blocks that read from and write to the registered channels. Each `go` block will begin executing immediately in background threads. The "server" block will wait for and reply to three requests (`<!` blocks until it receives a value), replying with "pong" each time. Concurrently, the "client" block will make three "ping" requests, awaiting a reply before moving on to the next request. Finally, after both blocks are done working, they each close their channels using `close!`.

The `register-socket!` function can be given an already-created ZeroMQ socket, but typically you would have the library create a socket for you by passing the `:socket-type` and a `:configurator`. The configurator is a function that is passed the raw ZeroMQ socket object. This function is run on the socket after it is created in order to connect/bind addresses, set pub/sub subscriptions, and otherwise configure the socket.

The implicit context supporting `register-socket!` can only handle one incoming/outgoing message at a time. If you need sockets to work in parallel (i.e., you don't want to miss a small control message just because you're slurping in a 10 GB message on another socket), then you'll need multiple `zmq-async` contexts.

## See Also

- Rich Hickey's "Language of the System" talk (*http://bit.ly/lang-of-system*), wherein he outlines the benefits of queues
- The ZeroMQ guide (*http://bit.ly/zmq-guide*) for architectural patterns and advice
- Recipe 3.11, "Decoupling Consumers and Producers with core.async" on page 148
- The introductory blog post (*http://bit.ly/core-async-post*) for `core.async`, which provides a good overview

# 5.9. Creating a TCP Client

by Luke VanderHart

## Problem

You want to open a TCP connection to a remote host, on a particular port.

## Solution

Use Java interop to create an instance of `java.net.Socket` and connect to a remote host.

For example, the following code uses a `Socket` to create a TCP connection and send an HTTP GET request, returning the result as a string:

```
(require '[clojure.java.io :as io])
(import '[java.io StringWriter]
        '[java.net Socket])

(defn send-request
  "Sends an HTTP GET request to the specified host, port, and path"
  [host port path]
  (with-open [sock (Socket. host port)
              writer (io/writer sock)
              reader (io/reader sock)
              response (StringWriter.)]
    (.append writer (str "GET " path "\n"))
    (.flush writer)
    (io/copy reader response)
    (str response)))
```

This function obtains instances of `java.io.Writer` and `java.io.Reader` to send and receive data to and from the remote server. By appending strings that conform to the HTTP specification to the writer, it forms a rudimentary HTTP client and executes a GET request to the specified endpoint. The results are then copied into an instance of `java.io.StringWriter` using the `clojure.java.io/copy` utility function, and returned as a string.

Invoking `(send-request "google.com" 80 "/")` at the REPL should return a very long string, consisting of the entire HTTP response that is the Google home page.

## Discussion

This example uses the `clojure.java.io` namespace to obtain instances of `java.io.Writer` and `java.io.Reader` to read and write textual data to/from the network socket. In point of fact, `Socket` instances are not actually limited to textual data, and it would be possible to obtain raw binary input and output streams just as easily using `clojure.java.io/input-stream` and `clojure.java.io/output-stream`, respectively. Since HTTP is a textual protocol, however, it makes more sense to use the higher-level features of `Reader` and `Writer`.

This example uses HTTP because it's a protocol that many readers are familiar with. In the real world, using a raw TCP socket for HTTP requests is almost certainly a terrible idea. There are a plethora of libraries that provide a much higher-level interface to HTTP requests and responses, and encapsulate a lot of pesky details such as escaping, encoding, and formatting.

Also note that the reader, the writer, and the socket itself are bound within the context of a `with-open` macro. This guarantees that the `close` method is called when they are finished, which releases the TCP connection. If the connection is not released, it will continue to consume resources on both the client and the server and may be subject to termination on the remote side.

When returning lazy sequences from a `with-open` context, it is important to fully realize those sequences using `doall`. This is because resources opened by `with-open` are *only* available inside the `with-open` block. The `doall` function fully realizes a collection, retaining its entire contents in memory:

```
(realized? (range 100))
;; -> false

(realized? (doall (range 100)))
;; -> true
```

Depending on your application, you may prefer to use the `doseq` macro. Instead of retaining the entire sequence, `doseq` executes its body for each element of the sequence. This is useful if you need to cause side effects for each element of a sequence, but need to hang on to the entire thing:

```
(doseq [n (range 3)]
  (println n))
;; *out*
;; 0
;; 1
;; 2
```

## See Also

- Recipe 5.10, "Creating a TCP Server" on page 247
- Wikipedia on the TCP protocol (*http://bit.ly/wiki-tcp*)

# 5.10. Creating a TCP Server

by Luke VanderHart

## Problem

You want to open up a socket on a port to use as a low-level TCP server.

## Solution

Use Java interop on the `java.net.ServerSocket` class to create a TCP listener. Use the functions in `clojure.java.io` to obtain input and output streams (or readers and writers) to read and write data to the socket:

```
(require '[clojure.java.io :as io])
(import '[java.net ServerSocket])

(defn receive
  "Read a line of textual data from the given socket"
  [socket]
  (.readLine (io/reader socket)))

(defn send
  "Send the given string message out over the given socket"
  [socket msg]
  (let [writer (io/writer socket)]
      (.write writer msg)
      (.flush writer)))

(defn serve [port handler]
  (with-open [server-sock (ServerSocket. port)
              sock (.accept server-sock)]
    (let [msg-in (receive sock)
          msg-out (handler msg-in)]
      (send sock msg-out))))
```

This code defines three functions. `receive` and `send` deal with reading and writing string data from and to a socket, using the `clojure.java.io/reader` and `clojure.java.io/writer` functions. Both of these accept a `java.net.Socket` as an argument and will return a `java.io.Reader` or `java.io.Writer` built from the socket's input and output streams.

`server` handles actually creating an instance of `ServerSocket` on a particular port. It also takes a handler function, which will be used to process the incoming request and determine a response message.

After creating an instance of `ServerSocket`, `server` immediately calls its `accept` method, which blocks until a TCP connection is established. When a client connects, it returns the session as an instance of `java.net.Socket`.

It then passes the socket to the `receive` function, which opens up a reader on it and blocks until it receives a full line of input, terminated by a newline character (`\n`). When it receives one, it calls the handler function with the resulting value, and calls `send` to send the response using a writer opened on the same socket. `send` also calls the `flush` method on the writer to ensure that all the data is actually sent back to the client, instead of being buffered in the `Writer` instance.

After sending the response, the `serve` method returns. Because it used the `with-open` macro when creating the server socket and the TCP session socket, it will invoke the `close` method on each before returning, which disconnects the client and ends the session.

To try it out, invoke the `serve` function in the REPL. For a simple example, use `(serve 8888 #(.toUpperCase %))`. Note that it won't return right away; it blocks, waiting for a client to connect.

To connect to the server you can use a *telnet* client, which is installed by default on nearly every operating system. To use it, open up a command-line window:

```
$ telnet localhost 8888
Trying ::1...
Connected to localhost.
Escape character is '^]'.
```

At this point you can type anything you like (in the following example, the input is "Hello, World!"). When you finish, make sure you type Enter or Return to send a newline character:

```
$ telnet localhost 8888
Trying ::1...
Connected to localhost.
Escape character is '^]'.
Hello, World!
HELLO, WORLD!Connection closed by foreign host
```

As you can see, as soon as you type a newline, the server responds with the uppercase version of your input (as per the handler function) and then immediately terminates the connection. In the REPL, you will find that the `serve` function has finally returned.

## Discussion

This example uses readers and writers, which deal solely in textual data, to make the concepts of working with sockets easier to demonstrate. Of course, an actual socket is not limited to strings and can send and receive any kind of binary data.

To do this, simply use the `clojure.java.io/input-stream` and `clojure.java.io/output-stream` functions instead of the `clojure.java.io/reader` and `clojure.java.io/writer` functions, respectively, which return `java.io.InputStream` and `java.io.OutputStream` objects. These provide APIs for reading and writing raw bytes, rather than just strings and characters.

One thing you may have noticed about the example is that, unlike a traditional server, it doesn't actually continue to accept incoming connections after the `serve` function returns. For ongoing use, typically you'd like to be able to serve multiple incoming connections.

Fortunately, this is relatively straightforward to do given the concurrency tools that Clojure provides. Modifying the `serve` function to work as a persistent server requires three changes:

- Run the server on a separate thread so it doesn't block the REPL.
- Don't close the server socket after handling the first request.
- After handling a request, loop back to immediately handle another.

Also, because the server will be running on a non-REPL thread, it would be good to provide a mechanism for terminating the server other than killing the whole JVM.

The modified code looks like this:

```
(defn serve-persistent [port handler]
  (let [running (atom true)]
    (future
      (with-open [server-sock (ServerSocket. port)]
        (while @running
          (with-open [sock (.accept server-sock)]
            (let [msg-in (receive sock)
                  msg-out (handler msg-in)]
              (send sock msg-out))))))
    running))
```

The key feature of this code is that it launches the server socket asynchronously inside a future and calls the `accept` method inside of a loop. It also creates an atom called `running` and returns it, checking it each time it loops. To stop the server, reset the atom to `false`, and the loop will break:

```
(def a (serve-persistent 8888 #(.toUpperCase %)))
;; -> #'my-server/a

;; Server is running, will respond to multiple requests

(reset! a false)
;; -> false
;; Server is stopped, will stop serving requests after the next one
```

### When to Use Sockets

As you can see from these examples, raw server sockets are a fairly low-level networking construct. Using them effectively means either creating your own data protocol or reimplementing an existing one, and handling all the fiddly bits of connecting, flushing, and disconnecting input and outputs streams yourself.

If your communication needs can be met by some existing protocol or communication technique (such as HTTP, SSH, or a message queue), you should almost certainly use that instead. There are widely available servers and libraries for these protocols that allow programming at a much higher level of abstraction, with much better performance and resiliency.

Still, understanding how all these different techniques work on a low level is valuable. At least as far as the JVM is concerned, most networking code ultimately bottoms out in calls to the raw socket mechanisms described in this recipe. Understanding how they work is key to understanding how higher-level networking tools (such as HTTP requests or JMS queues) actually work.

## See Also

- The API documentation (*http://bit.ly/javadoc-server-socket*) for `ServerSocket` and `Socket` objects in Java
- The API documentation (*http://bit.ly/clj-java-io-api*) for the `clojure.java.io` namespace
- Recipe 5.9, "Creating a TCP Client" on page 245
- Wikipedia on the TCP protocol (*http://bit.ly/wiki-tcp*)

# 5.11. Sending and Receiving UDP Packets

by Luke VanderHart

## Problem

You want to send asynchronous UDP packets from your application, or receive them.

## Solution

Use Java interop with the `java.net.DatagramSocket` and `java.net.DatagramPacket` classes to send and receive UDP messages.

The following example demonstrates functions that send and receive short strings encoded into UDP packets:

```
(import '[java.net DatagramSocket
                   DatagramPacket
                   InetSocketAddress])

(defn send
  "Send a short textual message over a DatagramSocket to the specified
  host and port. If the string is over 512 bytes long, it will be
  truncated."
  [^DatagramSocket socket msg host port]
  (let [payload (.getBytes msg)
        length (min (alength payload) 512)
        address (InetSocketAddress. host port)
        packet (DatagramPacket. payload length address)]
    (.send socket packet)))

(defn receive
  "Block until a UDP message is received on the given DatagramSocket, and
  return the payload message as a string."
  [^DatagramSocket socket]
  (let [buffer (byte-array 512)
        packet (DatagramPacket. buffer 512)]
    (.receive socket packet)
    (String. (.getData packet)
             0 (.getLength packet))))

(defn receive-loop
  "Given a function and DatagramSocket, will (in another thread) wait
  for the socket to receive a message, and whenever it does, will call
  the provided function on the incoming message."
  [socket f]
  (future (while true (f (receive socket)))))
```

The `send` function is fairly straightforward—most of its content is devoted to constructing a byte array as a payload for the `DatagramPacket` and invoking constructor forms. The most interesting thing is its limitation of the payload size to 512 bytes, using the `length` argument to the `DatagramPacket` constructor. This is because it generally isn't safe to attempt to send over 512 bytes of payload in a single UDP packet; although some network infrastructures may support it, others do not.

The `receive` function creates an incoming byte array, adds it to a mutable empty `DatagramPacket` instance, and invokes the `DatagramSocket.receive` method on the socket. When incoming data is received, the `receive` method will return after populating the instance of `DatagramPacket`. The Clojure code then constructs and returns a new `String` using the populated range of the byte array (that is, between 0 and the value reported by the `DatagramPacket.getLength` method).

Because the `receive` function blocks and only returns a single value, it isn't particularly useful for accepting multiple messages or using from the REPL. `receive-loop` wraps the `receive` function, calling it repeatedly on a separate thread. Whenever it returns a value, it invokes the supplied function, then loops back to wait for more input.

To execute this code, you'll first need to create an instance of `DatagramSocket`. At the REPL:

```
(def socket (DatagramSocket. 8888))
;; -> #'udp/socket
```

This creates a UDP socket on the specified port (in this case, 8888).

Next, start up a listener using the `receive-loop` function. For this example, simply pass it the `println` function so it will print out all received values:

```
(receive-loop socket println)
;; -> #<core$future_call$reify__6267@2783890e: :pending>
```

Then you can send a message! If you started the listener thread with `receive-loop` properly, you should see it print out the incoming message immediately:

```
(send socket "hello, world!" "localhost" 8888)
;; *out*
;; hello, world!
;;
;; -> nil
```

In this case, sending to *localhost*, the message transmission happens so quickly that the message is actually received before the `send` function even returns.

### Discussion

Unlike TCP, UDP (the User Datagram Protocol) is an *asynchronous* protocol that makes no guarantees regarding the order in which messages arrive, whether their contents are correct, or even if they arrive at all. In exchange, UDP typically has a lower per-packet latency than protocols like TCP, since it does not need to perform error checking or recovery.

Before you decide to use UDP, make sure your application is designed to continue working even if packets are dropped or corrupted.

Because UDP uses asynchronous messages as its model, it is fairly easy to use `core.async` to wrap the raw `DatagramSocket` instances. `core.async` provides a very nice channel abstraction that lets you consume and produce inherently asynchronous events (such as UDP messages) in a clean, managed way.

### Multicast UDP

UDP is also capable of sending the same datagram packet to multiple destinations using a technique called *UDP multicast*. To use multicast, create an instance of `java.net.MulticastSocket` instead of `java.net.DatagramSocket`.

A full explanation of how to use `MulticastSocket` is very well documented on Oracle's website (*http://bit.ly/javadoc-multicast-socket*) and would be redundant to reproduce here, since it is straightforward Java interop. After reading the preceding example, extending it to `MulticastSocket` should be relatively self-explanatory.

## See Also


- Recipe 3.11, "Decoupling Consumers and Producers with core.async" on page 148
- Recipe 5.9, "Creating a TCP Client" on page 245
- Recipe 5.10, "Creating a TCP Server" on page 247

- The `java.net.MulticastSocket` API documentation (*http://bit.ly/javadoc-multicast-socket*)

# CHAPTER 6
# Databases

## 6.0. Introduction

Storing data in a database is not an uncommon task for developers—in this day and age, it's practically a given. As with nearly every language under the sun, there is a bevy of drivers and clients to interact with databases from Clojure. What sets Clojure apart, however, is its ability to *compose*.

As we've said before in this book: in Clojure, data is king. You'll find many of the database client libraries do a little legwork to connect you to the datastore, then promptly get out of your way. Such libraries don't do so out of laziness (at least, we hope), but rather out of the principle of separation of concerns: *I'll handle connecting to the database; you handle the domain (your data).* In fact, the best APIs are built out of data, providing only one or two functions and letting you manipulate queries and data to be inserted directly as Clojure data structures.

In this chapter, we'll visit a wide number of databases and techniques, including the SQLs, full-text search, Mongo, Redis, and Datomic.

Datomic (*http://www.datomic.com/*) is one of the more interesting recent developments in the database landscape. Invented and maintained by Rich Hickey (who you will probably recognize as the same person who wrote Clojure itself), it is a scalable, transactional, value-oriented, time-aware database built around the same principles and philosophies as Clojure. If you like Clojure, you should definitely give Datomic a try, both as your application's datastore and also as a learning tool to further explore functional, data-oriented programming.

# 6.1. Connecting to an SQL Database

by Tom Hicks; originally submitted by Simone Mosciatti

## Problem

You want to connect your program to an SQL database.

## Solution

Use the `clojure.java.jdbc` library for JDBC-based access to SQL databases.

To follow along with this recipe, you'll need a running SQL database and an existing table to connect to. We suggest PostgreSQL.[1]

After you have PostgreSQL running (presumably on *localhost:5432*), run the following command to create a database for this recipe:

```
# On Mac:
$ /Applications/Postgres93.app/Contents/MacOS/bin/createdb cookbook_experiments

# Everyone else:
$ createdb cookbook_experiments
```

Before starting, add `[org.clojure/java.jdbc "0.3.0"]` to your project's dependencies. You'll also need a JDBC driver for the RDBMS of your choice. If you're following along with this sample, use `[org.postgresql/postgresql "9.2-1003-jdbc4"]`. To start a REPL using `lein-try`, enter the following Leiningen command:

```
$ lein try org.clojure/java.jdbc "0.3.0" \
           java-jdbc/dsl "0.1.0" \
           org.postgresql/postgresql "9.2-1003-jdbc4"
```

To interact with a database using `clojure.java.jdbc`, all you need is a connection specification. This specification takes the form of a plain Clojure map with values indicating the database driver type, location, and authentication credentials:

```
(def db-spec {:classname "org.postgresql.Driver"
              :subprotocol "postgresql"
              :subname "//localhost:5432/cookbook_experiments"
              ;; Not needed for a non-secure local database...
              ;; :user "bilbo"
              ;; :password "secret"
              })
```

1. Mac users: visit *http://postgresapp.com/* to download an easy-to-install DMG. Everyone else: you'll find a guide for your operating system on the PostgreSQL wiki (*http://bit.ly/postgres-install*).

Create a relation in the specified database by invoking the `clojure.java.jdbc/create-table` function with the specification and any number of column specifications:

```
(require '[clojure.java.jdbc :as jdbc]
         '[java-jdbc.ddl :as ddl])

(jdbc/db-do-commands db-spec false
  (ddl/create-table
     :tags
     [:id :serial "PRIMARY KEY"]
     [:name :varchar "NOT NULL"]))
;; -> (0)
```

Many other functions that query and manipulate a database, such as `clojure.java.jdbc/insert!`, take a database specification directly as their first argument:

```
(require '[java-jdbc.sql :as sql])

(jdbc/insert! db-spec :tags
                      {:name "Clojure"}
                      {:name "Java"})
;; -> ({:name "Clojure", :id 1} {:name "Java", :id 2})

(jdbc/query db-spec (sql/select * :tags (sql/where {:name "Clojure"})))
;; -> ({:name "Clojure", :id 1})
```

## Discussion

The `clojure.java.jdbc` library provides functions that wrap the basic capabilities of the Java JDBC specification. The additional `java-jdbc.sql` and `java-jdbc.ddl` namespaces from the `java-jdbc/dsl` project implement small DSLs to generate basic SQL DML and DDL statements.

Because it relies upon Java JDBC, the `clojure.java.jdbc` library is usable with many of the most popular SQL databases, including Apache Derby, HSQLDB, Microsoft SQL Server, MySQL, PostgreSQL, and SQLite.

The parameters necessary to set up and access a data source are called the *database specification* (often abbreviated "db-spec") and are provided in a simple Clojure map. The specification usually includes such parameters as the driver class name, the subprotocol for a particular RDBMS type, the hostname, the port number, the database name, and the username and password.

The `clojure.java.jdbc` library also permits several other forms of data source specification, including Java URIs, already-open connections, JNDI connections, and plain strings. For example, a complete URI string may be provided under the `:connection-uri` key:

```
;; As a spec string
(def db-spec
  "jdbc:postgresql://bilbo:secret@localhost:5432/cookbook_experiment")

;; As a connection URI map...
;; with a username and password...
(def db-spec
  {:connection-uri (str "jdbc:postgresql://localhost:5432/cookbook_experiments?"
                        "user=bilbo&password=secret")})

;; or without
(def db-spec
  {:connection-uri "jdbc:postgresql://localhost:5432/cookbook_experiments"})
```

Database records are represented as Clojure maps, with the table's column names used as keys. Retrieval of a set of database records produces a sequence of maps that can then be processed with all the normal Clojure functions:

```
(jdbc/query db-spec (sql/select * :tags))
;; -> ({:name "Clojure", :id 1}
;     {:name "Java", :id 2})

(filter #(not (.endsWith (:name %) "ure"))
        (jdbc/query db-spec (sql/select * :tags)))
;; -> ({:name "Java", :id 2})
```

There are other Clojure libraries to access relational databases, and each provides a different abstraction and DSL for the manipulation of SQL data and expressions, such as Korma. The `clojure.java.jdbc` library, however, covers a large portion of everyday database access needs.

## See Also

- See Recipe 6.2, "Connecting to an SQL Database with a Connection Pool" on page 259, to learn about pooling connections to an SQL database with `c3p0` and `clojure.java.jdbc`.
- See Recipe 6.3, "Manipulating an SQL Database" on page 262, to learn about using `clojure.java.jdbc` to interact with an SQL database.
- Visit the `clojure.java.jdbc` GitHub repository (*https://github.com/clojure/java.jdbc*) for more detailed information on the library.
- Visit the `java-jdbc/dsl` GitHub repository (*https://github.com/seancorfield/jsql*) for more information on the SQL query generation capabilities it provides. Alternatively, investigate the Honey SQL (*https://github.com/jkk/honeysql*), SQLingvo (*https://github.com/r0man/sqlingvo*), or Korma (*http://sqlkorma.com/*) libraries for SQL query generation. Korma is covered in Recipe 6.4, "Simplifying SQL with Korma" on page 268.

# 6.2. Connecting to an SQL Database with a Connection Pool

by Tom Hicks and Filippo Diotalevi

## Problem

You would like to connect to an SQL database efficiently using a connection pool.

## Solution

Use the BoneCP connection and statement pooling library to wrap your JDBC-based drivers, creating a pooled data source. The pooled data source is then usable by the `clojure.java.jdbc` library, as described in Recipe 6.1, "Connecting to an SQL Database" on page 256.

To follow along with this recipe, you'll need a running SQL database and an existing table to connect to. We suggest PostgreSQL.[2]

After you have PostgreSQL running (presumably on *localhost:5432*), run the following command to create a database for this recipe:

```
# On Mac:
$ /Applications/Postgres93.app/Contents/MacOS/bin/createdb cookbook_experiments

# Everyone else:
$ createdb cookbook_experiments
```

Before starting, add the BoneCP dependency (`[com.jolbox/bonecp "0.8.0.RELEASE"]`), as well as the appropriate JDBC libraries for your RDBMS, to your project's dependencies. You'll also need a valid SLF4J logger. Alternatively, you can follow along in a REPL using `lein-try`:

```
$ lein try com.jolbox/bonecp "0.8.0.RELEASE" \
           org.clojure/java.jdbc "0.3.0" \
           java-jdbc/dsl "0.1.0" \
           org.postgresql/postgresql "9.2-1003-jdbc4" \
           org.slf4j/slf4j-nop  # Just do not log anything
```

First, create a database specification containing the parameters for accessing the database. This includes keys for the initial and maximum pool sizes, as well as the number of partitions:

```
(def db-spec {:classname "org.postgresql.Driver"
              :subprotocol "postgresql"
```

2. Mac users: visit *http://postgresapp.com/* to download an easy-to-install DMG. Everyone else: you'll find a guide for your operating system on the PostgreSQL wiki (*http://bit.ly/postgres-install*).

```
              :subname "//localhost:5432/cookbook_experiments"
              :init-pool-size 4
              :max-pool-size 20
              :partitions 2})
```

To create a pooled BoneCPDataSource object, define a function (for convenience) that uses the parameters in the database specification map:

```
(import 'com.jolbox.bonecp.BoneCPDataSource)

(defn pooled-datasource [db-spec]
  (let [{:keys [classname subprotocol subname user password
                init-pool-size max-pool-size idle-time partitions]} db-spec
        min-connections (inc (int (/ init-pool-size partitions)))
        max-connections (inc (int (/ max-pool-size partitions)))
        cpds (doto (BoneCPDataSource.)
                   (.setDriverClass classname)
                   (.setJdbcUrl (str "jdbc:" subprotocol ":" subname))
                   (.setUsername user)
                   (.setPassword password)
                   (.setMinConnectionsPerPartition min-connections)
                   (.setMaxConnectionsPerPartition max-connections)
                   (.setPartitionCount partitions)
                   (.setStatisticsEnabled true)
                   (.setIdleMaxAgeInMinutes (or idle-time 60)))]
       {:datasource cpds}))
```

Use the convenience function to define a pooled data source for connecting to your database:

```
(def pooled-db-spec (pooled-datasource db-spec))

pooled-db-spec
;; -> {:datasource #<BoneCPDataSource ...>}
```

Pass the database specification as the first argument to any clojure.java.jdbc functions that query or manipulate your database:

```
(require '[clojure.java.jdbc :as jdbc]
         '[java-jdbc.ddl :as ddl]
         '[java-jdbc.sql :as sql])

(jdbc/db-do-commands pooled-db-spec false
  (ddl/create-table
    :blog_posts
    [:id :serial "PRIMARY KEY"]
    [:title "varchar(255)" "NOT NULL"]
    [:body :text]))
;; -> (0)

(jdbc/insert! pooled-db-spec
              :blog_posts
              {:title "My first post!" :body "This is going to be good!"})
```

```
;; -> ({:body "This is going to be good!", :title "My first post!", :id 1})

(jdbc/query pooled-db-spec
            (sql/select * :blog_posts (sql/where{:title "My first post!"})))
;; -> ({:body "This is going to be good!", :title "My first post!", :id 1})
```

## Discussion

As shown in the solution, the `clojure.java.jdbc` library can create database connections from JDBC data sources, which allows connections to be easily pooled by the BoneCP or other pooling libraries.

The BoneCP library wraps existing JDBC classes to allow the creation of efficient data sources. It can adapt traditional unpooled drivers and data sources by augmenting them with transparent pooling of `Connection` and `PreparedStatement` instances.

While the library offers several ways to create data sources, most users will find the examples provided here to be the easiest.

BoneCP offers several dozen configuration parameters that control the operation of the data source and its connections. Luckily, most of these configuration parameters have built-in defaults. Parameters may be specified to control such facets as the min, max, and initial pool size; the number of idle connections; the age of connections; transaction handling; the use of `PreparedStatement` pooling; and if, when, and how pooled connections are tested.

Pooled data resources (threads and database connections) may be released by calling the `close` method on the `BoneCPDataSource` class of the library. Attempting to reuse the pooled data source after it is closed will result in an SQL exception:

```
(.close (:datasource pooled-db-spec))
;; -> nil
```

## See Also

- Recipe 6.1, "Connecting to an SQL Database" on page 256, to learn about basic database connections with `clojure.java.jdbc`
- Recipe 6.3, "Manipulating an SQL Database" on page 262, to learn about using `clojure.java.jdbc` to interact with an SQL database
- The BoneCP documentation (*http://bit.ly/bonecp-doc*) and GitHub repository (*https://github.com/wwadge/bonecp*)
- The `clojure.java.jdbc` GitHub repository (*https://github.com/clojure/java.jdbc*) for more detailed information on the library

# 6.3. Manipulating an SQL Database

by Tom Hicks

## Problem

You want your Clojure program to manipulate tables and records in an SQL database.

## Solution

Use the `clojure.java.jdbc` library for JDBC-based access to SQL databases.

To follow along with this recipe, you'll need a running SQL database and an existing table to connect to. We suggest PostgreSQL.[3]

After you have PostgreSQL running (presumably on *localhost:5432*), run the following command to create a database for this recipe:

```
# On Mac:
$ /Applications/Postgres93.app/Contents/MacOS/bin/createdb cookbook_experiments

# Everyone else:
$ createdb cookbook_experiments
```

Before starting, add `[org.clojure/java.jdbc "0.3.0"]` and `[java-jdbc/dsl "0.1.0"]` to your project's dependencies. You'll also need a JDBC driver for the RDBMS of your choice. If you're following along with this sample, use `[org.postgresql/postgresql "9.2-1003-jdbc4"]`. To start a REPL using `lein-try`, enter the following Leiningen command:

```
$ lein try org.clojure/java.jdbc "0.3.0" \
           java-jdbc/dsl "0.1.0" \
           org.postgresql/postgresql "9.2-1003-jdbc4"
```

Then, define how the database should be accessed:

```
(def db-spec {:classname "org.postgresql.Driver"
              :subprotocol "postgresql"
              :subname "//localhost:5432/cookbook_experiments"})
```

To create a new table, use the `java-jdbc.ddl/create-table` function to generate the necessary DDL statement, and then pass the statement to the `jdbc/db-do-commands` function to execute it:

3. Mac users: visit *http://postgresapp.com/* to download an easy-to-install DMG. Everyone else: you'll find a guide for your operating system on the PostgreSQL wiki (*http://bit.ly/postgres-install*).

```
(require '[clojure.java.jdbc :as jdbc]
         '[java-jdbc.ddl :as ddl])

(jdbc/db-do-commands db-spec
  (ddl/create-table :fruit
    [:name "varchar(16)" "PRIMARY KEY"]
    [:appearance "varchar(32)"]
    [:cost :int "NOT NULL"]
    [:unit "varchar(16)"]
    [:grade :real]))
;; -> (0)
```

Insert complete records into a table using the `clojure.java.jdbc/insert!` function, invoking it with a vector of the column values for each row. Be sure to provide the column values in the order in which the columns were declared in the table:

```
(jdbc/insert! db-spec :fruit
  nil ; column names omitted
  ["Red Delicious" "dark red" 20 "bushel" 8.2]
  ["Plantain" "mild spotting" 48 "stalk" 7.4]
  ["Kiwifruit" "fresh"  35 "crate" 9.1]
  ["Plum" "ripe" 12 "carton" 8.4])
;; -> (1 1 1 1)
```

To query the database, generate the SQL for the query with the `java-jdbc.sql/select` function, then invoke `clojure.java.jdbc/query` with the result:

```
(require '[java-jdbc.sql :as sql])

(jdbc/query db-spec
  (sql/select * :fruit (sql/where {:appearance "ripe"})))
;; -> ({:grade 8.4, :unit "carton", :cost 12, :appearance "ripe", :name "Plum"})
```

If you no longer need a particular table, invoke `clojure.java.dbc/jdb-do-commands` with the appropriate DDL statements generated by `java-jdbc.ddl/drop-table`:

```
(jdbc/db-do-commands db-spec
  (ddl/create-table :delete_me
    [:name "varchar(16)" "PRIMARY KEY"]))

(jdbc/db-do-commands db-spec (ddl/drop-table :delete_me))
;; -> (0)
```

## Discussion

The `clojure.java.jdbc` library provides functions that wrap the basic capabilities of the Java JDBC specification. The `java-jdbc/dsl` project's `java-jdbc.sql` and `java-jdbc.ddl` namespaces implement small DSLs to generate basic SQL DML and DDL statements.

java-jdbc/dsl used to be a part of clojure.java.jdbc, but was removed to keep the API of the core library as small as possible.

The java-dbc.ddl/create-table function generates the DDL needed to create a table. The arguments are a table name and a vector for each column specification. At the time of this writing, table-level specifications are not yet supported.

#### Inserting and updating records

Records may be inserted into a table in a variety of ways. In addition to the vector method illustrated, the clojure.java.jdbc/insert! function can accept one or more maps with column names as keys:

```
(jdbc/insert! db-spec :fruit
  {:name "Banana" :appearance "spotting" :cost 35}
  {:name "Tomato" :appearance "rotten" :cost 10 :grade 1.4}
  {:name "Peach" :appearance "fresh" :cost 37 :unit "pallet"})
;; -> ({:grade nil, :unit nil, :cost 35, :appearance "spotting", :name "Banana"}
;;     {:grade 1.4, :unit nil, :cost 10, :appearance "rotten", :name "Tomato"}
;;     {:grade nil, :unit "pallet", :cost 37, :appearance "fresh",
;;      :name "Peach"})
```

If you want to insert rows but only specify some columns' values, you can invoke clojure.java.jdbc/insert! with a vector of column names followed by one or more vectors containing values for those columns:

```
(jdbc/insert! db-spec :fruit
  [:name :cost]
  ["Mango" 84]
  ["Kumquat" 77])
;; -> (1 1)
```

To update existing records, invoke clojure.java.jdbc/update! with a map of column names to new values. The optional java-jdbc.sql/where clause controls which rows will be updated:

```
(jdbc/update! db-spec :fruit
  {:grade 7.0 :appearance "spotting" :cost 75}
  (sql/where {:name "Mango"}))
;; -> (1)
```

#### Transactions

Database transactions are available to ensure that multiple operations are performed atomically (i.e., all or none). The clojure.java.jdbc/with-db-transaction macro creates a transaction-aware connection from the database specification. Use the transaction-aware connection for the duration of the transaction:

```
;; Insert two new fruits atomically
(jdbc/with-db-transaction [trans-conn db-spec]
  (jdbc/insert! trans-conn :fruit {:name "Fig" :cost 12})
  (jdbc/insert! trans-conn :fruit {:name "Date" :cost 14}))
;; -> ({:grade nil, :unit nil, :cost 14, :appearance nil, :name "Date"})
```

If an exception is thrown, the transaction is rolled back:

```
;; Query how many items the table has now
(defn fruit-count
  "Query how many items are in the fruit table."
  [db-spec]
  (let [result (jdbc/query db-spec (sql/select "count(*)" :fruit))]
    (:count (first result))))

(fruit-count db-spec)
;; -> 11

(jdbc/with-db-transaction [trans-conn db-spec]
  (jdbc/insert! trans-conn :fruit
    [:name :cost]
    ["Grape" 86]
    ["Pear" 86])
  ;; At this point the insert! call is complete, but the transaction
  ;; is not. An exception will cause the transaction to roll back,
  ;; leaving the database unchanged.
  (throw (Exception. "sql-test-exception")))
;; -> Exception sql-test-exception ...

;; The table still has the same number of items
(fruit-count db-spec)
;; -> 11
```

Transactions can be explicitly set to roll back with the `clojure.java.jdbc/db-set-rollback-only!` function. This setting can be unset with the `clojure.java.jdbc/db-unset-rollback-only!` function and tested with the `clojure.java.jdbc/is-rollback-only` function:

```
(fruit-count db-spec)
;; -> 11

(jdbc/with-db-transaction [trans-conn db-spec]
  (jdbc/db-set-rollback-only! trans-conn)
  (jdbc/insert! trans-conn :fruit {:name "Pear" :cost 69}))
;; -> ({:grade nil, :unit nil, :cost 69, :appearance nil, :name "Pear"})

;; The table still has the same number of items
(fruit-count db-spec)
;; -> 11
```

### Reading and processing records

Database records are returned from queries as Clojure maps, with the table's column names used as keys. Retrieval of a set of database records produces a sequence of maps that can then be processed with all the normal Clojure functions. Here, we query all the records in the fruit table, gathering the name and grade of any low-quality fruit:

```
(->> (jdbc/query db-spec (sql/select "name, grade" :fruit))
     ;; Filter all fruits by fruits with grade < 3.0
     (filter (fn [{:keys [grade]}] (and grade (< grade 3.0))))
     (map (juxt :name :grade)))
;; -> (["Tomato" 1.4])
```

The preceding example uses the SQL DSL provided by the `java-jdbc.sql` namespace. The DSL implements a simple abstraction over the generation of SQL statements. At present, it provides some basic mechanisms for selects, joins, `where` clauses, and `order-by` clauses:

```
(defn fresh-fruit []
  (jdbc/query db-spec
    (sql/select [:f.name] {:fruit :f}
      (sql/where {:f.appearance "fresh"})
      (sql/order-by :f.name))))

(fresh-fruit)
;; -> ({:name "Kiwifruit"} {:name "Peach"})
```

The use of the SQL DSL is entirely optional. For more direct control, a vector containing an SQL query string and arguments can be passed to the `query` function. The following function also finds low-quality fruit but does it by passing a quality threshold value directly to the SQL statement:

```
(defn find-low-quality [acceptable]
  (jdbc/query db-spec
              ["select name, grade from fruit where grade < ?" acceptable]))

(find-low-quality 3.0)
;; -> ({:grade 1.4, :name "Tomato"})
```

The `jdbc/query` function has several optional keyword parameters that control how it constructs the returned result set. The `:result-set-fn` parameter specifies a function that is applied to the entire result set (a lazy sequence) before it is returned. The default argument is the `doall` function:

```
(defn hi-lo [rs] [(first rs) (last rs)])

;; Find the highest- and lowest-cost fruits
(jdbc/query db-spec
            ["select * from fruit order by cost desc"]
            :result-set-fn hi-lo)
```

```
;; -> [{:grade nil, :unit nil, :cost 77, :appearance nil, :name "Kumquat"}
;;     {:grade 1.4, :unit nil, :cost 10, :appearance "rotten", :name "Tomato"}]
```

The `:row-fn` parameter specifies a function that is applied to each result row as the result is constructed. The default argument is the `identity` function:

```
(defn add-tax [row] (assoc row :tax (* 0.08 (row :cost))))

(jdbc/query db-spec
            ["select name,cost from fruit where cost = 12"]
            :row-fn add-tax)
;; -> ({:tax 0.96, :cost 12, :name "Plum"} {:tax 0.96, :cost 12, :name "Fig"})
```

The Boolean `:as-arrays?` parameter indicates whether to return the results as a set of vectors or not. The default argument value is `false`:

```
(jdbc/query db-spec
            ["select name,cost,grade from fruit where appearance = 'spotting'"]
            :as-arrays? true)
;; -> ([:name :cost :grade] ["Banana" 35 nil] ["Mango" 75 7.0])
```

Finally, the `:identifiers` parameter takes a function that is applied to each column name in the result set. The default argument is the `clojure.string/lower-case` function, which lowercases the table's column names before they are converted to keywords. If your application needs to perform some different conversion of column names, provide an alternate function using this keyword parameter.

The `clojure.java.jdbc` library is a good choice for quick and easy access to most popular relational databases. Its use of Clojure's vectors and maps to represent records blends well with Clojure's emphasis on data-oriented programming. Novice users of SQL can conveniently utilize the provided DSLs while expert users can more directly construct and execute complex SQL statements.

## See Also

- See Recipe 6.1, "Connecting to an SQL Database" on page 256, to learn about basic database connections with `clojure.java.jdbc`.
- See Recipe 6.2, "Connecting to an SQL Database with a Connection Pool" on page 259, to learn about pooling connections to an SQL database with BoneCP and `clojure.java.jdbc`.
- Visit the `clojure.java.jdbc` GitHub repository (*https://github.com/clojure/java.jdbc*) for more detailed information on the library.
- Visit the `java-jdbc/dsl` GitHub repository (*https://github.com/seancorfield/jsql*) for more information on the SQL query generation capabilities it provides. Alternatively, investigate the Honey SQL (*https://github.com/jkk/honeysql*), SQLingvo (*https://github.com/r0man/sqlingvo*), or Korma (*http://sqlkorma.com/*) libraries for

SQL query generation. Korma is covered in Recipe 6.4, "Simplifying SQL with Korma" on page 268.

## 6.4. Simplifying SQL with Korma

by Dmitri Sotnikov and Chris Allen

### Problem

You want to work with data stored in a relational database without writing SQL by hand.

### Solution

Use Korma as a DSL for generating SQL queries and traversing relationships.

Before starting, add `[korma "0.3.0-RC6"]` and `[org.postgresql/postgresql "9.2-1002-jdbc4"]` to your project's dependencies or start a REPL using `lein-try`:

```
$ lein try korma org.postgresql/postgresql
```

To follow along with this recipe, you'll need a running SQL database and an existing table to connect to. We suggest PostgreSQL.[4]

After you have PostgreSQL running (presumably on *localhost:5432*), run the following command to create a database for this recipe:

```
# On Mac:
$ /Applications/Postgres.app/Contents/MacOS/bin/createdb learn_korma

# Everyone else:
$ createdb learn_korma
```

To connect to the `learn_korma` database, use `defdb` with the `postgres` helper. Because Korma is a rather large DSL, it is acceptable to `:refer :all` its contents into model namespaces:

```
(require '[korma.db :refer :all])

(defdb db
  (postgres {:db "learn_korma"}))
```

To interact with a table in your database, define and create what Korma calls *entities*. Here you'll define an entity for blog posts:

4. Mac users: visit *http://postgresapp.com/* to download an easy-to-install DMG. Everyone else: you'll find a guide for your operating system on the PostgreSQL wiki (*http://bit.ly/postgres-install*).

```
(defentity posts
  (pk :id)
  (table :posts) ; Table name
  (entity-fields :title :content)) ; Default fields to SELECT
```

Normally you'd use a proper migration library for your schema, but for the sake of simplicity, we'll create a table manually. Use the `exec-raw` function to execute raw SQL statements against the database. You should only do this where strictly necessary:

```
(def create-posts (str "CREATE TABLE posts "
                       "(id serial, title text, content text,"
                       "created_on timestamp default current_timestamp);"))

(exec-raw create-posts)
```

Now that the `posts` table exists, you can invoke `insert` against `posts` with a map's `values` to add records to the database. Each record is represented by a map. The names of the keys in the map must match the names of the columns in the database:

```
(insert posts
        (values nil {:title "First post" :content "blah blah blah"}))
```

To retrieve values from the database, query using `select`. Successful queries will return a sequence of maps, each containing keys representing the column names:

```
(select posts (limit 1))
;; -> [{:created_on #inst "2013-11-01T19:21:10.652920000-00:00",
;;      :content "blah blah blah",
;;      :title "First post",
;;      :id 1}]
```

To correct or change existing records, use the `update` macro. Invoke `update` against `posts`, providing a `set-fields` declaration to specify what should change and a `where` declaration narrowing what records to make those changes to:

```
(update posts
        (set-fields {:title "Best Post"})
        (where {:title "First post"}))
;; -> {:title "Best Post", :id 1 ...}
```

The `delete` macro works similarly to `update`, but doesn't take a `set-fields` declaration:

```
(delete posts
        (where {:title "Best Post"}))

(select posts)
;; -> []
```

## Discussion

Korma provides a simple and intuitive way to construct SQL queries from Clojure. The advantage of using Korma is that the queries are written as regular code instead of SQL strings. You can easily compose queries and abstract common operations.

Korma exposes these abilities through its entity system. Entities are an abstraction over traditional SQL tables that mask the complexity of SQL's crufty and complicated DDL (data definition language). Via the `defentity` macro, you have access to all of the power of traditional SQL, packaged in a readable, Clojure-based DSL.

When defining entities with `defentity`, you can pass in a number of options. Some common options include `table` to specify a table name, `pk` to specify the default ID field (primary key), `entity-fields` to specify the default fields for SELECT statements, or even `db` to specify which database the entity belongs in.

Entities also simplify defining relations between tables. Entity declaration statements such as `has-one`, `has-many`, `belongs-to`, and `many-to-many` define relationships to other entities. Consider adding an author to each of our blog posts:

```
;; Create authors, assuming posts has an author_id
(defentity authors
  ;; By default, foreign-key will be :authors_id, but that is a little
  ;; awkward
  (has-many posts {:fk :author_id}))

;; Redefine posts such that it assumes it has an author_id
(defentity posts
  (belongs-to authors {:fk :author_id}))

;; Create the authors table
(exec-raw "CREATE TABLE authors (id serial, name text);")

;; Add the authors_id field to posts
(exec-raw "ALTER TABLE posts ADD COLUMN author_id int;")

(def ryan (insert authors (values {:name "Ryan"})))
ryan
;; -> {:name "Ryan", :id 1}

(insert posts (values [{:title "My first post!", :author_id (:id ryan)}
                       {:title "My second post.", :author_id (:id ryan)}]))
(select posts
        (where {:author_id (:id ryan)}))
;; -> [{:author_id 1,
;;        ...
;;        :title "My first post!",
;;        :id 4}
;;       {:author_id 1,
;;        ...
```

```
;;       :title "My second post.",
;;       :id 5}]
```

Stemming from its entity system, Korma provides DSL versions of common SQL statements such as `select`, `update`, `insert`, and `delete`. One of the most interesting query types is `select`, which provides support for most every SELECT statement option, include simplified table joins (via its relation helpers). Some notable helpers include `aggregate`, `join`, `order`, `group`, and `having`. Chances are, if it is an SQL statement feature, Korma has a helper for it.

Korma's DSL isn't only convenient, it's also composable. Using `select*` instead of `select` returns a query as a value, instead of an evaluated result. You can pipeline query values through regular `select` helpers to build up or store partial queries. Finally, invoke `select` on a query value to execute it and receive its result:

```
(defn authors-posts
  "Retrieve all posts for a person with a given name"
  [name]
  (-> (select* posts)
      (with authors)
      (where {:authors.name name})))

;; Find the title of all posts by the author named "Ryan"
(-> (authors-posts "Ryan")
    (where (like :title "%second%"))
    (fields :title)
    select)
;; -> [{:title "My second post."}]
```

Another convenience Korma provides is default connections. You may have noticed in the examples that we never referred to the `db` we defined. When only a single connection is defined, it will be used by default and you don't have to pass it explicitly. If you like, you can define multiple connections and wrap series of statements in a `with-db` call:

```
(with-db db
  (select (authors-posts "Ryan")))
```

## See Also

- The official Korma project page (*http://sqlkorma.com/docs*)

# 6.5. Performing Full-Text Search with Lucene

by Osbert Feng

## Problem

You want to support flexible full-text search over an unstructured or semistructured dataset using Lucene. For example, you want to return all people in the United States that have "Clojure" anywhere in their job descriptions.

## Solution

Use Clucy (*https://github.com/weavejester/clucy*), a Clojure wrapper for Lucene. Clucy provides the tools to build and query indexes from within a Clojure process.

To follow along with this recipe, create a new project (**`lein new text-search`**), add `[clucy "0.4.0"]` to its dependencies, and start a REPL using **`lein repl`**.[5]

The following code creates and queries a simple in-memory index:

```
(require '[clucy.core :as clucy])

(def index (clucy/memory-index))
;; -> #'user/index


(clucy/add index
   {:name "Alice" :description "Clojure expert"
    :location "North Carolina, United States"}
   {:name "Bob" :description "Clojure novice"
    :location "Berlin, Germany"}
   {:name "Eve" :description "Eavesdropper"
    :location "Maryland, United States"})
;; -> nil

(clucy/search index "description:clojure AND location:\"united states\"" 10)
;; -> ({:name "Alice",
;;       :location "North Carolina, United States",
;;       :description "Clojure expert"})
```

## Discussion

Lucene is a Java library for information retrieval. To use Lucene, you generate documents and index them for later retrieval. Documents consist of fields and terms. In this ex-

5. We would normally suggest using `lein-try`, but the plug-in is currently incompatible with Clucy.

ample, the documents are quite small, but Lucene is capable of efficiently indexing large numbers of very large documents as well.

Clucy wraps Lucene in a convenient manner for use in Clojure and is capable of generating Lucene documents directly from simple Clojure maps, where keys map to fields and values map to textual data to be indexed.

`clucy.core/search` takes an index, a query string, and the number of results to return as parameters. Lucene is able to efficiently query in part because it is not necessary to return all matching documents, just the top `n` best matches.

Clucy does not work as well out of the box with nested values in your maps. Be sure to flatten out values into simple strings for proper indexing and retrieval.

This example uses a `memory-index`, which stores the index in system memory. In most real applications, you'll want to persist the index to disk, which allows it to grow larger than the available memory and allows you to restart your process without re-indexing. Clucy lets you construct a Lucene disk index via the `disk-index` function:

```
(def index (clucy.core/disk-index "/tmp/index"))
```

As part of the process for generating documents, Lucene calls an analyzer on your strings to generate tokens for indexing. The default `StandardAnalyzer` is sufficient for most purposes and can be customized with a list of "stop words" to be ignored during token generation:

```
(import 'org.apache.lucene.analysis.standard.StandardAnalyzer)
;; -> org.apache.lucene.analysis.standard.StandardAnalyzer

(import 'org.apache.lucene.analysis.util.CharArraySet)
;; -> org.apache.lucene.analysis.util.CharArraySet

(def stop-words
  (doto (CharArray. clucy.core/*version* 3 true)
    (.add "do")
    (.add "not")
    (.add "index")))

(binding [clucy.core/*analyzer* (StandardAnalyzer.
                                  clucy.core/*version*
                                  stop-words)]
  ;; Invoke index add and search forms here, within the binding
  )
```

However, in other situations you may need to use a different analyzer or write your own. For example, the `EnglishAnalyzer` uses Porter stemming and other techniques better suited to taking into account pluralization or possessives:

```
(import org.apache.lucene.analysis.en.EnglishAnalyzer)
;; -> org.apache.lucene.analysis.en.EnglishAnalyzer

(binding [clucy.core/*analyzer* (EnglishAnalyzer. clucy.core/*version*)]
  ;; Invoke index add and search forms here, within the binding
  )
```

The basic search query syntax is `field:term`. By default, multiple clauses will perform an `OR` search, so an explicit `AND` is required if both clauses must be true.

If no field is specified, there is an implicit field `_content` that indexes all map values. Documents returned are ordered by Lucene's default relevance algorithm, which takes into account term frequency, distance, and document length:

```
(clucy.core/search index "clojure united states" 10)
;; -> ({:name "Alice",
;;       :location "North Carolina, United States",
;;       :description "Clojure expert"}
;;      {:name "Eve",
;;       :location "Maryland, United States",
;;       :description "Eavesdropper"}
;;      {:name "Bob",
;;       :location "Berlin, Germany",
;;       :description "Clojure novice"})
```

## See Also

- The Lucene project home page (*http://lucene.apache.org/*)
- The Clucy GitHub repository (*https://github.com/weavejester/clucy*)

# 6.6. Indexing Data with ElasticSearch

by Michael Klishin

## Problem

You want to index data using the ElasticSearch (*http://elasticsearch.org*) indexing and search engine.

## Solution

Use Elastisch (*http://bit.ly/clj-elastisch*), a minimalistic Clojure wrapper around the ElasticSearch Java APIs.

In order to successfully work through the examples in this recipe, you should have ElasticSearch installed and running on your local system. You can find details on how to install it on the ElasticSearch website (*http://bit.ly/cc-es-setup*).

ElasticSearch supports multiple transports (e.g., HTTP, native Netty-based transport, and Memcached). Elastisch supports HTTP and native transports. This recipe will use an HTTP transport client for the examples and explain how to switch to the native transport in the discussion section.

To follow along with this recipe, add `[clojurewerkz/elastisch "1.2.0"]` to your project's dependencies, or start a REPL using `lein-try`:

```
$ lein try clojurewerkz/elastisch
```

Before you can index and search with Elastisch, it is necessary to tell Elastisch what ElasticSearch node to use. To use the HTTP transport, you use the `clojurewerkz.elastisch.rest/connect!` function that takes an endpoint as its sole argument:

```
(require '[clojurewerkz.elastisch.rest :as esr])

(esr/connect! "http://127.0.0.1:9200")
```

### Indexing

Before data can be searched over, it needs to be indexed. Indexing is the process of scanning the text and building a list of search terms and data structures called a *search index*. Search indexes allow search engines such as ElasticSearch to efficiently retrieve relevant documents for a query.

The process of indexing involves a few steps:

1. Create an index.
2. [Optional] Define mappings (how documents should be indexed).
3. Submit documents for indexing via HTTP or other APIs.

To create an index, use the `clojurewerkz.elastisch.rest.index/create` function:

```
(require '[clojurewerkz.elastisch.rest.index :as esi])

(esr/connect! "http://127.0.0.1:9200")

;; Create an index with the given settings and no custom mapping types
(esi/create "test1")

;; Create an index with custom settings
(esi/create "test2" :settings {"number_of_shards" 1}))
```

A full explanation of the available indexing settings is outside the scope of this recipe. Please refer to the Elastisch documentation on indexing (*http://bit.ly/clj-es-indexing*) for full details.

### Creating mappings

*Mappings* define the fields in a document and what the indexing characteristics are for each field. Mapping types are specified when an index is created using the `:mapping` option:

```
(esr/connect! "http://127.0.0.1:9200")

;; Mapping types map structure is the same as in the ElasticSearch API reference
(def mapping-types {"person"
                    {:properties {:username   {:type "string" :store "yes"}
                                  :first-name {:type "string" :store "yes"}
                                  :last-name  {:type "string"}
                                  :age        {:type "integer"}
                                  :title      {:type "string"
                                               :analyzer "snowball"}
                                  :planet     {:type "string"}
                                  :biography  {:type "string"
                                               :analyzer "snowball"
                                               :term_vector
                                               "with_positions_offsets"}}}})

(esi/create "test3" :mappings mapping-types)))
```

### Indexing documents

To add a document to an index, use the `clojurewerkz.elastisch.rest.document/create` function. This will cause a document ID to be generated automatically:

```
(require '[clojurewerkz.elastisch.rest.document :as esd])

(esr/connect! "http://127.0.0.1:9200")

(def mapping-types {"person"
                    {:properties {:username   {:type "string" :store "yes"}
                                  :first-name {:type "string" :store "yes"}
                                  :last-name  {:type "string"}
                                  :age        {:type "integer"}
                                  :title      {:type "string" :analyzer "snowball"}
                                  :planet     {:type "string"}
                                  :biography  {:type "string"
                                               :analyzer "snowball"
                                               :term_vector
                                               "with_positions_offsets"}}}})

(esi/create "test4" :mappings mapping-types)
```

```
(def doc {:username "happyjoe"
          :first-name "Joe"
          :last-name "Smith"
          :age 30
          :title "The Boss"
          :planet "Earth"
          :biography "N/A"})


(esd/create "test4" "person" doc)
;; => {:ok true, :_index people, :_type person,
;;     :_id "2vr8sP-LTRWhSKOxyWOi_Q", :_version 1}
```

`clojurewerkz.elastisch.rest.document/put` will add a document to the index but expects a document ID to be provided:

```
(esr/put "test4" "person" "happyjoe" doc)
```

## Discussion

Whenever a document is added to the ElasticSearch index, it is first analyzed.

*Analysis* is a process of several stages:

- Tokenization (breaking field values into *tokens*)
- Filtering or modifying tokens
- Combining tokens with field names to produce *terms*

How exactly a document was analyzed defines what search queries will match (find) it. ElasticSearch is based on Apache Lucene (*http://lucene.apache.org*) and offers several analyzers developers can use to achieve the kind of search quality and performance they need. For example, different languages require different analyzers: English, Mandarin Chinese, Arabic, and Russian cannot be analyzed the same way.

It is possible to skip performing analysis for fields and specify whether field values are stored in the index or not. Fields that are not stored still can be searched over but will not be included into search results.

ElasticSearch allows users to define exactly how different kinds of documents are indexed, analyzed, and stored.

ElasticSearch has excellent support for *multitenancy*: an ElasticSearch cluster can have a virtually unlimited number of indexes and mapping types. For example, you can use a separate index per user account or organization in a SaaS (Software as a Service) product.

There are two ways to index a document with ElasticSearch: you can submit a document for indexing without an ID or update a document with a provided ID, in which case if the document already exists, it will be updated (a new version will be created).

While it is fine and common to use automatically created indexes early in development, manually creating indexes lets you configure a lot about how ElasticSearch will index your data and, in turn, what kinds of queries it will be possible to execute against it.

How your data is indexed is primarily controlled by *mappings*. They define which fields in documents are indexed, if/how they are analyzed, and if they are stored. Each index in ElasticSearch may have one or more *mapping types*. Mapping types can be thought of as tables in a database (although this analogy does not always stand). Mapping types are the heart of indexing in ElasticSearch and provide access to a lot of ElasticSearch functionality.

For example, a blogging application may have types such as *article*, *comment*, and *person*. Each has distinct *mapping settings* that define a set of fields documents of the type have, how they are supposed to be indexed (and, in turn, what kinds of queries will be possible over them), what language each field is in, and so on. Getting mapping types right for your application is the key to a good search experience. It also takes time and experimentation.

Mapping types define document fields and their core types (e.g., string, integer, or date/time). Settings are provided to ElasticSearch as a JSON document, and this is how they are documented on the ElasticSearch site (*http://bit.ly/cc-es-mapping*).

With Elastisch, mapping settings are specified as Clojure maps with the same structure (schema). A very minimalistic example:

```
{"tweet" {:properties {:username  {:type "string" :index "not_analyzed"}}}}
```

Here is a brief and very incomplete list of things that you can define via mapping settings:

- Document fields, their types, and whether they are analyzed
- Document time to live (TTL)
- Whether a document type is indexed
- Special fields (`"_all"`, default field, etc.)
- Document-level boosting (*http://bit.ly/cc-es-boost-field*)
- Timestamp field (*http://bit.ly/cc-es-timestamp-field*)

When an index is created using the `clojurewerkz.elastisch.rest.index/create` function, mapping settings are passed with the `:mappings` option, as seen previously.

When it is necessary to update mapping for an index, you can use the `clojurewerkz.elastisch.rest.index/update-mapping` function:

```
(esi/update-mapping "myapp_development" "person"
                    :mapping {:properties
                              {:first-name {:type "string" :store "no"}}})
```

In a mapping configuration, settings are passed as maps where keys are names (strings or keywords) and values are maps of the actual settings. In this example, the only setting is `:properties`, which defines a single field—a string that is not analyzed:

```
{"tweet" {:properties {:username  {:type "string" :index "not_analyzed"}}}}
```

There is much more to the indexing and mapping options, but that's outside the scope of a single recipe. See the Elastisch indexing documentation (*http://bit.ly/clj-es-indexing*) for an exhaustive list of the capabilities provided.

## See Also

- The official ElasticSearch guide (*http://bit.ly/cc-es-guide*)
- The Elastisch home page (*http://bit.ly/clj-elastisch*)

# 6.7. Working with Cassandra

by Alex Petrov

## Problem

You want to work with data stored in Cassandra.

## Solution

Use the Cassaforte (*http://clojurecassandra.info/*) library to connect to a Cassandra cluster and work with the records in the database.

In order to successfully work through the examples in this recipe, you should have Cassandra installed. You can find details on how to install Cassandra on the Getting-Started page of the wiki (*http://wiki.apache.org/cassandra/GettingStarted*).

To follow along with this recipe, add `[clojurewerkz/cassaforte "1.1.0"]` to your project's dependencies, or start a REPL using `lein-try`:

```
$ lein try clojurewerkz/cassaforte
```

In order to connect to your Cassandra cluster and create and use your first keyspace, you will need the `clojurewerkz.cassaforte.client`, `clojurewerkz.cassaforte.cql`, and `clojurewerkz.cassaforte.query` namespaces.

`clojurewerkz.cassaforte.client` is responsible for connection—the other two provide an easy interface to execute queries:

```
(require '[clojurewerkz.cassaforte.client :as client]
         '[clojurewerkz.cassaforte.cql :as cql]
         '[clojurewerkz.cassaforte.query :as q])

;; Connect to 2 nodes in a cluster
(client/connect! ["localhost" "another.node.local"])

;; Create a keyspace named `cassaforte_keyspace`, using
;; the Simple Replication Strategy and a replication factor of 2
(cql/create-keyspace "cassaforte_keyspace"
                     (q/with {:replication
                              {:class "SimpleStrategy"
                               :replication_factor 2 }}))

;; Switch to the keyspace
(cql/use-keyspace "cassaforte_keyspace")
```

Now, you can create tables and start inserting data into them. For that, invoke the `create-table` and `insert` functions of the `clojurewerkz.cassaforte.cql` namespace:

```
(cql/create-table "users"
                  (q/column-definitions {:name :varchar
                                         :city :varchar
                                         :age  :int
                                         :primary-key [:name]}))
```

Now, insert several users into the table:

```
(cql/insert "users" {:name "Alex" :city "Munich" :age (int 26)})
(cql/insert "users" {:name "Robert" :city "Brussels" :age (int 30)})
```

You can access these records using a `select` query. For example, if you want to retrieve all the users from the table or use `limit` in your query, you can run:

```
;; Will retrieve all users
(cql/select "users")

;; Will retrieve top 10 users
(cql/select "users" (q/limit 10))
```

Alternatively, if you want to retrieve information about a single person by a given `name`, you can add a `where` clause to it:

```
(cql/select "users" (q/where :name "Alex"))
```

## Discussion

Cassandra is an open source implementation of many of the ideas in Amazon's landmark Dynamo Paper (*http://bit.ly/dynamo-pdf*). It's a key/value datastore, and it's not aware of any relationships between tables and data points. Cassandra is a distributed datastore and is designed to be highly available. For that, it replicates data within the cluster. The data is stored redundantly on multiple nodes. If one node fails, data is still available for retrieval from a different node or multiple nodes.

Cassandra starts making sense when your data is rather big. Because it was built for distribution, you can scale your reads and writes, and fine-tune and manage your database's consistency and availability. Cassandra handles network partitions well, so even if several of your nodes are unavailable for some time, you will still be able to read and write data until the network partition heals. If your dataset is rather small, you don't expect it to grow significantly anytime soon, and you need to run many ad hoc queries against the dataset, then Cassandra may not make sense.

Consistency and availability are tunable values. You can get better availability by sacrificing data consistency: due to network partitions, not all the nodes will hold the latest snapshot of data at all times, but you'll be still able to respond to writes and receive reads. If you choose to have strong consistency, conversely, the latency will increase, since more nodes should respond successfully for reads and writes. Eventual consistency guarantees that, if no conflicting writes are made for the data point, eventually all nodes will hold the latest value.

Like most datastores, Cassandra has concepts of separate databases (*keyspaces* in Cassandra terminology). Every keyspace holds tables (sometimes called *column families*). Tables hold rows, and rows consist of columns. Each column has a key (column name), value, write timestamp, and time to live.

Cassandra uses two different communication protocols: an older binary protocol called Thrift, and CQL (Cassandra Query Language). All query operators in Cassaforte generate CQL code under the hood. Here are a couple of examples of how these operations translate to CQL internally:

```
(cql/select "users" (q/where :name "Alex"))
;; SELECT * FROM users WHERE name='Alex';

(cql/insert "users" {:name "Alex" :city "Munich" :age (int 26)})
;; INSERT INTO users (name, city) VALUES ('Munich', 26);
```

There's much more to Cassandra than just creating tables and inserting values. If you want to update records in your database, you can call the `update` function:

```
(cql/update "users"
            {:city "Berlin"}
            (q/where :name "Alex"))
```

Deleting records from the database is just as easy:

```
;; Will delete just one user
(cql/delete :users (q/where :name "Alex"))

;; Will delete all users whose names match within IN clause
(cql/delete :users (q/where :name [:in ["Alex" "Robert"]]))
```

If you'd like to execute some arbitrary CQL statements, outside of Cassaforte's macro-based DSL, you can pass a string to the `client/execute` function:

```
(client/execute
  "INSERT INTO users (name, city, age) VALUES ('Alex', 'Munich', 19);")
```

For each issued write, you can specify an optional time to live to expire the data after a certain period of time. This is useful for caching and for data that you only want to hold for a certain period of time (like user sessions). For example, if you want the record to live for just 60 seconds, you can run:

```
(cql/insert "users" {:name "Alex" :city "Munich" :age (int 26)}
                    (q/using :ttl 60))
```

Another concept that people like about Cassandra is distributed counters. Counter columns provide an efficient way to count or sum anything you need. This is achieved by using atomic increment/decrement operations on values. In order to create a table with a counter from Cassaforte, you can use the `:counter` column type:

```
(cql/create-table :scores
                  (q/column-definitions {:username :varchar
                                         :score    :counter
                                         :primary-key [:username]}))
```

You can increment and decrement counters by using the `increment-by` and `decrement-by` queries:

```
(cql/update :scores
            {:score (q/increment-by 50)}
            (q/where :name "Alex"))

(cql/update :scores
            {:score (q/decrement-by 5)}
            (q/where :name "Robert"))
```

## See Also

- The Cassaforte documentation (*http://clojurecassandra.info*)

# 6.8. Working with MongoDB

by Clinton Dreisbach

## Problem

You want to work with data stored in MongoDB.

## Solution

Use Monger (*http://clojuremongodb.info/*) to connect to MongoDB and search or manipulate the data. Monger is a Clojure wrapper around the Java MongoDB driver.

Before using Mongo from your Clojure code, you must have a running instance of MongoDB to connect to. See MongoDB's installation guide (*http://bit.ly/mongodb-install*) for instructions on how to install MongoDB on your local system.

When you're ready to write a Clojure MongoDB client, start a REPL using `lein-try`:

```
$ lein try com.novemberain/monger
```

To connect to MongoDB, use the `monger.core/connect!` function. This will store your connection in the `*mongodb-connection*` dynamic var. If you want to get a connection to use without storing it in a dynamic var, you can use `monger.core/connect` with the same options:

```
(require '[monger.core :as mongo])

;; Connect to localhost
(mongo/connect! {:host "127.0.0.1" :port 27017})

;; Disconnect when you are done
(mongo/disconnect!)
```

Once you are connected, you can insert and query documents easily:

```
(require '[monger.core :as mongo]
         '[monger.collection :as coll])
(import '[org.bson.types ObjectId])

;; Set the database in the *mongodb-database* var
(mongo/use-db! "mongo-time")

;; Insert one document
(coll/insert "users" {:name "Jeremiah Forthright" :state "TX"})

;; Insert a batch of documents
(coll/insert-batch "users" [{:name "Pete Killibrew" :state "KY"}
                            {:name "Wendy Perkins" :state "OK"}
                            {:name "Steel Whitaker" :state "OK"}
                            {:name "Sarah LaRue" :state "WY"}])

;; Find all documents and return a com.mongodb.DBCursor
(coll/find "users")

;; Find all documents matching a query and return a DBCursor
(coll/find "users" {:state "OK"})

;; Find documents and return them as Clojure maps
(coll/find-maps "users" {:state "OK"})
```

```
;; -> ({:_id #<ObjectId 520...>, :state "OK", :name "Wendy Perkins"}
;;     {:_id #<ObjectId 520...>, :state "OK", :name "Steel Whitaker"})

;; Find one document and return a com.mongodb.DBObject
(coll/find-one "users" {:name "Pete Killibrew"})

;; Find one document and return it as a Clojure map
(coll/find-one-as-map "users" {:name "Sarah LaRue"})
;; -> {:_id #<ObjectId 520...>, :state "WY", :name "Sarah LaRue"}
```

## Discussion

MongoDB, especially with Monger, can be a natural choice for storing Clojure data. It stores data as BSON (binary JSON), which maps well to Clojure's own vectors and maps.

There are several ways to connect to Mongo, depending on how much you need to customize your connection and whether you have a map of options or a URI:

```
;; Connect to localhost, port 27017 by default
(mongo/connect!)

;; Connect to another machine
(mongo/connect! {:host "192.168.1.100" :port 27017})

;; Connect using more complex options
(let [options (mongo/mongo-options :auto-connect-retry true
                                   :connect-timeout 15
                                   :socket-timeout 15)
      server (mongo/server-address "192.168.1.100" 27017)]
  (mongo/connect! server options))

;; Connect via a URI
(mongo/connect-via-uri! (System/genenv "MONGOHQ_URL"))
```

When inserting data, giving each document an `_id` is optional. One will be created for you if you do not have one in your document. It often makes sense to add it yourself, however, if you need to reference the document afterward:

```
(require '[monger.collection :as coll])
(import '[org.bson.types ObjectId])

(let [id (ObjectId.)
      user {:name "Lola Morales"}]
  (coll/insert "users" (assoc user :_id id))
  ;; Later, look up your user by id
  (coll/find-map-by-id "users" id))
;; -> {:_id #<ObjectId 521...>, :name "Lola Morales"}
```

In its idiomatic usage, Monger is set up to work with one connection and one database, as `monger.core/connect!` and `monger.core/use-db!` set dynamic vars to hold their information.

It is easy to work around this, though. You can use `binding` to set these explicitly around code. In addition, you can use the `monger.multi.collection` namespace instead of `monger.collection`. All functions in the `monger.multi.collection` namespace take a database as their first argument:

```
(require '[monger.core :as mongo]
         '[monger.multi.collection :as multi])

(mongo/connect!)

;; use-db! takes a string for the database, as it is a convenience function,
;; but for monger.multi.collection and other functions, we need to use
;; get-db to get the database
(let [stats-server (mongo/connect "stats.example.org")
      app-db (mongo/get-db "mongo-time")
      geo-db (mongo/get-db "geography")]

  ;; Record data in our stats server
  (binding [mongo/*mongodb-connection* stats-server]
    (multi/insert (mongo/get-db "stats") "access"
                  {:ip "127.0.0.1" :time (java.util.Date.)}))

  ;; Find users in our application DB
  (multi/find-maps app-db "users" {:state "WY"})

  ;; Insert a square in our geography DB
  (multi/insert geo-db "shapes"
                {:name "square" :sides 4
                 :parallel true :equal true}))
```

The basic find functions in `monger.collection` will work for simple queries, but you will soon find yourself needing to make more complex queries, which is where `monger.query` comes in. This is a domain-specific language for MongoDB queries:

```
(require '[monger.query :as q])

;; Find users, skipping the first two and getting the next three.
(q/with-collection "users"
  (q/find {})
  (q/skip 2)
  (q/limit 3))

;; Get all the users from Oklahoma, sorted by name.
;; You must use array-map with sort so you can keep keys in order.
(q/with-collection "users"
  (q/find {:state "OK"})
  (q/sort (array-map :name 1)))

;; Get all users not from Oklahoma or with names that start with "S".
(q/with-collection "users"
  (q/find {"$or" [{:state {"$ne" "OK"}}
                  {:name #"^S"}]}))
```

## See Also

- The Monger documentation (*http://clojuremongodb.info/*)
- CongoMongo (*https://github.com/aboekhoff/congomongo*), another Clojure library for working with MongoDB that you might consider

# 6.9. Working with Redis

by Jason Webb

## Problem

You want to work with data in Redis.

## Solution

Use Carmine (*https://github.com/ptaoussanis/carmine*) to connect to and interact with Redis.

To use this recipe, you should first install Redis and have it running locally. You can find details on how to install Redis at the official Redis download page (*http://redis.io/download*). If you are on Windows, you will want to look at the Microsoft Open Tech GitHub Redis project (*https://github.com/MSOpenTech/redis*).

To follow along with this recipe, add `[com.taoensso/carmine "2.2.0"]` to your project's dependencies, or start a REPL using `lein-try`:

```
$ lein try com.taoensso/carmine
```

To use Carmine, you must first define a connection spec:

```
(def server-connection {:pool {:max-active 8}
                        :spec {:host     "localhost"
                               :port     6379
                               ;;:password ""
                               :timeout  4000}})
```

Carmine supports all of the Redis commands, and the names (for the most part) match the Redis documentation. Use the `wcar` function and the connection specification `server-connection` to send all the Redis commands you already know and love:

```
(require '[taoensso.carmine :as car :refer (wcar)])

(wcar server-connection (car/set "Nick" "Nack"))
;; -> "OK"
```

```
(wcar server-connection (car/get "Nick"))
;; -> "Nack"
(wcar server-connection (car/hset "founder" "name" "Tim"))
;; -> 0
(wcar server-connection (car/hset "founder" "age" 59))
;; -> 0
(wcar server-connection (car/hgetall "founder"))
;; -> [name Tim age 59]
```

Passing in multiple commands will pipeline them and return the results together as a vector:

```
(wcar server-connection (car/set "paddywhacks" 0)
                        (car/incr "paddywhacks")
                        (car/get "paddywhacks"))
;; -> ["OK" 1 "1"]
```

## Discussion

Redis describes itself as a *data structure server*. With data structures similar to the core data structures in Clojure, they make a natural pairing for a wide range of problems. Redis's speed and key/value storage make it especially useful for caching and memoization applications (more on that later).

You can remove some boilerplate by wrapping the call to `wcar` in a macro that passes the connection specification for you:

```
(defmacro wcar* [& body] `(car/wcar server-connection ~@body))

(wcar* (car/set "Nick" "Nack"))
;; -> "OK"
(wcar* (car/get "Nick"))
;; -> "Nack"
```

Serialization is handled automatically and for most cases just works. Simply pass in the data you want to store, and Carmine will automatically serialize/deserialize it for you:

```
(wcar* (car/set "some-key" {:event "An Event", :timestamp (new java.util.Date)})
       (car/get "some-key"))
;; -> [OK {:event An Event, :timestamp #inst "2013-08-18T21:31:33.993-00:00"}]
```

This works great as long as you stick to core Clojure data types. However, if you need to support storing custom data types, you will need to deal with the underlying serialization library, called Nippy. For more information, see the Nippy GitHub project (*https://github.com/ptaoussanis/nippy*).

Redis is great to use as a memoization storage backend. Obviously, there are some serious trade-offs to consider when weighing against an in-memory solution, such as the `core.cache` library. But for the right situation, it can be an incredible boost. Consider, for example, memoizing a function that hits an external web service to fetch the current weather. With minimal effort, multiple servers can share the latest data and even have stale data automatically expire and refresh. The following is an example for just such a situation:

```
(defn redis-memoize
  "Convert a function to one that is memoized using Redis as storage."
  [key-prefix ttl-seconds connection-spec f]
  (fn [& args]
    (let [key-name [key-prefix args]]
      (if-let [found-result (wcar connection-spec (car/get key-name))]
        found-result
        (let [new-result (apply f args)]
          (wcar connection-spec (car/set key-name new-result)
                                (car/expire key-name ttl-seconds))
          new-result)))))
```

This makes a couple of assumptions worth noting. First, it assumes that the arguments for the function being memoized are supported by Nippy (see the earlier serialization example). Second, it assumes that the memoized data should be expired after a specified number of seconds. To use `redis-memoize`, simply pass in a function. The following is a highly contrived example that uses the `server-connection` defined previously:

```
(defn square [x]
  (printf "Ran square for: %s\n" x)
  (* x x))

(def redis-squared
  (redis-memoize "squared" 10 server-connection square))

(redis-squared 99)
;; -> Ran square for: 99
;; -> 9801
(redis-squared 99)
;; -> 9801
```

In addition to the features showcased earlier, Carmine includes (among other things) a message queue, distributed locks, a Ring session store, and even an implementation of DynamoDB (which is in alpha at the time of writing). These features are outside the scope of this recipe, but they're well documented and straightforward to use. Consult the Carmine GitHub project (*https://github.com/ptaoussanis/carmine*) for more information.

## See Also

- The Carmine GitHub project (*https://github.com/ptaoussanis/carmine*) for more information about Carmine
- The official Redis documentation (*http://redis.io/commands*) for a complete list of Redis commands

- The Nippy GitHub project (*https://github.com/ptaoussanis/nippy*) for information about serialization
- The Clojure core documentation (*http://bit.ly/clj-memoize-doc*) for documentation of the `memoize` function

# 6.10. Connecting to a Datomic Database

by Robert Stuttaford

## Problem

You need to connect to a Datomic database.

## Solution

Before starting, add `[com.datomic/datomic-free "0.8.4218"]` to your project's dependencies or start a REPL using `lein-try`:

```
$ lein try com.datomic/datomic-free
```

To create and connect to an in-memory database, use `database.api/create-database` and `datomic.api/connect`:

```
(require '[datomic.api :as d])

(def uri "datomic:mem://sample-database")

(d/create-database uri)
;; -> true

(def conn (d/connect uri))

conn
;; -> #<LocalConnection datomic.peer.LocalConnection@49384d99>
```

Once you have a connection, you can use it to get a database *value* with `datomic.api/db`. This value is used to query a database:

```
(def db (d/db (d/connect uri)))

db
;; -> datomic.db.Db@7b7fea26
```

You can also use the connection to transact data using `datomic.api/transact`:

```
;; Transact the schema for your Next Big Thing
(def my-great-schema []) ; This vector intentionally left blank
(d/transact (d/connect uri) my-great-schema)
```

## Discussion

You'll notice in the solution that we not only connected to a database, but we created it too. This pattern is common when using in-memory databases, as no in-memory databases exist in a fresh JVM. It is not strictly necessary to call `create-database` if the database already exists, but it is safe to do so—`create-database` is idempotent and will return `false` if one already exists. When connecting to a database that isn't in memory, it is necessary for the relevant transactor and storage service to be running.

The return value of `d/connect` is used when querying a database value or when transacting data. It is also used when reading the transaction log, when consuming the transaction report queue, or when performing administrative tasks such as requesting an indexing job, garbage collecting storage, and disposing of resources associated with the connection.

Connections are thread-safe and are cached by URI internally, so there is no need to pool connections yourself. There is no performance overhead for creating many connections to the same URI.

### Storage services

Datomic transactor processes have a limit on the number of concurrently connected peer processes. Datomic Free has a limit of two peers per transactor. For nondistributed applications, this may well be sufficient. If you're building a larger service, then you may need a Datomic Pro license for more peers.

There are several options for storage services that back Datomic. Three are built-in, and the rest use external services. Datomic Free includes access to the in-memory and `:free` storage backends. Datomic Pro and Pro Starter Edition include access to all services.

### Built-in storage options

The built-in storage options are:

- In local memory: `"datomic:mem://[db-name]"`
- Free, for use with Datomic Free, subject to a two-peer limit: `"datomic:free://host[:port]/[db-name]"`
- Dev, for use with Datomic Pro, subject to the licensed peer limit: `"datomic:dev://host[:port]/[db-name]"`

Free and Dev can also be configured to use alternate ports for storage: `"datomic:free://host[:port]/[db-name]?h2-port=[port]&h2-web-port=[port]"`.

By default, these ports will be one and two more than the transactor port, respectively.

### External storage service options

Several external storage options also exist. These include:

- DynamoDB: "datomic:ddb://[aws-region]/[dynamodb-table]/[db-name]?aws_access_key_id=[XXX]&aws_secret_key=[YYY]"
- Riak: "datomic:riak://host[:port]/bucket/dbname[?interface=http|protobuf]" (default is protobuf)
- Couchbase: "datomic:couchbase://host/bucket/dbname[?password=xxx]"
- Infinispan: "datomic:inf://[cluster-member-host:port]/[db-name]"
- SQL: "datomic:sql://[db-name][?jdbc-url]"

For SQL storage services, the map format can be used instead of the string format. This is useful when specifying objects that can't be embedded in URI strings, like Data Sources. The format for the SQL map is:

```
{:protocol :sql                          ;; keyword or string
 :db-name "[db-name]"                    ;; keyword or string
 :data-source aDataSourceObject
  ;; OR
 :factory aCallableReturningConnection}
```

## See Also

- Recipe 6.11, "Defining a Schema for a Datomic Database" on page 291
- Recipe 6.12, "Writing Data to Datomic" on page 295
- Datomic Pro Starter Edition (*http://bit.ly/datatomic-starter*), for free access to all service storages and the Datomic Console

# 6.11. Defining a Schema for a Datomic Database

by Robert Stuttaford

## Problem

You need to define how your data will be modeled in Datomic. For example, you need to model users and their user groups, relating the two in some way.

## Solution

Datomic schemas are defined in terms of *attributes*. It's probably easiest to jump straight to an example.

To follow along with this recipe, complete the steps in the solution in Recipe 6.10, "Connecting to a Datomic Database" on page 289. After doing this, you should have an in-memory database and connection, `conn`, to work with.

Consider the attributes a user might have:

- One email address, which must be unique to the database
- One name, which we index for fast search
- Any number of roles (guest, author, and editor)

To define this schema, create a vector with attribute maps for email, name, and role, as well as insertions of the three static roles:

```
(def user-schema
  [{:db/doc "User email address"
    :db/ident :user/email
    :db/valueType :db.type/string
    :db/cardinality :db.cardinality/one
    :db/unique :db.unique/identity
    :db/id #db/id[:db.part/db]
    :db.install/_attribute :db.part/db}

   {:db/doc "User name"
    :db/ident :user/name
    :db/valueType :db.type/string
    :db/cardinality :db.cardinality/one
    :db/index true
    :db/id #db/id[:db.part/db]
    :db.install/_attribute :db.part/db}

   {:db/doc "User roles"
    :db/ident :user/roles
    :db/valueType :db.type/ref
    :db/cardinality :db.cardinality/many
    :db/id #db/id[:db.part/db]
    :db.install/_attribute :db.part/db}

   [:db/add #db/id[:db.part/user] :db/ident :user.roles/guest]
   [:db/add #db/id[:db.part/user] :db/ident :user.roles/author]
   [:db/add #db/id[:db.part/user] :db/ident :user.roles/editor]])
```

We define a group as having:

- One UUID, which must be unique to the database
- One name, which we index for fast search
- Any number of related users

Define the group as follows:

```
(def group-schema
  [{:db/doc "Group UUID"
    :db/ident :group/uuid
    :db/valueType :db.type/uuid
    :db/cardinality :db.cardinality/one
    :db/unique :db.unique/value
    :db/id #db/id[:db.part/db]
    :db.install/_attribute :db.part/db}

   {:db/doc "Group name"
    :db/ident :group/name
    :db/valueType :db.type/string
    :db/cardinality :db.cardinality/one
    :db/index true
    :db/id #db/id[:db.part/db]
    :db.install/_attribute :db.part/db}

   {:db/doc "Group users"
    :db/ident :group/users
    :db/valueType :db.type/ref
    :db/cardinality :db.cardinality/many
    :db/id #db/id[:db.part/db]
    :db.install/_attribute :db.part/db}])
```

Finally, `transact` both schema definitions into a database via a connection:

```
(require '[datomic.api :as d])

@(d/transact (d/connect "datomic:mem://sample-database")
             (concat user-schema group-schema))
;; -> {:db-before datomic.db.Db@25b48c7b,
;;     :db-after datomic.db.Db@5d81650c,
;;     :tx-data [#Datum{:e ... :a ... :v ... :tx  :added true}, ...],
;;     :tempids {-... ..., ...}}
```

## Discussion

A Datomic schema is represented as Clojure data and is added to the database in a transaction, just like any other data we would store. The `:db.install/_attribute :db.part/db` key/value pair is used by the transactor to make the schema available to the rest of the system.

The schema is placed in the `:db.part/db` database partition, a partition reserved for schemas. All user data is placed in user partition(s)—either the default of `:db.part/user` or a custom partition. Partitions are useful for optimizing how indexes sort data, which is useful for optimizing a query. Schema entities require that at least `:db/ident`, `:db/valueType`, and `:db/cardinality` values are present.

Aside from the schema, Datomic does not enforce how attributes are combined for any given entity. Datomic only requires that a schema be defined up front, enforcing type and uniqueness constraints at runtime.

Use namespaces in schema `:db/ident` values to help classify entities (such as `user` in `:user/email`). Datomic doesn't do anything specific with namespaces, so using them is optional. There are several options for `:db/valueType`, listed in Table 6-1.

*Table 6-1. :db/valueType options*

| | | |
|---|---|---|
| `:db.type/keyword` | `:db.type/string` | `:db.type/long` |
| `:db.type/boolean` | `:db.type/bigint` | `:db.type/float` |
| `:db.type/double` | `:db.type/bigdec` | `:db.type/instant` |
| `:db.type/ref` | `:db.type/uuid` | `:db.type/uri` |
| `:db.type/bytes` | | |

See the Datatomic schema documentation (*http://docs.datomic.com/schema.html*) for an exhaustive listing of their semantics.

Attributes with `:db/valueType :db.type/ref` can only have other entities as their value(s). You use this type to model relationships between entities. Datomic does not enforce which entities are related to on a given `:db/valueType :db.type/ref` attribute. Any other entity can be related to—this means that entities can relate to themselves!

You also use `:db/valueType :db.type/ref` and lone `:db/ident` values to model enumerations, such as the user roles that you defined. These enumerations are not actually schemas; they are normal entities with a single attribute, `:db/ident`. An entity's `:db/ident` value serves as a shorthand for that entity; you may use this value in lieu of the entity's `:db/id` value in transactions and queries.

Attributes with `:db/valueType :db.type/ref` and `:db/unique` values are implicitly indexed as though you had added `:db/index true` to their definitions.

It is also possible to use Lucene full-text indexing on string attributes, using `:db/fulltext true` and the system-defined `fulltext` function in Datalog.

There are two options for specifying a uniqueness constraint at `:db/unique`:

`:db.unique/value`
: Disallows attempts to insert a duplicate value for a different entity ID.

`:db.unique/identity`
: Designates that the attribute value is unique to each entity and enables "upserts"; any attempts to insert a duplicate value for a temporary entity ID will cause all attributes associated with that temporary ID to be merged with the entity already in the database.

In the case where you are modeling entities with subentities that only exist in the context of those entities, such as order items on an order or variants for a product, you can use `:db/isComponent` to simplify working with such subentities. It can only be used on attributes of type `:db.type/ref`.

When you use the `:db.fn/retractEntity` function in a transaction, any entities on the value side of such attributes for the retracted entity will also be retracted. Also, when you use `d/touch` to realize all the lazy keys in an entity map, component entities will be realized too. Both the retraction and realization behaviors are recursive.

By default, Datomic stores all past values of attributes. If you do not wish to keep past values for a particular attribute, use `:db/noHistory true` to have Datomic discard previous values. Using this attribute is much like using a traditional update-in-place database.

## See Also

- Recipe 6.12, "Writing Data to Datomic" on page 295, for more information on transacting datoms (schemas!)

# 6.12. Writing Data to Datomic

by Robert Stuttaford

## Problem

You need to add data to your Datomic database.

## Solution

Use a Datomic connection to transact data.

To follow along with this recipe, complete the steps in the solutions to Recipe 6.10, "Connecting to a Datomic Database" on page 289, and Recipe 6.11, "Defining a Schema for a Datomic Database" on page 291.

After doing this, you will have a connection, `conn`, and a schema installed against which you can insert data:

```
(require '[datomic.api :as d :refer [q db]])

(def tx-data [{:db/id (d/tempid :db.part/user)
               :user/email "fowler@acm.org"
               :user/name "Martin Fowler"
               :user/roles [:user.roles/author :user.roles/editor]}])
```

```
@(d/transact conn tx-data)

(q '[:find ?name
     :where [?e :user/name ?name]]
   (:db-after tx-result))
;; -> #{["Martin Fowler"]}
```

## Discussion

This map-based syntax for representing the data expands to a series of `:db/add` statements. This transaction is identical to the previous one:

```
(def new-id (d/tempid :db.part/user))
new-id
;; -> #db/id[:db.part/user -1000013]

(def tx-data2 [[:db/add new-id :user/email "ryan@cognitect.com"]
               [:db/add new-id :user/name "Ryan Neufeld"]
               [:db/add new-id :user/roles [:user.roles/author
                                            :user.roles/editor]]])

(def tx-result @(d/transact conn tx-data2)) ;; Keep this for later...

(q '[:find ?name
     :where [?e :user/name ?name]]
   (db conn))
;; -> #{["Ryan Neufeld"] ["Martin Fowler"]}
```

Of course, you can use statements like these yourself, or you can use the map syntax shown in the solution. You can also mix the two. This is how you would transact multiple entries (e.g., `(d/transact conn [person1-map person2-map])`).

One difference you'll note between the map and the expanded form is the lack of a `:db/add` statement for the `:db/id` key. In the expanded form, this value comes immediately after the action (`:db/add`) and *must* be identical between all statements to correlate attributes to a single entity. When specifying an entity as a map, you provide a single ID, which the transactor transparently affixes to each attribute.

What is an appropriate ID? Any new entities are assigned temporary, negative ID values, which can be used to model relationships within the transaction. Upon successfully completing a transaction, all the temporary IDs are assigned in-storage positive ID values. When working with code, the correct approach is to use the `datomic.api/tempid` function to obtain a temporary ID. The `datomic.api/tempid` function takes a partition keyword and an optional ID number as its arguments; for most purposes, `:db.part/user` will suffice.

When working with nonexecutable data, you'll need to use the data-literal form for temporary IDs. The literal `#db/id [:db.part/user]` is equivalent to `(d/tempid :db.part/user)`. This form is most useful when you store transaction data in an *.edn* file, which is most often the case with schema definitions. Again, you should use `d/tempid` in your code—the `#db/id` literal will evaluate once at compile time, which means that any code that expects the ID value to change from one execution to the next will fail, because it'll only ever have one value.

Consider our example file, *user-bootstrap.edn*:

```
[{:db/id #db/id [:db.part/user]
  :user/email "fowler@acm.org"
  :user/name "Martin Fowler"
  :user/roles [:user.roles/author :user.roles/editor]}]
```

When a transaction completes, you'll receive a completed future. If you prefer to transact asynchronously, you can use `d/transact-async` instead, which will return its future immediately. In this case, as with all futures, when you dereference it, it will block until the transaction completes. Either way, dereferencing the future returns a map, with four keys:

`:db-before`
: The value of the database just before the transaction was committed

`:db-after`
: The value of the database just after the transaction was committed

`:tx-data`
: A vector of all the datoms that were transacted

`:tempids`
: A mapping of the temporary IDs to the in-storage IDs, one per temporary ID in the transaction

You can use the `:db-after` database to query the database directly after the transaction:

```
(def db-after-tx (:db-after tx-result))

(q '[:find ?name :in $ ?email :where
     [?entity :user/email ?email]
     [?entity :user/name ?name]]
   db-after-tx
   "fowler@acm.org")
;; -> #{["Martin Fowler"]}
```

You can use the `:tempids` map to find the in-storage IDs for any new entities you care about, much like you would when retrieving the last insert ID in SQL databases. Invoke `datomic.api/resolve-tempid` with the `:db-after` value, the `:tempids` value, and the original temporary ID to retrieve the realized ID:

```
(d/resolve-tempid db-after-tx (:tempids tx-result) new-id)
;; -> 17592186045421
```

## See Also

- Recipe 6.11, "Defining a Schema for a Datomic Database" on page 291
- Recipe 6.13, "Removing Data from a Datomic Database" on page 298
- Recipe 6.14, "Trying Datomic Transactions Without Committing Them" on page 300

# 6.13. Removing Data from a Datomic Database

by Robert Stuttaford

## Problem

You need to remove data from your Datomic database.

## Solution

To remove a value for an attribute, you should use the `:db/retract` operation in transactions.

To follow along with this recipe, complete the steps in the solutions to Recipe 6.10, "Connecting to a Datomic Database" on page 289, and Recipe 6.11, "Defining a Schema for a Datomic Database" on page 291. After doing this, you will have a connection, `conn`, and a schema installed against which you can insert data.

To start things off, add a user, Barney Rubble, and verify that he has an email address:

```
(def new-id (d/tempid :db.part/user))

(def tx-result @(d/transact conn
                            [{:db/id new-id
                              :user/name "Barney Rubble"
                              :user/email "barney@example.com"}]))

(def after-tx-db (:db-after tx-result))

(def barney-id (d/resolve-tempid after-tx-db
                                 (:tempids tx-result)
                                 new-id))

barney-id
;; -> 17592186045429

(d/q '[:find ?email :in $ ?entity-id :where
       [?entity-id :user/email ?email]]
     after-tx-db
```

```
     barney-id)
;; -> #{["barney@rubble.me"]}
```

To retract Barney's email, transact a transaction with the `:db/retract` operation:

```
(def retract-tx-result @(d/transact conn [[:db/retract barney-id
                                            :user/email "barney@example.com"]]))

(def after-retract-db (:db-after retract-tx-result))

(d/q '[:find ?email :in $ ?entity-id :where
       [?entity-id :user/email ?email]]
     after-retract-db
     barney-id)
;; -> #{}
```

To retract entire entities, use the `:db.fn/retractEntity` built-in transactor function:

```
(def retract-entity-tx-result
  @(d/transact conn [[:db.fn/retractEntity barney-id]]))

(def after-retract-entity-db (:db-after retract-entity-tx-result))

(d/q '[:find ?entity-id :in $ ?name :where
       [?entity-id :user/name ?name]]
     after-retract-entity-db
     "Barney Rubble")
;; -> #{}
```

## Discussion

When using `:db/retract`, you provide the value to retract so that in the case of cardinality-many attributes, it's clear which value to retract from the set of values for that attribute. Regardless of the cardinality, if you provide a value that isn't in storage, nothing will be retracted. This means that you have to know what value you want to retract; you can't simply retract everything for an attribute by only providing the entity ID and the attribute.

If you retract values for an attribute that does *not* use `:db/noHistory`, you will be able to query past database values to find past values for the attribute.

If you retract values for an attribute that uses `:db/noHistory`, that data will be *permanently deleted.*

When using `:db.fn/retractEntity`, all attribute values for all the attributes on that entity will be retracted, as will all `:db/ref` attributes that have the entity as a value. Any component entities of the entity being retracted will themselves be recursively retracted.

You'll find that the actual entity ID itself is not retracted, but that it will have no attributes associated with it. This is because once an entity is created, it cannot be retracted. Removing all the attributes and references to the entity has the same effect as if it had been permanently removed, though!

If you need to permanently remove data due to legal concerns or because the data in question falls outside of your domain-specified retention period, use excision (*http://bit.ly/datomic-excision*) to remove the data permanently.

## See Also

- The Datomic blog post (*http://bit.ly/datomic-excision*) covering the excision feature

# 6.14. Trying Datomic Transactions Without Committing Them

by Robert Stuttaford

## Problem

You want to test a transaction prior to committing it using Datalog or the entity API.

## Solution

Build your transaction as usual, but instead of calling `d/transact` or `d/transact-async`, use `d/with` to produce an in-memory database that includes the changes your transaction provides.

To follow along with this recipe, complete the steps in the solutions to Recipe 6.10, "Connecting to a Datomic Database" on page 289, and Recipe 6.11, "Defining a Schema for a Datomic Database" on page 291. After doing this, you will have a connection, `conn`, and a schema installed against which you can insert data.

First, add some data to the database about Fred Flintstone. As of about 4000 BCE, Fred didn't have an email, but we at least know his name:

```
(require '[datomic.api :as d])

(def new-id (d/tempid :db.part/user))


(def tx-result @(d/transact conn
                            [{:db/id new-id
                              :user/name "Fred Flintstone"}]))
```

Fast-forward to today: Fred is thawed, after having been frozen in ice for 6,000 years, and he gets his first email address. Prepare a transaction to add an email to the Fred entity:

```
;; Grab Fred's ID from the original transaction
(def fred-id (d/resolve-tempid (:db-after tx-result)
                               (:tempids tx-result)
                               new-id))

fred-id
;; -> 17592186045421

(def add-freds-email-tx [[:db/add fred-id
                          :user/email "twinkletoes@example.com"]])
```

Now, prepare an in-memory database with this new transaction applied. First, get the current database value to use as a basis, then create an in-memory database. Finally, grab the `:db-after` value so that you can test that the email was properly added:

```
(defn db-with
  "Return a new database with tx applied"
  [db tx]
  (-> (d/with db tx)
      :db-after))

(def db-after (db-with (d/db conn) add-freds-email-tx))
```

Compare the value of Fred's email in the current database with that of Fred's email in the in-memory database:

```
(defn users-email
  "Retrieve a user's email given the user's name."
  [db name]
  (-> (d/q '[:find ?email
            :in $ ?name
            :where
            [?entity :user/name ?name]
            [?entity :user/email ?email]]
          db
          name)
      ffirst))

(users-email db-after "Fred Flintstone")
;; -> "twinkletoes@example.com"

(users-email (d/db conn) "Fred Flintstone")
;; -> nil
```

As you can see, the current database remains unaffected by this transaction, but the database at `db-after` now displays the new value.

## Discussion

Databases produced by `d/with` can be used with any of the other API functions that accept a database, including `d/with` itself. This means that you can layer multiple transactions on top of one another without first having to commit them to the transactor!

One of the things that makes Datomic so powerful is its ability to treat a database as a value. For this reason, the helper functions we've written take a database as an argument, not a connection. Now it is not only possible to query the current database, but other values of the database as well.

## See Also

- Recipe 6.12, "Writing Data to Datomic" on page 295, for more general information on transacting data

# 6.15. Traversing Datomic Indexes

by Alan Busby and Ryan Neufeld

## Problem

You want to execute simple Datomic queries with high performance.

## Solution

Use the `datomic.api/datoms` function to directly access the core Datomic indexes in your database.

To follow along with this recipe, complete the steps in the solutions to Recipe 6.10, "Connecting to a Datomic Database" on page 289, and Recipe 6.11, "Defining a Schema for a Datomic Database" on page 291. After doing this, you will have a connection, `conn`, and a schema installed against which you can insert data.

For example, to quickly find the entities that have the provided attribute and value set, invoke `datomic.api/datoms`, specifying the `:avet` index (attribute, value, entity, transaction) and the desired attribute and value:

```
(require '[datomic.api :as d])

(d/transact conn [{:db/id (d/tempid :db.part/user)
                   :user/name "Barney Rubble"
                   :user/email "barney@example.com"}])

(defn entities-with-attr-val
  "Return entities with a given attribute and value."
```

```
  [db attr val]
  (->> (d/datoms db :avet attr val)
       (map :e)
       (map (partial d/entity db))))


(def barney (first (entities-with-attr-val (d/db conn)
                                           :user/email
                                           "barney@example.com")))

(:user/email barney)
;; -> "barney@example.com"
```

This will only work for attributes where `:db/index` is `true` or `:db/unique` is not `nil`.

To quickly determine all of the attributes an entity has, use the `:eavt`-ordered index:

```
(defn entities-attrs
  "Return attrs of an entity"
  [db entity]
  (->> (d/datoms db :eavt (:db/id entity))
       (map :a)
       (map (partial d/entity db))
       (map :db/ident)))

(entities-attrs (d/db conn) barney)
;; -> (:user/email :user/name)
```

To quickly find entities that refer, via `:db.type/ref`, to a provided entity, use the `:vaet`-ordered index:

```
;; Add a person that refers to a :user.roles/author role
(d/transact conn [{:db/id (d/tempid :db.part/user)
                   :user/name "Ryan Neufeld"
                   :user/email "ryan@rkn.io"
                   :user/roles [:user.roles/author :user.roles/editor]}])

(defn referring-to
  "Find all entities referring to an entity as a certain attribute."
  [db entity]
  (->> (d/datoms db :vaet (:db/id entity) )
       (map :e)
       (map (partial d/entity db))))

(def author-entity (d/entity (d/db conn) :user.roles/author))

;; The names of all users with a :user.roles/author role
```

```
(map :user/name (referring-to (d/db conn) author-entity))
;; -> ("Ryan Neufeld")
```

## Discussion

For simple lookup queries, like "find by attribute" or "find by value", nothing beats Datomic's raw indexes in terms of performance. The `datomic.api/datoms` interface provides access to all of Datomic's indexes and conveniently lets you dive in any number of levels, "biting off" only the data you need.

As with most Datomic functions, `datoms` takes a `db` as its first argument. You'll note that in our examples, and elsewhere in the book, we too accept a database as a value, and not a connection—this idiom allows API users to perform varying numbers of operations on the same database value. You should always try to do this yourself.

The second argument to `datoms` indicates the particular index you want to access. Each value is a permutation of the letters `e` (entity), `a` (attribute), `v` (value), and `t` (transaction). The order of the letters in an index indicates how it is indexed. For example, `:eavt` should be traversed by entity, then attribute, and so on and so forth. The four indexes and what they include are as follows:

`:eavt`
: An entity-first index that includes all datoms. This index provides a view over your database very much like a traditional relational database.

`:aevt`
: An attribute-then-entity index that includes all datoms. This index provides columnar access to your database, much like a data warehouse.

`:avet`
: An attribute-value index that only includes attributes where `:db/index` is `true`. Incredibly useful as a lookup index (e.g., "I need the entity with an email of *foo@example.com*").

`:vaet`
: A value-first index that only includes `:db.type/ref` values. This is a very interesting index that can be used to treat your data a bit like a graph database.

After specifying an index ordering, you can optionally provide any number of components to pre-traverse the index. This serves to reduce the number of elements returned. For example, specifying just an attribute component for AVET traversal will return any entity with that attribute. Specifying an attribute and a value component, on the other hand, will return only entities with that specific attribute and value pair.

What is returned by `datoms` is a stream of `Datum` objects. Each datum responds to `:a`, `:e`, `t`, `:v`, and `:added` as functions.

## See Also

- Recipe 6.12, "Writing Data to Datomic" on page 295

CHAPTER 7

# Web Applications

## 7.0. Introduction

Web application development is the breadwinner for many languages nowadays; Clojure is no exception. In the annual 2013 State of Clojure Survey (*http://bit.ly/clojure-survey-2013*), web development ranked first for the question, "In which domains are you applying Clojure and/or ClojureScript?"

Much of the Clojure web development community today centers around Ring (*https://github.com/ring-clojure/ring*), an HTTP server library very much akin to Ruby's Rack (*http://rack.github.io/*). Starting with the introduction to Ring in Recipe 7.1, "Introduction to Ring" on page 307, you'll find a full complement of recipes here that will get you up to speed in no time.

Following Ring, the chapter takes a tour of the other Clojure web development ecosystems available at the time of writing, covering a few templating and HTML-manipulation libraries and a number of alternative web frameworks.

## 7.1. Introduction to Ring

by Adam Bard

### Problem

You need to write an HTTP service with Clojure.

### Solution

Clojure has no built-in HTTP server, but the de facto standard for serving basic, synchronous HTTP requests is the Ring library.

To follow along with this recipe, clone the *https://github.com/clojure-cookbook/ringtest* repository and overwrite *src/ringtest.clj*:

```
(ns ringtest
  (:require
    [ring.adapter.jetty :as jetty]
    clojure.pprint))

;; Echo (with pretty-print) the request received
(defn handler [request]
  {:status 200
   :headers {"content-type" "text/clojure"}
   :body (with-out-str (clojure.pprint/pprint request))})

(defn -main []
  ;; Run the server on port 3000
  (jetty/run-jetty handler {:port 3000}))
```

## Discussion

Ring (*https://github.com/ring-clojure/ring*) is the basis for most web applications in Clojure. It provides a low-level and straightforward request/response API, where requests and responses are plain old Clojure maps.

Ring applications are architected around *handlers*: functions that accept requests and return responses. The preceding example defines a single handler that just echoes the response it receives.

A basic response map consists of three keys: `:status`, the status code of the response; `:headers`, an optional string-string map of the response headers you want; and `:body`, the string you want as your response body. Here, `:status` is `200` and `:body` is a pretty-printed string of the request. Therefore, the following sample response from hitting the URL *http://localhost:3000/test/path/?qs=1* on the author's machine demonstrates the structure of a request:

```
{:ssl-client-cert nil,
 :remote-addr "0:0:0:0:0:0:0:1",
 :scheme :http,
 :request-method :get,
 :query-string "qs=1",
 :content-type nil,
 :uri "/test/path/",
 :server-name "localhost",
 :headers
 {"accept-encoding" "gzip,deflate,sdch",
  "connection" "keep-alive",
  "user-agent"
  "Mozilla/5.0 (Macintosh; Intel Mac OS X 10_8_4) AppleWebKit/537.36
  (KHTML, like Gecko) Chrome/28.0.1500.71 Safari/537.36",
  "accept-language" "en-US,en;q=0.8",
```

```
 "accept"
 "text/html,application/xhtml+xml,application/xml;q=0.9,*/*;q=0.8",
 "host" "localhost:3000",
 "cookie" ""},
:content-length nil,
:server-port 3000,
:character-encoding nil,
:body #<HttpInput org.eclipse.jetty.server.HttpInput@43efe432>}
```

You can see that this is comprehensive, but low level, with the salient features of the request parsed into Clojure data structures without additional abstraction. Typically, additional code or libraries are used to extract meaningful information from this data structure.

The `jetty` adapter is used to run an embedded Jetty server. Ring also comes with adapters to run as a servlet in any Java servlet container.

Note that the call to `run-jetty` is synchronous and will not return as long as the server is running. If you call it from the REPL, you should wrap it in a future (or use some other concurrency mechanism) so the server runs on another thread and your REPL does not become unresponsive.

## See Also

- Ring's GitHub repository (*https://github.com/ring-clojure/ring*)

# 7.2. Using Ring Middleware

by Adam Bard

## Problem

You'd like to build a transformation to be automatically applied to Ring requests or responses. For example, Ring gives you query strings, but you'd really rather work with a parsed map.

## Solution

Since Ring works with regular Clojure data and functions, you can easily define middlewares as functions returning functions. In this case, define a middleware that modifies the request by adding a parsed version of the query string to the request before passing it on to the handler.

To follow along with this recipe, clone the *https://github.com/clojure-cookbook/ringtest* repository and overwrite *src/ringtest.clj*:

```
(ns ringtest
  (:require
    [ring.adapter.jetty :as jetty]
    [clojure.string :as str]
    clojure.pprint))

(defn parse-query-string
  "Parse a query string to a hash-map"
  [qs]
  (if (> (count qs) 0) ; Don't operate on nils or empty strings
    (apply hash-map (str/split qs #"[&=]"))))

(defn wrap-query
  "Add a :query parameter to incoming requests that contains a parsed
  version of the query string as a hash-map"
  [handler]
  (fn [req]
    (let [parsed-qs (parse-query-string (:query-string req))
          new-req (assoc req :query parsed-qs)]
      (handler new-req))))

(defn handler [req]
  (let [name (get (:query req) "name")]
    {:status 200
     :body (str "Hello, " (or name "World"))}))

(defn -main []
  ;; Run the server on port 3000
  (jetty/run-jetty (wrap-query handler) {:port 3000}))
```

## Discussion

Since Ring handlers operate on regular Clojure maps, it's very easy to write a middleware that wraps a handler. Here, we write a middleware that modifies the request before passing it to the handler. If the original request looked like this:

```
{:query-string "x=1&y=2"
 ; ... and the rest
 }
```

then the request received by the handler becomes:

```
{:query-string "x=1&y=2"
 :query {"x" "1" "y" "2"}
 ; ... and the rest
 }
```

However, you don't need to write your own middleware for this. Ring provides a number of middlewares to add to your apps, including one called `wrap-params` that does the same as the middleware we just wrote, but better. From the Ring documentation (*http://bit.ly/clj-wrap-params*):

**wrap-params**

Middleware to parse urlencoded parameters from the query string and form body (if the request is a urlencoded form). Adds the following keys to the request map:

:query-params - a map of parameters from the query string

:form-params - a map of parameters from the body

:params - a merged map of all types of parameter

Takes an optional configuration map. Recognized keys are:

:encoding - encoding to use for url-decoding. If not specified, uses the request character encoding, or "UTF-8" if no request character encoding is set.

You are in no way limited to using one middleware. Usually, you'll at least want to use the cookie, session, and parameter middleware. One concise way to wrap your handler with several middlewares is to use the -> macro:

```
(require '[ring.middleware.session :refer [wrap-session]])
(require '[ring.middleware.cookies :refer [wrap-cookies]])
(require '[ring.middleware.params :refer [wrap-params]])
(def wrapped-handler
  (-> handler
    wrap-cookies
    wrap-params
    wrap-session))
```

## See Also

- Ring's middleware concepts documentation (*http://bit.ly/ring-middleware*)

# 7.3. Serving Static Files with Ring

by Clinton Dreisbach

## Problem

You want to serve static files through your Ring application.

## Solution

Use `ring.middleware.file/wrap-file`:

```
(require '[ring.middleware.file :refer [wrap-file]])

;; Serve all files from your public directory
(def app
  (wrap-file handler "/var/webapps/public"))
```

## Discussion

wrap-file wraps another web request handler so that you will serve a static file if one exists in the specified directory, and call the handler if the requested file does not exist.

wrap-file is only one way to serve static files. If you only want to serve up a particular file, ring.util.response/file-response will return a handler that serves up that file:

```
(require '[ring.util.response :refer [file-response]])

;; Serve README.html
(file-response "README.html")

;; Serve README.html from the public/ directory
(file-response "README.html" {:root "public"})

;; Serve README.html through a symlink
(file-response "README.html" {:allow-symlinks? true})
```

Often, you will want to bundle your static files with your application. In that case, it makes more sense to serve files from your classpath rather than from a specific directory. For this, use ring.middleware.resource/wrap-resource:

```
(require '[ring.middleware.resource :refer [wrap-resource]])

(def app
  (wrap-resource handler "static"))
```

This will serve all files under a directory called *static* in your classpath. You can put the *static* directory under *resources/* in a Leiningen project and have your static files packaged with JAR files you generate from that project.

You may want to wrap any file responses with ring.middleware.file-info/wrap-file-info. This Ring middleware checks the modification date and the type of the file, setting the Content-Type and Last-Modified headers. wrap-file-info needs to wrap around wrap-file or wrap-resource.

## See Also

- Recipe 4.4, "Accessing Resource Files" on page 173
- Recipe 7.8, "Routing Requests with Compojure" on page 320

# 7.4. Handling Form Data with Ring

by Adam Bard

## Problem

You want your app to accept user input using an HTML form.

## Solution

Use `ring.middleware.params/wrap-params` to add incoming HTTP form parameters to incoming request maps.

To follow along with this recipe, clone the *https://github.com/clojure-cookbook/ringtest* repository and overwrite *src/ringtest.clj*:

```
(ns ringtest
  (:require
    [ring.adapter.jetty :as jetty]
    [ring.middleware.params :refer [wrap-params]]))

(def greeting-form
  (str
    "<html>"
    "  <form action='' method='post'>"
    "    Enter your name: <input type='text' name='name'><br/>"
    "    <input type='submit' value='Say Hello'>"
    "  </form>"
    "</html>"))

(defn show-form []
  {:body greeting-form
   :status 200 })

(defn show-name
  "A response showing that we know the user's name"
  [name]
  {:body (str "Hello, " name)
   :status 200})

(defn handler
  "Show a form requesting the user's name, or greet them if they
  submitted the form"
  [req]
  (let [name (get-in req [:params "name"])]
    (if name
      (show-name name)
      (show-form))))
```

```
(defn -main []
  ;; Run the server on port 3000
  (jetty/run-jetty (wrap-params handler) {:port 3000}))
```

## Discussion

`wrap-params` is a Ring middleware that handles the retrieval of query string and form parameters from raw requests. It adds three keys to the request:

`:query-params`
: Contains a map of the parsed query string parameters

`:form-params`
: Contains a map of form body parameters

`:params`
: Contains the contents of both `:query-params` and `:form-params` merged together

In the preceding example we used `:form-params`, so our handler will only respond with a greeting on POST requests containing form-encoded parameters. If we had used `:params`, we would have had the option of also passing a URL query string with a `"name"` parameter. `:params` works with any kind of parameter (form- or URL-encoded). `:form-params` only works for form parameters.

Note that the form keys are passed in as strings, not keywords.

## See Also

- Recipe 7.2, "Using Ring Middleware" on page 309
- Ring's parameters documentation (*http://bit.ly/ring-parameters*)

# 7.5. Handling Cookies with Ring

by Adam Bard

## Problem

Your web application needs to read or set cookies on the user's browser (for example, to remember a user's name).

## Solution

Use the `ring.middleware.cookies/wrap-cookies` middleware to add cookies to your requests.

To follow along with this recipe, clone the *https://github.com/clojure-cookbook/ringtest* repository and overwrite *src/ringtest.clj*:

```
(ns ringtest
  (:require
    [ring.adapter.jetty :as jetty]
    [ring.middleware.cookies :refer [wrap-cookies]]
    [ring.middleware.params :refer [wrap-params]]))

(defn set-name-form
  "A response showing a form for the user to enter their name."
  []
  {:body "<html>
           <form action=''>
             Name: <input type='text' name='name'>
             <input type='submit'>
           </form>
         </html>"
   :status 200
   :content-type "text/html"})

(defn show-name
  "A response showing that we know the user's name"
  [name]
  {:body (str "Hello, " name)
   :cookies {"name" {:value name}} ; Preserve the cookies
   :status 200 })

(defn handler
  "If we know the user's name, show it; else, show a form to get it."
  [req]
  (let [name (or
               (get-in req [:cookies "name" :value])
               (get-in req [:params "name"]))]
    (if name
      (show-name name)
      (set-name-form))))

(def wrapped-handler
  (-> handler
      wrap-cookies
      wrap-params))

(defn -main []
  ;; Run the server on port 3000
  (jetty/run-jetty wrapped-handler {:port 3000}))
```

## Discussion

This example uses the `wrap-cookies` and `wrap-params` middlewares included with `ring-core`. The first time users visit a page, it shows them a form to enter their names.

Once entered, it stores the user's name in a cookie and displays it instead, until the cookie is removed.

The example uses `wrap-cookies` to retrieve the user's stored name from the cookie map, or, if it's not there, `wrap-params` to retrieve the user's name from the request parameters.

Ring's cookie middleware simply adds an extra parameter, `:cookies`, onto the incoming request map, and sets any cookies you pass out as the `:cookies` parameter on the response. The `:cookies` parameter is a map that looks something like this:

```
{"name" {:value "Some Guy"}}
```

You can add other optional parameters to each cookie, along with `:value`. From the Ring cookie documentation (*http://bit.ly/ring-cookies*):

> As well as setting the value of the cookie, you can also set additional attributes:
>
> - `:domain`—restrict the cookie to a specific domain
> - `:path`—restrict the cookie to a specific path
> - `:secure`—restrict the cookie to HTTPS URLs if true
> - `:http-only`—restrict the cookie to HTTP if true (not accessible via e.g. JavaScript)
> - `:max-age`—the number of seconds until the cookie expires
> - `:expires`—a specific date and time the cookie expires

## See Also

- Recipe 7.2, "Using Ring Middleware" on page 309
- Ring's cookies documentation (*http://bit.ly/ring-cookies*)

# 7.6. Storing Sessions with Ring

by Adam Bard

## Problem

You need to store secure data about a logged-in user as state on the server.

## Solution

Use `ring.middleware.session/wrap-session` to add sessions to your Ring application.

To follow along with this recipe, clone the *https://github.com/clojure-cookbook/ringtest* repository and overwrite *src/ringtest.clj*:

```
(ns ringtest
  (:require
    [ring.adapter.jetty :as jetty]
    [ring.middleware.session :refer [wrap-session]]
    [ring.middleware.params :refer [wrap-params]]))

(def login-form
  (str
    "<html>"
    "  <form action='' method='post'>"
    "    Username: <input type='text' name='username'><br/>"
    "    Password: <input type='text' name='password'><br/>"
    "    <input type='submit' value='Log In'>"
    "  </form>"
    "</html>"))

(defn show-form []
  {:body login-form
   :status 200 })

(defn show-name
  "A response showing that we know the user's name"
  [name session]
  {:body (str "Hello, " name)
   :status 200
   :session session })

(defn do-login
  "Check the submitted form data and update the session if necessary"
  [params session]
  (if (and (= (params "username") "jim")
           (= (params "password") "password"))
    (assoc session :user "jim")
    session))


(defn handler
  "Log a user in, or not"
  [{session :session params :form-params :as req}]
  (let [session (do-login params session)
        username (:user session)]

    (if username
      (show-name username session)
      (show-form))))

(def wrapped-handler
  (-> handler
      wrap-session
```

```
        wrap-params))

(defn -main []
  ;; Run the server on port 3000
  (jetty/run-jetty wrapped-handler {:port 3000}))
```

## Discussion

Ring's session middleware (*http://bit.ly/ring-sessions*) has an API similar to the cookies API. You get session data from the `:session` request map, and set it by including a `:session` key in the response map. Whatever you pass to `:session` is up to you, but usually you'll want to use a map to store keys and values.

Behind the scenes, Ring sets a cookie called `ring-session`, which contains a unique ID identifying the session. When a request comes in, the session middleware gets the session ID from the request, then reads the value of the session from some session store.

Which session store the middleware uses is configurable. The default is to use an in-memory session store, which is useful for development but has the side effect of losing sessions whenever you restart the app. Ring includes an encrypted cookie store as well, which *is* persistent, and you can get third-party libraries for many popular storages, including Memcached (*http://bit.ly/ring-session-memcached*) and Redis (*https://github.com/wuzhe/clj-redis-session*). You can write your own, too, to store your sessions in any database.

You can set your store by passing an options map with a `:store` parameter to `wrap-session`:

```
(wrap-session handler {:store (my-store)}))
```

To set the value of `:session`, just pass it along with your response. If you don't need the session changed, leave `:session` out of your response. If you want to actually clear the session, pass `nil` as the value of the `:session` key.

## See Also

- Recipe 7.2, "Using Ring Middleware" on page 309
- Ring's sessions documentation (*http://bit.ly/ring-sessions*)

# 7.7. Reading and Writing Request and Response Headers in Ring

by Luke VanderHart and Adam Bard

## Problem

You need to read or write HTTP request or response headers.

## Solution

Read from the `:headers` key in a Ring request map, or `assoc` values onto the response map before returning from a Ring handler function.

To follow along with this recipe, clone the *https://github.com/clojure-cookbook/ringtest* repository and overwrite *src/ringtest.clj*:

```
(ns ringtest
  (:require
    [ring.adapter.jetty :as jetty]))

(defn user-agent-as-json
  "A handler that returns the User-Agent header as a JSON
   response with an appropriate Content-Type"
  [req]
  {:body (str "{\"user-agent\": \"" (get-in req [:headers "user-agent"]) "\"}")
   :headers {"Content-Type" "application/json"}
   :status 200})

(defn -main []
  ;; Run the server on port 3000
  (jetty/run-jetty user-agent-as-json {:port 3000}))
```

## Discussion

This example defines a Ring handler that returns the incoming `User-Agent` header as a JSON response. It gets the `User-Agent` from the request header map, and uses a `Content-Type` header in the response to indicate to the client that it should be parsed as JSON.

Ring passes request headers as a `:headers` parameter in the request map, and accepts a `:headers` parameter in response maps as well. The keys and values of the headers map should both be strings. Clojure keywords are not supported.

You can use Ring to set any header that is valid in HTTP (*http://bit.ly/http-header-fields*).

According to RFC-2616 (*http://bit.ly/rfc2616*), header names are *not* case sensitive. To make it easier to consistently `get` values from the request map, no matter what their case, Ring passes in all header values as lowercase, regardless of what the client sent. You may wish to *send* headers using the actual capitalization used in the specification, though, just in case the client you're communicating with is not compliant (following the classic robustness principle: "Be conservative in what you send; be liberal in what you accept").

## See Also

- Ring's concepts documentation (*http://bit.ly/ring-concepts*)

# 7.8. Routing Requests with Compojure

by Adam Bard

## Problem

You want an easy way to route URLs to specific Ring handler functions.

## Solution

Use the Compojure library (*https://github.com/weavejester/compojure*) to add routing to your app.

To follow along with this recipe, clone the *https://github.com/clojure-cookbook/ringtest* repository and overwrite *src/ringtest.clj*:

```
(ns ringtest
  (:require
    [compojure.core :refer [defroutes GET]]
    [ring.adapter.jetty :as jetty]))

;; View functions
(defn view [x]
  (str "<h1>" x "</h1>"))

(defn index []
  (view "Hello"))

(defn index-fr []
  (view "Bonjour"))

;; Routing
(defroutes main-routes
  (GET "/" [] (index))
  (GET "/en/" [] (index))
  (GET "/fr/" [] (index-fr))
  (GET "/:greeting/" [greeting] (view greeting)))

;; Server
(defn -main []
 (jetty/run-jetty main-routes {:port 3000}))
```

## Discussion

Compojure is a routing library that lets you define routes for your app. It does this via the `defroutes` macro, which produces a Ring handler function.

Here, we define four routes:

`/`
: Displays "Hello"

`/en/`
: Also displays "Hello"

`/fr/`
: Displays "Bonjour"

`/:greeting/`
: Echoes the greeting passed by the user

The last view is an example of Compojure's URL parameter syntax. The section of the URL identified by `:greeting` is passed along to the view, which displays it for the user. So, visiting *http://localhost:3000/Buenos%20Dias/* displays "Buenos Dias" in response.

One caveat to be aware of is that Compojure routes are sensitive to a trailing slash: a route defined as `/users/:user/blog/` will not match the URL *http://mysite.com/users/fred/blog*, but it *will* match *http://mysite.com/users/fred/blog/*.

The `[]` in each route is actually syntactic sugar for intercepting these parameters. You can also use `req` or any other symbol to get the whole request:

```
(defroutes main-routes-2
  (GET "/" req (some-view req)))
```

You can even use Clojure's destructuring syntax[1] to extract parts of the request. For example, if you're using the `wrap-params` middleware, you can grab the parameters and pass them to a function:

```
(defroutes main-routes-2
  (GET "/" {params :params} (some-other-view params)))
```

It is important to realize that Compojure works on top of Ring. Your views should still return Ring response maps (although Compojure will wrap strings you return with a basic 200 response).

1. If you're not familiar with Clojure's destructuring syntax, we suggest reading Jay Fields's "Clojure: Destructuring" blog post (*http://bit.ly/destructuring*). For a more extensive resource, pick up a copy of *Clojure Programming* (*http://www.clojurebook.com/*) (O'Reilly) by Chas Emerick, Brian Carper, and Christophe Grand, which covers destructuring in depth.

You can also define routes for other types of HTTP requests by specifying the route using the relevant Compojure directive: `compojure.core/POST` and `compojure.core/PUT` are most commonly used, in addition to `compojure.core/GET`.

Compojure provides a few other helpful tools, such as `compojure.route` (*http://bit.ly/compojure-route*), which provides helpers for serving resources, files, and 404 responses; and `compojure.handler` (*http://bit.ly/compojure-handler*), which bundles a number of Ring middlewares into one convenient wrapper.

## See Also

- The Compojure website (*http://compojure.org*)

# 7.9. Performing HTTP Redirects with Ring

by Craig McDaniel

## Problem

In a Ring application, you need to return an HTTP response code that will redirect the browser to another URL.

## Solution

To redirect a Ring request, use the `redirect` function in the `ring.util.response` namespace.

To follow along with this recipe, clone the *https://github.com/clojure-cookbook/ringtest* repository and overwrite *src/ringtest.clj*:

```
(ns ringtest
  (:require
   [ring.adapter.jetty :as jetty]
   [ring.util.response :as response]))

(defn redirect-to-github
  "A handler that redirects all requests"
  [req]
  (response/redirect "http://github.com/"))

(defn -main []
  ;; Run the server on port 3000
  (jetty/run-jetty redirect-to-github {:port 3000}))
```

## Discussion

The `ring.util.response` namespace contains a function for redirecting to a URL. This URL can be generated dynamically from the request map (using parameters from `wrap-params`, headers, etc.). Underneath, this function simply creates a response map with a 302 `:status` value and a location header containing the URL to redirect to.

According to the HTTP specification, if the response method is a POST, PUT, or DELETE, it should be assumed that the server received the request, and the client should issue a GET request to the URL in the location header. This is an important caveat when writing REST services. Fortunately, the specification provides a 307 status code, which should signal to clients that the request should be redirected to the new location using the original method and body. To do this, simply return a response map in the handler function like so:

```
(defn redirect-to-github
  [req]
  {:status 307
   :headers {"Location" "http://github.com"}
   :body ""})
```

## See Also

- Ring's concepts documentation (*http://bit.ly/ring-concepts*)

# 7.10. Building a RESTful Application with Liberator

by Eric Normand

## Problem

You want to build a RESTful (RFC 2616–compliant) web application on top of Ring and Compojure at a higher level of abstraction, by defining resources.

## Solution

Use Liberator (*https://github.com/clojure-liberator/liberator*) to create HTTP-compliant, RESTful web apps.

To follow along with this recipe, create a new project using the command **`lein new liberator-test`**.

Inside your *project.clj*, add the following dependencies to your `:dependencies` key:

```
[compojure "1.0.2"]
[ring/ring-jetty-adapter "1.1.0"]
[liberator "0.9.0"]
```

Then, modify *src/liberator_test/core.clj* to match the following contents:

```
(ns liberator-test.core
  (:require [compojure.core :refer [defroutes ANY]]
            [ring.adapter.jetty :as jetty]
            [liberator.core :refer [defresource]]))

;; Resources

(defresource root
   :available-media-types #{"text/plain"})

;; Routing
(defroutes main-routes
  (ANY "/" [] root))

;; Server
(defn -main []
 (jetty/run-jetty main-routes {:port 3000}))
```

## Discussion

Liberator (*https://github.com/clojure-liberator/liberator*) is a library for developing HTTP-compliant web servers. It handles content negotiation, status codes, and standard request methods on RESTful resources. It decides what status to respond with using a decision tree, which follows the HTTP spec.

Liberator does not handle routing, so another library needs to be used. In this recipe, Compojure was used. Since Liberator does a better job of handling the request method (GET, PUT, POST, etc.), you should use `ANY` in your Compojure routes. You could also use a different routing library, such as Clout (*https://github.com/weavejester/clout*), Moustache (*https://github.com/cgrand/moustache*), or the playnice (*https://github.com/ericnormand/playnice*) router.

The `defresource` form defines a web resource, which is modeled as a Ring handler. You can therefore pass the resource as the last argument to Compojure routes.

Liberator resources are set up with sensible defaults. The default for the available media types is the empty set, so it needs to be set to something; otherwise, Liberator will return a 406 "Not Acceptable" response. In this recipe it is set to respond with `text/plain` as the MIME type. The default response is "OK," which you will see if you run the recipe and point a browser at *http://localhost:3000*.

## See Also

- Recipe 7.1, "Introduction to Ring" on page 307, for information on setting up Ring
- Recipe 7.8, "Routing Requests with Compojure" on page 320, for more information on Compojure routes
- Liberator's home page (*http://bit.ly/clj-liberator*)

# 7.11. Templating HTML with Enlive

by Luke VanderHart

## Problem

You want to create HTML dynamically based on a template, without using traditional mixed code or DSL-style templating.

## Solution

Use Enlive (*https://github.com/cgrand/enlive*), a Clojure library that takes a selector-based approach to templating HTML. Unlike other template frameworks like PHP, ERB, and JSP, it doesn't mix code and text. And unlike systems like Haml or Hiccup, it doesn't use specialized DSLs. Instead, templates are plain old HTML files, and Enlive uses Clojure code to target specific areas for replacement or duplication based on incoming data.

To follow along with this recipe, start a REPL using `lein-try`:

```
$ lein try enlive
```

To begin, create a file *post.html* to serve as an Enlive template:

```
<html>
  <head><title>Page Title</title></head>
  <body>
    <h1>Page Title</h1>
    <h3>By <span class="author">Mickey Mouse</span></h3>
    <div class="post-body">
      Lorem ipsum etc...
    </div>
  </body>
</html>
```

Place this file in the *resources/* directory, if you're using Enlive in the context of a project.

The following Clojure code defines an Enlive template based on the contents of *post.html*:

```
(require '[net.cgrand.enlive-html :as html])

;; Define the template
(html/deftemplate post-page "post.html"
  [post]
  [:title] (html/content (:title post))
  [:h1] (html/content (:title post))
  [:span.author] (html/content (:author post))
  [:div.post-body] (html/content (:body post)))

;; Some sample data
(def sample-post {:author "Luke VanderHart"
                  :title "Why Clojure Rocks"
                  :body "Functional programming!"})
```

To apply the template to the data, invoke the function defined by `deftemplate`. Since it returns a sequence of strings, in most applications you'll probably want to concatenate the results into a single string:

```
(reduce str (post-page sample-post))
```

Here's the formatted output:

```
<html>
  <head><title>Why Clojure Rocks</title></head>
  <body>
    <h1>Why Clojure Rocks</h1>
    <h3>By <span class="author">Luke VanderHart</span></h3>
    </h3><div class="post-body">Functional programming!</div>
  </body>
</html>
```

See the following discussion section for a detailed explanation of the `deftemplate` macro and what is actually happening in this code.

#### Repeating elements

The preceding code simply replaces the values of certain nodes in the emitted HTML. In real scenarios, another common task is to *repeat* certain items from input HTML, one repetition for each item in the input data. For this task, Enlive provides *snippets*, which are selections from an input HTML that can then be repeated as many times as desired in the output of another template:

```
(def sample-post-list
  [{:author "Luke VanderHart"
    :title "Why Clojure Rocks"
    :body "Functional programming!"}
   {:author "Ryan Neufeld"
    :title "Clojure Community Management"
```

```
    :body "Programmers are like..."}
   {:author "Rich Hickey"
    :title "Programming"
    :body "You're doing it completely wrong."}])

(html/defsnippet post-snippet "post.html"
  {[:h1] [[:div.post-body (html/nth-of-type 1)]]}
  [post]
  [:h1] (html/content (:title post))
  [:span.author] (html/content (:author post))
  [:div.post-body] (html/content (:body post)))

(html/deftemplate all-posts-page "post.html"
  [post-list]
  [:title] (html/content "All Posts")
  [:body] (html/content (map post-snippet post-list)))
```

Invoking the defined `all-posts-page` function now returns an HTML page populated with all three sample posts:

```
(reduce str (all-posts-page sample-post-list))
```

Here's the formatted output:

```
<html>
  <head><title>All Posts</title></head>
  <body>
    <h1>Why Clojure Rocks</h1>
    <h3>By <span class="author">Luke VanderHart</span></h3>
    <div class="post-body">Functional programming!</div>
    <h1>Clojure Community Management</h1>
    <h3>By <span class="author">Ryan Neufeld</span></h3>
    <div class="post-body">Programmers are like...</div>
    <h1>Programming</h1>
    <h3>By <span class="author">Rich Hickey</span></h3>
    <div class="post-body">You're doing it completely wrong.</div>
  </body>
</html>
```

In this example, the `defsnippet` macro defines a snippet over a range of elements in the input HTML, from the `<h1>` element to the `<div class="post-body">`.

Then, the `deftemplate` for `all-posts-page` uses the result of mapping `post-snippet` over the content of the body element. Since there are three posts in the sample input data, the snippet is evaluated three times, and there are three posts output in the resulting HTML.

## Discussion

Enlive can be slightly difficult to get the hang of, compared to some other libraries. There are several contributing factors to this:

- It has a more novel conceptual approach than other templating systems (although it bears a lot of similarity to some other non-Clojure templating techniques, such as XSLT).
- It utilizes functional programming techniques to the fullest, including liberal use of higher-order functions.
- It's a large library, capable of many things. The subset of features required to accomplish a particular task is not always evident.

In general, the best way to get past these issues and experience the power and flexibility that Enlive can provide is to understand all the different parts individually, and what they do. Then, composing them into useful templating systems becomes more manageable.

### Enlive and the DOM

First of all, it is important to understand that Enlive does not operate on HTML text directly. Instead, it first parses the HTML into a Clojure data structure representing the DOM (Document Object Model). For example, the HTML fragment:

```
<div id="foo">
  <span class="bar">Hello!</span>
</div>
```

would be parsed into the Clojure data:

```
{:tag :html,
  :attrs nil,
  :content
  ({:tag :body,
    :attrs nil,
    :content
    ({:tag :div,
      :attrs {:id "foo"},
      :content
      ({:tag :span, :attrs {:class "bar"}, :content ("Hello!")})})})}
```

This is more verbose, but it is easier to manipulate from Clojure. You won't necessarily have to deal with these data structures directly, but be aware that anywhere Enlive says it operates on an element or a node, it means the Clojure data structure for the element, not the HTML string.

### Templates

The most important element of these examples is the `deftemplate` macro. `deftemplate` takes a symbol as a name, a classpath-relative path to an HTML file, an argument list, and a series of *selector* and *transform function* pairs. It emits a function, bound to the same name and of the specified arguments, which, when called, will return the resulting HTML as a sequence of strings.

An Enlive *selector* is a Clojure data structure that identifies a specific node in the input HTML file. They are similar to CSS selectors in operation, although somewhat more capable. In the example in the solution, `[:title]` selects each `<title>` element, `[:span.author]` each `<span>` with `class="author"`, etc. More selector forms are described in the following subsection.

A template *transform function* takes an Enlive node and returns a modified node. Our example uses Enlive's `content` utility function, which returns a function that swaps the contents of a node with the value given as its argument.

The return value is not itself a string, but a sequence of strings, each one a small fragment of HTML code. This allows the underlying data structure to be transformed to a string representation lazily. For simplicity, our example just reduces the string concatenation function `str` across the results, but this is actually not optimally performant. To build a string most efficiently, use the Java `StringBuilder` class, which uses mutable state to build up a `String` object with the best possible performance. Alternatively, forego the use of strings altogether and pipe the result seq of the template function directly into an output `Writer`, which most web application libraries (including Ring) can use as the body of an HTTP response (the most common destination for templated HTML).

### Selectors

Enlive selectors are data structures that identify one or more HTML nodes. They describe a *pattern* of data—if the pattern matches any nodes in the HTML data structure, the selector will select those nodes. A selector may select one, many, or zero nodes from a given HTML document, depending on how many matches the pattern has.

The full reference for valid selector forms is quite complex, and beyond the scope of this recipe. See the formal selector specification (*http://bit.ly/enlive-syntax*) for complete documentation.

The following selector patterns should be sufficient to get you started:

`[:div]`
: Selects all `<div>` element nodes.

`[:div.sidebar]`
: Selects all `<div>` element nodes with a CSS class of `"sidebar"`.

`[:div#summary]`
: Selects the `<div>` element with an HTML ID of `"summary"`.

`[:p :span]`
: Selects all `<span>` elements that are descendants of `<p>` elements.

`[:div.menu :ul :li :span]`
: Selects only `<span>` elements inside an `<li>` element inside a `<ul>` element inside a `<div>` element with a CSS style of `"menu"`.

`[[:div (nth-child 2)]]`
: Selects all `<div>` elements that are the second children of their parent elements. The double square brackets are not a typo—the inner vector is used to denote a logical *and* condition. In this case, the matched element must be a `<div>`, *and* the `nth-child` predicate must hold true.

Other predicates besides `nth-child` are available, as well as the ability to define custom predicates. See the Enlive documentation for more details.

Finally, there is a special type of selector called a *range* selector that is not specified by a vector, but rather by a map literal (in curly braces). The range selector contains two other selectors and inclusively matches all the nodes between the two matched nodes, in document order. The starting node is in key position in the map literal and the ending node is in value position, so the selector `{[:.foo] [:.bar]}` will match all nodes between nodes with an ID of "foo" and an ID of "bar".

The example in the solution uses a range selector in the `defsnippet` form to select all the nodes that are part of the same logical blog post, even though they aren't wrapped in a common parent element.

### Snippets

A snippet is similar to a template, in that it produces a function based on a base HTML file. However, snippets have two major differences from templates:

1. Rather than always rendering the entire HTML file like a template does, snippets render only a portion of the input HTML. The portion to be rendered is specified by an Enlive selector passed as the third argument to the `defsnippet` macro, right after the name and the path to the HTML file.
2. The return values of the emitted functions are Enlive data structures rather than HTML strings. This means that the results of rendering a snippet can be returned directly from the transform function of a template or another snippet. This is where Enlive starts to show its power; snippets can be recycled and reused extensively and in different combinations.

Other than these differences, the `defsnippet` form is identical to `deftemplate`, and after the selector, the rest of the arguments are the same—an argument vector and a series of selector and transform function pairs.

### Using Enlive for scraping

Because of its emphasis on selectors and use of plain, unannotated HTML files, Enlive is extremely useful not just for templating and producing HTML, but also for parsing and scraping data from HTML from any source.

To use Enlive to extract data from HTML, you must first parse the HTML file into an Enlive data structure. To do this, invoke the `net.cgrand.enlive-html/html-resource` function on the HTML file. You may specify the file as a `java.net.URL`, a `java.io.File`, or a string indicating a classpath-relative path. The function will return the parsed Enlive data structure representing the HTML DOM.

Then, you can use the `net.cgrand.enlive-html/select` function to apply a selector to the DOM and extract specific data. Given a node and a selector, `select` will return only the matched nodes. You can then use the `net.cgrand.enlive-html/text` function to retrieve the text content of a node.

For example, the following function will return a sequence of the most recent `n` comic titles in the XKCD archives:

```
(defn comic-titles
  [n]
  (let [dom (html/html-resource
             (java.net.URL. "http://xkcd.com/archive"))
        title-nodes (html/select dom [:#middleContainer :a])
        titles (map html/text title-nodes)]
    (take n titles)))

(comic-titles 5)
;; -> ("Oort Cloud" "Git Commit" "New Study"
       "Telescope Names" "Job Interview")
```

### When to use Enlive

As an HTML templating system, Enlive has two primary value propositions over its alternatives in the Clojure ecosystem.

First, the templates are pure HTML. This makes it much easier to work with HTML designers: they can hand their HTML mockups directly to a developer without having to deal with inline markup code, and developers can use them directly without manually slicing them (outside of code, that is). Furthermore, the templates themselves can be viewed in a browser statically, meaning they can serve as their own wireframes. This eliminates the burden of keeping a web project's visual prototypes in sync with the code.

Secondly, because it uses real Clojure functions and data structures instead of a custom DSL, Enlive exposes the full power of the Clojure language. There are very few situations where you should feel limited by Enlive's capabilities, since it is always possible to extend it using only standard Clojure functions and macros, operating on familiar persistent, immutable data structures.

## See Also

- The Enlive documentation (*http://bit.ly/enlive-wiki*)
- David Nolen's Enlive tutorial (*https://github.com/swannodette/enlive-tutorial*)
- The Enlive mailing list (*http://bit.ly/enlive-group*)
- Alternative templating libraries Selmer (Recipe 7.12, "Templating with Selmer" on page 332) and Hiccup (Recipe 7.13, "Templating with Hiccup" on page 336)

# 7.12. Templating with Selmer

by Dmitri Sotnikov

## Problem

You want to create server-side page templates using syntax similar to that of Django and Jinja. You want to be able to insert dynamic content and use template inheritance to structure the templates.

## Solution

Use the Selmer library (*https://github.com/yogthos/Selmer*) to create your template and call it with a context map containing the dynamic content.

To follow along with this recipe, start a REPL using `lein-try`:

```
$ lein try selmer
```

A Selmer template is an HTML file with special tags that is populated with dynamic content at runtime. A simple template (*base.html*) might look like the following:

```
<!DOCTYPE html>
<html lang="en">
  <body>
    <header>

      <h1>{{header}}</h1>

      <ul id="navigation">

        {% for item in nav-items %}
        <li>
            <a href="{{item.link}}">{{item.name}}</a>
        </li>
        {% endfor %}

      </ul>
    </header>
```

```
  </body>
</html>
```

The template can then be rendered by calling the `selmer.parser/render-file` function:

```
(require '[selmer.parser :refer [render-file]])

(println
  (render-file "base.html"
               {:header "Hello Selmer"
                :nav-items [{:name "Home" :link "/"}
                            {:name "About" :link "/about"}]}))
```

When `render-file` runs, it will populate the tags with the content provided. The value will be returned as a string, suitable for use as the response body in a Ring application (for example). Here the result is simply printed to standard output, for easy inspection.

We can apply filters to variables for additional post-processing at runtime. Here, we use the `upper` filter to convert our heading to uppercase:

```
<h1>{{header|upper}}</h1>
```

We can extract parts of the template into individual snippets using the `include` tag. For example, if we wanted to define the header in a separate file *header.html*:

```
<header>

  <h1>{{header}}</h1>

  <ul id="navigation">

    {% for item in nav-items %}
    <li>
        <a href="{{item.link}}">{{item.name}}</a>
    </li>
    {% endfor %}

  </ul>
</header>
```

we could then include it as follows:

```
<!DOCTYPE html>
<html lang="en">
  <body>

    {% include "header.html" %}

  </body>
</html>
```

The `include` tag will simply be replaced by the contents of the file it points to when the template is compiled.

We can also extend our base template when we create individual pages. To do that, we first define a block in our base template. This will serve as an anchor for the child template to override:

```
<!DOCTYPE html>
<html lang="en">
  <body>

    {% include "header.html" %}

    {% block content %}
    {% endblock %}

  </body>
</html>
```

The child template will reference the parent using the `extends` tag and define its own content for the `content` block:

```
{% extends "base.html" %}

{% block content %}

<h1>This is the home page of the site</h1>
<p>some exciting content follows</p>

{% endblock %}
```

## Discussion

Selmer provides a powerful and familiar templating tool with many tags and filters for easily accomplishing many common tasks. It separates the view logic from presentation by design.

Selmer is also performant because it compiles the templates and ensures that only the dynamic content needs to be evaluated when serving a request.

### Selmer concepts

Selmer includes two types of elements, *variables* and *tags*.

Variables are used to render values from the context map on the page. The `{{` and `}}` are used to indicate the start and end of a variable.

In many cases, you may wish to post-process the value of a variable. For example, you might want to convert it to uppercase, pluralize it, or parse it as a date. Variable filters (described in the following subsection) are used for this purpose.

Tags are used to add various functionality to the template, such as looping and conditions. We already saw examples of the `for`, `include`, and `extends` tags. The tags use `{%` and `%}` to define their content.

The default tag characters might conflict with client-side frameworks such as AngularJS. In this case, we can specify custom tags by passing a map containing any of the following keys to the parser:

```
:tag-open
:tag-close
:filter-open
:filter-close
:tag-second
:custom-tags
:custom-filters
```

If we wanted to use [ and ] as our opening and closing tags, we could call the `render` function as follows:

```
(render (str "[% for ele in foo %] "
             "{{I'm not a tag, but the next one is}} [{ele}] [%endfor%]")
        {:foo [1 2 3]}
        {:tag-open \[
         :tag-close \]})
```

The `render` function works just like `render-file`, except that it accepts the template content as a string.

### Defining filters

Selmer provides a rich set of filters that allow decorating of the dynamic content. Some of the filters include `capitalize`, `pluralize`, `hash`, `length`, and `sort`.

However, if you need a custom filter that's not part of the library, you can trivially add one yourself. For example, if we wanted to parse Markdown using the `markdown-clj` library (*https://github.com/yogthos/markdown-clj*) and display it on the page, we could write the following filter:[2]

```
(require '[markdown.core :refer [md-to-html-string]]
         '[selmer.filters/add-filter!])

(add-filter! :markdown md-to-html-string)
```

We can now use this filter in our templates to render our Markdown content:

```
<h2>Blog Posts</h2>
<ul>
  {% for post in posts %}
```

2. You'll need to restart a new REPL with `lein-try` including `markdown-clj` to try this.

```
    <li>{{post.title|markdown|safe}}</li>
{% endfor %}
</ul>
```

Note that we had to chain the `markdown` filter with the `safe` filter. This is due to the fact that Selmer escapes variable content by default. We can change our filter definition to indicate that its content does not need escaping as follows:

```
(add-filter! :markdown (fn [s] [:safe (md-to-html-string s)]))
```

#### Defining tags

Again, we can define custom tags in addition to those already present in the library. This is done by calling the `selmer.parser/add-tag!` function.

Let's say we wish to add a tag that will capitalize its contents:

```
(require '[selmer.parser :refer [add-tag!]])

(add-tag! :uppercase
          (fn [args context-map content]
            (.toUpperCase (get-in content [:uppercase :content])))
          :enduppercase)

(render "{% uppercase %}foo {{bar}} baz{% enduppercase %}" {:bar "injected"})
```

#### Inheritance

We already saw some examples of template inheritance. Each template can extend a single template and include any number of templates in its content.

The templates can extend templates that themselves extend other templates. In this case, the blocks found in the outermost child will override any other blocks with the same name.

### See Also

- The Selmer GitHub repository (*https://github.com/yogthos/Selmer*)

## 7.13. Templating with Hiccup

by Ryan Neufeld

### Problem

You want to create HTML dynamically based on a template, written in pure Clojure data.

## Solution

Use Hiccup, a library for representing and rendering HTML templates made up of regular Clojure data structures.

To follow along with this recipe, start a REPL using `lein-try`:

```
$ lein try hiccup
```

Hiccup represents HTML nodes as vectors. The first entry of the vector is the element's name; the second is an optional map of the element's attributes; and any remaining entries are the element's body:

```
;; <h1 class="header">My Page Title</h1> in Hiccup...
[:h1 {:class "header"} "My Page Title"]

;; <ul>
;;   <li>lions</li>
;;   <li>tigers</li>
;;   <li>bears</li>
;; </ul> in Hiccup...
[:ul
  [:li "lions"]
  [:li "tigers"]
  [:li "bears"]] ;; oh my!
```

Render any Hiccup data structure to HTML using the `hiccup.core/html` function:

```
(require '[hiccup.core :refer [html]])
(html [:h1 {:class "header"} "My Page Title"])
;; -> "<h1 class=\"header\">My Page Title</h1>"
```

Since nodes are represented as regular Clojure data, you can leverage any of Clojure's built-in functions or techniques to yield Hiccup-compliant vectors:

```
(def pi 3.14)
(html [:p (str "Pi is approximately: " pi)])
;; -> "<p>Pi is approximately: 3.14</p>"

(html [:ul
        (for [animal ["lions" "tigers" "bears"]]
          [:li animal])])
;; -> "<ul><li>lions</li><li>tigers</li><li>bears</li></ul>"
```

Using all of the preceding techniques, it's possible to create a simple function to dynamically populate the contents of a minimal blog page using only Clojure functions and data:

```
(defn blog-index
  "Render a blog's index as Hiccup data"
  [title author posts]
  [:html
    [:head
```

```
      [:title title]]
    [:body
      [:h1 title]
      [:h2 (str "By " author)]
      (for [post posts]
        [:article
          [:h3 (:title post)]
          [:p (:content post)]])]])

(-> (blog-index "My First Blog"
                "Ryan"
                [{:title "First post!" :content "I'm here!"}
                 {:title "Second post." :content "Yawn, bored."}])

    html)
```

Formatted output:

```
<html>
  <head>
    <title>My First Blog</title>
  </head>
  <body>
    <h1>My First Blog</h1>
    <h2>By Ryan</h2>
    <article>
      <h3>First post!</h3>
      <p>I'm here!</p>
    </article>
    <article>
      <h3>Second post.</h3>
      <p>Yawn, bored.</p>
    </article>
  </body>
</html>"
```

## Discussion

Hiccup is an easy, "no muss, no fuss" way of templating and rendering HTML from raw functions and data. This comes in particularly handy when you don't have the time to learn a new DSL or you prefer to work exclusively with Clojure.

An HTML node is represented in Hiccup as a vector of a few elements:

- The node's name, represented as a keyword (e.g., `:h1`, `:article`, or `:body`)
- An optional map of the node's attributes, with attribute names represented as keywords (e.g., `{:href "/posts/"}` or `{:id "post-1" :class "post"}`)
- Any number of other nodes or string values constituting the node's body

Invoke `hiccup.core/html` with a single node, snippet, or entire page to render its contents as HTML. For content with special characters that should be escaped, wrap values in a `hiccup.core/h` invocation:

```
(require '[hiccup.core :refer [h]])
(html [:a {:href (h "/post/my<crazy>url")}])
;; -> "<a href=\"/post/my&amp;lt;crazy&amp;gt;url\"></a>"
```

Hiccup also has basic support for rendering forms. Use `form-to` and a bevy of other helpers in the `hiccup.form` namespace to simplify rendering form tags:

```
(require '[hiccup.form :as f])

(f/form-to [:post "/posts/new"]
  (f/hidden-field :user-id 42)
  (f/text-field :title)
  (f/text-field :content))
;; -> [:form {:method "POST", :action #<URI /posts/new>}
;;      [:input {:type "hidden"
;;               :name "user-id"
;;               :id "user-id"
;;               :value 42}]
;;      [:input {:type "text"
;;               :name "title"
;;               :id "title"
;;               :value nil}]
;;      [:input {:type "text"
;;               :name "content"
;;               :id "content"
;;               :value nil}]]
```

## See Also

- Hiccup's GitHub repository (*https://github.com/weavejester/hiccup/*), API documentation (*http://bit.ly/hiccup-docs*), and wiki (*http://bit.ly/hiccup-wiki*).
- If you have more complicated needs from your templating engine—like consuming and populating existing HTML files—you'll need sharper tools such as Enlive (Recipe 7.11, "Templating HTML with Enlive" on page 325) or Selmer (Recipe 7.12, "Templating with Selmer" on page 332).

# 7.14. Rendering Markdown Documents

by Dmitri Sotnikov

## Problem

You need to render a Markdown document.

## Solution

Use the `markdown-clj` library (*https://github.com/yogthos/markdown-clj*) to render Markdown documents.

To follow along with this recipe, start a REPL using `lein-try`:

```
$ lein try markdown-clj
```

Use `markdown.core/md-to-html` to read a Markdown document and generate a string containing HTML:

```
(require '[markdown.core :as md])

(md/md-to-html "input.md" "output.html")

(md/md-to-html (input-stream "input.md") (output-stream "test.txt"))
```

Use `markdown.core/md-to-html-string` to convert a string with Markdown content to its HTML representation:

```
(md/md-to-html-string
  "# This is a test\n\nsome code follows:\n```\n(defn foo [])\n```")

<h1> This is a test</h1><p>some code follows:</p><pre>
&#40;defn foo &#91;&#93;&#41;
</pre>
```

## Discussion

Markdown is a popular lightweight markup language that's easy to read and write and can be converted to structurally valid HTML.

Since Markdown leaves many aspects of rendering the HTML open to interpretation, it's not guaranteed that different parsers will produce the same representation. This can be a problem if you render a Markdown preview on the client using one parser and then later generate HTML on a server using a different parser. By virtue of compiling to both Clojure and ClojureScript, `markdown-clj` avoids this problem. With it, you can use the same parser on both the server and the client and be guaranteed that the documents will be rendered consistently.

Let's take a look at more examples of using the library. The code blocks can be annotated with language hints. In this case, the `pre` tags will be decorated with a class compatible with the SyntaxHighlighter (*http://alexgorbatchev.com/SyntaxHighlighter/*):

```
(md/md-to-html-string (str "# This is a test\n\nsome code follows:\n"
                           "```clojure\n(defn foo [])\n```"))

<h1> This is a test</h1><p>some code follows:</p><pre class="brush: clojure">
&#40;defn foo &#91;&#93;&#41;
</pre>
```

markdown-clj supports all the standard Markdown tags, with the exception of reference-style links (because the parser uses a single pass to generate the document).

The markdown.core/md-to-html processes the input line by line, and the entirety of the content does not need to be stored in memory when processing. On the other hand, both the md-to-html-string and md-to-html functions load the entire contents into memory.

The parser accepts additional formatting options. These include :heading-anchors, :code-style, :custom-transformers, and :replacement-transformers.

When the :heading-anchors keyis set to true, an anchor will be generated for each heading tag:

```
(md/md-to-html-string "###foo bar BAz" :heading-anchors true)
```

```
<h3>
  <a name=\"heading\" class=\"anchor\" href=\"#foo&#95;bar&#95;baz></a>
  foo bar BAz
</h3>
```

The :code-style key allows overriding the default style hint for code blocks:

```
(md/md-to-html-string "```clojure\n(defn foo [])\n```"
                      :code-style #(str "class=\"" % "\""))
```

```
<pre class="clojure">
&#40;defn foo &#91;&#93;&#41;
</pre>
```

We can specify transformers for custom tags by using the :custom-transformers key. The transformer function should accept the text parameter, which is the current line, and the state parameter, which contains the current state of the parser. The state can be used to store information such as what tags are active:

```
(defn capitalize [text state]
  [(.toUpperCase text) state])
```

```
(md/md-to-html-string "#foo" :custom-transformers [capitalize])
```

```
<H1>FOO</H1>
```

Finally, we can provide a custom set of transformers to replace the built-in ones using the :replacement-transformers key:

```
(markdown/md-to-html-string "#foo" :replacement-transformers [capitalize])
```

## See Also

- The markdown-clj GitHub repository (*https://github.com/yogthos/markdown-clj*) for more information on the library

# 7.15. Building Applications with Luminus

by Dmitri Sotnikov

## Problem

You want to quickly create a typical Ring/Compojure web application structure to get a fast start on a new web development project.

## Solution

Use the Luminus Leiningen template when creating a new project.

At the command line, type:

```
$ lein new luminus myapp
```

This will create a new Ring/Compojure application with a skeletal namespace and resource directory structure that is ready to be packaged as standalone Java Archive (JAR) or Web Archive (WAR) file that can be deployed on an application server.

You can start the application in development mode by running:

```
$ lein ring server
```

## Discussion

Luminus doesn't do anything you couldn't do yourself, but provides a standardized set of libraries and boilerplate for creating common Ring/Compojure applications.

The template generates a standard directory structure within your project, defines a main handler for your application, adds `lein-ring` hooks for it in the *project.clj* file, provides a default logging configuration, and sets up the default routes.

When creating the application, you can add functionality by specifying profiles that extend the generated code to include the relevant stubs. The following are some examples of initializing the application with default configurations for different databases:

```
$ lein new luminus app1 +h2

# Or, with PostgreSQL:
$ lein new luminus app2 +postgres

# Or ClojureScript!
$ lein new luminus app3 +cljs

# You can also specify multiple profiles simultaneously:
$ lein new luminus app4 +cljs +postgres
```

The resulting application is structured using the following namespaces.

The `<app-name>.handler` namespace contains `init` and `destroy` functions. These will be called when the application is starting up and shutting down, respectively. It also contains the `app` handler function that's used by Ring to initialize the route handlers.

The `<app-name>.routes` namespace is used to house the core logic of the application. Here is where you would define the application routes and their handlers. The `<app-name>.routes.home` namespace contains the routes for the default */* and */about* pages.

The layout for the site is generated by the `render` function in the `<app-name>.views.layout` namespace. The HTML templates for the pages can be found under *src/<app-name>/views/templates/*. Luminus uses Selmer (*https://github.com/yogthos/Selmer*), introduced in Recipe 7.12, "Templating with Selmer" on page 332, as its default templating engine.

Any miscellaneous helpers will be found under the `<app_name>.views.util` namespace.

When a database profile is selected, the `<app_name>.models.db` and `<app_name>.models.schema` namespaces will be created. The `schema` namespace is reserved for table definitions, while the `db` namespace houses the functions dealing with the application model.

The application can be packaged as a standalone JAR file using **`lein ring uberjar`** or as a WAR file using **`lein ring uberwar`**.

## See Also

- The Luminus project page (*http://www.luminusweb.net/*)

# CHAPTER 8
# Performance and Production

## 8.0. Introduction

You've spent all of this time developing your next big thing: what's next but to ship it to the wild? Whether it is a product, internal service, or library, the last (and most important) step is delivering the fruits of your labor to your audience.

It's easy for developers to forget that code-complete is only the beginning of an actual application's life cycle. A successful project will spend much more time in production than it will in development, and stability and maintainability are premium features.

This is a chapter all about really finishing your work and building something that will run as painlessly as possible for years to come. Be the task performance, logging, release, or long-term maintenance, it's all important in shipping something that is truly excellent. There is certainly a lot to worry about when your baby finally leaves home; we hope these recipes help you get it right.

## 8.1. AOT Compilation

by Luke VanderHart

### Problem

You want to deliver your code as precompiled JVM bytecode in *.class* files, rather than as Clojure source code.

### Solution

Use the `:aot` (ahead of time) compilation key in your project's *project.clj* file to specify which namespaces should be compiled to *.class* files. The value of the `:aot` key is a vector of either symbols indicating specific namespaces to be compiled, or regular expression literals specifying that any namespace with a matching name should be compiled. Alternatively, instead of a vector, you can use the keyword `:all` as a value, which will AOT-compile every namespace in the project:

```
:aot [foo.bar foo.baz]

;; or...
:aot [#"foo\.b.+"] ; Compile all namespaces starting with "foo.b"

;; or...
:aot :all
```

Note that if your project has specified a `:main` namespace, Leiningen will AOT-compile it by default, regardless of whether it is present in an `:aot` directive.

Once your project is configured for AOT compilation, you can compile it by invoking **`lein compile`** at the command line. All emitted classes will be placed in the *target/classes* directory, unless you've overridden the output directory with the `:target-path` or `:compile-path` options.

## Discussion

It's important to understand that AOT compilation does *not* change how the code actually runs. It's no faster or different. All Clojure code is compiled to the same bytecode before execution; AOT compilation merely means that it happens at a singular, defined point in time instead of on demand as the program loads and runs.

However, although it isn't any faster, it can be a great tool in the following situations:

- You want to deliver the application binary, but you don't want to include the original source code with it.
- To marginally speed up an application's start time (since the Clojure code won't have to be compiled on the fly).
- You need to generate classes loadable directly from Java for interop purposes.
- For platforms (such as Android) that do not support custom class loaders for running new bytecode at runtime.

You may observe that there is more than one emitted class file for each AOT-compiled namespace. In fact, there will be separate Java classes for each function, the namespace itself, and any additional `gen-class`, `deftype`, or `defrecord` forms. This is actually not dissimilar from Java itself; it has always been the case that inner classes are compiled to separate class files, and Clojure functions are effectively anonymous inner classes from the JVM's point of view.

## See Also

- Clojure's official documentation on AOT compilation (*http://clojure.org/compilation*)
- Recipe 8.2, "Packaging a Project into a JAR File" on page 347

# 8.2. Packaging a Project into a JAR File

by Alan Busby

## Problem

You want to package a project into an executable JAR.

## Solution

Use the Leiningen build tool to package your application as an *uberjar*, a JAR file that includes an application and all of its dependencies.

To follow along with this recipe, create a new Leiningen project:

```
$ lein new foo
```

Configure the project to be executable by adding `:main` and `:aot` parameters to the project's *project.clj* file:

```
(defproject foo "0.1.0-SNAPSHOT"
  :description "FIXME: write description"
  :url "http://example.com/FIXME"
  :license {:name "Eclipse Public License"
            :url "http://www.eclipse.org/legal/epl-v10.html"}
  :dependencies [[org.clojure/clojure "1.5.1"]]
  :main foo.core
  :aot :all)
```

To finish making the project executable, add a `-main` function and `:gen-class` declaration to *src/foo/core.clj*. Remove the existing `foo` function:

```
(ns foo.core
  (:gen-class))

(defn -main  [& args]
  (->> args
       (interpose " ")
       (apply str)
       (println "Executed with the following args: ")))
```

Run the application using the **`lein run`** command to verify it is functioning correctly:

```
$ lein run 1 2 3
```

To package the application with all of its dependencies included, invoke **`lein uberjar`**:

```
$ lein uberjar
Created /tmp/foo/target/uberjar/foo-0.1.0-SNAPSHOT.jar
Created /tmp/foo/target/foo-0.1.0-SNAPSHOT-standalone.jar
```

Execute the generated *target/foo-0.1.0-SNAPSHOT-standalone.jar* file by passing it as the `-jar` option to the `java` executable:

```
$ java -jar target/foo-1.0.0-standalone.jar 1 2 3
Executed with the following args:  1 2 3
```

## Discussion

Executable JAR files provide an excellent method to package a program so it can be provided to users, called by cron jobs, combined with other Unix tools, or used in any other scenario where command-line invocation is useful.

Under the hood, an executable JAR is like any other JAR file in that it contains a collection of program resources such as class files, Clojure source files, and classpath resources. Additionally, an executable JAR contains metadata indicating which class contains the `main` method as a `Main-Class` tag in its internal manifest file.

A Leiningen uberjar is a JAR file that contains not only your program, but all the dependencies bundled in as well. When Leiningen builds an uberjar, it can detect from the `:main` entry in *project.clj* that your program supplies a `-main` function and writes an appropriate manifest that will ensure that the emitted JAR file is executable.

The `:gen-class` in your namespace and the `:aot` Leiningen option are required to precompile your Clojure source file into a JVM class file, since the "Main-Class" manifest entry doesn't know how to reference or compile Clojure source files.

### Packaging JARs Without Their Dependencies

Not only does Leiningen make it possible to package a project *with* its dependencies, it also makes it possible to package it *without* its dependencies.

The `jar` command packages a project's code without any of its upstream dependencies. Not even Clojure itself is included in the JAR file—you'll need to BYOC.[1]

By invoking the command **`lein jar`** in the `foo` project, you'll generate *target/foo-0.1.0-SNAPSHOT.jar*:

```
$ lein jar
Created /tmp/foo/target/jar/target/foo-0.1.0-SNAPSHOT.jar
```

1. Bring your own Clojure!

Listing the contents of the JAR file using the **unzip** command,[2] you can see that very little is packaged—just a Maven *.pom* file, generated JVM class files, and the project's miscellany:

```
$ unzip -l target/foo-0.1.0-SNAPSHOT.jar
Archive:  target/foo-0.1.0-SNAPSHOT.jar
  Length      Date    Time    Name
 --------    ----    ----    ----
      113  12-06-13 10:26   META-INF/MANIFEST.MF
     2595  12-06-13 10:26   META-INF/maven/foo/foo/pom.xml
       91  12-06-13 10:26   META-INF/maven/foo/foo/pom.properties
      292  12-06-13 10:26   META-INF/leiningen/foo/foo/project.clj
      292  12-06-13 10:26   project.clj
      229  12-06-13 10:26   META-INF/leiningen/foo/foo/README.md
    11220  12-06-13 10:26   META-INF/leiningen/foo/foo/LICENSE
        0  12-06-13 10:26   foo/
     1210  12-06-13 10:26   foo/core$_main.class
     1304  12-06-13 10:26   foo/core$fn__16.class
     1492  12-06-13 10:26   foo/core$loading__4910__auto__.class
     1755  12-06-13 10:26   foo/core.class
     2814  12-06-13 10:26   foo/core__init.class
      162  12-04-13 14:54   foo/core.clj
 --------                   -------
    23569                   14 files
```

The *target/foo-0.1.0-SNAPSHOT-standalone.jar* listing, on the other hand, includes over 3,000 files.[3]

Since the packaged *pom.xml* file includes a listing of the project's dependencies, build tools like Leiningen or Maven can resolve these dependencies on their own. This allows for efficient packaging of libraries. Can you imagine if each and every Clojure library included the entirety of its dependencies? It would be a bandwidth nightmare.

Because of this property, lean JAR files such as this are what is deployed to remote repositories when you use the `lein deploy` command.[4]

Without its dependencies included—namely, Clojure—you'll need to do a bit more work to run the *foo* application. First, download Clojure 1.5.1 (*http://clojure.org/downloads*). Then invoke `foo.core` via the `java` command, including *clojure-1.5.1.jar* and *foo-0.1.0-SNAPSHOT.jar* on the classpath (via the `-cp` option):

2. Available on most Unix-based systems.

3. All of which we won't be committing to print. Take a look for yourself with the command **`lein uberjar && unzip -l target/foo-0.1.0-SNAPSHOT-standalone.jar`**.

4. See Recipe 8.9, "Releasing a Library to Clojars" on page 369, for more information on releasing libraries.

```
# Download Clojure
$ wget \
  http://repo1.maven.org/maven2/org/clojure/clojure/1.5.1/clojure-1.5.1.zip
$ unzip clojure-1.5.1.zip

# Execute the application
$ java -cp target/foo-0.1.0-SNAPSHOT.jar:clojure-1.5.1/clojure-1.5.1.jar \
       foo.core \
       1 2 3
Executed with the following args:  1 2 3
```

## See Also

- Recipe 3.6, "Running Programs from the Command Line" on page 132, to learn about running Clojure programs from Leiningen
- Recipe 8.1, "AOT Compilation" on page 345
- `lein-bin` (*https://github.com/Raynes/lein-bin*), a Leiningen plug-in for producing standalone console executables that work on OS X, Linux, and Windows

# 8.3. Creating a WAR File

by Luke VanderHart

## Problem

You want to deploy a Clojure web application built using Ring as a standard web archive (WAR) file in a commonly used Java EE container such as Tomcat, JBoss, or WebLogic.

## Solution

Assuming you are using Ring or a framework based on Ring (such as Compojure), the easiest way to structure your project to build as a WAR file is to use the `lein-ring` plug-in for Leiningen. Say that your project has a Ring handler function defined in a namespace called `warsample.core`,[5] like so:

```
(ns warsample.core)

(defn handler [request]
  {:status 200
   :headers {"content-type" "text/html"}
   :body "<h1>Hello, world!</h1>"})
```

5. If you don't happen to already have a similarly named project, and you want to follow along, create a new one with **`lein new warsample`**.

To configure the project with `lein-ring`, add the following key/value pairs to your Leiningen *project.clj* file:

```
:plugins [[lein-ring "0.8.8"]]
:ring {:handler warsample.core/handler}
```

You'll also need to make sure that your application declares a dependency on the `javax.servlet/servlet-api` library. Most web app libraries do include a transitive dependency, which you can verify by running **`lein deps :tree`**. If no other library you're using includes it, you can include it yourself by adding `[javax.servlet/servlet-api "2.5"]` to the `:dependencies` key in *project.clj*.

The `:plugins` key specifies that the project uses the `lein-ring` plug-in, and the map under the `:ring` key specifies configuration options specific to `lein-ring`. The only required option is `:handler`, which indicates the var name of the application's primary Ring handler function.

`lein-ring` provides a handy way to run your application locally, for development and testing. At the command line, simply type:

```
$ lein ring server
```

An embedded Jetty server will be started, serving your Ring application (on port 3000 by default, though you can change this in the `lein-ring` options). It will also open your operating system's default browser to that page.

Once you think the application is running correctly, you can build a WAR file using the **`lein ring war`** or **`lein ring uberwar`** commands. Both take the name of the WAR file to emit:

```
$ lein ring war warsample.war

$ lein ring uberwar warsample-with-deps.war
```

`lein ring war` builds a WAR file containing only your application code, not any transitive dependencies, whereas `lein ring uberwar` will build a WAR file containing bundled JAR files for every dependency as well.

Both these commands will generate all the necessary configuration and wiring (such as a *WEB-INF* directory and a *web.xml* file) before building the WAR. See the discussion section for some options you can pass to `lein ring` that will influence how these artifacts are generated.

After issuing the WAR build command, you will find the WAR file you created in your project's *target* directory. This is a perfectly normal WAR file that you can deploy just as if it were a standard J2EE WAR. Every application server is different, so check the documentation for your preferred system to see how to deploy a WAR file. If you have an operations team responsible for production deployments, you will definitely want to check with them to make sure you adhere to their processes and best practices.

## Discussion

It is crucial to understand the difference between a bare WAR file generated using `lein ring war` and an "uberwar" generated by `lein ring uberwar`, and when to use each.

A bare WAR file does not contain any of your project's dependencies; it contains only the application code itself. This means that your program will *not work* unless you make sure that each and every JAR file your program depends on, *including Clojure itself*, is present on your web application's shared library path. Exactly how to do this depends on the application server you're using—you'll have to refer to your system's documentation to determine how to make them available.

An "uberwar," on the other hand, includes all the JARs your program depends on in the WAR archive as a *bundled library* under the *WEB-INF/lib* subfolder. Compliant application servers are capable of running each application (each deployed WAR file) in its own class loader context and will make the bundled JARs available only to their applications.

Typically, an uberwar is a safer choice. It spares you from much of the effort of manually curating your libraries, and better reflects how your application's classpath probably looked in development.

The cost of an uberwar, however, is that a single library may be loaded multiple times if it is bundled by multiple applications. If you are running 10 applications, all of which use (say) Compojure, the server will actually load the Compojure code into the JVM's class space 10 times, once for each application. Some organizations running resource-constrained or high-performance deployments prefer to ensure that there is minimal redundancy in application dependencies. If this is the case, then you may have to fall back to using a non-uber WAR file and managing your dependencies in your application server's shared library pool by hand.

### Dependency Collisions

Although modern J2EE application servers do a pretty good job of keeping the classpaths and bundled libraries of different applications isolated from one another, you do have to be careful of the scenario where your application depends on a library that is part of the core J2EE *platform*, such as JDBC, the Servlet API, various XML libraries like JAX-*, StAX, JMS, etc.

These classes are usually provided by the application container itself, and if your application refers to them, those references will resolve to the instance provided by the container rather than the version your application has bundled. If they are exactly the same, well and good; but if there is a version mismatch that includes breaking changes in the class API, you may encounter cryptic errors as your application tries to call into classes that are different than the ones it was built against.

In this scenario, you will need to reconcile the dependency versions used by your application container and your application to make sure they are compatible.

### Other lein-ring options

`lein-ring` provides some additional options you can set in the `:ring` configuration map in *project.clj* to fine-tune how WAR files are generated. For an exhaustive description, see the `lein-ring` project page (*https://github.com/weavejester/lein-ring*).

A few of the more useful ones are shown in Table 8-1.

*Table 8-1. lein-ring WAR options*

| Key | Description | Default |
|---|---|---|
| `:war-exclusions` | A sequence of regexes of files to exclude from the target WAR | All hidden files |
| `:servlet-class` | The name of the generated `Servlet` class | |
| `:servlet-name` | The name of the servlet in *web.xml* | The name of the handler function |
| `:url-pattern` | The URL of the servlet mapping in *web.xml* | /* |
| `:web-xml` | A specific *web.xml* file to use instead of the generated one | |

### Building WAR files from scratch

If you aren't using Ring, or if you have a good reason not to use the `lein-ring` plug-in, you can still create a WAR file, but the process is much more hands-on. Fortunately, a WAR file is essentially a JAR file with a different extension and some additional internal structure and configuration files, so you can use the standard `lein jar` tool to generate one—provided you add the following files at the appropriate locations in the archive.

You'll also need to define some AOT classes implementing `javax.servlet.Servlet` yourself, and have these call into your Clojure application. Then you'll need to wire them up to the application server using a deployment descriptor (*web.xml*).

The structure of a WAR file is:

```
<war root>
|-- <static resources>
|-- WEB-INF
    |-- web.xml
    |-- <app-server-specific deployment descriptors>
    |-- lib
    |   |-- <bundled JAR libraries>
    |-- classes
        |-- <AOT compiled .class files for servlets, etc.>
        |-- <.clj source files>
```

A full explanation of all of these elements is beyond the scope of this recipe. For more information, see Oracle's J2EE tutorial (*http://bit.ly/java-wars*) on packaging web archives.

Other web server libraries (for example, Pedestal Server) that include tooling for Leiningen will also often have a utility for building WAR files—check the documentation of the library you're using.

## See Also

- Recipe 8.1, "AOT Compilation" on page 345
- Recipe 8.2, "Packaging a Project into a JAR File" on page 347
- `lein-ring`'s project page (*https://github.com/weavejester/lein-ring*)
- Oracle's J2EE tutorial (*http://bit.ly/javaee-tut*)

# 8.4. Running an Application as a Daemon

by Ryan Neufeld

## Problem

You want to run a Clojure application as a daemon (i.e., you want your application to run in the background) in another system process.

## Solution

Use the Apache Commons Daemon library to write applications that can be executed in a background process. Daemon consists of two parts: the `Daemon` interface, which your application must implement, and a system application[6] that runs `Daemon`-compliant applications as daemons.

Begin by adding the Daemon dependency to your project's *project.clj* file. If you don't have an existing project, create a new one with the command **`lein new my-daemon`**. Since Daemon is a Java-based system, enable AOT compilation so that class files are generated:

```
(defproject my-daemon "0.1.0-SNAPSHOT"
  :description "FIXME: write description"
  :url "http://example.com/FIXME"
  :license {:name "Eclipse Public License"
            :url "http://www.eclipse.org/legal/epl-v10.html"}
```

6. `jsvc` on Unix systems; `procrun` on Windows.

```
  :dependencies [[org.clojure/clojure "1.5.1"]
                 [org.apache.commons/commons-daemon "1.0.9"]]
  :main my-daemon.core
  :aot :all)
```

To implement the `org.apache.commons.daemon.Daemon` interface, add the appropriate `:gen-class` declaration and interface functions to one of your project's namespaces. For a minimally functional daemon, implement `-init`, `-start`, and `-stop`. For best results, provide a `-main` function to enable smoke testing of your application without touching the `Daemon` interface:

```
(ns my-daemon.core
  (:import [org.apache.commons.daemon Daemon DaemonContext])
  (:gen-class
    :implements [org.apache.commons.daemon.Daemon]))

;; A crude approximation of your application's state
(def state (atom {}))

(defn init [args]
  (swap! state assoc :running true))

(defn start []
  (while (:running @state)
    (println "tick")
    (Thread/sleep 2000)))

(defn stop []
  (swap! state assoc :running false))

;; Daemon implementation

(defn -init [this ^DaemonContext context]
  (init (.getArguments context)))

(defn -start [this]
  (future (start)))

(defn -stop [this]
  (stop))

(defn -destroy [this])

;; Enable command-line invocation
(defn -main [& args]
  (init args)
  (start))
```

Package all of the necessary dependencies and generated classes by invoking the Leiningen `uberjar` command:

```
$ lein uberjar
Compiling my-daemon.core
Created /tmp/my-daemon/target/my-daemon-0.1.0-SNAPSHOT.jar
Created /tmp/my-daemon/target/my-daemon-0.1.0-SNAPSHOT-standalone.jar
```

Before proceeding, test your application by running it with `java`:

```
$ java -jar target/my-daemon-0.1.0-SNAPSHOT-standalone.jar
tick
tick
tick
# ... Type Ctrl-C to stop the madness
```

Once you've verified your application works correctly, install `jsvc`.[7] Finally, the moment of truth. Run your application as a daemon by invoking `jsvc` with all of the requisite parameters—the absolute path of your Java home directory, the uberjar, the output log file, and the namespace where your `Daemon` implementation resides:[8]

```
$ sudo jsvc -java-home "$JAVA_HOME" \
            -cp "$(pwd)/target/my-daemon-0.1.0-SNAPSHOT-standalone.jar" \
            -outfile "$(pwd)/out.txt" \
            my_daemon.core
# Nothing!

$ sudo tail -f out.txt
tick
tick
tick
# ... Ctrl-C to exit

# Quit the daemonized process by adding the -stop flag
$ sudo jsvc -java-home "$JAVA_HOME" \
            -cp "$(pwd)/target/my-daemon-0.1.0-SNAPSHOT-standalone.jar" \
            -stop \
            my_daemon.core
```

If all is well, *out.txt* should now contain a couple of ticks. Congratulations! Daemon can be a little hard to get set up, but once you have it running, it works fantastically. If you encounter any problems launching a daemon using `jsvc`, use the `-debug` flag to output more detailed diagnostic information.

7. On OS X we suggest using Homebrew (*http://brew.sh/*) to `brew install jsvc`. If you're using Linux, you'll likely find a `jsvc` package in your favorite package manager. Windows users will need to install and use `procrun` (*http://bit.ly/daemons-procrun*).

8. Don't worry, we'll capture all this in a shell script soon.

You'll find a full working copy of the `my-daemon` project at *https://github.com/clojure-cookbook/my-daemon*.

## Discussion

Have no illusions, daemonizing Java-based services is *hard*; yet, for over 10 years, Java developers have been using Apache Commons Daemon to this end. Why reinvent the wheel with a separate Clojure tool? One of Clojure's core strengths is its ability to breathe new life into old tunes, and Daemon is one such "old tune."

Not all tunes are created equal, however. Where some Java libraries require a little Java interop, Daemon requires a lot. Daemonizing an application with Apache Commons Daemon requires getting two parts *just right*. The first part is creating a class that implements the `Daemon` interface and packaging it as a JAR file. The `Daemon` interface consists of four methods, called at different points in an daemonized application's life cycle:

`init(DaemonContext context)`
: Invoked as your application is initializing. This is where you should set up any initial state for your application.

`start()`
: Invoked after `init`. This is where you should begin performing work. `jsvc` expects `start()` to complete quickly, so you should kick-off work in a `future` or Java `Thread`.

`stop()`
: Invoked when a daemon has been instructed to stop. This is where you should halt whatever processing you began in `start`.

`destroy()`
: Invoked after `stop`, but before the JVM process exits. In a traditional Java program, this is where you would free any resources you had acquired. You may be able to skip this method in Clojure applications if you've properly structured your application. It doesn't hurt to include an empty function to prevent `jsvc` from complaining.

It's easy enough to create a record (with `defrecord`) that implements the `Daemon` interface—but that isn't enough. `jsvc` expects a `Daemon`-implementing *class* to exist on the classpath. To provide this, you must do two things: first, you need to enable ahead-of-time (AOT) compilation for your project—setting `:aot :all` in your *project.clj* will accomplish this. Second, you need to commandeer a namespace to produce a class via the `:gen-class` namespace directive. More specifically, you need to generate a class that implements the `Daemon` interface. This is accomplished easily enough using `:gen-class` in conjunction with the `:implements` directive:

```
(ns my-daemon.core
  ;; ...
  (:gen-class
    :implements [org.apache.commons.daemon.Daemon]))
```

Having set up `my-daemon.core` to generate a `Daemon`-implementing class upon compilation, the only thing left is to implement the methods themselves. Prefacing a function with a dash (e.g., `-start`) indicates to the Clojure compiler that a function is in fact a Java method. Further, since the `Daemon` methods are *instance* methods, each function includes one additional argument, the present `Daemon` instance. This argument is traditionally denoted with the name `this`.

In our simple `my-daemon` example, most of the method implementations are rather plain, taking no arguments other than `this` and delegating work to regular Clojure functions. `-init` deserves a bit more attention, though:

```
(defn -init [this ^DaemonContext context]
  (init (.getArguments context)))
```

The `-init` method takes an additional argument: a `DaemonContext`. This argument captures the command-line arguments the daemon was started with in its `.getArguments` property. As implemented, `-init` invokes the `.getArguments` method on `context`, passing its return value along to the regular Clojure function `init`.

On that topic, why delegate every `Daemon` implementation to a separate Clojure function? By separating participation in the `Daemon` interface from the inner workings of your application, you retain the ability to invoke it in other ways. With this separation of concerns, it becomes much easier to test your application, via either integration tests or direct invocation. The `-main` function utilizes these Clojure functions to allow you to verify that your application behaves correctly in isolation of daemonization.

With all of the groundwork for a Daemon-compliant application laid, the only remaining step is packaging the application. Leiningen's `uberjar` command completes all of the necessary preparations for running your application as a daemon: compiling `my-daemon.core` to a class, gathering dependencies, and packaging them all into a standalone JAR file.

Last but not least, you need to run the darn thing. Since JVM processes don't generally play nicely with low-level system calls, Daemon provides system applications, `jsvc` and `procrun`, that act as intermediaries between the JVM and your computer's operating system. These applications, generally written in C, are capable of invoking the appropriate system calls to fork and execute your application in a background process. For simplicity, we'll limit our discussion to the `jsvc` tool for the remainder of the recipe.

Both of these tools have a dizzying number of configuration options, but only a handful of them are actually necessary for getting the ball rolling. At a minimum, you must provide the location of your standalone JAR (`-cp`), your Java installation (`-java-home`), and the desired class to execute (the final argument). Other relevant options include `-pidfile`, `-outfile`, and `-errfile`; these specify where the process's ID, `STDOUT`, and `STDERR` output will be written to, respectively. Any arguments following the name of the class to invoke will be passed into `-init` as a `DaemonContext`.

A more complete example:

```
$ sudo jsvc -java-home "$JAVA_HOME" \
            -cp "$(pwd)/target/my-daemon-0.1.0-SNAPSHOT-standalone.jar" \
            -pidfile /var/run/my-daemon.pid \
            -outfile "/var/log/my-daemon.out" \
            -errfile "/var/log/my-daemon.err" \
            my_daemon.core \
            "arguments" "to" "my-daemon.core"
```

Once you've started a daemon with `jsvc`, you can halt it by re-running `jsvc` with the `-stop` option included.

Since `jsvc` *relaunches* your application in a completely new process, it carries none of its original execution context. This means no environment variables, no current working directory, nothing; the process may not even be running as the same user. Because of this, it is extremely important to specify arguments to `jsvc` with their absolute paths and correct permissions in place.

For our sample, we've opted to use `sudo` to make this a less painful experience, but in production you should set up a separate user with more limited permissions. The running user should have write access to the *.pid*, *.out*, and *.err* files, and read access to Java and the classpath.

`jsvc` and its ilk can be fickle beasts—the slightest misconfiguration will cause your daemon to fail silently, without warning. We highly suggest using the `-debug` and `-nodetach` flags while developing and configuring your daemon until you're *sure* things work correctly.

Once you've nailed an appropriate configuration, the final step is to automate the management of your daemon by writing a *daemon script*. A good daemon script captures configuration parameters, file paths, and common operations, exposing them in a clean, noise-free skin. Instead of the long `jsvc` commands you executed before, you would simply invoke **`my-daemon start`** or **`my-daemon stop`**. In fact, many Linux distributions use similar scripts to manage system daemons. To implement your own `jsvc` daemon script, we suggest reading Sheldon Neilson's "Creating a Java Daemon (System Service) for Debian using Apache Commons Jsvc" (*http://www.neilson.co.za/?p=253*).

## See Also

- The `Daemon` documentation (*http://bit.ly/commons-api*)
- The contents of the `jsvc` manpage, accessible via **`jsvc -help`**
- `procrun` (*http://bit.ly/daemons-procrun*), a Daemon runner for Windows
- `lein-daemon` (*https://github.com/arohner/lein-daemon*), a Leiningen plug-in for creating daemons that can be managed via a `lein daemon` command inside your project
- Recipe 8.1, "AOT Compilation" on page 345, for more information on AOT compilation
- Recipe 8.2, "Packaging a Project into a JAR File" on page 347, for more information on packaging JAR files
- Meikel Brandmeyer's blog post "gen-class—how it works and how to use it" (*http://bit.ly/gen-class-post*)
- Stuart Sierra's Component (*https://github.com/stuartsierra/component*) library, a tiny framework for managing the life cycle of software components

# 8.5. Alleviating Performance Problems with Type Hinting

by Ryan Neufeld

## Problem

You have functions that get called very often, and you want to optimize performance for those methods.

## Solution

One of the easiest ways to increase performance for a given function is to eliminate Java reflection. Enable `warn-on-reflection` to diagnose excessive reflection:

```
(defn column-idx
  "Return the index number of a column in a CSV header row"
  [header-cols col]
  (.indexOf (vec header-cols) col))

(def headers (clojure.string/split "A,B,C" #","))
(column-idx headers "B")
;; -> 1
```

```
(set! *warn-on-reflection* true)

(defn column-idx
  "Return the index number of a column in a CSV header row"
  [header-cols col]
  (.indexOf (vec header-cols) col))
;; Reflection warning, NO_SOURCE_PATH:1:1 - call to indexOf can't be resolved.

;; 100,000 non-hinted executions...
(time (dotimes [_ 100000] (column-idx headers "B")))
;; "Elapsed time: 329.258 msecs"
```

Once you've identified reflection, add type hints to your argument list preceding each argument in the form `<^Type> <arg>`:

```
(defn column-idx
  "Return the index number of a column in a CSV header row"
  [^java.util.List header-cols col]
  (.indexOf header-cols col))

;; 100,000 properly hinted executions
(time (dotimes [_ 100000] (column-idx headers "B")))
;; "Elapsed time: 27.779 msecs"
```

When you have groups of functions that interact together, you may see reflection warnings in spite of your properly hinted arguments. Add type hints to the argument list itself to hint the types of the functions' return values:

```
;; As a simple example, imagine you want to compare the result
;; of two function calls

(defn some-calculation [x] 42)

(defn same-calc? [x y] (.equals (some-calculation x)
                                (some-calculation y)))
;; Reflection warning, NO_SOURCE_PATH:1:24 - call to equals can't be resolved.

;; Now type-hint the return value of some-calculation
(defn some-calculation ^Integer [x] 42)

(defn same-calc? [x y] (.equals (some-calculation x)
                                (some-calculation y)))

;; Look Ma, no reflection warnings!
```

## Discussion

In highly performant code, it is often the case that you'll choose to fall back to Java for increased performance. There is an impedance mismatch between Clojure and Java, however; Java is strongly typed, whereas Clojure is not. Because of this, (almost) every time you invoke a Java function in Clojure, it needs to reflect on the type of the provided arguments in order to select the appropriate Java method to invoke. For seldom-invoked methods, this isn't too big of a deal, but for methods executed frequently, the cost of reflection can pile up quickly.

Type hinting short-circuits this reflection. If you've hinted *all* of the arguments to a Java function, the Clojure compiler will no longer perform reflection. Instead, the function application will directly invoke the appropriate Java function. Of course, if you've gotten your types wrong, your methods may not work properly; improperly hinted functions may throw a type-cast exception.

What about when you have a sequence of values, all of a uniform type? Clojure provides a number of special hints for these cases, namely `^ints`, `^floats`, `^longs`, and `^doubles`. Hinting these types will allow you to pass whole arrays as arguments to Java functions and not provoke reflection for sequences.

## Unchecked Math

You may have noticed Clojure puts training wheels on all of its numeric types too, upgrading types liberally to avoid overflows. This isn't without a cost, of course, as Clojure needs to check on every operation to make sure you aren't overflowing containers. If you need even more to-the-metal performance and happen to have nerves of steel yourself, then you may want to look at *unchecked math*.[9]

Setting `unchecked-math` to `true` will disable this safety, causing addition, subtraction, multiplication, division, and `inc/dec` to occur without overflow checks. This in effect reverts numeric behavior to a C-like state where it is possible to overflow a positive integer to a negative one:

```
;; With checked math, you cannot overflow an integer
(inc Long/MAX_VALUE)
;; ArithmeticException integer overflow  ...

(set! *unchecked-math* true)

;; Now integers are free to overflow
(inc Long/MAX_VALUE)
;; -> -9223372036854775808
```

`unchecked-math` isn't absolute, however; it is possible for boxed types to sneak into your operation, forcing checked math to occur. Combine `unchecked-math` with type hinting to ensure your math is truly unchecked—at your own risk, of course!

9. To accurately measure performance improvements from `unchecked-math`, we suggest using a tool like Criterium (*https://github.com/hugoduncan/criterium*). Benchmarking code with `time` can be tricky and often yields misleading results (or none at all).

## See Also

- Chapter 1, *Primitive Data*
- Recipe 8.6, "Fast Math with Primitive Java Arrays" on page 363

# 8.6. Fast Math with Primitive Java Arrays

by Jason Wolfe

## Problem

You need to perform fast numerical operations over significant amounts of data.

## Solution

Primitive Java arrays are the canonical way to store large collections of numbers compactly and do math over them quickly (often 100 times faster than Clojure sequences). The `hiphip` (array) (*https://github.com/Prismatic/hiphip*) library is a quick and easy way to manipulate primitive arrays of `double`, `long`, `float`, or `int` members.

Before starting, add `[prismatic/hiphip "0.1.0"]` to your project's dependencies or start a REPL using `lein-try`:

```
$ lein try prismatic/hiphip
```

Use one of `hiphip`'s `amap` macros to perform fast math on typed arrays. `amap` uses a parallel binding syntax similar to `doseq`:

```
(require 'hiphip.double)

(defn map-sqrt [xs]
  (hiphip.double/amap [x xs] (Math/sqrt x)))

(seq (map-sqrt (double-array (range 1000))))
;; -> (2.0 3.0 4.0)

(defn pointwise-product
  "Produce a new double array with the product of corresponding elements of
  xs and ys"
  [xs ys]
  (hiphip.double/amap [x xs y ys] (* x y)))
(seq (pointwise-product (double-array [1.0 2.0 3.0])
                        (double-array [2.0 3.0 4.0])))
;; -> (2.0 6.0 12.0)
```

To modify an array in place, use one of `hiphip`'s `afill!` macros:

```
(defn add-in-place!
  "Modify xs, incrementing each element by the corresponding element of ys"
  [xs ys]
  (hiphip.double/afill! [x xs y ys] (+ x y)))

(let [xs (double-array [1.0 2.0 3.0])]
  (add-in-place! xs (double-array [0.0 1.0 2.0]))
  (seq xs))
;; -> (1.0 3.0 5.0)
```

For faster `reduce`-like operations, use one of `hiphip`'s `areduce` and `asum` macros:

```
(defn dot-product [ws xs]
  (hiphip.double/asum [x xs w ws] (* x w)))

(dot-product (double-array [1.0 2.0 3.0])
             (double-array [2.0 3.0 4.0]))
;; -> 20.0
```

We'd love to throw in a quick `time` benchmark to demonstrate the gains, but the JVM is a fickle beast when it comes to optimizations. We suggest using Criterium (*https://github.com/hugoduncan/criterium*) when benchmarking to avoid common pitfalls.

To see Criterium benchmarks of `hiphip`, see w01fe's *bench.clj* gist (*http://bit.ly/hiphip-bench*).

## Discussion

Most of the time, Clojure's sequence abstraction is all you need to get the job done. The preceding `dot-product` can be written succinctly in ordinary Clojure, and this is generally what you should try first:

```
(defn dot-product [ws xs]
  (reduce + (map * ws xs))
```

Once you identify a bottleneck in your mathematical operations, however, primitive arrays may be the only way to go. The preceding `dot-product` implementation can be made more than 100 times faster by using `asum`, primarily because `map` produces sequences of *boxed* Java `Double` objects. In addition to the cost of constructing an intermediate sequence, all arithmetic operations on boxed numbers are significantly slower than on their primitive counterparts.

`hiphip`'s `amap`, `afill!`, `reduce`, and `asum` macros (among others) are available for `int`, `long`, `float`, and `double` types. If you wanted to use `reduce` over an array of floats, for example, you would use `hiphip.float/reduce`. These macros define the appropriate type hints and optimizations per type.

Clojure also comes with built-in functions (*http://clojure.org/java_interop#Java%20Interop-Arrays*) for operating on arrays, although greater care must be taken to ensure maximal performance (via appropriate type hints and use of `*unchecked-math*`):

```
(set! *unchecked-math* true)
(defn map-inc [^doubles xs]
  (amap xs i ret (aset ret i (inc (aget xs i)))))
```

Working with primitive arrays in Clojure isn't for the faint of heart: if you don't get *everything* right, you can easily end up with code that's both much uglier and no faster (or even slower) than the straightforward sequence version. The biggest issue to watch out for is reflection, which can easily bring you from 100 times faster to 10 times slower with one small typo or missing type hint.

If you're up to the challenge, you should keep these tips in mind:

- Use `*warn-on-reflection*` religiously, but be aware that it won't warn you about many of the ways your code can be slow.
- A solid profiler, or at least a comprehensive benchmark suite, is a must; otherwise you won't know which function is using 99% of your runtime.
- Especially if you're not using `hiphip`, experiment with `*unchecked-math*`; it almost always makes your code faster, if you're willing to give up the safety of overflow checks.
- If you want your array code to go fast under Leiningen (*http://bit.ly/lein-tiered-compilation*), you probably want to add the following to your *project.clj*: `:jvm-opts ^:replace []`.

## See Also

- `hiphip` comes with a comprehensive suite of benchmarks (*http://bit.ly/hiphip-tests*) of its and Clojure's array operations for the main primitive types, including performance comparisons with handcoded Java alternatives.
- Vertigo (*https://github.com/ztellman/vertigo*) goes beyond simple arrays of primitives to full C-style structs, which may be a good choice if you need to manipulate structured data (i.e., not just sequences of `doubles`) with maximal performance.
- Recipe 8.5, "Alleviating Performance Problems with Type Hinting" on page 360, to learn more about type hinting and unchecked math.
- Recipe 8.7, "Simple Profiling with Timbre" on page 366, to learn about using Timbre to output profiling statistics from your code.

# 8.7. Simple Profiling with Timbre

by Ambrose Bonnaire-Sergeant

## Problem

You want fine-grained statistics on the running time and invocation counts of your code.

## Solution

Use Timbre (*https://github.com/ptaoussanis/timbre*) to insert profiling macros into your code that won't incur a performance penalty in production.

Before starting, add `[com.taoensso/timbre "2.6.3"]` to your project's dependencies or start a REPL using `lein-try`:

```
$ lein try com.taoensso/timbre
```

Use the macros in the `taoensso.timbre.profiling` namespace to collect benchmarking metrics in development:

```
(require '[taoensso.timbre.profiling :as p])

(defn bench-me [f]
  (p/p :bench/bench-me
    (let [_ (p/p :bench/sleep
              (Thread/sleep 10))
          n (p/p :bench/call-f-once
              (f))
          _ (p/p :bench/call-f-10-times-outer
              (dotimes [_ 10]
                (p/p :bench/call-f-10-times-inner
                  (f))))]
      (iterate f n))))

(p/profile :info :Bench-f
  (bench-me
    (fn ([] (p/p :bench/no-arg-f) 100)
        ([a] (p/p :bench/one-arg-f) +))))
```

Here we define a Clojure function `bench-me`, which is called with a higher-order function `f` that takes zero or one argument.

Timbre outputs rich profiling information in a convenient table:

```
2013-Aug-25 ... Profiling :taoensso.timbre.profiling/Bench-f
                         Name  Calls    Min    Max  MAD   Mean Time%  Time
             :bench/bench-me      1   13ms   13ms  0ns   13ms    95  13ms
                :bench/sleep      1   11ms   11ms  0ns   11ms    76  11ms
:bench/call-f-10-times-outer      1  970μs  970μs  0ns  970μs     7 970μs
          :bench/call-f-once      1  610μs  610μs  0ns  610μs     4 610μs
```

```
:bench/call-f-10-times-inner     10    20μs  214μs  35μs    39μs       3  394μs
             :bench/no-arg-f     11     5μs  163μs  26μs    20μs       2  215μs
                [Clock] Time                                         100   14ms
              Accounted Time                                         186   26ms
```

## Discussion

Profiling with Timbre is a great solution for Clojure-only profiling. Standard JVM profiling tools like YourKit and JVisualVM provide more comprehensive information on Java methods but come with a greater performance penalty.

Timbre's profiling is most useful when profiling a specific area of code, rather than using profiling as an exploratory tool for tuning performance. As profiling markers are just macros, they are flexible. For example, you could record how many times a particular `if` branch was taken, all without leaving Clojure or suffering from mangled Clojure function names via YourKit or JVisualVM.

If profiling is deemed useful enough to keep in your code base, it is good practice to use the profiling macros via a namespace alias. `p`, while conveniently named, is prone to being shadowed by local bindings if used without an explicit namespace. In the solution we used the alias `p`, so each call to `p` becomes `p/p`.

Remember, you should not be hesitant to add profiling statements: there is no performance penalty for code involving `taoensso.timbre.profiling/p` if tracing is not enabled. This means you can leave tracing code in production, which is useful if you want to profile the same code later, or if the profiling comments make your code clearer.

## See Also

- Profiling with Timbre (*http://bit.ly/timbre-profiling*)

# 8.8. Logging with Timbre

by Alex Miller

## Problem

You want to add logging to your application code.

## Solution

Use Timbre (*https://github.com/ptaoussanis/timbre*) to configure your logger and add logging messages to your code.

Before starting, add `[com.taoensso/timbre "2.7.1"]` to your project's dependencies or start a REPL using `lein-try`:

```
$ lein try com.taoensso/timbre
```

To write a function that writes log messages, use the Timbre functions `info`, `error`, etc:

```
(require '[taoensso.timbre :as log])

(defn div-4 [n]
  (log/info "Starting")
  (try
    (/ 4 n)
    (catch Throwable t
      (log/error t "oh no!"))
    (finally
      (log/info "Ending"))))
```

The `div-4` function takes a single argument and returns 4/n.

The `log/info` calls will create a log message output at the "info" level. Similarly, the `log/error` call will create a log message at the "error" output level. Passing an exception as the first argument will cause the stack trace to be printed as well.

If you call `div-4` with values that will succeed or throw an error, you will see output like the following in your REPL:

```
(div-4 2)
;; -> 2
;; *out*
;; 2013-Nov-22 10:34:11 -0500 laptop INFO [user] - Starting
;; 2013-Nov-22 10:34:11 -0500 laptop INFO [user] - Ending

(div-4 0)
;; -> 2013-Nov-22 10:34:47 -0500 laptop ERROR [user] -
;;      oh no! java.lang.ArithmeticException: Divide by zero
;; -> nil
;; *out*
;; 2013-Nov-22 10:34:21 -0500 laptop INFO [user] - Starting
;; 2013-Nov-22 10:34:21 -0500 laptop ERROR [user] -
;;   oh no! java.lang.ArithmeticException: Divide by zero
;; ... Exception stacktrace
;; 2013-Nov-22 10:34:21 -0500 laptop INFO [user] - Ending
```

## Discussion

Timbre is a great way to get started with logging in your code. Using a log library allows you to specify later where the output will go, possibly to more than one location or filtered by namespace.

Timbre writes logs to any number of configured "appenders" (output destinations). By default, a single appender is configured to write to standard out.

For example, to add a second appender for a file, you can dynamically modify the configuration by enabling the preconfigured `spit` appender:

```
;; Turn it on
(log/set-config! [:appenders :spit :enabled?] true)
;; Set the log file location
(log/set-config! [:shared-appender-config :spit-filename] "out.log")
```

Note that the output file's directory must exist and the user must be able to write to the file. Once this configuration has been completed, any log messages will be written to both the console and the file.

The available logging levels are `:trace`, `:debug`, `:info`, `:warn`, `:error`, and `:fatal`. The default log level is set to `:debug`, so all logging levels greater than or equal to `:debug` will be recorded (everything but `:trace`).

To change the logging level at runtime, change the configuration:

```
(log/set-level! :warn)
```

While Timbre is an excellent library for simple logging in your Clojure app, it may not be sufficient if you are integrating with many Java libraries. There are a variety of popular Java logging frameworks and logging facades. If you wish to leverage the existing Java logging infrastructure, you might find the `tools.logging` framework more suitable.

## See Also

- Timbre Readme (*http://bit.ly/clj-timbre*)
- Logging with `tools.logging` (*http://bit.ly/clj-tools-logging*)

# 8.9. Releasing a Library to Clojars

by Ryan Neufeld; originally submitted by Simon Mosciatti

## Problem

You've built a library in Clojure, and you want to release it to the world.

## Solution

One of the easiest places to release libraries to is Clojars (*https://clojars.org*), a community repository for open source libraries. To get started, sign up for an account (*https://clojars.org/register*). If you don't already have an SSH key, the GitHub guide "Generating SSH Keys" (*http://bit.ly/ssh-keys*) is an excellent resource.

Once you have an account set up, you're ready to publish any Leiningen-based project. If you don't have a project to publish, generate one with the command **`lein new my-first-project-<firstname>-<lastname>`**, replacing `<firstname>` and `<lastname>` with your own name.

You can now use the command **`lein deploy clojars`** to release your library to Clojars:

```
$ lein deploy clojars
WARNING: please set :description in project.clj.
WARNING: please set :url in project.clj.
No credentials found for clojars (did you mean `lein deploy clojars`?)
See `lein help deploy` for how to configure credentials.
Username: # ❶
Password: # ❷
Wrote .../my-first-project-ryan-neufeld/pom.xml
Created .../my-first-project-ryan-neufeld-0.1.0-SNAPSHOT.jar
Could not find metadata my-first-project-ryan-neufeld:
    .../0.1.0-SNAPSHOT/maven-metadata.xml \
    in clojars (https://clojars.org/repo/)
Sending .../my-first-project-ryan-neufeld-0.1.0-20131113.123334-1.pom (3k)
    to https://clojars.org/repo/
Sending .../my-first-project-ryan-neufeld-0.1.0-20131113.123334-1.jar (8k)
    to https://clojars.org/repo/
Could not find metadata my-first-project-ryan-neufeld:.../maven-metadata.xml \
    in clojars (https://clojars.org/repo/)
Sending my-first-project-ryan-neufeld/.../0.1.0-SNAPSHOT/maven-metadata.xml (1k)
    to https://clojars.org/repo/
Sending my-first-project-ryan-neufeld/.../maven-metadata.xml (1k)
    to https://clojars.org/repo/
```

❶ Enter your Clojars username, then press Return.

❷ Enter your Clojars password, then press Return.

After this command has completed, your library will be available both on the Web (*https://clojars.org/my-first-project-ryan-neufeld*) and as a Leiningen dependency (`[my-first-project-ryan-neufeld "0.1.0-SNAPSHOT"]`).

## Discussion

Releasing a library doesn't get much easier than this; just create an account and press the Big Red Button. Together, Leiningen and Clojars make it trivially easy for members of the Clojure community such as yourself to release their libraries to the masses.

In this example, you released a simple, uniquely named library with little care for versioning, release strategies, or adequate metadata. In a real project, you should pay attention to these matters to be a good open source citizen.

The easiest change is adding appropriate metadata and a website. In your *project.clj* file, add an accurate `:description` and `:url`. If you don't have a website for your project, consider linking to your project's GitHub page (or other public SCM "landing page").

Less easy is having consistent version numbers for your project. We suggest a scheme called Semantic Versioning (*http://semver.org*), or "semver." The semver scheme prescribes a version number of three parts, *major*, *minor*, and *patch*, joined with periods. This ends up looking like "0.1.0" or "1.4.2". Each version position indicates a certain level of stability and consistency across releases. Releases sharing a major version should be API-compatible; bumping the major version says, "I have fundamentally changed the API of this library." The minor version indicates when new, backward-compatible functionality has been added. Finally, the patch version indicates when bug fixes have been made.

It certainly takes discipline to follow Semantic Versioning, but when you do, you make it easier for your fellow developers to understand your library versions and trust them to behave in a way they expect.

Code signing is another important concern in the deployment process. Signing the artifacts you release lets your users know the artifacts were created by someone they trust (you) and contain exactly what you intended (i.e., they have not be tampered with). Leiningen includes the facilities to sign release artifacts using GPG and include the relevant *.asc* signature files in `lein deploy` publications. Enabling code signing is described in the GNU Privacy Guard (GPG) section of Leiningen's deploying libraries guide (*http://bit.ly/lein-deploy-gpg*).

## See Also

- The Clojars wiki (*http://bit.ly/clojars-wiki*), a bountiful source of information on releasing libraries to Clojars
- Leiningen's own deploying libraries guide (*http://bit.ly/lein-deploy*), which covers code signing and how to deploy to repositories other than Clojars
- The output of the `lein help deploy` command

# 8.10. Using Macros to Simplify API Deprecations

by Michael Fogus

## Problem

You want to use Clojure macros to deprecate API functions and report existing deprecations.

## Solution

When maintaining a library that other programmers rely on to get their work done, it behooves you to be thoughtful when making changes. In the process of fixing bugs and making improvements to your library, you will eventually wish to change its public interface. Making changes to a public-facing portion of your library is no small matter, but assuming that you've determined its necessity, then you'll want to *deprecate* the functions that are obsolete. The term "deprecate" basically means that a given function should be avoided in favor of some other, newer function.

For an example, take the case of the Clojure contrib library `core.memoize` (*https://github.com/clojure/core.memoize*). Without going into detail about what `core.memoize` does, it's fine to know that at one point a segment of its public-facing API was a function named `memo-fifo` that looked like the following:

```
(defn memo-fifo
  ([f] ... )
  ([f limit] ... )
  ([f limit base] ... ))
```

Obviously, the implementation has been elided to highlight only the parts that were planned for change in a later version—namely, the function's name and its available argument vectors. The details of the new API are not important, but they were different enough to cause potential confusion to the users. In a case like this, simply making the change without due notice in a new version would have been bad form and genuine cause for bitterness.

Therefore, the question arises: what can you do in the case where a feature is planned for deprecation that not only supports existing code in the interim, but also provides fair warning to the users of your library of a future breaking change? In this section, we'll discuss using macros to provide a nice mechanism for deprecating library functions and macros with minimal fuss.

In the case of the planned deprecation of `memo-fifo`, the new function, named simply `fifo`, was changed not only in name but also in its provided arities. When deprecating portions of a library, it's often a good idea to print warning messages that point to the new, preferred function to use instead. Therefore, to start on the way to deprecating `memo-fifo`, the following function, `!!`, was created to print a warning:

```
(defn ^:private !! [c]
  (println "WARNING - Deprecated construction method for"
           c
           "cache; preferred way is:"
           (str "(clojure.core.memoize/" c
                " function <base> <:"
                c "/threshold num>)")))
```

When passed a symbol, the `!!` function prints a message like this one:

```
(!! 'fifo)

;; WARNING - Deprecated construction method for fifo cache;
;; preferred way is:
;; (clojure.core.memoize/fifo function <base> <:fifo/threshold num>)
```

Not only does the deprecation message indicate that the function called is deprecated, but it also points to the function that should be used instead. As far as deprecation messages go, this one is solid, although your own purposes may call for something different. In any case, to insert this warning on every call to `memo-fifo`, we can create a simple macro to inject the call to `!!` into the body of the function's definition, as shown here:

```
(defmacro defn-deprecated [nom _ alt ds & arities]
  `(defn ~nom ~ds                                  ; ❶
     ~@(for [[args body] arities]                  ; ❷
         (list args `(!! (quote ~alt)) body))))    ; ❸
```

❶ Create a `defn` call with the given name and docstring.

❷ Loop through the given function arities.

❸ Insert a call to `!!` as the first part of the body.

We'll talk a bit about the goals of the `defn-deprecated` macro in the following discussion section, but for now, you can see how it works:

```
(defn-deprecated memo-fifo :as fifo
  "DEPRECATED: Please use clojure.core.memoize/fifo instead."
  ([f] ... )
  ([f limit] ... )
  ([f limit base] ... )
```

The only changes to the definition of `memo-fifo` are the use of the `defn-deprecated` macro instead of `defn` directly, the use of the `:as fifo` directive, and the addition (or change) of the docstring to describe the deprecation. The `defn-deprecated` macro takes care of assembling the parts in the macro body to print the warning on use:

```
(def f (memo-fifo identity 32))
;; WARNING - Deprecated construction method for fifo cache;
;; preferred way is:
;; (clojure.core.memoize/fifo function <base> <:fifo/threshold num>)
```

The warning message will only display once for every call to `memo-fifo`, and due to the nature of that function, that should be sufficient.

## Discussion

There are different ways to handle the same situation besides using macros. For example, the `!!` function could have taken a function and a symbol and wrapped the function, inserting a deprecation warning in passing:

```
(defn depr [fun alt]
  (fn [& args]                                          ; ❶
    (println
      "WARNING - Deprecated construction method for"
      alt
      "cache; preferred way is:"
      (str "(clojure.core.memoize/" alt
           " function <base> <:"
           alt "/threshold num>)"))
    (apply fun args)))                                  ; ❷
```

❶ Return a function that prints the deprecation message before calling the deprecated function.

❷ Call the deprecated function.

This new implementation of `!!` would work in the following way:

```
(def memo-fifo (depr old-memo-fifo 'fifo))
```

Thereafter, calling the `memo-fifo` function will print the deprecation message. Using a higher-order function like this is a reasonable way to avoid the potential complexities of using a macro. However, we chose the macro version for a number of reasons, explained in the following sections.

### Preserving stack traces

Let's be honest: the exception stack traces that Clojure can produce can at times be painful to deal with. If you decide to use a higher-order function like `depr`, be aware that if an exception occurs in its execution, another layer of stack trace will be added. By using a macro like `!!` that delegates its operation directly to `defn`, you are ensured that the stack trace will remain unadulterated (so to speak).

### Metadata

Using a near 1-for-1 replacement macro like `defn-deprecated` allows you to preserve the metadata on a function. Observe:

```
(defn-deprecated ^:private memo-foo :as bar
  "Does something."
  ([] 42))

(memo-foo)
;; WARNING - Deprecated construction method for bar cache;
;; preferred way is:
;; (clojure.core.memoize/bar function <base> <:bar/threshold num>)
;;=> 42
```

Because `defn-deprecated` defers the bulk of its behavior to `defn`, any metadata attached to its elements automatically gets forwarded on and attached as expected:

```
(meta #'memo-foo)

;;=> {:arglists ([]), :ns #<Namespace user>,
;;    :name memo-foo, :private true, :doc "Does something.",
;;    ...}
```

Using the higher-order approach does not automatically preserve metadata:

```
(def baz (depr foo 'bar))

(meta #'baz)
;;=> {:ns #<Namespace user>, :name baz, ...}
```

Of course, you could copy over the metadata if so desired, but why do so when the macro approach takes cares of it for you?

### Faster call site

The `depr` function, because it's required to handle any function that you give it, needed to use `apply` at its core. While in the case of the `core.memoize` functions this was not a problem, it may become so in the case of functions requiring higher performance. In reality, though, the use of `println` will likely overwhelm the cost of the `apply`, so if you really need to deprecate a high-performance function, then you might want to consider the following approach instead.

### Compile-time warnings

The operation of `defn-deprecated` is such that the deprecation warning is printed every time the function is called. This could be problematic if the function requires high speed.

Very few things slow a function down like a console print. Therefore, we can change `defn-deprecate` slightly to report its warning at compile time rather than runtime:

```
(defmacro defn-deprecated [nom _ alt ds & arities]
  (!! alt)                        ; ❶
  `(defn ~nom ~ds ~@arities))  ; ❷
```

❶ Print the warning when the macro is accessed.

❷ Delegate function definition to `defn` without adulteration.

Observe the compile-time warning:

```
(defn-deprecated ^:private memo-foo :as bar
  "Does something."
  ([] 42))

;; WARNING - Deprecated construction method for bar cache;
;; preferred way is:
;; (clojure.core.memoize/bar function <base> <:bar/threshold num>)
;;=> #'user/memo-foo
```

```
(memo-foo)
42
```

This approach will work well if you distribute libraries as source code rather than as compiled programs.

#### Turning it off

The real beauty of macros is not that they allow you to change the semantics of your programs, but that they allow you to avoid doing so whenever it's not appropriate. For example, when using macros, you can run any code available to Clojure at compile time. Thankfully, the full Clojure language is available at compile time. Therefore, we can check a Boolean flag attached to a namespace as metadata to decide whether to report a compile-time deprecation warning. We can change the newest `defn-deprecated` to illustrate this technique:

```
(defmacro defn-deprecated
  [nom _ alt ds & arities]
  (let [silence? (:silence-deprecations (meta clojure.core/*ns*))] ; ❶
    (when-not silence?  ; ❷
     (!! alt)))
  `(defn ~nom ~ds ~@arities))
```

❶ Look up the metadata on the current namespace.

❷ Only report the deprecation warning if the flag is not set to silence mode.

The `defn-deprecated` macro checks the status of the `:silence-deprecations` metadata property on the current namespace and reports (or not) the deprecation warning based on it. If you wind up using this approach, then you can turn off the deprecation warning on a per-namespace basis by adding the following to your `ns` declaration:

```
(ns ^:silence-deprecations my.awesome.lib)
```

Now, any use of `defn-deprecated` in that namespace will not print the warning. Future versions of Clojure will provide a cleaner way of creating and managing compile-time flags, but for now this is a decent compromise.

## See Also

- The official macro documentation (*http://clojure.org/macros*)

CHAPTER 9
# Distributed Computation

## 9.0. Introduction

With the advent of cheaper and cheaper storage, we're inclined to store more and more data. As this data grows larger and larger, it becomes increasingly difficult to utilize to its full potential. In response, numerous new techniques have emerged in the last decade or so for dealing with such quantities of data.

The primary focus of this chapter is one such technique, MapReduce (*http://bit.ly/mapreduce-paper*), developed at Google in the early 2000s. Functional even in name, this technique uses `map` and `reduce` in parallel across multiple machines at tremendous scale to process data at phenomenal speeds. In this chapter, we'll be covering Cascalog (*http://cascalog.org/*), a data-processing library built on top of Hadoop (*http://hadoop.apache.org/*), which is an open source MapReduce implementation.

We'll also briefly cover Storm (*http://storm-project.net/*), a real-time stream-processing library in use at several tech giants such as Twitter, Groupon, and Yahoo!.

### Cascalog

Cascalog defines a DSL based on Datalog, the same query language that backs Datomic (*http://www.datomic.com/*). It might seem strange at first, but you will be thinking in Datalog in no time. Once you've wet your feet with these recipes, visit the Cascalog wiki (*http://bit.ly/cascalog-wiki*) for more information on writing your own queries.

Cascalog provides a concise syntax for describing data-processing jobs. Transformations and aggregates are easy to express in Cascalog. Joins are particularly simple. You might like the Cascalog syntax so much that you use it even for local jobs.

You can run your Cascalog jobs in a number of different ways. The easiest way is to run jobs locally. When running jobs locally, Cascalog uses Hadoop's local mode, completing the entire job on your own computer. You get the benefit of parallelism, without the hassle of setting up a cluster.

Once your jobs outgrow local mode, you'll need to start running them on a Hadoop cluster. Having your own cluster is a lot of fun, but it can take a fair amount of work (and money!) to set up and maintain. If you don't need a cluster very often, you might consider running your job on link to Amazon Elastic MapReduce (*http://aws.amazon.com/elasticmapreduce/*) (EMR). EMR provides on-demand Hadoop clusters the same way EC2 provides on-demand servers. You'll need an Amazon Web Services account to run the job, but it isn't difficult. You can read exactly how to do it later, in Recipe 9.7, "Running a Cascalog Job on Elastic MapReduce" on page 403. Whether you run your job on EMR or on your own cluster, you will package up your code into an uberjar (see Recipe 8.2, "Packaging a Project into a JAR File" on page 347), then send it to Hadoop for execution. It is surprisingly simple to get hundreds of computers working on your task.

# 9.1. Building an Activity Feed System with Storm

by Travis Vachon

## Problem

You want to build an activity stream processing system to filter and aggregate the raw event data generated by the users of your application.

## Solution

Streams are a dominant metaphor for presenting information to users of the modern Internet. Used on sites like Facebook and Twitter and mobile apps like Instagram and Tinder, streams are an elegant tool for giving users a window into the deluge of information generated by the applications they use every day.

As a developer of these applications, you want tools to process the firehose of raw event data generated by user actions. They must offer powerful capabilities for filtering and aggregating data and must be arbitrarily scalable to serve ever-growing user bases. Ideally they should provide high-level abstractions that help you organize and grow the complexity of your stream-processing logic to accommodate new features and a complex world.

Clojure offers just such a tool in Storm (*http://storm-project.net/*), a distributed real-time computation system that aims to be for real-time computation what Hadoop is for batch computation. In this section, you'll build a simple activity stream processing system that can be easily extended to solve real-world problems.

First, create a new Storm project (*http://storm.incubator.apache.org/*) using its Leiningen template:

```
$ lein new cookbook-storm-project feeds
```

In the project directory, run the default Storm topology (which the `lein` template has generated for you):

```
$ cd feeds
$ lein run -m feeds.topology/run!
Compiling feeds.TopologySubmitter
...
Emitting: spout default [:bizarro]
Processing received message source: spout:4, stream: default, id: {}, [:bizarro]
Emitting: stormy-bolt default ["I'm bizarro Stormy!"]
Processing received message source: stormy-bolt:5,
  stream: default, id: {}, [I'm bizarro Stormy!]
Emitting: feeds-bolt default ["feeds produced: I'm bizarro Stormy!"]
```

This generated example topology just babbles example messages incoherently, which probably isn't what you want, so begin by modifying the "spout" to produce realistic events.

In Storm parlance, the "spout" is the component that inserts data into the processing system and creates a data stream. Open *src/feeds/spouts.clj* and replace the `defspout` form with a new spout that will periodically produce random user events such as one might see in an online marketplace (in a real application, of course, you'd hook this up to some source of real data rather than a random data generator):

```
(defspout event-spout ["event"]
  [conf context collector]
  (let [events [{:action :commented, :user :travis, :listing :red-shoes}
                {:action :liked, :user :jim, :listing :red-shoes}
                {:action :liked, :user :karen, :listing :green-hat}
                {:action :liked, :user :rob, :listing :green-hat}
                {:action :commented, :user :emma, :listing :green-hat}]]
    (spout
     (nextTuple []
       (Thread/sleep 1000)
       (emit-spout! collector [(rand-nth events)])))))
```

Next, open *src/feeds/bolts/clj*. Add a bolt that accepts a user and an event and produces a tuple of `(user, event)` for each user in the system. A bolt consumes a stream, does some processing, and emits a new stream:

```
(defbolt active-user-bolt ["user" "event"] [{event "event" :as tuple} collector]
       (doseq [user [:jim :rob :karen :kaitlyn :emma :travis]]
    (emit-bolt! collector [user event]))
  (ack! collector tuple))
```

Now add a bolt that accepts a user and an event and emits a tuple if and only if the user is following the user who triggered the event:

```
(defbolt follow-bolt ["user" "event"] {:prepare true}
  [conf context collector]
  (let [follows {:jim #{:rob :emma}
                 :rob #{:karen :kaitlyn :jim}
                 :karen #{:kaitlyn :emma}
                 :kaitlyn #{:jim :rob :karen :kaitlyn :emma :travis}
                 :emma #{:karen}
                 :travis #{:kaitlyn :emma :karen :rob}}]
    (bolt
     (execute [{user "user" event "event" :as tuple}]
              (when ((follows user) (:user event))
                (emit-bolt! collector [user event]))
              (ack! collector tuple)))))
```

Finally, add a bolt that accepts a user and an event and stores the event in a hash of sets like `{:user1 #{event1 event2} :user2 #{event1 event2}}`—these are the activity streams you'll present to users:

```
(defbolt feed-bolt ["user" "event"] {:prepare true}
  [conf context collector]
  (let [feeds (atom {})]
    (bolt
     (execute [{user "user" event "event" :as tuple}]
              (swap! feeds #(update-in % [user] conj event))
              (println "Current feeds:")
              (clojure.pprint/pprint @feeds)
              (ack! collector tuple)))))
```

This gives you all the pieces you'll need, but you'll still need to assemble them into a computational topology. Open up *src/feeds/topology.clj* and use the topology DSL to wire the spouts and bolts together:

```
(defn storm-topology []
  (topology
   {"events" (spout-spec event-spout)}

   {"active users" (bolt-spec {"events" :shuffle} active-user-bolt :p 2)
    "follows" (bolt-spec {"active users" :shuffle} follow-bolt :p 2)
    "feeds" (bolt-spec {"follows" ["user"]} feed-bolt :p 2)}))
```

You'll also need to update the `:require` statement in that file:

```
(:require [feeds
           [spouts :refer [event-spout]]
           [bolts :refer [active-user-bolt follow-bolt feed-bolt]]]
          [backtype.storm [clojure :refer [topology spout-spec bolt-spec]]
                          [config :refer :all]])
```

Run the topology again. Feeds will be printed to the console by the final bolts in the topology:

```
$ lein run -m feeds.topology/run!
```

## Discussion

Storm's Clojure DSL doesn't look like standard Clojure. Instead, it uses Clojure's macros to extend the language to the domain of stream processing. Storm's stream processing abstraction consists of four core primitives:

*Tuples*
: Allow programmers to provide names for values. Tuples are dynamically typed lists of values.

*Spouts*
: Produce tuples, often by reading from a distributed queue.

*Bolts*
: Accept tuples as input and produce new tuples—these are the core computational units of a Storm topology.

*Streams*
: Used to wire spouts to bolts and bolts to other bolts, creating a computational topology. Streams can be configured with rules for routing certain types of tuples to specific instances of bolts.

The following subsections review the components of our system to give a better picture of how these primitives work together.

### event-spout

`defspout` looks much like Clojure's standard `defn`, with one difference—the second argument to `defspout` is a list of names that will be assigned to elements of each tuple this spout produces. This lets you use tuples like vectors or maps interchangeably. The third argument to `defspout` is a list of arguments that will be bound various components of Storm's operational infrastructure.

In the case of the `event-spout` spout, only `collector` is used:

```
(defspout event-spout ["event"]
  [conf context collector]
```

`defspout`'s body will be evaluated once, when the spout instance is created, which gives you an opportunity to create in-memory state. Usually this will be a connection to a database or distributed queue, but in this case you'll create a list of events this spout will produce:

```
(let [events [{:action :commented, :user :travis, :listing :red-shoes}
              {:action :liked, :user :jim, :listing :red-shoes}
              {:action :liked, :user :karen, :listing :green-hat}
              {:action :liked, :user :rob, :listing :green-hat}
              {:action :commented, :user :emma, :listing :green-hat}]]
```

This call to spout creates an instance of a spout with the given implementation of nextTuple. This implementation simply sleeps for one second and then uses emit-spout! to emit a one-element tuple consisting of a random event from the preceding list:

```
(spout
 (nextTuple []
   (Thread/sleep 1000)
   (emit-spout! collector [(rand-nth events)])))))
```

nextTuple will be called repeatedly in a tight loop, so if you create a spout that polls an external resource, you may need to provide your own backoff algorithm to avoid excess load on that resource.

You can also implement the spout's ack method to implement a "reliable" spout that will provide message-processing guarantees. For more information on reliable spouts, see Storm's spout implementation for the Kestrel queueing system, storm-kestrel (*https://github.com/nathanmarz/storm-kestrel*).

### active-user-bolt

Every time a user takes an action in this system, the system needs to determine whether each other user in the system will be interested in it. Given a simple interest system like Twitter, where users express interest in a single way (i.e., user follows), you could simply look at the follower list of the user who took the action and update feeds accordingly. In a more complex system, however, interest might be expressed by having liked the item the action was taken against, following a collection that the item has been added to, or following the seller of the item. In this world, you need to consider a variety of factors for each user in the system for every event and determine whether the event should be added to that user's feed.

The first bolt starts this process by generating a tuple of (user, event) for each user in the system every time an event is generated by the event-spout:

```
(defbolt active-user-bolt ["user" "event"] [{event "event" :as tuple} collector]
  (doseq [user [:jim :rob :karen :kaitlyn :emma :travis]]
    (emit-bolt! collector [user event]))
  (ack! collector tuple))
```

defbolt's signature looks very similar to defspout. The second argument is a list of names that will be assigned to tuples generated by this bolt, and the third argument is a list of parameters. The first parameter will be bound to the input tuple, and may be destructured as a map or a vector.

The body of this bolt iterates through a list of users in the system and emits a tuple for each of them. The last line of the body calls ack! on this tuple, which allows Storm to track message processing and restart processing when appropriate.

### follow-bolt

The next bolt is a *prepared bolt*; that is, one that maintains in-memory state. In many cases, this would mean maintaining a connection to a database or a queue, or a data structure aggregating some aspect of the tuples it processes, but this example maintains a complete list of the followers in the system in memory.

This bolt looks more like the spout definition. The second argument is a list of names, the third argument is a map of bolt configuration options (importantly, these set `:prepare` to `true`), and the fourth argument is the same set of operational arguments received in `defspout`:

```
(defbolt follow-bolt ["user" "event"] {:prepare true}
  [conf context collector]
```

The body of the bolt first defines the list of followers, and then provides the actual bolt definition inside a call to `bolt`:

```
  (let [follows {:jim #{:rob :emma}
                 :rob #{:karen :kaitlyn :jim}
                 :karen #{:kaitlyn :emma}
                 :kaitlyn #{:jim :rob :karen :kaitlyn :emma :travis}
                 :emma #{:karen}
                 :travis #{:kaitlyn :emma :karen :rob}}]
    (bolt
     (execute [{user "user" event "event" :as tuple}]
              (when ((follows user) (:user event))
                (emit-bolt! collector [user event]))
              (ack! collector tuple)))))
```

Note that the tuple argument is inside the bolt's definition of `execute` in this case and may be destructured as usual. In cases where the event's user is not following the user in the tuple, it does not emit a new tuple and simply acknowledges that it received the input.

As noted earlier, this particular system could be implemented much more simply by querying whatever datastore tracks follows and simply adding a story to the feed of each follower. Anticipating a more complicated system, however, provides a massively extensible architecture. This bolt could easily be expanded to a collection of scoring bolts, each of which would evaluate a user/event pair based on its own criteria and emit a tuple of (`user`, `event`, `score`). A score aggregation bolt would receive scores from each scoring bolt and choose to emit a tuple once it received scores from each type of scoring bolt in the system. In this world, adjusting the factors determining the makeup of a user's feed and their relative weights would be trivial—indeed, production experience with just such a system was, in the opinion of the authors, delightful (see the Rising Tide project page (*https://github.com/utahstreetlabs/risingtide*) on GitHub).

### feed-bolt

The final bolt aggregates events into feeds. Since it only receives (`user`, `event`) tuples that the "scoring system" has approved, it needs only add the event to the existing list of events it has received for the given user:

```
(let [feeds (atom {})]
  (bolt
   (execute [{user "user" event "event" :as tuple}]
            (swap! feeds #(update-in % [user] conj event))
            (println "Current feeds:")
            (clojure.pprint/pprint @feeds)
            (ack! collector tuple))))
```

This toy topology simply prints the current feeds every time it receives a new event, but in the real world it would persist feeds to a durable datastore or a cache that could efficiently serve the feeds to users.

Note that this design can be easily extended to support event digesting; rather than storing each event separately, it could aggregate an incoming event with other similar events for the user's convenience.

As described, this system has one enormous flaw: by default, Storm tuples are delivered to exactly one instance of each bolt, and the number of instances in existence is not defined in the bolt implementation. If the topology operator adds more than one `feed-bolt`, we may have events for the same user delivered to different bolt instances, giving each bolt a different feed for the same user.

Happily, this flaw is addressed by Storm's support for *stream grouping*, which is defined in the Storm topology definition.

### Topology

The topology definition is where the rubber meets the road. Spouts are wired to bolts, which are wired to other bolts, and the flow of tuples between them can be configured to give useful properties to the computation.

This is also where you define the component-level parallelism of the topology, which provides a rough sketch of the true operational parallelism of the system.

A topology definition consists of spout specifications and bolt specifications, each of which is a map from names to specifications.

Spout specifications simply give a name to a spout implementation:

```
{"events" (spout-spec event-spout)}
```

Multiple spouts can be configured, and the specification may define the parallelism of the spout:

```
{
  "events" (spout-spec event-spout)
  "parallel-spout" (spout-spec a-different-more-parallel-spout :p 2)
}
```

This definition means the topology will have one instance of `event-spout` and two instances of `a-different-more-parallel-spout`.

Bolt definitions get a bit more complicated:

```
"active users" (bolt-spec {"events" :shuffle} active-user-bolt :p 2)
"follows" (bolt-spec {"active users" :shuffle} follow-bolt :p 2)
```

As with the spout spec, you must provide a name for the bolt and specify its parallelism. In addition, bolts require specifying a *stream grouping*, which defines (a) from which component the bolt receives tuples and (b) how the system chooses which in-memory instance of the bolt to send tuples to. Both of these cases specify `:shuffle`, which means tuples from "events" will be sent to a random instance of `active-user-bolt`, and tuples from "active users" will be sent to a random instance of `follow-bolt`.

As noted, `feed-bolt` needs to be more careful:

```
"feeds" (bolt-spec {"follows" ["user"]} feed-bolt :p 2)
```

This bolt spec specifies a *fields grouping* on "user". This means that all tuples with the same "user" value will be sent to the same instance of `feed-bolt`. This stream grouping is configured with a list of field names, so field groupings may consider the equality of multiple field values when determining which bolt instance should process a given tuple.

Storm also supports stream groupings that send tuples to all instances and groupings that let the bolt producing a tuple determine where to send it. Combined with the groupings already seen, these provide an enormous amount of flexibility in determining how data flows through your topology.

Each of these component specifications supports a parallelism option. Because the topology does not specify the physical hardware upon which it will run, these hints cannot be used to determine the true parallelism of the system, but they are used by the cluster to determine how many in-memory instances of the specified components to create.

### Deployment

The real magic of Storm comes out in deployment. Storm gives you the tools to build small, independent components that make no assumptions about how many identical instances are running in the same topology. This means that the topology itself is essentially infinitely scalable. The edges of the system, which receive data from and send data to external components like queues and databases, are not necessarily as scalable, but in many cases, strategies for scaling these services are well understood.

A simple deployment strategy is built into the Storm library:

```
(doto (LocalCluster.)
  (.submitTopology "my first topology"
                   {TOPOLOGY-DEBUG (Boolean/parseBoolean debug)
                    TOPOLOGY-WORKERS (Integer/parseInt workers)}
                   (storm-topology)))
```

`LocalCluster` is an in-memory implementation of a Storm cluster. You can specify the number of *workers* it will use to execute the components of your topology and submit the topology itself, at which point it begins polling the `nextTuple` methods of the topology's spouts. As spouts emit tuples, they are propagated through the system to complete the topology's computation.

Submitting the topology to a configured cluster is nearly as simple, as you can see in *src/feeds/TopologySubmitter.clj*:

```
(defn -main [& {debug "debug" workers "workers" :or {debug "false" workers "4"}}]
  (StormSubmitter/submitTopology
   "feeds topology"
   {TOPOLOGY-DEBUG (Boolean/parseBoolean debug)
    TOPOLOGY-WORKERS (Integer/parseInt workers)}
   (storm-topology)))
```

This file uses Clojure's Java interop to generate a Java class with a `main` method. Because the *project.clj* file specifies that this file should be ahead-of-time compiled, when you use `lein uberjar` to build a JAR suitable for submission to the cluster, this file will be compiled to look like a normal Java class file. You can upload this JAR to the machine running Storm's *Nimbus* daemon and submit it for execution using the `storm` command:

```
$ storm jar path/to/thejariuploaded.jar feeds.TopologySubmitter "workers" 5
```

This command will tell the cluster to allocate five dedicated workers for this topology and begin polling `nextTuple` on all of its spouts, as it did when you used `LocalCluster`. A cluster may run any number of topologies simultaneously—each worker is a physical JVM and may end up running instances of many different bolts and spouts.

The full details of setting up and running a Storm cluster are out of the scope of this recipe, but they are documented extensively on Storm's wiki.

### Conclusion

We've only touched on a fraction of the functionality Storm has to offer. Built-in distributed remote procedure calls allow users to harness the power of a Storm cluster to make synchronous requests that trigger a flurry of activity across hundreds or thousands of machines. Guaranteed data-processing semantics allow users to build extremely robust systems. Trident, a higher-level abstraction over Storm's primitives, provides breathtakingly simple solutions to complicated real-time computing problems. A detailed runtime console provides crucial insight into the runtime characteristics of a fully operational Storm cluster. The power provided by this system is truly remarkable.

Storm is also a fantastic example of Clojure's ability to be extended to a problem domain. Its constructs idiomatically extend Clojure syntax and allow the programmer to stay within the domain of real-time processing, without needing to deal with low-level language formalities. This allows Storm to truly get out of the way. The majority of the code in a well-written Storm topology's code base is focused on the problem at hand. The result is concise, maintainable code and happy programmers.

## See Also

- Storm's website (*http://storm-project.net/*)
- The Storm project template (*http://bit.ly/storm-template*)
- `storm-deploy` (*https://github.com/nathanmarz/storm-deploy*), a tool for easy Storm deployment
- Rising Tide (*https://github.com/utahstreetlabs/risingtide*), the feed generation service on which this recipe is based

# 9.2. Processing Data with an Extract Transform Load (ETL) Pipeline

by Alex Robbins

## Problem

You need to change the format of large amounts of data from JSON lists to CSV for later processing. For example, you want to turn this input:

```
{"name": "Clojure Programming", "authors": ["Chas Emerick",
                                            "Brian Carper",
                                            "Christophe Grand"]}
{"name": "The Joy of Clojure", "authors": ["Michael Fogus", "Chris Houser"]}
```

into this output:

```
Chas Emerick,Brian Carper,Christophe Grand
Michael Fogus,Chris Houser
```

## Solution

Cascalog allows you to write distributed processing jobs that can run locally for small jobs or on a Hadoop cluster for larger jobs.

To follow along with this recipe, create a new Leiningen project:

```
$ lein new cookbook
```

Modify your new project's *project.clj* file by adding the `cascalog` dependency, setting up the `:dev` profile, and enabling AOT compilation for the `cookbook.etl` namespace. Your *project.clj* file should now look like this:

```
(defproject cookbook "0.1.0-SNAPSHOT"
  :description "FIXME: write description"
  :url "http://example.com/FIXME"
  :license {:name "Eclipse Public License"
            :url "http://www.eclipse.org/legal/epl-v10.html"}
  :dependencies [[org.clojure/clojure "1.5.1"]
                 [cascalog "1.10.2"]
                 [org.clojure/data.json "0.2.2"]]
  :profiles {:dev {:dependencies [[org.apache.hadoop/hadoop-core "1.1.2"]]}}
  :aot [cookbook.etl])
```

Create the file *src/cookbook/etl.clj* and add a query to it:

```
(ns cookbook.etl
  (:require [cascalog.api :refer :all]
            [clojure.data.json :as json]))

(defn get-vec
  "Wrap the result in a vector for Cascalog to consume."
  [m k]
  (vector
   (get m k)))

(defn vec->csv
  "Turn a vector into a CSV string. (Not production quality)."
  [v]
  (apply str (interpose "," v)))

(defmain Main [in out & args]
  (?<-
    (hfs-textline out :sinkmode :replace)
    [?out-csv]
    ((hfs-textline in) ?in-json)
    (json/read-str ?in-json :> ?book-map)
    (get-vec ?book-map "authors" :> ?authors)
    (vec->csv ?authors :> ?out-csv)))
```

Create a file with input data in *samples/books/books.json*:

```
{"name": "Clojure Cookbook", "authors": ["Ryan", "Luke"]}
```

The full contents of this solution are available on GitHub in the Cascalog samples (*http://bit.ly/cc-cascalog-samples*) repository.

To retrieve a copy of the working project, clone the project from GitHub and check out the `etl-sample` branch:

```
$ git clone https://github.com/clojure-cookbook/cascalog-samples.git
$ cd cascalog-samples
$ git checkout etl-sample
```

You can now execute the job locally with **`lein run`**, providing an input and output file:

```
$ lein run -m cookbook.etl.Main samples/books/books.json samples/books/output

# Or, on a Hadoop cluster
$ lein uberjar
$ hadoop jar target/cookbook-standalone.jar cookbook.etl.Main \
  books.json books.csv
```

The results in *samples/books/output/part-00000* are as follows:

```
Ryan,Luke
```

## Discussion

While it would be easy to write a script that converted JSON to CSV, it would be a lot of work to convert the script to run across many computers. Writing the transform script using Cascalog allows it to run in local mode or distributed mode with almost no modification.

There are a lot of new concepts and syntax in the preceding small example, so let's break it down piece by piece.

In this recipe, the data flows through the functions roughly in order. The first line uses the `defmain` macro (from Cascalog) to define a class with a `-main` function that lets you run the query over Hadoop. In this case, the class with a `-main` function is called `Main`, but that is not required. `defmain` allows you to create several Hadoop-enabled queries in the same file:

```
(defmain Main [in out & args]
```

Inside the `Main` function is a Cascalog operator, `?<-`,[1] that defines and executes a query:

```
(?<-
```

1. While queries *look* like regular Clojure, they are in fact a DSL. If you're not familiar with Cascalog queries, learn more in Nathan Marz's "Introducing Cascalog" article (*http://bit.ly/cascalog-intro-post*).

This operator takes an output location (called a "tap" in Cascalog), a result vector, and a series of logic predicates. The next line is the destination, the place the output will be written to. The same functions are used to create input and output taps:

```
(hfs-textline out :sinkmode :replace)
```

This example uses `hfs-textline`, but many other taps exist. You can even write your own.

Use `:sinkmode :replace` in your output tap, and Cascalog will replace any existing output. This helps while you are rerunning the query to debug it. Otherwise, you will have to remove the output file every time you want to rerun.

This is a list of all the logic variables that should be returned from this query:

```
[?out-csv]
```

In this case, these are the logic variables that will be dumped into the output location. Cascalog knows these are special logic variables because their names begin with a `?` or a `!`.

When thinking about logic variables, it helps to think of them as containing all possible valid values. As you add predicates, you either introduce new logic variables that are (hopefully) linked to existing variables, or you add constraints to existing logic variables.

The next line defines the input tap. The JSON data structures will be read in one line at a time from the location specified by `in`. Each line will be stored into the `?in-json` logic var, which will flow through the rest of the logic predicates:

```
((hfs-textline in) ?in-json)
```

`read-str` parses the JSON string found in `?in-json` into a hash map, which is stored into `?book-map`:

```
(json/read-str ?in-json ?book-map)
```

Now you pull the authors out of the map and store the vector into its own logic variable. Cascalog assumes vector output means binding multiple logic vars. To outsmart Cascalog, wrap the output in an extra vector for Cascalog to consume:

```
(get-vec ?book-map "authors" ?authors)
```

Finally, you convert the vector of authors into valid CSV using the `vec->csv` function. Since this line produces values for the `?out-csv` logic variable, which is named in the output line earlier, the query will produce the output:

```
(vec->csv ?authors ?out-csv)))
```

Cascalog is a great tool for building an extract transform load (ETL) pipeline. It allows you to spend more time thinking about your data and less time thinking about the mechanics of reading files, distributing work, or managing dependencies. When writing your own ETL pipelines, it might help to follow this process:

1. Finalize the input format(s).
2. Finalize the output format(s).
3. Start working from the input format, keeping track of the current format for each step.

## See Also

- Ian Rumford's blog post "Using Cascalog for Extract Transform and Load" (*http://bit.ly/cascalog-etl-post*)
- `core.logic` (*https://github.com/clojure/core.logic*), a logic programming library for Clojure

# 9.3. Aggregating Large Files

by Alex Robbins

## Problem

You need to generate aggregate statistics from terabytes of log files. For example, for a simple input log file (`<date>,<URL>,<USER-ID>`):

```
20130512020202,/,11
20130512020412,/,23
20130512030143,/post/clojure,11
20130512040256,/post/datomic,23
20130512050910,/post/clojure,11
20130512051012,/post/clojure,14
```

you want to output aggregate statistics like this:

```
{
"URL"  {"/"              2
        "/post/datomic"  1
        "/post/clojure"  3}
"User" {"23" 2
        "11" 3
        "14" 1}
"Day"  {"20130512" 6}
}
```

## Solution

Cascalog allows you to write distributed processing jobs that run locally or on a Hadoop cluster.

To follow along with this recipe, clone the Cascalog samples GitHub repository (*http://bit.ly/cc-cascalog-samples*) and check out the `aggregation-begin` branch. This will give you a basic Cascalog project as created in Recipe 9.2, "Processing Data with an Extract Transform Load (ETL) Pipeline" on page 387:

```
$ git clone https://github.com/clojure-cookbook/cascalog-samples.git
$ cd cascalog-samples
$ git checkout aggregation-begin
```

Now add `[cascalog/cascalog-more-taps "2.0.0"]` to the project's dependencies and set the `cookbook.aggregation` namespace to be AOT-compiled. *project.clj* should look like this:

```
(defproject cookbook "0.1.0-SNAPSHOT"
  :description "FIXME: write description"
  :url "http://example.com/FIXME"
  :license {:name "Eclipse Public License"
            :url "http://www.eclipse.org/legal/epl-v10.html"}
  :dependencies [[org.clojure/clojure "1.5.1"]
                 [cascalog "2.0.0"]
                 [cascalog/cascalog-more-taps "2.0.0"]
                 [org.clojure/data.json "0.2.2"]]
  :profiles {:dev {:dependencies [[org.apache.hadoop/hadoop-core "1.1.2"]]}}
  :aot [cookbook.etl
        cookbook.aggregation])
```

Create the file *src/cookbook/aggregation.clj* and add an aggregation query to it:

```
(ns cookbook.aggregation
  (:require [cascalog.api :refer :all]
            [cascalog.more-taps :refer [hfs-delimited]]))

(defn init-aggregate-stats [date url user]
  (let [day (.substring date 0 8)]
    {"URL"  {url 1}
     "User" {user 1}
     "Day"  {date 1}}))

(def combine-aggregate-stats
  (partial merge-with (partial merge-with +)))

(defparallelagg aggregate-stats
  :init-var    #'init-aggregate-stats
  :combine-var #'combine-aggregate-stats)

(defmain Main [in out & args]
  (?<-
```

```
    (hfs-textline out :sinkmode :replace)
    [?out]
    ((hfs-delimited in :delimiter ",") ?date ?url ?user)
    (aggregate-stats ?date ?url ?user :> ?out)))
```

Add some sample data to the file *samples/posts/posts.csv*:

```
20130512020202,/,11
20130512020412,/,23
20130512030143,/post/clojure,11
20130512040256,/post/datomic,23
20130512050910,/post/clojure,11
20130512051012,/post/clojure,14
```

The full contents of this solution are available in the `aggregation-complete` branch of the Cascalog samples (*http://bit.ly/cc-cascalog-samples*) repository.

Check out that branch to retrieve a full working copy with sample data:

```
$ git checkout aggregation-complete
```

You can now execute the job locally:

```
$ lein run -m cookbook.aggregation.Main \
  samples/posts/posts.csv samples/posts/output

# Or, on a Hadoop cluster
$ lein uberjar
$ hadoop jar target/cookbook-standalone.jar \
             cookbook.aggregation.Main \
             samples/posts/posts.csv samples/posts/output
```

The results in *samples/posts/output/part-00000*, formatted for readability, are as follows:

```
{
"URL"  {"/"              2
        "/post/datomic"  1
        "/post/clojure"  3}
"User" {"23" 2
        "11" 3
        "14" 1}
"Day"  {"20130512" 6}
}
```

## Discussion

Cascalog makes it easy to quickly generate aggregate statistics. Aggregate statistics can be tricky on some MapReduce frameworks. In general, the map phase of a MapReduce job is well distributed across the cluster. The reduce phase is often less well distributed. For instance, a naive implementation of the aggregation algorithm would end up doing all of the aggregation work on a single reducer. A 2,000-computer cluster would be as slow as a 1-computer cluster during the reduce phase if all the aggregation happened on one node.

Before you start writing your own aggregator, check through the source of `cascalog.logic.ops`. This namespace has many useful functions and probably already does what you want to do.

In our example, the goal is to count occurrences of each URL. To create the final map, all of the URLs need to end up in one reducer. A naive MapReduce program implementation would use an aggregation over all the tuples. That means you'd be doing all the work on only one node, with the computation taking just as long as it would on a single computer.

The solution is to use Hadoop's *combiner* function. Combiners run on the result of the map phase, before the output is sent to the reducers. Most importantly, the combiner runs on the mapper nodes. That means combiner work is spread across the entire cluster, like map work. When the majority of the work is done during the map and combiner phases, the reduce phase can run almost instantly. Cascalog makes this very easy. Many of the built-in Cascalog functions use combiners under the covers, so you'll be writing highly optimized queries without even trying. You can even write your own functions to use combiners using the `defparallelagg` macro.

Cascalog often works with vars instead of the values of those vars. For example, the call to `defparallelagg` takes quoted arguments. The `#'` syntax means that the var is being passed, not the value that the var refers to. Cascalog passes the vars around instead of values so that it doesn't have to serialize functions to pass them to the mappers and reducers. It just passes the name of the var, which is looked up in the remote execution environment. This means you won't be able to dynamically construct functions for some parts of the Cascalog workflow. Most functions need to be bound to a var.

`defparallelagg` is kind of confusing at first, but the power to write queries that leverage combiners makes it worth learning. You need to provide two vars that point to functions to the `defparallelagg` call: `init-var` and `combine-var`. Note that both arguments are being passed as vars, not function values, so you need to prepend a `#'` to the names. The `init-var` function needs to take the input data and change it into a format that can be easily processed by the `combine-var` function. In this case, the recipe changes the data into a map of maps that can easily be merged. Merging maps is an easy way to write parallel aggregators. The `combine-var` function needs to be commutative and associative. The function is called with two instances of the output of the `init-var` function. The return value will be passed as an argument to later invocations of the `combine-`

var function. Pairs of output will be combined until there is only one output left, which is the final output.

What follows is an explanation of the query, bit by bit.

First, require the Cascalog functions you'll need:

```
(ns cookbook.aggregation
  (:require [cascalog.api :refer :all]
            [cascalog.more-taps :refer [hfs-delimited]]))
```

Then define a function, `init-aggregate-stats`, that takes a date, URL, and user and returns a map of maps. The second level of maps has keys that correspond to the observed values. This is the `init` function, which takes each row and prepares it for aggregation:

```
(defn init-aggregate-stats [date url user]
  (let [day (.substring date 0 8)]
    {"URL"  {url 1}
     "User" {user 1}
     "Day"  {date 1}}))
```

The `combine-aggregate-stats` function takes the output of invoking the `init-aggregate-stats` function on all the inputs and combines it. This function will be called over and over, combining the output of `init-aggregate-stats` function calls and the output of other invocations of itself. Its output should be of the same form as its input, since this function will be called on pairs of output until there is only one piece of data left. This function merges the nested maps, adding the values together when they are in the same key:

```
(def combine-aggregate-stats
  (partial merge-with (partial merge-with +)))
```

`aggregate-stats` takes the two previous functions and turns them into a Cascalog parallel-aggregation operation. Note that you pass the vars, not the functions themselves:

```
(defparallelagg aggregate-stats
  :init-var    #'init-aggregate-stats
  :combine-var #'combine-aggregate-stats)
```

Finally, set up `Main` to define and execute a query that invokes the `aggregate-stats` operation across input from `in`, writing it to `out`:

```
(defmain Main [in out & args]
  ;; This defines and executes a Cascalog query.
  (?<-
    ;; Set up the output path.
    (hfs-textline out :sinkmode :replace)
    ;; Define which logic variables will be output.
    [?out]
    ;; Set up the input path, and define the logic vars to bind to input.
```

```
    ((hfs-delimited in) ?date ?url ?user)
    ;; Run the aggregation operation.
    (aggregate-stats ?date ?url ?user :> ?out)))
```

If the aggregate you want to calculate can't be defined using `defparallelagg`, Cascalog provides some other options for defining aggregates. However, many of them don't use combiners and could leave you with almost all the computation happening in a small number of reducers. The computation will probably finish, but you are losing a lot of the benefit of distributed computation. Check out the source of `cascalog.logic.ops` to see what the different options are and how you can use them.

## See Also

- The source of `cascalog.logic.ops` (*http://bit.ly/cascalog-ops*), a namespace with many predefined operations (including aggregators)

# 9.4. Testing Cascalog Workflows

by Alex Robbins

## Problem

You love testing your code. You love writing Cascalog jobs. You hate trying to test your Cascalog jobs.

## Solution

Midje-Cascalog (*http://bit.ly/midje-cascalog*) provides a small amount of extra functionality that makes writing tests for Cascalog jobs quite easy. To follow along with this recipe, clone the Cascalog samples GitHub repository (*http://bit.ly/cc-cascalog-samples*) and check out the `testing-begin` branch. This will give you a basic Cascalog project as created in Recipe 9.2, "Processing Data with an Extract Transform Load (ETL) Pipeline" on page 387.

Now add the Midje plug-in and Midje-Cascalog dependency to the `:dev` profile in your *project.clj*. The `:profiles` key should now look like this:

```
(defproject cookbook "0.1.0-SNAPSHOT"
  ;; ...
  :profiles {:dev {:dependencies [[org.apache.hadoop/hadoop-core "1.1.2"]
                                  [cascalog/midje-cascalog "2.0.0"]]
                   :plugins [[lein-midje "3.1.1"]]}})
```

Create a simple query in *src/cookbook/test_me.clj* to write a test against:

```
(ns cookbook.test-me
  (:require [cascalog.api :refer :all]))

(defn capitalize [s]
  (.toUpperCase s))

(defn capitalize-authors-query [author-path]
  (<- [?capitalized-author]
    ((hfs-textline author-path) ?author)
    (capitalize ?author :> ?capitalized-author)))
```

You can now write a test for this query in *test/cookbook/test_me_test.clj*:

```
(ns cookbook.test-me-test
  (:require [cookbook.midje-cascalog :refer :all]
            [midje
              [sweet :refer :all]
              [cascalog :refer :all]]))

(fact "Query should return capitalized versions of the input names."
  (capitalize-authors-query :author-path) => (produces [["LUKE VANDERHART"]
                                                        ["RYAN NEUFELD"]])
  (provided
    (hfs-textline :author-path) => [["Luke Vanderhart"]
                                    ["Ryan Neufeld"]]))
```

The full contents of this solution are available in the `testing-complete` branch of the Cascalog samples repository (*http://bit.ly/cc-cascalog-samples*).

Check out that branch to retrieve a full working copy with sample data:

```
$ git checkout testing-complete
```

Finally, run the tests with **`lein midje`**:

```
$ lein midje
2013-11-09 12:19:27.844 java[3620:1703] Unable to load realm info from
  SCDynamicStore
All checks (1) succeeded.
```

## Discussion

Unit testing is an important aspect of software craftsmanship. However, unit testing Hadoop workflows is difficult, to say the least. Most distributed computing development is done using trial and error, with only limited manual testing happening before the workflow is considered "good enough" and put into production use. You shouldn't let your code quality slip, but testing distributed code can be difficult. Midje-Cascalog makes it easy to test different parts of your Cascalog workflow by making it dead simple to mock out the results of subqueries.

In the solution outlined, you are testing a simple query. It reads lines from the input path, capitalizes them, and outputs them. Normally, you'd need to make sure part of the test wrote some test data into a file, reference that file in the test, then clean up and delete the file. Instead, using Midje-Cascalog, you mock the `hfs-textline` call.

`fact` is provided by the Midje library, which is well worth learning on its own. It is an alternative to `deftest` from `clojure.test`. Here, you state the test as a call, followed by an arrow and then the `produces` function. `produces` lets you write out the results of a query as a vector of vectors. Having established the test, you use `provided` to outline the functions you want to mock. This lets you test only the function in question, and not the functions it depends on. Testing your Cascalog workflows is as important as testing any other part of your application. With Midje-Cascalog, this is actually possible.

## See Also

- Recipe 10.2, "Testing with Midje" on page 410
- The Midje-Cascalog documentation (*http://bit.ly/midje-cascalog*) on GitHub

# 9.5. Checkpointing Cascalog Jobs

by Alex Robbins

## Problem

Your long-running Cascalog jobs throw errors, then need to be completely restarted. You waste time waiting for steps to rerun when the problem was later in the workflow.

## Solution

Cascalog Checkpoint (*http://bit.ly/cascalog-checkpoint*) is an excellent library that provides the ability to add checkpoints to your Cascalog job. If a step fails, the job is restarted at that step, instead of restarting from the beginning.

In an existing Cascalog project, such as the one generated by Recipe 9.2, "Processing Data with an Extract Transform Load (ETL) Pipeline" on page 387, add `[cascalog/cascalog-checkpoint "1.10.2"]` to your project's dependencies and set the `cookbook.checkpoint` namespace to be AOT-compiled.

Then use Cascalog Checkpoint's `workflow` macro to set up your job. A hypothetical four-step job would look something like this:

```
(ns cookbook.checkpoint
  (:require [cascalog.api :refer :all]
            [cascalog.checkpoint :refer [workflow]]))

(defmain Main [in-path out-path & args]
  (workflow ["/tmp/log-parsing"]
    step-1 ([:temp-dirs parsed-logs-path]
            (parse-logs in-path parsed-logs-path))
    step-2 ([:temp-dirs [min-path max-path]]
            (get-min parsed-logs-path min-path)
            (get-max parsed-logs-path max-path))
    step-3 ([:deps step-1 :temp-dirs log-sample-path]
            (sample-logs parsed-logs-path log-sample-path))
    step-4 ([:deps :all]
            (summary parsed-logs-path
                     min-path
                     max-path
                     log-sample-path
                     out-path))))
```

## Discussion

Cascalog jobs often take hours to run. There are few things more frustrating than a typo in the last step breaking a job that has been running all weekend. Cascalog Checkpoint provides the `workflow` macro, which allows you to restart a job from the last step that successfully completed.

The `workflow` macro expects its first argument, `checkpoint-dir`, to be a vector with a path for temporary files. The output of each step is temporarily stored in folders inside this path, along with some files to keep track of what steps have successfully completed.

After the first argument, `workflow` expects pairs of step names and step definitions. A step definitions is a vector of options, followed by as many Cascalog queries as desired for that step. For example:

```
step-3 ([:deps step-1 :temp-dirs [log-sample-path log-other-sample-path]]
        (sample-logs parsed-logs-path log-sample-path)
        (other-sample-logs parsed-logs-path log-other-sample-path))
```

This step definition defines `step-3`. It depends on `step-1`, so it won't run until `step-1` has completed. This step creates two temporary directories for its queries. Both `:deps` and `:temp-dirs` can be either a symbol or a vector of symbols, or can be omitted. After the options vector, you can include one or many Cascalog queries; in this case, there are two queries.

`:deps` can take several different values. `:last`, which is the default value, makes the step depend on the step before it. `:all` makes the step depend on all previously defined steps. Providing a symbol, or vector of symbols, makes that step depend on that particular step or steps. A step won't run until everything it depends upon has completed. If several steps have their dependencies met, they will all run in parallel.

Every symbol provided to `:temp-dirs` is turned into a directory within the temp directory. Later steps can use these directories to read data output by earlier steps. These directories are cleaned up once the workflow successfully runs all the way through. Until then, these directories hold the output from the different steps so the workflow can resume from the last incomplete step.

If you want to restart a step that successfully completed, delete the file at *<checkpoint-dir>/<step-name>*. The `:temp-dirs` from the step definitions can be found in *<checkpoint-dir>/data/<temp-dir>*, in case you need to delete or modify the data there.

Another method for dealing with errors is providing error taps for your Cascalog queries. Cascalog will put the input tuples that cause errors in a query into the error tap (for different processing or to dump for manual inspection). With error taps in place, a couple of malformed inputs won't bring down your entire workflow.

Checkpointing your Cascalog jobs is a little bit of extra work initially, but it'll save you a lot of time. Things will go wrong. The cluster will go down. You'll discover typos and edge cases. It is wonderful to be able to restart your job from the last step that worked, instead of waiting for the entire thing to rerun every time.

## See Also

- The `cascalog.checkpoint` project page (*http://bit.ly/cascalog-checkpoint*) on GitHub

# 9.6. Explaining a Cascalog Query

by Alex Robbins

## Problem

Your Cascalog job runs very slowly and you aren't sure why.

## Solution

Use the `cascalog.api/explain` function to print out a DOT file of your query. You can follow along by launching a REPL in an existing project, like that created in Recipe 9.2, "Processing Data with an Extract Transform Load (ETL) Pipeline" on page 387:

```
(require '[cascalog.api :refer [explain <-]])

(explain "slow-query.dot" (<- [?a ?b] ([[1 2]] ?a ?b)))
```

Next, you'll want to view the DOT file. There are many ways to do that, but the easiest is probably by using `dot`, one of the Graphviz tools, to convert a DOT file to a PNG or GIF:

```
$ dot -Tpng -oslow-query.png slow-query.dot
```

Now open *slow-query.png* (shown in Figure 9-1) to see a diagram of your query.

## Discussion

Cascalog workflows compile into Cascading workflows. Cascading (*http://www.cascading.org/*) is a Java library that wraps Hadoop, providing a flow-based plumbing abstraction. The query graph in the DOT file will have different Cascading elements as nodes.

The `explain` function here is analogous to the EXPLAIN command in many SQL implementations. `explain` causes Cascalog to print out the query plan. And as with the output from an SQL EXPLAIN, you might have to work to understand exactly what you are seeing.

The biggest thing to look for is that the basic flow of the query is what you expected. Make sure that you aren't rerunning some parts of your query. Cascalog makes it easy to reuse queries, but often you want to run the query, save the results, then reference the saved results from other queries instead of running it once for every time its output is used.

You can also work to match up the phases from your query plan to a job as it is running. This is tricky, because the phases won't correspond exactly to your output map. However, when you succeed, you'll be able be able to track down the slow phases.

In general, to keep your Cascalog queries fast, make sure you are using all of the nodes in your cluster. That means keeping the work in small, evenly sized units. If one map input takes 1,000 times as long to run as the other 40 inputs, your whole job will wait on the one mapper to finish. Working to split the long map job into 1,000 smaller jobs would make the job run much faster, since it could be distributed across the entire cluster instead of running on a single node. It is particularly easy to accidentally have nearly the entire job end up in one reducer. This is easy to see happening in the Hadoop job tracker, when nearly all the reducers are done and the job is waiting on one or two reducers to finish. To fix this, do as much reduce work as possible during the map phase using aggregators, and then make sure that the remaining reduce work isn't all piling up into a small number of reducers.

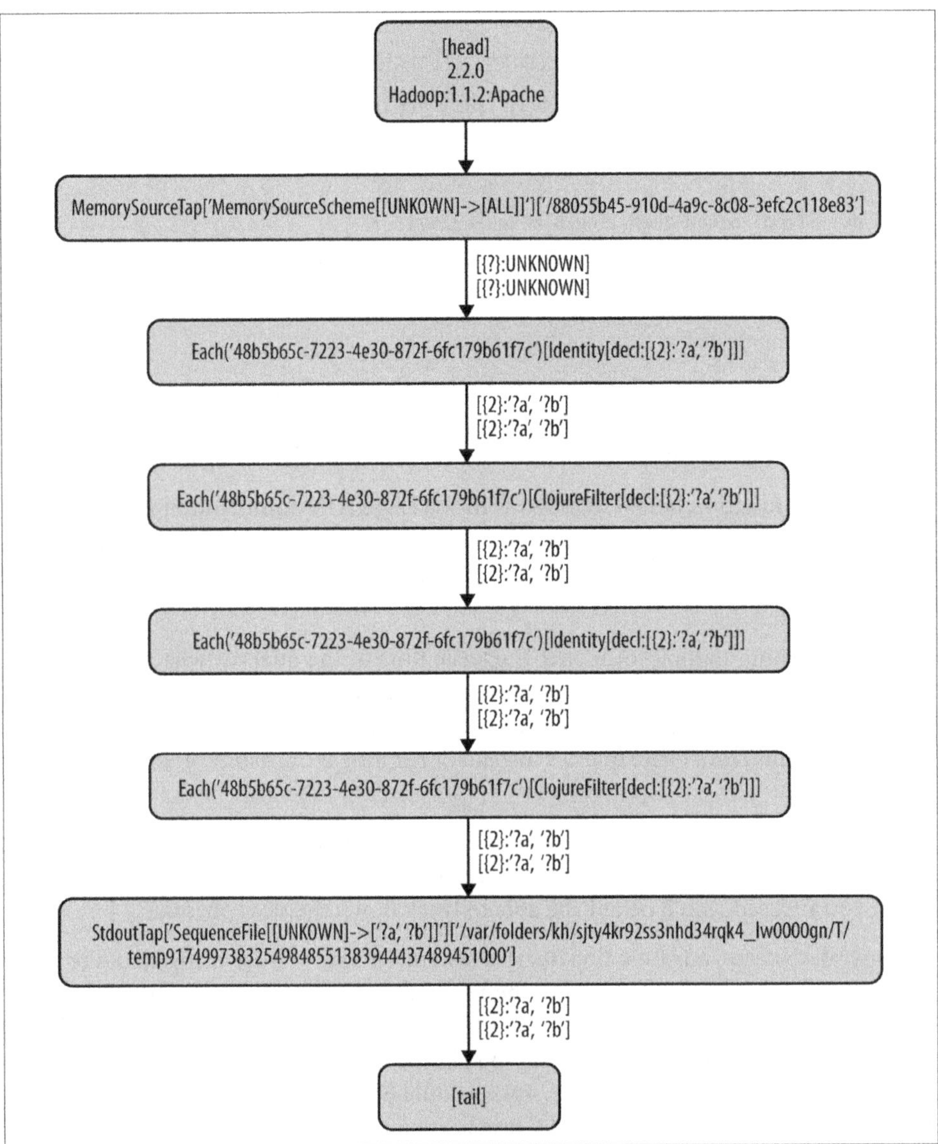


*Figure 9-1. slow-query.png*

## See Also

- Recipe 9.3, "Aggregating Large Files" on page 391
- "Cascading Flow Visualization" (*http://bit.ly/cascalog-flow-vis*) on Cascalog wiki

# 9.7. Running a Cascalog Job on Elastic MapReduce

by Alex Robbins

## Problem

You have a large amount of data to process, but you don't have a Hadoop cluster.

## Solution

Amazon's Elastic MapReduce (*http://aws.amazon.com/elasticmapreduce/*) (EMR) provides on-demand Hadoop clusters. You'll need an Amazon Web Services account (*http://aws.amazon.com/*) to use EMR.

First, write a Cascalog job as you normally would. There are a number of recipes in this chapter that can help you create a complete Cascalog job. If you don't have your own, you can clone Recipe 9.2, "Processing Data with an Extract Transform Load (ETL) Pipeline" on page 387:

```
$ git clone https://github.com/clojure-cookbook/cascalog-samples.git
$ cd cascalog-samples
$ git checkout etl-sample
```

Once you have a Cascalog project, package it into an uberjar:

```
$ lein compile
$ lein uberjar
```

Next, upload the generated JAR (*target/cookbook-0.1.0-SNAPSHOT-standalone.jar* if you're following along with the ETL sample) to S3. If you haven't ever uploaded a file to S3, follow the S3 documentation to "Create a Bucket" (*http://bit.ly/create-bucket*) and for "Adding an Object to a Bucket" (*http://bit.ly/add-object-bucket*). Repeat this process to upload your input data. Take note of the path to the JAR and the input data location.

To create your MapReduce job, visit *https://console.aws.amazon.com/elasticmapreduce/* and select "Create New Job Flow" (Figure 9-2). Once you're in the new job flow wizard, choose the "Custom JAR" job type. Select "Continue" and enter your JAR's location and arguments. "JAR Location" is the S3 path you noted earlier. "JAR Arguments" are all of the arguments you would normally pass when executing your JAR. For example, using the Cascalog samples repository, the arguments would be the fully qualified class name to execute, `cookbook.etl.Main`, an *s3n://* URI for input data, and an *s3n://* URI for the output.

The next few wizard windows allow you to specify additional configuration options for the job. Select "Continue" until you reach the review phase and start your job.

After your job has run, you should be able to retrieve the results from S3. Elastic MapReduce also allows you to set up a logging path to help with debugging if your job doesn't complete like you expect.

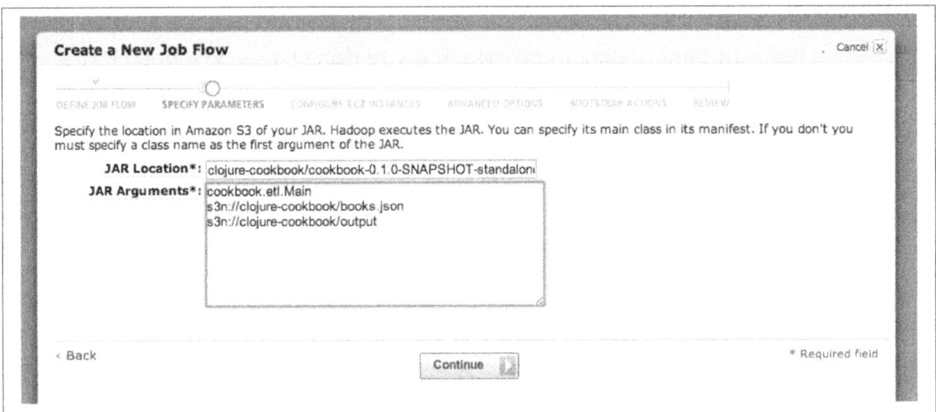


*Figure 9-2. Specifying parameters in the new job flow wizard*

## Discussion

Amazon's EMR is a great solution if you have big Cascalog jobs but you don't have to run them very often. Maintaining your own Hadoop cluster can take a fair amount of time and money. If you can keep the cluster busy, it is a great investment. If you only need it a couple of times a month, you might be better off using EMR for on-demand Hadoop clusters.

## See Also

- Recipe 9.2, "Processing Data with an Extract Transform Load (ETL) Pipeline" on page 387, to learn about building a simple Cascalog job
- Amazon's "Launch a Custom JAR Cluster" (*http://bit.ly/emr-jar-cluster*) documentation

# CHAPTER 10
# Testing

## 10.0. Introduction

It's one thing to trust your code is correct today, but how will you feel about it in a week? A month? A year? When you're long gone? For this kind of trust, we write tests for our code. A well-written suite of tests is a statement to yourself and to anyone that comes after you: "This is how this application works, now and so long as this test passes."

In addition to tests, several other tools have recently sprung up in the Clojure space aimed at improving program reliability. Often, these focus on validating that data looks as expected to guard programs from receiving input they don't know how to handle. These solutions range from optional static typing with algebraic types analyzed at compile time, down to simple preconditions.

Admittedly, testing is a bit of a hot-button topic in the Clojure community right now. People are starting to question whether these tests are worthwhile, or if there's a better way to think about program verification. In recent years, techniques such as REPL-driven development, property-based testing, and optional typing have all popped up to fill perceived voids in the testing landscape.

This chapter covers all of the above. As much as we'd love to push the envelope, nothing beats a good old-fashioned unit test suite from time to time. At the same time, as we build more and more gargantuan applications, it is clear that simple unit tests are not always sufficient. We hope that regardless of your skill level or focus, you'll find new tools to add to your testing arsenal in this chapter.

# 10.1. Unit Testing

by Daniel Gregoire

## Problem

You want to test individual units of Clojure code.

## Solution

Clojure includes a unit-testing framework in its `clojure.test` namespace. It provides ways to name and group tests, make assertions, report results, and orchestrate test suites.

For demonstration, imagine you had a `capitalize-entries` function that capitalized values in a map. To test this function, define a test using `clojure.test/deftest`:

```
;; A function in namespace com.example.core
(defn capitalize-entries
  "Returns a new map with values for keys 'ks' in the map 'm' capitalized."
  [m & ks]
  (reduce (fn [m k] (update-in m [k] clojure.string/capitalize)) m ks))

;; The corresponding test in namespace com.example.core-test
(require '[clojure.test :refer :all])

;; In a real test namespace, you would also :refer all of the target namespace
;; (require '[com.example.core :refer :all])

(deftest test-capitalize-entries
  (let [employee {:last-name "smith"
                  :job-title "engineer"
                  :level 5
                  :office "seattle"}]
    ;; Passes
    (is (= (capitalize-entries employee :job-title :last-name)
           {:job-title "Engineer"
            :last-name "Smith"
            :office "seattle"
            :level 5}))
    ;; Fails
    (is (= (capitalize-entries employee :office)
           {}))))
```

Run the test with the `clojure.test/run-tests` function:

```
(run-tests)
;; -> {:type :summary, :pass 1, :test 1, :error 0, :fail 1}
;; *out*
;; Testing user
;;
```

```
;; FAIL in (test-capitalize-entries) (NO_SOURCE_FILE:13)
;; expected: (= (capitalize-entries employee :office) {})
;;   actual: (not (= {:last-name "smith", :office "Seattle",
;;                    :level 5, :job-title "engineer"} {}))
;;
;; Ran 1 tests containing 2 assertions.
;; 1 failures, 0 errors.
```

## Discussion

The preceding example only scratches the surface of what `clojure.test` provides for unit testing. Let's take a bottom-up look at its other features.

First, you can improve reporting when an assertion fails by providing a second argument that explains what the assertion is intended to test. When you run this test, you will see an extended description of how the code was expected to behave:

```
(is (= (capitalize-entries {:office "space"} :office) {})
    "The employee's office entry should be capitalized.")
;; -> false
;; * out*
;; FAIL in clojure.lang.PersistentList$EmptyList@1 (NO_SOURCE_FILE:1)
;; The employee's office entry should be capitalized.
;; expected: (= (capitalize-entries {:office "space"} :office) {})
;;   actual: (not (= {:office "Space"} {}))
```

For testing a function like `capitalize-entries` thoroughly, several use cases need to be considered. To more concisely test numerous similar cases, use the `clojure.test/are` macro:

```
(deftest test-capitalize-entries
  (let [employee {:last-name "smith"
                  :job-title "engineer"
                  :level 5
                  :office "seattle"}]
    (are [ks m] (= (apply capitalize-entries employee ks) m)
         [] employee
         [:not-a-key] employee
         [:job-title] {:job-title "Engineer"
                       :last-name "smith"
                       :level 5
                       :office "seattle"}
         [:last-name :office] {:last-name "Smith"
                               :office "Seattle"
                               :level 5
                               :job-title "engineer"})))
```

The first two parameters to `are` set up a testing pattern: given a sequence of keys `ks` and a map `m`, call `capitalize-entries` for those keys on the original `employee` map and assert that the return value equals `m`.

Writing out multiple use cases in a declarative syntax makes it easier to catch errors and untreated edge cases, such as the `NullPointerException` that will be thrown for the `[:not-a-key] employee` assertion pair in the preceding test.

Unlike testing frameworks for other popular dynamic languages, Clojure's built-in assertions are minimal and simple. The `is` and `are` macros check test expressions for "truthiness" (i.e., that those expressions return neither `false` nor `nil`, in which case they pass). Beyond this, you can also check for `thrown?` or `thrown-with-msg?` to test that a certain `java.lang.Throwable` (error or exception) is expected:

```
(is (thrown? IndexOutOfBoundsException (nth [] 1)))
```

Above the level of individual assertions, `clojure.test` also provides facilities for calling functions before or after tests run. In the `test-capitalize-entries` test, we defined an ad hoc `employee` map for testing, but you could also read in external data to be shared across multiple tests by registering a data-loading function as a "fixture." The `clojure.test/use-fixtures` multimethod allows registering Clojure functions to be called either before or after each test, or before or after an entire namespace's test suite. The following example defines and registers three fixture functions:

```
(require '[clojure.edn :as edn])

(def test-data (atom nil))

;; Assuming you have a test-data.edn file...
(defn load-data "Read a Clojure map from test data in a file."
  [test-fn]
  (reset! test-data (edn/read-string (slurp "test-data.edn")))
  (test-fn))

(defn add-test-id "Add a unique id to the data before each test."
  [test-fn]
  (swap! test-data assoc :id (java.util.UUID/randomUUID))
  (test-fn))

(defn inc-count "Increment a counter in the data after each test runs."
  [test-fn]
  (test-fn)
  (swap! test-data update-in [:count] (fnil inc 0)))

(use-fixtures :once load-data)
(use-fixtures :each add-test-id inc-count)

;; Tests...
```

You can think about fixture functions as forming a pipeline through which each test is passed as a parameter, which we called `test-fn` in the preceding example. Take `inc-count`, for example. It is the job of this fixture to invoke the `test-fn` function, continuing the pipeline, and afterward, to increment a count (i.e., "do some work"). Each fixture decides whether to invoke `test-fn` before or after its own work (compare the `add-test-id` function with the `inc-count` function), while the `clojure.test/use-fixtures` multimethod controls whether each registered fixture function is run only once for all tests in a namespace or once for each test.

Finally, with a firm understanding of how to develop individual Clojure test suites, it is important to consider how you organize and run those suites as part of your project's build. Although Clojure allows defining tests for functions anywhere in your code base, you should keep your testing code in a separate directory that is only added to the JVM classpath when needed (e.g., during development and testing). It is conventional to name your test namespaces after the namespaces they test, so that a file located at *<project-root>/src/com/example/core.clj* with namespace `com.example.core` has a corresponding test file at *<project-root>/test/com/example/core_test.clj* with namespace `com.example.core-test`. To control the location of your source and test directories and their inclusion on the JVM classpath, you should use a build tool like Leiningen (*http://leiningen.org/*) or Maven (*http://maven.apache.org/*) to organize your project.

In Leiningen, the default directory for your tests is a top-level *<project-root>/test* folder, and you can run your project's tests with `lein test` at the command line. Without any additional arguments, the `lein test` command will execute all of the tests in a project:

```
$ lein test

lein test com.example.core-test
lein test com.example.util-test

Ran 10 tests containing 20 assertions.
0 failures, 0 errors.
```

To limit the scope of tests Leiningen runs, use the `:only` option, followed by a fully qualified namespace or function name:

```
# To run an entire namespace
$ lein test :only com.example.core-test

lein test com.example.core-test

Ran 5 tests containing 10 assertions.
0 failures, 0 errors.

# To run one specific test
$ lein test :only com.example.core-test/test-capitalize-entries

lein test com.example.core-test

Ran 1 tests containing 2 assertions.
0 failures, 0 errors.
```

## See Also

- The `clojure.test` API documentation (*http://bit.ly/clj-test-api*) contains full information on the unit-testing framework.
- If you are instead using Maven, use `clojure-maven-plugin` (*https://github.com/talios/clojure-maven-plugin*) to run Clojure tests. This plug-in will incorporate your Clojure tests located in the Maven standard *src/test/clojure* directory as part of the `test` phase in the Maven build life cycle. You can optionally use the plug-in's `clojure:test-with-junit` goal to produce JUnit-style reporting output for your Clojure test runs.

# 10.2. Testing with Midje

by Joseph Wilk

## Problem

You want to unit-test a function that integrates with external dependencies such as HTTP services or databases.

## Solution

Use Midje (*https://github.com/marick/Midje*), a testing framework that provides ways to mock functions and return fakes.

To follow along with this recipe, start a REPL using `lein-try`:

```
$ lein try midje clj-http
```

Here is an example function that makes an HTTP request:

```
;; A function in namespace com.example.core
(require '[clj-http.client :as http])

(defn github-profile [username]
  (let [response (http/get (str "https://api.github.com/users/" username))]
    (when (= (:status response) 200)
      (:body response))))

(github-profile "clojure-cookbook")
;; -> "{\"login\":\"clojure-cookbook\",\"id\":4176246, ...}"
```

To test the `github-profile` function, define a test using `midje.sweet/facts` and `midje.sweet/fact` in the corresponding test namespace:

```
;; In the com.example.core-test namespace...
(require '[midje.sweet :refer :all])
```

```
(facts "about successful requests"
  (fact "returns the response body"
    (github-profile "clojure-cookbook") => ..body..
    (provided
      (http/get #"/users/clojure-cookbook") =>
        {:status 200 :body ..body..})))
```

## Discussion

In Midje, `facts` associates a description with a group of tests, while `fact` maps to your test. Assertions in your `fact` take the form of:

```
;; actual => expected

10 => 10 ; This will pass
10 => 11 ; This will fail
```

Assertions behave a little differently than most testing frameworks. Within a `fact` body, every single assertion is checked, irrespective of whether a previous one failed.

Midje only provides mocks, not stubs. All functions specified in the `provided` body have to be called for the test to pass. Mocks use the same syntax as assertions, but with a slightly different meaning:

```
;; <function call & arguments to match> => <return value of function>

(provided (+ 10 10) => 0)
```

It is important to note you are not calling the `(+ 10 10)` function here—you are setting up a pattern. Every function call occurring in the test is checked to see if it matches this pattern. If it does match, Midje will not call the function, but will instead return `0`. When defining mocks with `provided`, there is a lot of flexibility in terms of how to match mock functions against real calls. In the preceding solution, for example, regular expressions are used. This expression instructs Midje to mock calls to `http/get` whose URLs end in */users/clojure-cookbook*:

```
;; The expectation
(http/get #"/users/clojure-cookbook$")

;; Would match
(http/get "http://localhost:4001/users/clojure-cookbook")
;; or
(http/get "https://api.github.com/users/clojure-cookbook")
```

Midje provides a lot of match-shaping functions that you can use to match against the arguments of a mock:

```
;; Match an argument list that contains 1
(provided
  (http/get (contains [1])) => :result)
```

```
;; Match against a custom fn that must return true
(provided
  (http/get (as-checker (fn [x] (x == 10)))) => :result)

;; Match against a single argument of any value
(provided
  (http/get anything) => :result)
```

From within a REPL, you can investigate all of Midje's checkers:

```
(require 'midje.repl)
(doc midje-checkers)
;; *out*
;; -------------------------
;; midje.sweet/midje-checkers
;;
;;  (facts "about checkers"
;;    (f) => truthy
;;    (f) => falsey
;;    (f) => irrelevant ; or `anything`
;;    (f) => (exactly odd?) ; when you expect a particular function
;;    (f) => (roughly 10 0.1)
;;    (f) => (throws SomeException #"with message")
;;    (f) => (contains [1 2 3]) ; works with strings, maps, etc.
;;    (f) => (contains [1 2 3] :in-any-order :gaps-ok)
;;    (f) => (just [1 2 3])
;;    (f) => (has every? odd?)
;;    (f) => (nine-of odd?) ; must be exactly 9 odd values.
;;    (f) => (every-checker odd? (roughly 9)) ; both must be true
;;    (f) => (some-checker odd? (roughly 9))) ; one must be true
```

You may have noticed in the solution that we used `..body..` instead of an actual response. This is something Midje refers to as a *metaconstant*.

A metaconstant is any name that starts and ends with two dots. It has no properties other than identity. Think of it as a fake or placeholder, where we do not care about the actual value or might be referencing something that does not exist yet. In our example, we don't really care what `..body..` is; we just care that it is the thing returned.

To add Midje to an existing project, add `[midje "1.5.1"]` to your development dependencies and `[lein-midje "3.1.2"]` to your development plug-ins. Your *project.clj* should look something like this:

```
(defproject example "1.0.0-SNAPSHOT"
  :profiles {:dev {:dependencies [[midje "1.5.1"]]
                   :plugins [[lein-midje "3.1.2"]]}})
```

Midje provides two ways to run tests: through a REPL, as you may have been doing, or through Leiningen. Midje actually encourages you to run all your tests through the REPL, as you develop them. One very useful way to run your tests is with the `midje.repl/autotest` function. This continuously polls the filesystem looking for changes in your project. When it detects these changes, it will automatically rerun the relevant tests:

```
(require '[midje.repl :as midje])

(midje/autotest) ; Start auto-testing

;; Other options are...
(midje/autotest :pause)
(midje/autotest :resume)
(midje/autotest :stop)
```

There are many more things you can do from the REPL with Midje. To find out more, read the docstring of `midje-repl` by running **`(doc midje-repl)`** in a REPL.

You can also run Midje tests through the Leiningen plug-in `lein-midje` (add as noted in *project.clj*). `lein-midje` allows you run tests at a number of granularities—all of your tests, all the tests in a group, or all the tests in a single namespace:

```
# Run all your tests
$ lein midje

# Run a group of namespaces
$ lein midje com.example.*

# Run a specific namespace
$ lein midje com.example.t-core
```

## See Also

- Recipe 10.1, "Unit Testing" on page 406, for information on more basic unit testing in Clojure
- The Midje GitHub repository (*https://github.com/marick/Midje*)

# 10.3. Thoroughly Testing by Randomizing Inputs

by Luke VanderHart

## Problem

You want to test a function using randomly generated inputs to ensure that it works in all possible scenarios.

## Solution

Use the `test.generative` library to specify a function's inputs, and test it across randomly generated values.

To follow along with this recipe, start a REPL using `lein-try`:

```
$ lein try org.clojure/test.generative "0.5.0"
```

Say you are trying to test the following function, which calculates the arithmetic mean of all the numbers in a sequence:

```
(defn mean
  "Calculate the mean of the numbers in a sequence"
  [s]
  (/ (reduce + s) (count s)))
```

The following `test.generative` code defines a *specification* for the `mean` function:

```
(require '[clojure.test.generative :as t]
         '[clojure.test.generative.runner :as r]
         '[clojure.data.generators :as gen])

(defn number
  "Return a random number, of a random type"
  []
  (gen/one-of gen/byte
              gen/short
              gen/int
              gen/long
              gen/float
              gen/double))

(defn seq-of-numbers
  "Return a list, seq, or set of numbers"
  []
  (gen/one-of (gen/list number)
              (gen/set number)
              (gen/vec number)))

(t/defspec mean-spec
  mean
  [^example.generative-tests/seq-of-numbers arg]
  (assert (number? %)))
```

To run the `mean-spec` specification, invoke the `run` function in the `clojure.test.generative.runner` namespace, passing in the number of threads upon which to run the simulation, the number of milliseconds to run, and the var referring to a spec.

Here's what happens when we run the previous example at the REPL:

```
(r/run 2 5000 #'example.generative-tests/mean-spec)
;; -> clojure.lang.ExceptionInfo: Generative test failed
```

This shows the behavior when the generative test fails. The exact details of the failure are returned as the data of a Clojure information-bearing exception; you must retrieve an instance of the exception itself and call `ex-data` on it to return the data map.

In the REPL, if you didn't explicitly catch the exception, you can use the special `*e` symbol to retrieve the most recent exception. Calling `ex-data` on it returns information on the test case that provoked the error:

```
(ex-data *e)
;; -> {:exception #<ArithmeticException java.lang.ArithmeticException:
;;     Divide by zero>, :iter 7, :seed -875080314,
;;     :example.generative-tests/mean-spec, :input [#{}]}
```

This states that after only seven iterations, using the random number seed –875080314, the function under test was passed `#{}` as input and threw a divide by zero error.

Once highlighted in this way, the problem is easy to see; the `mean` function will divide by zero if `(count s)` is zero. Fix the bug by rewriting the `mean` function to handle that case:

```
(defn mean
  [s]
  (if (zero? (count s))
    0
    (/ (reduce + 1.0 s) (count s))))
```

Rerunning now shows a passing test:

```
(r/run 2 5000 #'example.generative-tests/mean-spec)
;; -> {:iter 3931, :seed -1495229764, :test testgen-test.core/mean-spec}
;;    {:iter 3909, :seed -1154113663, :test testgen-test.core/mean-spec}
```

This output indicates that over the allotted 5 seconds, two threads ran about 3,900 iterations of the test each and did not encounter any errors or assertion failures.

## Discussion

There are two key parts to the preceding test definition: the `defspec` form itself, which defines the generative test, and the functions used to generate random data. In this case, the data generator functions are built from primitive data generation functions found in the `clojure.data.generators` namespace.

Generator functions take no arguments and return random values. Different functions produce different types of data. The `clojure.data.generators` namespace contains generator functions for all of Clojure's primitive types, as well as collections. It also contains functions for randomly choosing from a set of options; the `one-of` function used previously, for example, takes a number of generator functions and chooses a value from one at random.

The `defspec` macro takes three types of forms: a *function* to put under test, an *argument specification*, and a *body* containing one or more assertion forms.

The function under test is simply the function to call. Over the course of the generative test, it will be called many times, each time with different values.

The argument specification is a vector of argument names and should match the signature of the function under test. Each argument should have *metadata* attached. Specifically, it should have a `:tag` metadata key, mapped to the fully qualified name of a generator function. Each time the test driver calls the function, it will use a random value for each argument pulled from its corresponding generator function.

> ### Why :tag?
>
> You may find the use of `:tag` metadata a bit confusing. Normally, `:tag` is a type hint and returns a JVM *class*. In `test.generative`, it should be a *function* that can return any type of value you want to pass to the function under test.
>
> The motivation for reusing `:tag` in this way is mostly historical. `test.generative` is largely inspired by a library called QuickCheck, which is written in Haskell. Because Haskell is strongly and statically typed, QuickCheck truly can use the type signature as sufficient information on how to generate input data.
>
> The link isn't quite as strong in Clojure, and arguably is more confusing than helpful. Just remember that, in the context of `test.generative`, `:tag` refers not to the actual system type, but to a function that returns an object of the type(s) you want to pass to the function to test.

The body of a `defspec` simply contains expressions that may throw an exception if some condition is not met. It is executed on each iteration of the test, with the instantiated arguments available, and with the return value of the function under test bound to `%`. This example merely has a single assertion that the result is a number, for brevity, but you can have any number of assertions executing arbitrary checks.

An interesting difference between `test.generative` and traditional unit tests is that rather than specifying what tests to run and having them take as long as they do, in `test.generative` you specify how long to run, and the system will run as many random permutations of the test as it can fit into that time. This has the property of keeping test runtimes deterministic, while allowing you to trade off speed and comprehensiveness depending on the situation. For example, you might have tests run for five seconds in development, but thoroughly hammer the system for an hour every night on the continuous integration server, allowing you to find that (literally) one-in-a-million bug.

#### Running generative tests

While developing tests, running from the REPL is usually the most convenient. However, there are many other scenarios (such as testing commit hooks or on a CI) where running tests from the command line is required. For this purpose, `test.generative` provides a `-main` function in the `clojure.test.generative.runner` namespace that takes as a command-line argument one or more directories where generative tests can be found. It searches all the Clojure namespaces in those locations for generative testing specifications and executes them.

For example, if you've placed your generative tests in a *tests/generative* directory inside a Leiningen project, you could execute tests by running the following at the shell, from your project's root directory:

```
$ lein run -m clojure.test.generative.runner tests/generative
```

If you want to control the intensity of the test run, you can adjust the number of concurrent threads and the length of the run using the `clojure.test.generative.threads` and `clojure.test.generative.msec` JVM system properties. Using Leiningen, you must set these options in the `:jvm-opts` key in *project.clj* like so:

```
:jvm-opts ["-Dclojure.test.generative.threads=32"
           "-Dclojure.test.generative.msec=10000"]
```

`clojure.test.generative.runner/-main` will pick up any parameters provided in this way, and run accordingly.

## See Also

- The `test.generative` (*https://github.com/clojure/test.generative*) page on GitHub
- The QuickCheck Haskell library (*http://hackage.haskell.org/package/QuickCheck*)
- Recipe 10.4, "Finding Values That Cause Failure" on page 417, on SimpleCheck, a property-based testing library for Clojure with some overlap with `test.generative` and unique features

# 10.4. Finding Values That Cause Failure

by Luke VanderHart

## Problem

You want to specify properties of a function that should hold true for all inputs, and find input values that violate those properties.

## Solution

Use `simple-check` (*https://github.com/reiddraper/simple-check*). This is a property-specification library for Clojure that is capable of "shrinking" the input case to find the minimal failing input.[1]

To follow along with this recipe, add `[reiddraper/simple-check "0.5.3"]` to your project's dependencies, or start a REPL using `lein-try`:

```
$ lein try reiddraper/simple-check
```

Then, find a function to test. This example uses a contrived function that calculates the sum of the reciprocals of a sequence of numbers:

```
(defn reciprocal-sum [s]
  (reduce + (map (partial / 1) s)))
```

Here's the test code itself:

```
(require '[simple-check.core :as sc]
         '[simple-check.generators :as gen]
         '[simple-check.properties :as prop])

(def seq-of-numbers (gen/one-of [(gen/vector gen/int)
                                 (gen/list gen/int)]))

(def reciprocal-sum-check
  (prop/for-all [s seq-of-numbers]
    (number? (reciprocal-sum s))))
```

`seq-of-numbers` is a data generator composed of primitive generators found in the `simple-check.generators` namespace.

Unlike with `test.generative`, `simple-check` generators are more complicated than a single function that returns a value. Instead, they are data structures that define not only how random values are sampled, but how they converge on the "simplest" possible failing case.

A full discussion of creating custom `simple-check` generators (other than simple compositions of primitive generators) is beyond the scope of this recipe, but full documentation is available on the `simple-check` GitHub page (*https://github.com/reiddraper/simple-check*).

The actual test is defined using the `simple-check.properties/for-all` macro, which emits a property definition. It takes a binding form (similar to `let` or `for`) that specifies

1. It is important to note that `simple-check` finds a *local* minimum, not the *global* minimum.

the possible values to bind to one or more symbols, and a body. The body is what actually specifies the properties that must hold, and must return `true` if and only if the test passes for a particular set of values.

To run the test, invoke the `simple-check.core/quick-check` function, passing it the defined property:

```
(sc/quick-check 100 reciprocal-sum-check)
```

`quick-check` takes the number of samples to execute, and the property definition to execute. The body of the property definition will be sampled repeatedly, with randomized values bound to the symbols specified in the binding form.

As you may have already observed, the `reciprocal-sum` function has a problem: it will throw a "divide by zero" error if a zero is present in the input sequence. The `quick-check` function returns a data structure showcasing the problem:

```
{:result
 #<ArithmeticException java.lang.ArithmeticException: Divide by zero>,
 :failing-size 8,
 :num-tests 9,
 :fail [(5 0 0 -8 1 -2)],
 :shrunk
 {:total-nodes-visited 10,
  :depth 5,
  :result
  #<ArithmeticException java.lang.ArithmeticException: Divide by zero>,
  :smallest [(0)]}}
```

Fix the function by eliminating zero values:

```
(defn reciprocal-sum [s]
  (reduce + (map (partial / 1)
                 (filter (complement zero?) s))))
```

Rerunning the test now indicates success:

```
(sc/quick-check 100 reciprocal-sum-check)
;; -> {:result true, :num-tests 100, :seed 1384622907885}
```

## Discussion

`simple-check` has the very useful property of not only returning *a* failing sample input to a test, but returning the *minimal* failing sample. In the preceding example program, for instance, any time a zero occurs in the input sequence, it causes an error. However, merely from looking at the sequence `(5 0 0 -8 1 -2)`, it might not be apparent that zeros are the problem. Not knowing anything else about the function under test, the problem might be, for example, the negative numbers, or the value 5. `simple-check` returns not just any arbitrary failing input, but *the specific input* that will consistently cause the program to fail. As useful as it is to know that there is an input that will provoke failure, it's even more useful to know the specific problematic value. And, the larger and more complex the inputs to the function are, the more useful it is to be able to reduce the failing case.

> **test.generative and simple-check**
>
> You may have observed that `test.generative` (discussed in Recipe 10.3, "Thoroughly Testing by Randomizing Inputs" on page 413) and `simple-check` cover a lot of the same ground. They both generate a randomized distribution of inputs, and they both specify "success" conditions in terms of properties or qualities that must hold across all inputs and outputs, rather than specific examples.
>
> However, there are a few key differences. `simple-check` minimizes the failing input before returning, whereas `test.generative` bails the first time it sees a failure. However, the data generators of `test.generative` are simple functions, without any additionally specified behavior, which makes them much more flexible and easy to extend.
>
> `test.generative` also provides the ability to specify not only how many iterations of the test to run, but how long to test for, running as many tests as it can fit into the allotted time frame across multiple threads.
>
> Ultimately, both are valuable approaches that you should seriously consider when you want to really thoroughly test something. The decision between them should be mediated by your own specific needs: how large or complicated the inputs are, how much control you want over the running time, and how likely you are to need to extend the set of generated primitives.

## See Also

- Recipe 10.1, "Unit Testing" on page 406
- Recipe 10.3, "Thoroughly Testing by Randomizing Inputs" on page 413
- The `simple-check` project page (*https://github.com/reiddraper/simple-check*)
- "Introduction to QuickCheck" (*http://bit.ly/quickcheck-intro*) for information on the Haskell library that inspired `simple-check`

# 10.5. Running Browser-Based Tests

by Matthew Maravillas

## Problem

You want to run browser-based tests.

## Solution

Use Selenium WebDriver via the `clj-webdriver` library (*https://github.com/semperos/clj-webdriver*). This will allow you to use `clojure.test` to test your application's behavior in actual browser environments.

To follow along with this recipe, create a new Leiningen project:

```
$ lein new browser-testing
Generating a project called browser-testing based on the 'default' template.
```

Modify the new project's *project.clj* file to match the following:

```
(defproject browser-testing "0.1.0-SNAPSHOT"
  :profiles {:dev {:dependencies [[clj-webdriver "0.6.0"]]}}
  :test-selectors {:default (complement :browser)
                   :browser :browser})
```

Next, add a simple Selenium test to *test/browser_testing/core_test.clj*, overwriting its content:

```
(ns browser-testing.core-test
  (:require [clojure.test :refer :all]
            [clj-webdriver.taxi :as t]))

;; A simple fixture that sets up a test driver
(defn selenium-fixture
  [& browsers]
  (fn [test]
    (doseq [browser browsers]
      (println (str "\n[ Testing " browser " ]"))
      (t/set-driver! {:browser browser})
      (test)
      (t/quit))))

(use-fixtures :once (selenium-fixture :firefox))

(deftest ^:browser test-clojure
  (t/to "http://clojure.org")

  (is (= (t/title) "Clojure - home"))
  (is (= (t/current-url) "http://example.com/")))

(deftest ^:browser test-clojure-download
  (t/to "http://clojure.org")
  (t/click {:xpath "//div[@class='menu']/*/a[text()='Download']"})

  (is (= (t/title) "Clojure - downloads"))
  (is (= (t/current-url) "http://clojure.org/downloads"))
  (is (re-find #"Rich Hickey" (t/text {:id "foot"}))))
```

A complete version of this repository is available on GitHub (*https://github.com/clojure-cookbook/browser-testing*). Check out a copy locally to catch up:

```
$ git clone https://github.com/clojure-cookbook/browser-testing
$ cd browser-testing
```

Run the tests on the command line:

```
$ lein test :browser

lein test browser-testing.core-test

[ Testing :firefox ]

lein test :only browser-testing.core-test/test-clojure

FAIL in (test-clojure) (core_test.clj:20)
expected: (= (t/current-url) "http://example.com/")
  actual: (not (= "http://clojure.org/" "http://example.com/"))

Ran 2 tests containing 5 assertions.
1 failures, 0 errors.
Tests failed.
```

## Discussion

Browser tests verify that your application behaves as expected in your targeted browsers. They test the appearance and behavior of your application as rendered in the browser itself.

Manually testing applications in a browser is a tedious and repetitive task. The amount of time and effort required for a complete test run can be unmanageable for even a moderately sized project. Automating browser tests ensures they are run consistently and relatively quickly, resulting in reproducible errors and more frequent test runs. However, automated tests lack the visual inspection by a human inherent to manual tests. For example, a manual test could easily catch a positioning error that an automated test would likely miss if it were not explicitly tested for.

To write browser tests in Clojure, use the `clj-webdriver` library with your preferred test framework, such as `clojure.test`. `clj-webdriver` provides a clean Clojure interface to Selenium WebDriver, a tool used to control and automate browser actions.

Some additional configuration may be required to use Selenium WebDriver or `clj-webdriver` with your browsers of choice. See the Selenium WebDriver documentation (*http://bit.ly/cc-selenium*) and the `clj-webdriver` wiki (*http://bit.ly/clj-webdriver-wiki*).

Before you dive into testing, you can experiment with `clj-webdriver` at a REPL. Start up a REPL with `clj-webdriver` using `lein-try`:

```
$ lein try clj-webdriver "0.6.0"
```

Use the `clj-webdriver.taxi/set-driver!` function, selecting the Firefox WebDriver implementation (other options include `:chrome` or `:ie`, but these may require more setup):

```
(require '[clj-webdriver.taxi :as t])

(t/set-driver! {:browser :firefox})
;; -> #clj_webdriver.driver.Driver{:webdriver ...}
```

This will open the browser you picked, ready to receive commands. Try a few functions from the `clj-webdriver.taxi` namespace:

```
(t/to "http://clojure.org/")

(t/current-url)
;; -> "http://clojure.org/"

(t/title)
;; -> "Clojure - home"

(t/click {:xpath "//div[@class='menu']/*/a[text()='Download']"})
(t/current-url)
;; -> "http://clojure.org/downloads"

(t/text {:id "foot"})
;; -> "Copyright 2008-2012 Rich Hickey"
```

When you're finished, close the browser from the REPL:

```
(t/quit)
```

Your tests will use these functions to start up and run against the browser. To save yourself some work, you should set up the browser startup and teardown using a `clojure.test` fixture.

`clojure.test/use-fixtures` allows you to run functions around each individual test, or once around the namespace's test run as a whole. Use the latter, as restarting the browser for each test will be far too slow.

The `selenium-fixture` function uses `clj-webdriver`'s `set-driver!` and `quit` functions to start up a browser for each of the keywords it's provided and run the namespace's tests inside that browser:

```
(defn selenium-fixture
  [& browsers]
  (fn [test]
    (doseq [browser browsers]
```

```
    (t/set-driver! {:browser browser})
    (test)
    (t/quit))))

(use-fixtures :once (selenium-fixture :firefox))
```

It's important to note that using a `:once` fixture means the state of the browser will persist between tests. Depending on your particular application's behavior, you may need to guard against this when you write your tests by beginning from a common browser state for each test. For example, you might delete all cookies or return to a certain top-level page. If this is necessary, you may find it useful to write this common reset behavior as an `:each` fixture.

To begin writing tests, modify your project's *project.clj* file to include the `clj-webdriver` dependency in the `:dev` profile and `:test-selectors` for `:default` and `browser` convenience:

```
(defproject my-project "1.0.0-SNAPSHOT"
  ;; ...
  :profiles {:dev {:dependencies [[clj-webdriver "0.6.0"]]}}
  :test-selectors {:default (complement :browser)
                   :browser :browser})
```

Test selectors let you run groups of tests independently. This prevents slower browser tests from impacting the faster, more frequently run unit and lower-level integration tests.

In this case, you've added a new selector and modified the default. The new `:browser` selector will only match tests that have been annotated with a `:browser` metadata key. The default selector will now exclude any tests with this annotation.

With the fixture and test selectors in place, you can begin writing your tests. Start with something simple:

```
(deftest ^:browser test-clojure
  (t/to "http://clojure.org/")

  (is (= (t/title) "Clojure - home"))
  (is (= (t/current-url) "http://example.com/")))
```

Note the `^:browser` metadata attached to the test. This test is annotated as a browser test, and will only run when that test selector is chosen.

In this test, as in the REPL experiment, you navigate to a URL and check its title and URL. Run this test at the command line, passing the additional test selector argument to `lein test`:

```
$ lein test :browser

lein test browser-testing.core-test

[ Testing :firefox ]

lein test :only browser-testing.core-test/test-clojure

FAIL in (test-clojure) (core_test.clj:20)
expected: (= (t/current-url) "http://example.com/")
  actual: (not (= "http://clojure.org/" "http://example.com/"))

Ran 2 tests containing 5 assertions.
1 failures, 0 errors.
Tests failed.
```

Clearly, this test was bound to fail—replace `http://example.com/` with `http://clojure.org/` and it will pass.

This test is very basic. In most real tests, you'll load a URL, interact with the page, and verify that the application behaved as expected. Write another test that interacts with the page:

```
(deftest ^:browser test-clojure-download
  (t/to "http://clojure.org")
  (t/click {:xpath "//div[@class='menu']/*/a[text()='Download']"})

  (is (= (t/title) "Clojure - downloads"))
  (is (= (t/current-url) "http://clojure.org/downloads"))
  (is (re-find #"Rich Hickey" (t/text {:id "foot"}))))
```

In this test, after loading the URL, the browser is directed to click on an anchor located with an XPath selector. To verify that the expected page has loaded, the test compares the title and URL, as in the first test. Lastly, it finds the text content of the `#foot` element containing the copyright and verifies that the text includes the expected name.

`clj-webdriver` provides many other capabilities for interacting with your application. For more information, see the `clj-webdriver` wiki (*http://bit.ly/clj-webdriver-wiki*).

## See Also

- The `clj-webdriver` GitHub repository (*https://github.com/semperos/clj-webdriver*) and wiki (*http://bit.ly/clj-webdriver-wiki*)
- The Selenium project page (*http://bit.ly/selenium-project*)
- Recipe 10.1, "Unit Testing" on page 406, to learn more about unit testing in Clojure

# 10.6. Tracing Code Execution

by Stefan Karlsson

## Problem

You want to trace the execution of your code, in order to see what it is doing.

## Solution

Use the `tools.trace` (*https://github.com/clojure/tools.trace*) library's bevy of "trace" functions and macros to examine your code as it runs.

Before starting, add `[org.clojure/tools.trace "0.7.6"]` to your project's dependencies under the `:development` profile (in the vector at the `[:profiles :dev :dependencies]` path instead of the `[:dependencies]` path). Alternatively, start a REPL using `lein-try`:

```
$ lein try org.clojure/tools.trace
```

To examine a single value at execution, wrap that value in an invocation of `clojure.tools.trace/trace`:

```
(require '[clojure.tools.trace :as t])

(map #(inc (t/trace %))
     (range 3))
;; -> (1 2 3)
;; *out*
;; TRACE: 0
;; TRACE: 1
;; TRACE: 2
```

To examine multiple values without losing context of which trace is which, supply a descriptive name string as the first argument to `trace`:

```
(defn divide
  [n d]
  (/ (t/trace "numerator" n)
     (t/trace "denominator" d)))

(divide 4 6)
;; -> 2/3
;; *out*
;; TRACE numerator: 4
;; TRACE denominator: 6
```

## Discussion

At its core, the `tools.trace` library is all about introspecting upon the execution of a body of code. The `trace` function is the simplest and most low-level tracing operation. Wrapping a value in an invocation of `trace` does two things: it logs a tracer message to `STDOUT` and, most importantly, returns the original value unadulterated. `tools.trace` provides a number of other granularities for tracing execution.

Stepping up a level from simple values, you can define functions with `clojure.tools.trace/deftrace` instead of `defn` to trace the input to and output from the function you define:

```
(t/deftrace pow [x n]
  (Math/pow x n))

(pow 2 3)
;; -> 8.0
;; *out*
;; TRACE t815: (pow 2 3)
;; TRACE t815: => 8.0
```

It is not advisable to deploy production code with tracing in place. Tracing is most suited to development and debugging, particularly from the REPL. Include `tools.trace` in your *project.clj*'s `:dev` profile to make tracing available only to development tasks.

If you're trying to diagnose a difficult-to-understand exception, use the `clojure.tools.trace/trace-forms` macro to wrap an expression and pinpoint the origin of the exception. When no exception occurs, `trace-forms` prints no output and returns normally:

```
(t/trace-forms (* (pow 2 3)
                  (divide 1 (- 1 1))))
;; *out*
;; ...
;; ArithmeticException Divide by zero
;;   Form failed: (divide 1 (- 1 1))
;;   Form failed: (* (pow 2 3) (divide 1 (- 1 1)))
;;   clojure.lang.Numbers.divide (Numbers.java:156)
```

Apart from explicitly tracing values or functions, `tools.trace` also allows you to dynamically trace vars or entire namespaces. To add a trace function to a var, use `clojure.tools.trace/trace-vars`. To remove such a trace, use `clojure.tools.trace/untrace-vars`:

```
(defn add [x y] (+ x y))

(t/trace-vars add)
(add 2 2)
;; -> 4
;; *out*
;; TRACE t1309: (user/add 2 2)
;; TRACE t1309: => 4

(t/untrace-vars add)
(add 2 2)
;; -> 4
```

To trace or untrace an entire namespace, use `clojure.tools.trace/trace-ns` and `clojure.tools.trace/untrace-ns`, respectively. This will dynamically add tracing to or remove it from all functions and vars in a namespace. Even things defined *after* `trace-ns` is invoked will be traced:

```
(def my-inc inc)
(defn my-dec [n] (dec n))

(t/trace-ns 'user)

(my-inc (my-dec 0))
;; -> 0
;; TRACE t1217: (user/my-dec 0)
;; TRACE t1218: | (user/my-dec 0)
;; TRACE t1218: | => -1
;; TRACE t1217: => -1
;; TRACE t1219: (user/my-inc -1)
;; TRACE t1220: | (user/my-inc -1)
;; TRACE t1220: | => 0
;; TRACE t1219: => 0

(t/untrace-ns 'user)

(my-inc (my-dec 0))
;; -> 0
```

## See Also

- The `tools.trace` GitHub repository (*https://github.com/clojure/tools.trace*) for a full list of trace functions/macros

# 10.7. Avoiding Null-Pointer Exceptions with core.typed

by Ambrose Bonnaire-Sergeant

## Problem

You want to verify that your code handles `nil` correctly, eliminating potential null-pointer exceptions.

## Solution

Use `core.typed` (*https://github.com/clojure/core.typed*), an optional type system for Clojure, to annotate and check a namespace for misuses of `nil`.

To follow along with this recipe, create a file *core_typed_samples.clj* and start a REPL using `lein-try`:

```
$ touch core_typed_samples.clj
$ lein try org.clojure/core.typed
```

This recipe is a little different than others because `core.typed` uses on-disk files to check namespaces.

Consider, for example, that you are writing a function `handle-number` to process numbers. To verify that `handle-number` handles `nil` correctly, annotate it with `clojure.core.typed/ann` to accept the union (`U`) of the `nil` and `Number` types, returning a `Number`:

```
(ns core-typed-samples
  (:require [clojure.core.typed :refer [ann] :as t]))

(ann handle-number [(U nil Number) -> Number])
(defn handle-number [a]
  (+ a 20))
```

Verify the function's correctness at the REPL using `clojure.core.typed/check-ns`:

```
user=> (require '[clojure.core.typed :as t])
user=> (t/check-ns 'core-typed-samples)
# ...
Type Error (core-typed-samples:6:3) Static method clojure.lang.Numbers/add
could not be applied to arguments:

Domains:
```

```
        t/AnyInteger t/AnyInteger
        java.lang.Number java.lang.Number

Arguments:
        (U nil java.lang.Number) (Value 20)

Ranges:
        t/AnyInteger
        java.lang.Number

with expected type:
        java.lang.Number

in: (clojure.lang.Numbers/add a 20)
in: (clojure.lang.Numbers/add a 20)

ExceptionInfo Type Checker: Found 1 error  clojure.core/ex-info (core.clj:4327)
```

The current definition is unsafe. `check-ns` recognizes that `+` can only handle numbers, while the `handle-number` function accepts numbers *or* `nil`.

Protect the call to `+` by wrapping it in an `if` statement, returning `0` in the absence of `a`:

```
(ns core-typed-samples
  (:require [clojure.core.typed :refer [ann] :as t]))

(ann handle-number [(U nil Number) -> Number])
(defn handle-number [a]
  (if a
    (+ a 20)
    0))
```

Check the namespace with `check-ns` again:

```
user=> (t/check-ns 'core-typed-samples)
# ...
:ok
```

Now that there is no way `nil` could accidentally be passed to `+` by this code, a null-pointer exception is impossible.

## Discussion

`core.typed` is designed to avoid all misuses of `nil` or `null` in typed code. To achieve this, the concepts of the null pointer and reference types are separated. This is unlike in Java, where a type like `java.lang.Number` implies a "nullable" type.

In `core.typed`, reference types are implicitly non-nullable. To express a nullable type (such as in the preceding example), construct a *union type* of the desired type and `nil`. For example, a `java.lang.Number` in `core.typed` syntax is non-nullable; the union type

`(U nil java.lang.Number)` expresses the equivalent to a nullable `java.lang.Number` (the latter is closest to what `java.lang.Number` implies in Java type syntax).

This separation of concepts allows `core.typed` to throw a *type error* on any potential misuse of `nil`. The preceding solution threw a type error when type checking the equivalent expression: `(+ nil 20)`.

To better understand `core.typed` type errors, it is useful to note that some functions have *inline* definitions. `core.typed` fully expands all code before type checking, so it is common to see calls to the Java method `clojure.lang.Numbers/add` in type errors when user code invokes `clojure.core/+`.

It is also common to see *ordered intersection function types* in type errors. Our first type error claims that the arguments `(U Number nil)` and `(Value 20)` are not under either of the ordered intersection function domains, listed under "Domains." Notice two "Ranges" are provided, which correspond to the listed domains.

The full type of `clojure.lang.Numbers/add` is:

```
(Fn [t/AnyInteger t/AnyInteger -> t/AnyInteger]
    [Number Number -> Number])
```

Briefly, the function is "ordered" because it tries to match the argument types with each arity until one matches.

## See Also

- `core.typed` Home (*https://github.com/clojure/core.typed*) on GitHub.
- The `core.typed` API reference (*http://bit.ly/core-typed-doc*) (particularly the list of core-type aliases—for example, the entry for clojure.core.typed/AnyInteger (*http://bit.ly/anyinteger-doc*))
- The Types wiki page (*http://bit.ly/core-typed-types*), which documents valid types
- Recipe 10.8, "Verifying Java Interop Using core.typed" on page 431, and Recipe 10.9, "Type Checking Higher-Order Functions with core.typed" on page 435, for further examples of how to use `core.typed`

# 10.8. Verifying Java Interop Using core.typed

by Ambrose Bonnaire-Sergeant

## Problem

You want to verify that you are using Java libraries safely and unambiguously.

## Solution

Java provides a vast ecosystem that is a major draw for Clojure developers; however, it can be often be complex to use large, cumbersome Java APIs from Clojure.

To type-check Java interop calls, use `core.typed`.

To follow along with this recipe, create a file *core_typed_samples.clj* and start a REPL using `lein-try`:

```
$ touch core_typed_samples.clj
$ lein try org.clojure/core.typed
```

This recipe is a little different than others because `core.typed` uses on-disk files to check namespaces.

To demonstrate, choose a standard Java API function such as the `java.io.File` constructor.

Using the dot constructor to create new files can be annoying—wrap it in a Clojure function that takes a string `new-file`:

```
(ns core-typed-samples
  (:require [clojure.core.typed :refer [ann] :as t])
  (:import (java.io File)))

(ann new-file [String -> File])
(defn new-file [s]
  (File. s))
```

Setting `*warn-on-reflection*` when compiling this namespace will tell us that there is a reflective call to the `java.io.File` constructor. Checking this namespace at the REPL with `clojure.core.typed/check-ns` will report the same information, albeit in the form of a type error:

```
user=> (require '[clojure.core.typed :as t])
user=> (t/check-ns 'core-typed-samples)
# ...
ExceptionInfo Internal Error (core-typed-samples:6)
  Unresolved constructor invocation java.io.File.

Hint: add type hints.

in: (new java.io.File s)  clojure.core/ex-info (core.clj:4327)
```

Add a type hint to call the `public File(String pathname)` (*http://bit.ly/javadoc-file-constructor*) constructor:

```
(ns core-typed-samples
  (:require [clojure.core.typed :refer [ann] :as t])
  (:import (java.io File)))

(ann new-file [String -> File])
(defn new-file [^String s]
  (File. s))
```

Checking again, `core.type` is satisfied:

```
user=> (t/check-ns 'core-typed-samples)
# ...
:ok
```

`File` has a second single-argument constructor: `public File(URI uri)`. Enhance `new-file` to support `URI` or `String` filenames:

```
(ns core-typed-samples
  (:require [clojure.core.typed :refer [ann] :as t])
  (:import (java.io File)
           (java.net URI)))

(ann new-file [(U URI String) -> File])
(defn new-file [s]
  (if (string? s)
    (File. ^String s)
    (File. ^URI s)))
```

Even after relaxing the input type to `(U URI String)`, `core.typed` is able to infer that each branch has the correct type by following the `string?` predicate.

## Discussion

While `java.io.File` is a relatively small API, careful inspection of Java types *and* documentation is needed to confidently use foreign Java code correctly.

Though the `File` constructor is fairly innocuous, consider writing `file-parent`, a thin wrapper over the `getParent` method:

```
(ns core-typed-samples
  (:require [clojure.core.typed :refer [ann] :as t])
  (:import (java.io File)))

(ann file-parent [File -> String])
(defn file-parent [^File f]
  (.getParent f))
```

The preceding implementation is free from reflective calls, so... all good? No. Checking this function with `core.typed` tells another story; Java's return types are *nullable* and `core.typed` knows it. It is possible that `getParent` will return `nil` instead of a `String`:

```
user=> (t/check-ns 'core-typed-samples)
# ...
Type Error (core-typed-samples:7:3) Return type of instance method
java.io.File/getParent is (U java.lang.String nil), expected
java.lang.String.

Hint: Use `non-nil-return` and `nilable-param` to configure where
`nil` is allowed in a Java method call. `method-type` prints the
current type of a method.
in: (.getParent f)

Type Error (core-typed-samples:6) Type mismatch:

Expected:       java.lang.String

Actual:         (U String nil)
in: (.getParent f)

Type Error (core-typed-samples:6:1) Type mismatch:

Expected:       (Fn [java.io.File -> java.lang.String])

Actual:         (Fn [java.io.File -> (U String nil)])
in: (def file-parent (fn* ([f] (.getParent f))))

ExceptionInfo Type Checker: Found 3 errors clojure.core/ex-info ...
```

`core.typed` assumes all methods return nullable types, so it is a type error to annotate `parent` as `[File -> String]`. Each preceding type error reiterates that the annotation tried to claim a `(U nil String)` was a `String`, with the most specific (and useful) error being the first.

`core.typed` is designed to be pessimistic about Java code, while being accurate enough to avoid adding arbitrary code to "please" the type checker. For example, `core.typed` distrusts Java methods enough to assume all method parameters are non-nullable and the return type is nullable by default. On the other hand, `core.typed` knows Java constructors never return `null`.

If `core.typed` is too pessimistic for you with its nullable return types, you can override particular methods with `clojure.core.typed/non-nil-return`. Adding the following to the preceding code would result in a successful type check (check omitted for brevity):

```
(t/non-nil-return java.io.File/getName :all)
```

As of this writing, `core.typed` does not enforce static type overrides at runtime, so use `non-nil-return` and similar features with caution.

Sometimes the type checker might seem overly picky; in the solution, two type-hinted constructors were necessary. It might seem normal in a dynamically typed language to simply call `(File. s)` and allow reflection to resolve any ambiguity. By conforming to what `core.typed` expects, however, all ambiguity is eliminated from the constructors, and the type hints inserted enable the Clojure compiler to generate efficient bytecode.

It is valid to wonder why both type hints *and* `core.typed` annotations are needed to type-check ambiguous Java calls. A type hint is a directive to the compiler, while type annotations are merely for `core.typed` to consume during type checking. `core.typed` does not have influence over resolving reflection calls at compile time, so it chooses to assume all reflective calls are ambiguous instead of trying to guess what the reflection might resolve to at runtime. This simple rule usually results in faster, more explicit code, often desirable in larger code bases.

## See Also

- `core.typed` Home (*https://github.com/clojure/core.typed*) on GitHub
- The `core.typed` API reference (*http://bit.ly/core-typed-doc*)—particularly the documentation for `non-nil-return` and `nilable-param`
- Recipe 10.7, "Avoiding Null-Pointer Exceptions with core.typed" on page 429, and Recipe 10.9, "Type Checking Higher-Order Functions with core.typed" on page 435, for further examples of how to use `core.typed`

# 10.9. Type Checking Higher-Order Functions with core.typed

by Ambrose Bonnaire-Sergeant

## Problem

Clojure strongly encourages higher-order functions, but tools for verifying their use focus on runtime verification. You want earlier feedback, preferably at compile time.

## Solution

Use `core.typed` to type-check higher-order functions.

To follow along with this recipe, create a file *core_typed_samples.clj* and start a REPL using `lein-try`:

```
$ touch core_typed_samples.clj
$ lein try org.clojure/core.typed
```

This recipe is a little different than others because `core.typed` uses on-disk files to check namespaces.

To demonstrate `core.typed`'s abilities, define a typed higher-order function `hash-of?`, which accepts two predicates and returns a new predicate.

Use `clojure.core.typed/fn>` to return an anonymous function with type annotations attached:

```
(ns core-typed-samples
  (:require [clojure.core.typed :refer [ann fn>] :as t]))

(ann hash-of? [[Any -> Any] [Any -> Any] -> [Any -> Any]])
(defn hash-of? [ks? vs?]
  (fn> [m :- Any]
    (when (map? m)
      (and (every? ks? (keys m))
           (every? ks? (vals m))))))
```

Each argument to `hash-of?` has type `[Any -> Any]`: a single argument function taking anything and returning anything.

Verifying `hash-of?` confirms that the preceding type annotations are correct:

```
user=> (require '[clojure.core.typed :as t])
user=> (t/check-ns 'core-typed-samples)
# ...
:ok
```

Using the `clojure.core.typed/cf` macro, you can type-check individual forms at the REPL (or under test). Invoking `hash-of?` with two predicates verifies as expected, outputting the resulting type:

```
user=> (require '[core-typed-samples :refer [hash-of?]])
user=> (t/cf (hash-of? number? number?))
(Fn [Any -> Any])
```

Passing + as a predicate, however, is a type error:

```
user=> (t/cf (hash-of? + number?))
Type Error (user:1:7) Type mismatch:

Expected:       (Fn [Any -> Any])

Actual:         (Fn [t/AnyInteger * -> t/AnyInteger]
                    [java.lang.Number * -> java.lang.Number])

ExceptionInfo Type Checker: Found 1 error  clojure.core/ex-info (core.clj:4327)
```

This is because `hash-of?` takes a function with an `Any` parameter and `+` takes at most a `Number`.

## Discussion

While Clojure's built-in pre/post conditions are useful for defining anonymous functions that fail fast, these checks only provide feedback at runtime. Why not type-check our higher-order functions as well? `core.typed`'s type-checking abilities aren't limited to only data types—it can also type-check functions as types themselves.

By writing returning anonymous functions created with the `clojure.core.typed/fn>` form instead of `fn`, it is possible to annotate function objects with `core.typed`'s rich type-checking system. When defining functions with `fn>`, annotate types to its arguments with the `:-` operator. For example, `(t/fn> [m :- Map] ...)` would indicate an anonymous function that accepted a `Map` as its sole argument.

Beyond definition, it can also be useful to check the types of forms at the REPL. The `clojure.core.typed/cf` macro is a versatile REPL-oriented tool for on-demand type checking. It proves useful not only for checking your code, but also for investigating built-in functions. Invoking `cf` on any of Clojure's higher-order functions reveals their type signatures:

```
user=> (t/cf iterate)
(All [x]
  (Fn [(Fn [x -> x]) x -> (clojure.lang.LazySeq x)]))
```

The `All` around `iterate`'s type indicates that it is *polymorphic* in `x`. It reads, "for all types `x`, takes a function that accepts an `x` and returns an `x`, and takes an `x`, and returns a lazy sequence of `x`."

The `cf` macro can also detect when the wrong number of arguments are being passed to a function returned by another function:

```
user=> (t/cf (fn [] ((hash-of? + number?))))
Type Error (user:1:15) Type mismatch:

Expected:       (Fn [Any -> Any])

Actual:         (Fn [t/AnyInteger * -> t/AnyInteger]
                    [java.lang.Number * -> java.lang.Number])
in: ((core-typed-samples/hash-of? clojure.core/+ clojure.core/number?))

Type Error (user:1:14) Wrong number of arguments, expected 1 fixed
parameters, and got 0 for function [Any -> Any] and arguments []
in: ((core-typed-samples/hash-of? clojure.core/+ clojure.core/number?))

ExceptionInfo Type Checker: Found 2 errors  clojure.core/ex-info (core.clj:4327)
```

In this experiment, the faulty invocation of `hash-of?` is wrapped in an anonymous function. At the time of this writing, `core.typed` evaluates code before it type-checks it.

Without this, the raw invocation `((hash-of? + number?))` would return a regular Clojure `ArityException`.

## See Also

- The `core.typed` repository (*https://github.com/clojure/core.typed*) on GitHub
- The `core.typed` user guide (*https://github.com/clojure/core.typed/wiki/User-Guide*), in particular its sections on polymorphism and function annotations
- Recipe 10.7, "Avoiding Null-Pointer Exceptions with core.typed" on page 429, and Recipe 10.8, "Verifying Java Interop Using core.typed" on page 431, for further examples of how to use `core.typed`

# Index

## Symbols



## A



## B



*We'd like to hear your suggestions for improving our indexes. Send email to index@oreilly.com.*

## D

## E



## F

## G



## H

## I



## J

## N

## O



## P



## Q



## R

## S

## T

## U



## V



## W



## X



## Y



## Z

## About the Authors

**Luke VanderHart** is a Clojure and ClojureScript developer working with Cognitect, Inc. He is the coauthor of *Practical Clojure* (Apress) and *ClojureScript: Up and Running* (O'Reilly). He lives and works in Durham, NC.

**Ryan Neufeld** is a polyglot software developer and budding architect specializing in distributed systems and web applications. Whether it's tough technical issues or one of the softer elements of software engineering, Ryan relishes the opportunity to deliver results for customers. Ryan currently lives in Durham, NC, where he works as a developer at Cognitect, Inc.

## Colophon

The animal on the cover of *Clojure Cookbook* is an aardwolf (*Proteles cristata*), a small mammal with two separate populations in the plains of Eastern and Southern Africa. Though its name means "earth wolf" in the Afrikaans language, it is part of the hyena family. The aardwolf generally doesn't eat carrion like its larger cousins do—its diet mainly consists of insects (especially termites), which it catches with a long, sticky tongue.

Aardwolves have thick yellow or brown fur with dark stripes, with bushy tails and long manes that run along their necks and backs. The mane is used to make the aardwolves appear bigger and intimidate predators, since they are neither fast runners nor especially good fighters. They do have strong jaws, but their teeth have evolved for eating insects rather than attacking larger animals. They average 22–31 inches long, and weigh 15–22 pounds.

The aardwolf is nocturnal, and sleeps in underground burrows during the day. These animals are very territorial, and use scent glands to mark the area containing their dens (a mating pair may claim and rotate through multiple burrows, using only one or two at a time). The breeding season occurs in late June/early July, with a litter of 2–5 cubs born 90 days later.

Aardwolves are occasionally mistaken for hyenas and killed to protect livestock. However, many African farmers recognize the benefit of the animals in controlling the termite population and thus protecting crops. A single aardwolf can eat 200,000–300,000 termites per night.

The cover image is from Wood's *Animate Creation*. The cover fonts are URW Typewriter and Guardian Sans. The text font is Adobe Minion Pro; the heading font is Adobe Myriad Condensed; and the code font is Dalton Maag's Ubuntu Mono.

CPSIA information can be obtained at www.ICGtesting.com
Printed in the USA
BVOW11s1643070314

346982BV00002B/2/P